The Blackwell Reader in

CONTEMPORARY
SOCIAL
THEORY

B

The Blackwell Reader in

CONTEMPORARY SOCIAL THEORY

Edited by

Anthony Elliott

Copyright © Blackwell Publishers Ltd 1999; editorial introduction and arrangement copyright © Anthony Elliott 1999

First published 1999

2 4 6 8 10 9 7 5 3 1

Blackwell Publishers Inc.
350 Main Street
Malden, Massachusetts 02148
USA

Blackwell Publishers Ltd
108 Cowley Road
Oxford OX4 1JF
UK

Library of Congress Cataloging-in-Publication Data

The Blackwell reader in contemporary social theory / edited by Anthony Elliott.
    p. cm.
Includes bibliographical references and index.
ISBN 0–631–20649–3 (alk. paper). — ISBN 0–631–20650–7 (pbk. : alk. paper)
1. Sociology—Philosophy.   2. Social sciences—Philosophy.
I. Elliott, Anthony.
HM24.B533   1999
301'.01—dc21   98–47773
                                              CIP

British Library Cataloguing in Publication Data

A CIP catalogue record for this book is available from the British Library.

Typeset in 10½ on 12pt Palatino by
Grahame & Grahame Editorial, Brighton

Printed in Great Britain by TJ International, Padstow, Cornwall

Contents

Contents

Preface

In this book I have tried to offer a comprehensive overview of the principal concerns, and also dilemmas, of contemporary social theory. In selecting readings I have been guided by two main criteria. I have chosen from the work of a number of leading figures in contemporary intellectual life who are in very different ways at the cutting edge of thinking and research in social theory. But I have also tried to select materials which engage centrally with the immense personal and cultural transformations associated with the development of modern institutions, as well as the postmodern constitution and conditioning of modernity. Thus, in addition to the key contributions of well-known thinkers, such as Jürgen Habermas, Michel Foucault, Anthony Giddens and Julia Kristeva, I have also sought to introduce the reader to a variety of other authors, including Ulrich Beck and Elizabeth Beck-Gernsheim, Sander L. Gilman, Jeffrey Weeks and Seyla Benhabib.

I owe thanks to many people. In particular, I am indebted to Andrew Newton, who assisted me in editorial and administrative matters through the long gestation of this book. His great skill and commendable attention to detail have enhanced the finished text considerably, and I am deeply grateful for the support, assistance and many important contributions that he offered throughout. Many colleagues have offered help and suggestions along the way. Particularly deserving of mention are Anthony Giddens and John B. Thompson, both of whom have greatly influenced my own work in social theory. I would also like to thank the following informal reviewers and advisers: Steven Seidman, Bryan Turner, William Outhwaite, Ira Cohen, Jeffrey Prager, Steve Pile and Larry Ray. I am grateful to Jill Landeryou, of Blackwell Publishers, for commissioning the book. Also at Blackwell Publishers, many thanks to Susan Rabinowitz and Nicola Boulton.

Anthony Moran, Nick Stevenson, Kriss McKie, Fiore Inglese and Simone Skacej have been loyal friends, and I would like to express my thanks for the support they have given me over the years. Thanks also to Keith

Elliott, Jean Elliott and Deborah Maxwell, whom have been constant sources of encouragement and support. My greatest debt is – as always – to Nicola Geraghty.

Anthony Elliott
Melbourne, March 1999

Acknowledgments

The editor and publishers gratefully acknowledge the following for permission to reproduce copyright material:

The Estate of Roland Barthes for "Language and Speech" from *Elements of Sociology*, Jonathan Cape.

Routledge for Jacques Lacan, "The Mirror Stage as Formative of the Function of the I" from *Ecrits*. Reproduced by permission of Routledge, Inc.

Columbia University Press for Julia Kristeva, "Revolution in Poetic Language" from *The Kristeva Reader*, edited by Toril Moi. Copyright © 1986 by Columbia University Press. Reprinted with permission of the publisher.

MIT Press and Polity Press for Cornelius Castoriadis, "The Individual and Representations" originally published as "The Sense of Autonomy" and "The Question of Representation" from *The Imaginary Institution of Society*. Reprinted with permission of the publishers.

Georges Borchardt, Inc. and Penguin for Michel Foucault, "The Means of Correct Training" from *Discipline and Punish*. Copyright © 1975 by Editions Gallimard. Reprinted by permission of the publishers for the author.

Stanford University Press and Polity Press for Pierre Bourdieu, "Structures, *Habitus*, Practices" from *The Logic of Practice*, tr. Richard Nice. Reprinted with the permission of the publishers.

Polity Press and the University of California Press for Anthony Giddens, "Elements of the Theory of Structuration" from *The Constitution of Society*. Copyright © 1984. Reprinted with the permission of the publishers and author.

The University of Chicago Press for Alain Touraine, "Society Turns Back Upon

Itself" from *The Self-Production of Society*. Reprinted with the permission of the publishers.

Sage Publications for Niklas Luhmann, "The Concept of Society" from *Thesis Eleven*, Volume 31, pp. 67–80. Reprinted by permission of the publisher and author.

Blackwell Publishers for Ulrich Beck and Elizabeth Beck-Gernsheim, "Individualization and 'Precarious Freedoms': Perspectives and Controversies of a Subject-orientated Sociology" from S. Lash, P. Heelas, and P. Morris (eds), *Detraditionalization*. Reprinted with the permission of the publishers and authors.

Beacon Press for Jürgen Habermas, "The Uncoupling of System and Lifeworld" from *The Theory of Communicative Action, Volume II*. Copyright © 1981 by Suhrkamp Verlag. Reprinted by permission of Beacon Press, Boston.

MIT Press and Polity Press for Axel Honneth, "Patterns of Intersubjective Recognition: Love, Rights and Solidarity" from *The Struggle For Recognition*, 1995. Reprinted with the permission of the publishers.

MIT Press and Polity Press for Albrecht Wellmer, "Truth, Semblance, Reconciliation: Adorno's Aesthetic Redemption of Modernity" from *The Persistence of Modernity*, 1991. Reprinted with the permission of the publishers.

Routledge for Homi K. Bhabha, "DissemiNation" from *The Location of Culture*, 1994. Reprinted with the permission of the publishers.

Princeton University Press for Sander L. Gilman, "Sigmund Freud and the Epistemology of Race" from *Freud, Race and Gender*, 1993. Reprinted with the permission of the publishers.

Verso Publishers for Paul Gilroy, "Masters, Mistresses, Slaves, and the Antinomies of Modernity" from *The Black Atlantic*, 1993.

Routledge for Gayatri Chakravorty Spivak, "Subaltern Studies: Deconstructing Historiography" from *In Other Worlds*. Copyright © 1987. Reproduced by permission of Routledge, Inc.

The University of California Press for Nancy Chodorow, "Gender Personality and the Reproduction of Mothering" from *The Reproduction of Mothering: Psychoanalysis and the Sociology of Gender*. Copyright © 1978 The Regents of the University of California. Reprinted with the permission of the publishers.

Cornell University Press for Luce Irigaray, "This Sex Which Is Not One" from *This Sex Which is Not One*, 1985. Reprinted with the permission of the publishers.

Routledge for Judith Butler "Subjects of Sex/Gender/Desire" from *Gender Trouble*, 1991. Reprinted with the permission of the publishers.

Columbia University Press and Polity Press for Jeffrey Weeks, "Living with Uncertainty" from *Invented Moralities: Sexual Values in an Age of Uncertainty*. Copyright © 1993, Columbia University Press. Reprinted with the permission of the publishers.

Routledge and Cathy Miller Foreign Rights Agency for Donna J. Haraway, "Situated Knowledges: The Science Question in Feminism and the Privilege of Partial Perspective" from *Simians, Cyborgs and Women*. Reprinted with the permission of the publishers.

Blackwell Publishers for David Harvey, "Postmodernism" from *The Condition of Postmodernity*, 1989. Reprinted with the permission of the publishers and author.

Manchester University Press for Jean-François Lyotard, *The Postmodern Condition*. Reprinted with the permission of the publishers.

Duke University Press for Fredric Jameson, "The Cultural Logic of Late Capitalism" from *Postmodernism, or, the Cultural Logic of Late Capitalism*, 1991. Copyright © 1991, Duke University Press. All rights reserved. Reprinted with permission.

Blackwell Publishers and Routledge for Seyla Benhabib, "Feminism and the Question of Postmodernism" from *Situating the Self*, 1991. Reprinted with the permission of the publishers and author.

Cornell University Press and Blackwell Publishers for Zygmunt Bauman, "Postmodernity, or Living with Ambivalence" from *Modernity and Ambivalence*, 1991. Reprinted with the permission of the publishers and author.

The publishers apologize for any errors or omissions in the above list and would be grateful to be notified of any corrections that should be incorporated in the next edition or reprint of this book.

Introduction

Anthony Elliott

The Blackwell Reader in Contemporary Social Theory provides a systematic introduction to the leading themes, traditions, and trends in current social thought.
The focus is specifically on contemporary theoretical issues, developments, and
transitions facing the social sciences and the humanities today, with the
coverage of twentieth-century social theory stretching from traditions such
as critical theory, structuralism, and psychoanalysis to feminism, post-
structuralism, and postmodernism.

The breadth of the *Reader* is a reflection of that explosion in competing
versions of social theory which has occurred during the last few decades. This
diversification of approaches includes hermeneutics, systems analysis,
ethnomethodology, psychoanalytical theory, structuralism, queer theory,
post-Marxism, post-colonialism, post-structuralism, post-feminism, postmodernism; and, in case one concludes too quickly that the prefix "post" is
necessary to qualify these days as a substantive critical concern, we might also
add more recently developed types of thinking such as the theory of "world
risk society" associated with Ulrich Beck or the "theory of practice" associated
in particular with Pierre Bourdieu.

In this book there are six core critical issues around which I have organized
a survey of contemporary social theory. These issues form the backcloth for
an understanding of human inquiry and theoretical endeavour, and inform
questions of broad significance in social theory.

- Part I provides readings of various attempts to develop a sophisticated "theory of the
  subject" in conjunction with social analysis.
- Part II offers competing readings of the nature of social structures and institutions in
  the contemporary age.
- Part III examines the tradition of the Frankfurt School of social theorists, paying
  special attention to issues of political autonomy, justice, social conflict, solidarity, and
  aesthetics in contemporary critical theory.

- Part IV provides readings on the centrality of racial identity, difference, and multi-culturalism to issues of knowledge, politics, theory, justice, and methodology.
- Part V offers a diverse set of readings in contemporary feminist thought, debates about gender, and the theorizing of sexual difference.
- Part VI examines the modernity/postmodernity debate in the social sciences and the humanities, with readings on the relevance and import of this debate for a diagnosis of contemporary culture and alternative social futures.

It would be impossible in a brief introduction such as this to analyze in detail the framework of critical traditions and theoretical controversies which these core issues have generated throughout the social sciences and the humanities in recent decades. Nonetheless, in what follows I hope to signal some of the salient themes and concerns of these traditions of thought, stressing throughout how social theory can be brought to bear on some of the central problems of the late modern era.

1   The Theory of the Subject

Few areas of contemporary social and political thought are more controversial and important than the area staked out by the theory of the subject. To a considerable extent, it would be true to say that this interest in individual subjectivity, human agency, and the acting self emerged against an academic backdrop of mainstream social science which took such matters for granted. In orthodox social science in the 1950s and 1960s, two conceptual strands dominated. In behavioral approaches, the human subject was regarded as a product of organic wants and needs; hence, the dynamics of mind and action were not viewed as something requiring explication. In functionalist approaches, the individual was viewed as fully molded by society. Controlled by either biology or society, the acting subject was accorded little conceptual or political significance; in effect, the subject was treated as a cultural dope, without any capacity for self-understanding or self-reflection. A critical analysis of human subjectivity, by contrast, has emerged in various guises in social theory in recent decades, and this has been nowhere more obvious than in Continental traditions of social thought. The impact of Freudian psychoanalysis, structural linguistics and post-structuralism, in particular, has been of core importance in this respect, and has given rise to the idea of the "decentered subject."

"Decentered subjectivity" is a term worth exploring. It implies a profound mistrust in the reliability of consciousness as a basis for knowledge. Consciousness of self is a symptom of broader structural forces, sometimes described as language or the unconscious or social relations, and from this vantage point the Cartesian *cogito* ("I think, therefore I am") is rendered suspect. We can find a prefiguring of the "decentered subject," a term which takes off in much radical social theory after the impact of structuralist and post-structuralist linguistics, in the writings of Freud, Nietzsche, and Heidegger.

Each can be seen as questioning, in a profound manner, the philosophical privilege accorded to consciousness. According to each, subjectivity is not transparent: the "subject" is rather its own internal relations, constituted through the unconscious (Freud), the will to power (Nietzsche) or Being (Heidegger).

Freud, in particular, radicalizes the way in which we have come to think about self-identity. For in suggesting that dreams are the "royal road to the unconscious," Freud shows the ego not to be the master of its own home. The presence of unconscious desires were detected at work almost everywhere by Freud, in slips of the tongue, bungled actions, failures of memory, mis-interpretations, and misreadings. Unconscious desires for Freud have a predominantly sexual or libidinal content, and it is precisely for this reason that the ego blocks off knowledge defensively, shifting the energy that subsists in repressed desire to the moral prohibitions and restrictions of the superego. Ego, id and superego are the key agencies in Freud's model of the human mind, a model designed to help practitioners assist the mentally ill or disturbed. But psychoanalysis is much more than just a therapeutical practice. It is also a radical theory about the fundamental emotional creativity of human beings, focusing as it does on the passions and prohibitions that provide civilization with its basic structure. From this angle alone, Freud's work is instructive for rethinking the emotional dimensions of social life – dimensions which have been reductively and deterministically understood by traditional social thought.

Freudian psychoanalysis has come to exert a profound influence over contemporary social theory, especially in cultural analysis, feminist theory, and political studies.[1] A classic statement on the import of Freud for social theory is to be found in Herbert Marcuse's "The Obsolescence of the Freudian Concept of Man" (chapter 1). Marcuse, a leading member of the Frankfurt School, develops a powerful critical social theory of human subjectivity by weaving together the work of Freud, Weber, and Marx. As society undergoes vast technological and post-industrial transformation, says Marcuse, the internal dimensions of human experience alter. The Freudian picture of the human subject – divided between ego, id, and superego – becomes obsolescent. The Freudian self, suggests Marcuse, is dead. But there is nothing at all liberatory about this situation; indeed, the intertwining of advanced capitalism, bureau-cracy, and techno-science leads only to further emotional and sexual restrictions in the personal realm. Tracing how contemporary social relations warp the inner textures of self-identity and communal relations, Marcuse speaks of a "technological desublimation" – an internal vehicle of repression which gears the primary mental structure to the demands of advanced in-dustrial society. In this connection, psychological and political repression are deeply interconnected for Marcuse.

If Freudian theory has come to be associated with the dethroning of the sovereign subject, this is equally true of structuralist linguistics. The key book here is Ferdinand de Saussure's *Course in General Linguistics* (1916), a work which profoundly shaped the development of French structuralism and post-structuralism.[2] In developing a critique of meaning, Saussure paid special attention to what is social, as opposed to what is individual, in the production of language. According to Saussure, there is no intrinsic connection between a word and an object, like the term "dog" and the flesh and blood animal that lies in the back garden. Instead, meaning is constituted through the unity of a sound-image (or signifier) and a concept (or signified). For Saussure, the relation between signifier and signified is *radically arbitrary*. This notion of the arbitrary character of the sign does not mean, absurdly, that individual speakers can make whatever utterances they like in day-to-day conversation and interaction. On the contrary, individual speakers are strongly bound by the conventional usage of linguistic terms in order to be understood. Rather, the principle of relative arbitrariness refers to the internal composition of language as a structure. Language, he suggests, is composed of a set of binary oppositions of signifiers – "day" is only constituted as a sign in terms of its difference from "night," "black" from "white," and the like. Although in Saussure a certain indebtedness to psychology is still evident, the main focus is upon the analysis of language (*langue*) as a system of collective representations, rather than the actual substance of individual speech (*parole*). That is to say, Saussure was not so much concerned with the actual things about which people spoke, but rather with how a signifier comes to be isolated from other signifiers in the preservation of difference. "In language," as Saussure said, "there are only differences *without positive terms*. Whether we take the signified or the signifier, language has neither ideas nor sounds that existed before the linguistic system, but only conceptual and phonic differences that have issued from the system."[3] In this framework, therefore, language is considered as a system of values structured in terms of their internal and oppositional relations, and speech is the individual or subjective realization of language.

In extending the methods of analysis worked out by Saussure, social theorists influenced by structuralist linguistics seek to discern the complex, contradictory connections between language and the production of social life. This concern with signifying practices has come to be referred to as the "linguistic turn" of social theory, and anthropologist Claude Lévi-Strauss's *The Elementary Structures of Kinship* is widely considered one of the first main experiments in sociological semiotics. Linguists and social scientists, Lévi-Strauss contends, "do not merely apply the same methods, but are studying the same thing"[4] – a statement which underwrites the structure of language as of central importance to the explication of social life. This interest in and enthusiasm for linguistics can be characterized as a theoretical means for (1) the critique of a system of signs at any given point in time as an approach to the explication of meaning; and (2) the critical appraisal of objective structures which makes the speech of the human subject possible in the first place. In chapter 2, the French semiologist Roland Barthes traces out the main characteristics of Saussurian linguistics, and applies this theory to the study of personal life and social practices. Barthes's chapter is a good example of structuralist social theory, as it brings Saussurian concepts to bear upon the explication of social phenomena such as fashion, food, and furniture. Social life for Barthes is a complex "system of signs," a relation of relations.[5] Within this complex system can be found the decentered and dispersed human subject, navigating its way through a labyrinth of images, sounds, and texts. The human subject, from such a semiological angle, is a product of this continuous play among signs, of signs rationalized or naturalized, of language as a code. Barthes's principal contribution to social theory lies in the development of a semiological approach to understanding what society reveals about itself through the signs it produces.

It is in the marriage of structuralist linguistics and psychoanalytical concepts, however, that we find the most radical and comprehensive decentering of the human subject. The work of the French psychoanalyst Jacques Lacan is exemplary in this respect. Lacan, in a provocative "return to Freud," attempts to rework the main concepts of psychoanalysis in line with core Saussurian concepts, such as system, difference, and the arbitrary relation between signifier and signified. Lacan's writings are notoriously difficult and elusive. Notwithstanding this, Lacan's Freud has exercised considerable influence in contemporary social theory, from the structuralist Marxism of Louis Althusser to the deconstructive feminism of Luce Irigaray.[6] One of the most important features of Lacan's psychoanalysis is the idea that the unconscious, just like language, is an endless process of difference, lack and absence. For Lacan, as for Saussure, the "I" is a *linguistic shifter* that marks difference and division in the social field; there is always in speech a split between the self which utters "I" and the word "I" which is spoken. The human subject is structured by and denies this splitting, shifting from one signifier to another in a potentially endless play of desires. Language and the unconscious thus thrive on difference: signs fill in for the absence of actual objects at the level of the mind and in social exchange. This is central to Lacan's theory that social relations, or what he calls the Symbolic Order, depend on the repression of desire. "Civilization is built upon a renunciation of drives" wrote Freud, and Lacan's account of the unconscious/language relation is an impressive attempt to theorize this insight in terms of the intersubjective workings of desire and recognition.

The repression of desire then is at one with the very constitution of the self, and according to Lacan this is a process which leaves the human subject forever scarred or internally divided. In "The Mirror Stage as Formative of the Function of the I" (chapter 3), Lacan emphasizes the *narcissistic positioning* of the child on an imaginary level of perception. At some point between six and eighteen months, the child identifies with itself by seeing its image reflected in a mirror. The mirror-stage, Lacan argues, founds an imaginary identity through a narcissistic relationship to images and doubles. The child reacts with a sense of jubilation in seeing itself whole and complete in the mirror, yet this self-recognition is in fact a *misrecognition* since the child is still dependent upon other people for its own physical needs. The process of self-identification, because it occurs via a mirror which is outside and other, is actually one of alienation. In a word, the mirror *lies*. The very process of achieving self-identification, which is necessary to becoming a positioned subject in the social world, renders the child at odds with itself.

What are the gains of this decentering of the subject in structuralist and post-structuralist thought? To begin with, instead of taking consciousness as given, the psychoanalytic post-structuralism of Lacan represents a radical demystification of human subjectivity. Structure predates experience, the mirror frames imaginary perception: the individual subject is a product of the "discourse of the Other," that is signification. Lacan's argument that the subject finds an imaginary identity through an image granted by another represents a major advance on approaches which uncritically assume that the ego or the "I" is at the center of psychological functioning. In stressing that the "I" is an alienating fiction, a misrecognition that masks the split and fractured nature of unconscious desire, social theorists influenced by Lacan locate a sense of otherness at the heart of the self – a theme which runs deep in contemporary thought. The radical edge of such an approach is that it runs counter to much received wisdom, specifically the assumption that experience is unproblematic and that meaning is transparent. By highlighting that all self-knowledge is fractured and fragile – with the individual subject caught between imaginary traps of narcissistic mirroring and symbolic dislocations of language – structuralist and post-structuralist social theory underwrite the view that subject and society are discontinuous with each other. The social world may never seem the same again after having read Lacan, if only for the reason that his theories capture something of the strangeness that pervades the mundane and familiar in daily life.

A novel and critical engagement with Lacan's Freud is developed in an interesting way in the writings of Julia Kristeva.[7] Kristeva, a leading intellectual and practising psychoanalyst in France, develops what might best be termed a post-Lacanian account of processes of signification in "Revolution in Poetic Language" (chapter 4). Kristeva's critique of the subject is at once Lacanian (most notably in terms of her argument for the imaginary framing and symbolic decentring of the subject) and post-Lacanian (through her connection of psychic process to being and action). She explicitly reintroduces the Freudian notion of drives into the linguistic abstractions of Lacanian theory, termed the "semiotic", in order to account for the subject's psychic investment in the mirror stage as preparatory to the constitution of the "I". By the semiotic, Kristeva refers to a realm of prolinguistic experience – of drives, passions, feelings, bodily sensations, and rhythms experienced by the small infant in its pre-Oedipal relationship to the mother. According to Kristeva, these pre-Oedipal, semiotic psychic elaborations undergo repression with the child's entry to the social and cultural processes of the Symbolic Order of language. However, the repression of the semiotic in the Symbolic Order is never complete; semiotic forces cannot be shut off from culture. It is thus obvious to Kristeva that the signifying relations between subject and society are not eternally fixed or given. In order to counter the Lacanian view of the constitution of the subject as a subjectless process, she focuses instead on the structuration of the passions as central to experiences of autonomy and alienation, subjectivity and subjection. There is for Kristeva, in other words, a hiatus between the richly heterogeneous realm of semiotic psychic processes, and a structuralist notion of system in which language speaks the subject.

A related, but distinct, critique of the open-endedness of the signifying process is also to be found in Cornelius Castoriadis's reading of Freud and psychoanalysis. In "The Individual and Representation" (chapter 5), Castoriadis (in rejecting Lacan's linguistic reinterpretation of Freud) argues that human subjectivity cannot be meaningfully understood as a structuralization of the unconscious. Claiming that structuralism and post-structuralism provide no means of coping with the irreducible creativity of self and society, Castoriadis argues that unconscious imagination is an open-ended eruption of representations, drives, and passions. On the level of the individual, it is this radical creativity of the unconscious which accounts for the orientation of symbolism; and, on the level of society, for the affective structuring of institutions. In this connection, Castoriadis reads Freud's therapeutic maxim "Where id was, there ego shall be" not as the possibility of making the unconscious conscious, but rather as highlighting the relevance of unconscious passion to everything we do, and of recognizing that desire is a creative feature of human social life. Imagination, creation, and autonomy are for Castoriadis inextricably intertwined. He thus argues for a notion of autonomous selfhood that demands an interchange of conscious reflection and unconscious desire, the turning back of impulse and desire upon itself in order to effect an alteration in the relation of these psychical systems. This entails defining and thinking the self anew, which also means recognizing the central role of imagination in the life of the individual and in the life of society: difficult tasks, both.

2   Social Structure and Institutional Analysis

The problem of the relation between subject and structure, or individual and society, must be regarded as a core preoccupation of contemporary social thought. In general terms, it would be true to say that those schools of thought which have paid special attention to theorizing individual subjectivity and human action have contributed to a unique understanding of how action and interaction are structured by broader social, cultural, and political forces. This is most obviously true of those forms of contemporary social analysis which have drawn from psychoanalytical theory, both in the various attempts to delineate the unconscious motivation of action as well as the symbolic forms of interpersonal and cultural relations. Notwithstanding the importance of these dimensions of human experience for the social sciences and social theory, however, such frameworks encounter difficulty in providing conceptions of social structure or institutional explanation. Institutions certainly appear in the writings of major theorists of human subjectivity, such as Lacan, Kristeva, and Barthes, and in ways that problematize the connections between self

and society. But as understood from the standpoint of more orthodox sociological traditions, institutions are analyzed by these authors mostly in terms of
their symbolic or semiological meanings, and not in terms of power relations
or social transformations.

Other branches of social theory, such as structuralism and systems
approaches, have sought to remedy this neglect by taking institutional structure as the core ingredient of social explanation. Here there is an explicit
attempt to elucidate, in objective terms, the structures and representations
upon which social interaction depends but which it cannot explicitly grasp or
formulate. In such objectivistic approaches to social-scientific inquiry, there is
a methodological break with the immediate experience of individual agents
and a focus instead on pattern variables of the structural features of modern
industrial societies.

There is, of course, an important line of continuity here with classical social
thought. One central theoretical issue in classical sociology was concerned with
the intrusion of systemic or structural aspects of modern societies into forms of
social conduct, specifically the ways in which structures shaped both the
freedom and oppression of people. The view that economic structures are at
once determinant and dominant in social life is certainly evident in the writings
of Marx. "Human beings make their own history," wrote Marx, "but not in
circumstances of their own choosing."[8] Marx saw in the capitalist mode of
production a dynamic in which people are subjected to the dull compulsion
of oppressive economic relationships; writing about commodity fetishism in
Capital, he argued that the individual subject is caught up in a social logic of
mystified activity and ideology. A somewhat similar understanding of the
power of structures in the lives of people can be found in the writings of Weber.
While Weber held that reason unleashed social critique and the demise of traditional world-views, he too thought that the development of industrial
societies ultimately led to the self-destruction of individuality and human
agency. In Weber's sociology, the iron cage of modernity was a result of rationalization raised to the second power, in which agents functioned as mere cogs
in the machine of the bureaucratic state.

Broadly speaking, many forms of modern social theory have sought to
further explicate the role of structures in the maintenance of social order and
stability. *The Social System* (1951), written by Harvard sociologist Talcott
Parsons, became for many years a classic book for understanding how the
actions of individuals linked to the general social system, its variety of reproductive processes, and socialization patterns. Parsons' functionalism laid
primary stress upon a global system of common values and shared dispositions. In the face of increasing social conflict and political violence
throughout the 1960s and 1970s, however, sociologists found it increasingly
difficult to defend the Parsonian theoretical tradition, with its neglect of issues
of power and domination. As we will see, though, Parsonian theory has made
something of a resurgence in recent times,[9] especially in Europe – where both
Niklas Luhmann and Jürgen Habermas have deployed and refashioned

Parsonian system theory for the analysis of contemporary society. Indeed, Parsonian functionalism and systems-theoretic logic is increasingly deployed in contemporary social theory as an explanation for both social stability and social change.

But if such attempts to understand institutional structures as arising from more than repetitious patterns of human action have merit, they also have limitations of their own. The central limitation of objectivist social theories is that, by according priority to structure over action, a deterministic flavour is accorded to the social world and the practical activities of the individuals who make up the world. Many argue that this is especially obvious in the classical social theory of Emile Durkheim, in which society often appears as a force external to the agent, exercising constraint over individual action.[10] Yet the tendency to grant priority to the object (structure) over the subject (agent) is sustained in various guises in contemporary social thought, principally in the work of structuralist and systems-theory analysts. It might thus be said that, while sociologists concerned with structural-functionalism or systems approaches have managed to analyze the intrusion of systemic factors into domains of social activity, such theorists have managed less well with grasping how structural forces affect the production of everyday life in situated social settings. That this is the case is perhaps not too surprising, for as I have said most social theorists tend to resolve the problem of the relation between human action and social structure by prioritizing one term at the expense of the other. "Few questions in social theory," laments John B. Thompson, "remain as refractory to cogent analysis as the question of how, and in precisely what ways, the action of individual agents is related to the structural features of the societies of which they are parts."[11]

Michel Foucault is widely considered the major social theorist on the social organization of power, particularly in terms of the role of structures in the discipline and surveillance of subjective agency. In "The Means of Correct Training" (chapter 6), Foucault signals his debt to structuralism with his contention that discipline "makes" individuals. The exercise of power, writes Foucault, has increasingly shifted from spectacular, violent, and open forms of punishment in societies of the ancient world to more hidden, disciplinary, and monotonous types of coercive monitoring in modern societies. The prison, the army, the school, the mental asylum: these and other institutions deploy subtle methods of domination based on the continual monitoring, observing, recording, training, and disciplining of human subjects. Foucault's analysis of the rise of the disciplinary society, and in particular the ways in which contemporary methods of surveillance and domination differ from traditional forms of social control, has been tremendously influential in social theory. However, his thesis that the systematic imposition of domination in discourse and surveillance provides a comprehensive model for analyzing power relations in modern societies has also been found wanting. Some analysts have argued that Foucault accords the theme of surveillance too much weight; others argue that his model of power is too one-sided, focused only on how power is installed in institutions and not on those actually subjected to domination.[12] It should be pointed out that Foucault does underline that social practices and structures are always contested; ongoing resistance to power, he says, is everywhere. But it is not clear from this post-structuralist program that Foucault is able to adequately theorize an uncoercive relation to society, nor how power and domination interweave.

Foucault, it might be argued, treats the practical relationship of inner and outer nature, of self and society, as an objectivistic fact of structures. To the extent that this is so, his work preserves a series of oppositions and antinomies that have plagued social theory, such as the individual versus society, action versus structure, subject versus object. In recent decades, a variety of social theorists have sought to overcome these divisions. Perhaps the most original formulations of this transformation in contemporary social theory are to be found in the writings of Pierre Bourdieu and Anthony Giddens.[13] Essential to these attempts is the relating of self and society without prioritizing one term at the expense of the other. The conceptualization of such a relation, it is argued, requires attention not to how structure fixes action or how repetitive actions constitute structures, but rather how action is *structured* and *reproduced* in contexts of daily life.

In "Structures, *Habitus*, Practices" (chapter 7), Bourdieu identifies the conditions of those pre-conscious, ingrained, structured dispositions which inform the multiplicity of actions and practices which individuals carry out in the production and reproduction of social life. The idea of a disposition, or system of dispositions, is what Bourdieu calls "habitus" – a durably installed set of generating principles for making practical sense of the world and one's place in society. The human body, in particular, is regarded by Bourdieu as a key subjective site for such durable dispositions; the specific manner and distinctive characteristics of framed individual action – ranging from, say, differing ways of walking or talking, or thinking and feeling – is of capital importance to the structuring of social practices and representations. An individual from a middle-class background, for example, will most likely have inculcated certain dispositions which differ in crucial respects from those which actors of working-class backgrounds might display. This does not imply, stresses Bourdieu, that the social system can be seen as *determining* the activities or choices of individual subjects. On the contrary, actors have a multiplicity of strategies or tactics at their disposal in the generation of social conduct; in this sense, human agents are purposive, reflective beings. But Bourdieu certainly wishes to emphasize the influence of specific social contexts (or what he calls the "fields" or "markets" of the social domain) within which individuals act. In this connection, he speaks of both a "structuration of practices" and "structuring stuctures."

Another attempt to rethink the notions of, and the relations between, human action and social structure is undertaken by Anthony Giddens in "Elements of the Theory of Structuration" (chapter 8). Like Bourdieu, Giddens argues it is necessary for social theory to provide an account of the conditions and consequences of action as directly embroiled with structure. To do so, Giddens suggests that action and structure should be seen as complementary terms of a duality, the "duality of structure": social structures, he says, are *both medium and outcome* of the practices that constitute those structures. That is to say, social systems are viewed by Giddens as simultaneously enabling and constraining. The structuring properties of social systems, he suggests, at once render human action possible and, through the performance of action, serve to reproduce the structural properties of society. To talk of the "structuring properties" of social systems, as Giddens does, is to adopt a radical, and indeed novel, view of the ways in which structures work in relation to human subjects. Giddens does not view structures so much as things that exist in themselves as, to use his terminology, a "virtual order" of transformative relations that exhibit themselves only in instantiated social practices and memory traces. When Giddens writes of this virtual order of structures his analysis sometimes sounds reminisent of a post-structuralist critique of language – as a structuring of presences against a backdrop of absences. What distinguishes his theory of structuration from post-structuralist thought, however, is a strong conception of human agency. For Giddens, subjects necessarily know a great deal about the social world in which they recursively organize their practices; such practices, he says, are socially embedded as virtual order properties of structures. This mutual dependence of structure and agency is what Giddens calls the "recursive character" of social life, in which self-reflexivity and self-critique are defining features.

For the French sociologist of post-industrial society, Alain Touraine, it is precisely this recursive intertwining of the individual and the wider society that underpins "historicity" – the using of history to make history, the intervention of society in its own functioning. In "Society Turns Back upon Itself" (chapter 9), Touraine suggests that social theory is, above all, the study of historicity: the critical examination of those complex cultural forms in and through which each type of society invents its knowledge, functions as an agent of investment in cultural identities and social institutions, defines and relates to its own social creativity. "Society," says Touraine, "produces itself, imposes a meaning on its practices, turns back upon itself." The rise of the modern, of modernity, is for Touraine the complex history of a world in crisis – a world constantly being challenged, refined, re-examined and reinvigorated.

All institutional forms have a bearing on the subjective and personal aspects of social life, even if an individual subject is incapable of grasping the cultural and material formations in which they are embedded. The fact that every individual is situated within a structured realm of cultural practices, and the latter within a field of dominant social and symbolic systems, means that concentration upon the functional conditions of system properties is an essential task for social theorists. One of the most sophisticated and sustained attempts to enhance the primacy of system over action, while at the same time according the understanding of meaning and self-reference a central place in social analysis, is to be found in the writings of systems theorist Niklas

Luhmann. In "The Concept of Society" (chapter 10), Luhmann argues that the notion of society cannot be grasped through a subject/object dichotomy. Elaborating and refining the functionalist tradition in social theory, Luhmann views society as a multiplicity of system-environment relationships in which self-observation and self-description operate as the constitutive feature of communication-processing. Against a global backdrop of mass media and new communications technology, Luhmann's radical conceptual move is to underline the growing importance of self-referential systems, especially in terms of the increased complexity and differentiation of contemporary societies. Society, writes Luhmann, is a "self-describing object" – by which he means that the constitution of meaning arises out of the mutual observation of actions, practices, and codes that operate self-relatedly within institutional contexts. In this viewpoint, it is the repeated mirroring of self-observing – the interplay of self and other – which contributes to the self-maintenance of the system as well as the reproduction of meaning-processing systems.[14]

When social theorists today reflect on the changing relations between the individual and society, they generally do so in ways that are profoundly shaped by methodological concerns which underscore actor and/or system-based models of analysis. Yet for many social theorists, these issues cannot be worked out at the level of methodology alone. For some theorists the transformations of modernity, such as globalization and the changing character of the public sphere, directly impact upon the nature of the self as well as the textures of day-to-day social life – reshaping the very definition of what is meant by the constitution of personal and social life. According to German sociologists Ulrich Beck and Elisabeth Beck-Gernsheim, for example, the antithesis between individual and system-based social-theoretic perspectives is itself brought low by a new riskiness to risk, the consequences of which people confront everywhere around the globe. What Beck calls "risk society" – an emerging global technological world which generates a diversity of possible dangers, hazards, and futures – is said to bring people into a more active engagement with aspects of their lives, aspects that were previously the terrain of tradition or taken-for-granted norms.[15] In "Individualization and 'Precarious Freedoms': Perspectives and Controversies of a Subject-orientated Sociology" (chapter 11), Beck and Beck-Gernsheim examine the complex and contradictory ways in which risk society opens out to an expansion of choice, or an individual engagement with the self, with the body, with relationships and marriage, with gender, with work. This a process that Beck and Beck-Gernsheim call "individualization." To live in the late modern world, after the end of tradition, is to live in a society where life is no longer lived as fate or destiny; new demands, opportunities, and controls are being placed on people today, such that it is questionable whether collective or system units of meaning and action are socially significant. The rise of risk society, according to Beck and Beck-Gernsheim, is the living of lives increasingly decision-dependent and in need of justification, re-elaboration, reworking, and, above all, reinvention. As a consequence, problems of self/society cohesion – the integration of individualized individuals into the network of broader social relations – necessarily arise in novel forms at both the micro and macro levels.

3 Contemporary Critical Theory

The term "critical theory" refers to a series of core ideas worked out by the Institute for Social Research in Frankfurt (the "Frankfurt School") in the 1920s and 1930s. Preeminent among the first generation of Frankfurt critical theorists were Max Horkheimer (philosopher, sociologist, and leader of the Institute), Theodor Adorno (sociologist, philosopher, and musicologist), and Herbert Marcuse (philosopher and political theorist). While there were many other significant scholars associated with the Frankfurt School, including the literary critic Walter Benjamin and psychoanalyst Erich Fromm, it is in the writings of Horkheimer, Adorno, and Marcuse that the social-theoretical project of linking philosophy and the human sciences, of interweaving theoretical critique with empirical research, most strongly emerges.[16] Among the core issues central to the first generation of critical theorists were the following. What are the major social and political dimensions influencing the trajectory of twentieth-century history? What psychological and political factors underpinned the rise of fascism and Nazism? Why are tendencies towards bureaucracy, rationalization and authoritarianism increasingly prevalent throughout developed societies? And how might theoretical critique keep alive hope for alternative political possibilities, or social utopias? All of these issues remain important in contemporary critical theory, especially in the work of its key exponent, Jürgen Habermas. Others who have contributed to the contemporary recasting of critical theory include Axel Honneth, Albrecht Wellmer and Claus Offe. In order to sketch some of the core continuities and differences between the first and second generation of critical theorists, I want now to briefly examine the critique of power structures developed in Frankfurt philosophy.

Dialectic of Enlightenment, a book written by Horkheimer and Adorno in the 1940s and a foundational text of the critical theory canon, retraces the social-historical character of Reason, from its first appearance in *Genesis* via the Enlightenment through to its institutionalization in the capitalist world economy. With the mass destruction and human tragedy of World War II firmly in mind, Horkheimer and Adorno sought to develop a critical perspective on the application of reason to social life and politics. To do this, they coupled Max Weber's analysis of bureaucracy with Marx's critique of political economy. At the level of both theory and of politics, Horkheimer and Adorno contend that the Enlightenment, in the form of means-end or instrumental rationality, turns from a project of freedom into a new source of enslavement.

For Horkheimer and Adorno, the overall trend of development in western society is that of an expanding rationalization, an instrumental ordering of life in which there is a loss of moral meaning at the levels of society, culture, and personality. In the analyses of the first generation of critical theorists, this loss of meaning is captured by the term "totally administered society" – a term that Adorno gave further analytical clarity to when he spoke of a socio-psychological process of fragmentation, or "logics of disintegration." Linking Freudian psychoanalysis with Marxism, Horkheimer and Adorno propose a self-cancelling dynamic in which all identities and rationalities are constituted through a violent coercion of inner and outer nature. The broad argument is that, in the early phases of modernization, individuals repressed unconscious desires through the imposition of certain Oedipal prohibitions, resulting in a level of self-control which underpinned and reproduced asymmetrical relations of capitalist power. But not so in the administered world of post-liberal industrial societies. In post-liberal societies, changes in interpersonal structures mean that the family is no longer the principal agency of social repression. Instead, human subjects are increasingly brought under the sway of impersonal cultural symbols and technological forms, as registered in the rise of the culture industries (such as popular music, television and the like). The shift from liberal to post-liberal societies involves a wholesale destruction of the psychological dimension of experience: there is, according to Adorno, a socialization of the unconscious in the administered world which comes at the expense of the mediating agency of the Ego itself. The Janus-face of this process reveals itself as the repression of inner nature as the price of dominating external nature. "Man's domination over himself, which grounds his self-hood," write Horkheimer and Adorno, "is almost always the destruction of the subject in whose service it is undertaken; for the substance which is dominated, suppressed and dissolved through self-preservation is none other than that very life as a function of which the achievements of self-preservation are defined; it is, in fact, what is to be preserved."[17]

The idea of the self-destructive character of reason – that is, of a rationality that turns back on itself and creates a new realm of universal domination – is central to the tradition of Frankfurt critical theory, and also receives support, in various guises, from post-structuralist and postmodernist currents of social thought. It is also a core preoccupation of Habermas. Like Horkheimer and Adorno, Habermas is concerned to explore the interrelations between the conditions of social rationalization and the ways in which administrative struc-tures and economic markets come to dominate the lives of human subjects. However, unlike the first generation of critical theorists, Habermas seeks to move beyond the conceptual limitations of a subject-centered conception of rationality by deploying the concept of *communicative action*.[18] According to Habermas, the first generation of critical theorists developed a fatalistic vision of reason as self-mutilating since it was assumed that instrumental rationality applies writ large in all spheres of social action. By contrast, a conception of communicative rationality – which emphasizes the interactions *between* human subjects – prepares the way for a more differentiated social-theoretical analysis of human action and social systems – or so Habermas proposes.

In "The Uncoupling of System and Lifeworld" (chapter 12), Habermas begins by looking at the functionalist systems theory of Talcott Parsons and

Niklas Luhmann. He considers the ways in which functionalism permits an analysis of social rationalization, and considers the limitations of such a purely objectivistic approach to social systems. The theory of communicative action, as elaborated by Habermas in this chapter, draws from systems theory in order to analyze the financial and bureaucratic imperatives impinging upon the economy and state, and how these systems become increasingly self-reproducing through the impact of the objective steering media of money and power. According to Habermas, the analysis of systemic mechanisms which underpin the institutional complexes of modern culture is not the only methodological basis for social theory. For the reproduction of social life also involves personal identity, social integration, and cultural tradition, and it is for this reason that Habermas introduces the notion of life-world. For Habermas the life-world refers to both the public and private spheres, to those domains in which meaning and value reside, of deeply layered communicative interactions between subjects – such as the family, education, art, religion.

Habermas thus argues for a dualist theory of society in which he interweaves the concepts of system and life-world, without reducing one to the other. Habermas claims however that one can trace a *progressive uncoupling of system and life-world* with the shift from traditional to modern forms of social organization. This differentiation or uncoupling is a structural necessity of advanced modern societies: the operation of systemic mechanisms, such as state apparatuses and the market economy, uncoupled from interpersonal relations (that is, operating behind the back of individual agents) is a crucial feature of modernity. But there are also disturbing or pathological features arising from modern social development, and for Habermas these principally stem from the expansion of economic and political steering mechanisms into the interpersonal bases of the life-world – the destructive impact of capitalist reification upon interpersonal communication; the weakening of the public sphere through media homogenization; the increasing reliance of individuals upon expert knowledge (scientific, technological, psychotherapeutic) for self-understanding and the fostering of communal bonds. All of these forces threaten autonomous sociability says Habermas, as the communicative and consensual foundations of the life-world come under the increasing pressure and insidious influence of rationalization. Indeed, systems integration in modernity has become rationalized to such an extent that Habermas speaks of an "inner colonization of the life-world." Such a colonization can be resisted only through communicative reason. The critical involvement and political participation of individuals within the public sphere – in, for example, ecological, peace, and feminist social movements – is viewed by Habermas as an attempt to check and correct the current imbalances between life-world and system forces. New social movements, says Habermas, are primarily defensive in character, since they seek to defend the relentless colonization of the life-world against the systems.

Habermas's attempt to rethink the *interdependence* of socio-political grids and intersubjective communications has been crucial to the development of contemporary critical theory.[19] According to Axel Honneth, however, Habermas's critical theory of society fails to give adequate recognition to the complex dynamics of social interaction and conflict which are, in fact, vital to any reconquest of the life-world through communicative reason.[20] Questioning Habermas's emphasis on the spread of technocratic rationalization and scientific reason into more and more aspects of social life, Honneth affirms the need for critical theory to focus squarely on the interpretation of norms through which actors engage in both communication and conflict. The dynamic of social struggle, says Honneth, is structurally embedded within a moral or ethical space of social interactions; and it is by examining moral spacings of social interaction and conflict that Honneth wants to recover a notion of *praxis* for rethinking domains of intersubjective communication. In particular, the concepts of struggle, conflict and recognition are of core significance to understanding the restructurings of system and life-world in the contemporary era. In "Patterns of Intersubjective Recognition: Love, Rights and Solidarity" (chapter 13), Honneth adopts a number of psychoanalytic motifs and techniques in order to interpret anew intersubjective pathologies that result in instrumentally one-sided relational patterns of self-development. Honneth's adoption of psychoanalytic theory is, in some respects, a return to the project of linking Freud and Marx that was pursued by the first generation of critical theorists, especially Marcuse and Adorno. (Habermas has drawn from Freud, but in a methodological rather than substantive manner.)[21] Unlike the first generation of critical theorists, however, Honneth draws primarily from the object-relational school of psychoanalysis, an approach which is especially well suited to the *intersubjective focus* of contemporary critical theory. By examining reflexive communications about our needs, desires, cultural traditions, and social conflicts in this manner, Honneth underlines the point that an emancipated society and autonomous individuality imply one another.

The German philosopher Albrecht Wellmer, also an influential representative of contemporary critical theory, has rejected Habermas's claim that truth is a rational consensus. For Wellmer, consensus is not a criterion of truth; rather, the disclosure of truth may only come about through intersubjective engagement, through trying to understand others and to make ourselves understood. In "Truth, Semblance, Reconciliation: Adorno's Aesthetic Redemption of Modernity" (chapter 14), Wellmer seeks to insert Adorno's analysis of the truth content of works of art into an intersubjective paradigm of communicative rationality. That is to say, he undertakes a mediation between the first and second generations of critical theorists. Against Adorno's rather solitary, monadic conception of human subjectivity, Wellmer addresses the linguistic turn in critical theory developed by Habermas, arguing that an intersubjective approach highlights that the aesthetic realm offers a *potential for disclosing truth*. In this sense, the beauty of art consists, among other things, in its communicative possibilities. Wellmer's insertion of Adorno's work into Habermasian communication theory offers a novel approach to the aesthetic-expressive realm of social interaction, and a useful corrective to Habermas's downgrading of the aesthetic in favour of a dualistic framework split between instrumental and communicative reason.

4   Race, Multiculturalism, Difference

Recent debates on race, multiculturalism, and difference have fuelled discussions of social identities and values excluded or marginalized in the academic culture of the West. Issues of imperialism and decolonization, which have been substantially addressed through debates about the nation-state, nationalism, and the Third World, have served to highlight the exclusions and omissions of cultural identities and political formations from many of the core institutions of liberal, representative democracies. These debates have in turn underlined the Eurocentric bias of many western social theories, and extended appreciation of the interweaving of race, ethnicity, and cultural differences as sites for the production and politics of identity.

The participants in these debates are in considerable degree all struggling with a number of core questions and issues, many of which bear the strong imprint of current developments in social theory.[22] What are the connections between modernity and its racialized history of identity exclusions? How have racial exclusions and racist dominations become naturalized or normalized in the Eurocentered vision of western traditional thought? How might racist states of mind best be understood? What are the psychic roots of racist practices? How might social theory best develop a non-reductionist and anti-essentialist analysis of racist ideology and racialized discourse? What are the chances of multicultural diversity, and what threats of new racisms, in the postmodern, postcommunist, and post-colonial era of transnationalism? How might the current multiplicity of antiracisms be linked to critical theory and to social theory as a whole?

For many social theorists of differentiated cultural identities and the politics of race, neither the extension of mass consumer markets to previously excluded groups, nor the assimilation and integration of minority histories into dominant or mainstream sociopolitical contexts, seems an attractive model of antiracist development. For such critical antiracists, there is a danger in organizing selves, communities, and nations around a politics of identity, most obviously in terms of undermining commitments to diversity in the public, political domain. If too "inclusivist" or conformist a view is taken of what it means to hold a given identity, perspective or disposition, then we are never far from an unleashing of destructive, paranoid fantasy which underpins racist ideologies and the delegitimation of the political rights of others – or so it is argued. In an attempt to develop a new framework for antiracist practice, Homi K. Bhabha argues for the transformative power of what he calls "the supplementary space of doubling" in "DissemiNation: Time, narrative and the margins of the modern nation" (chapter 15). Drawing from a diverse range of social theorists, including Derrida, Lacan, Kristeva, and Foucault, Bhabha focuses on the political effects of various languages of national belonging. His political aim is to disrupt familiar or settled identity myths, primarily by focusing on the multiple forms in which "nation," "culture," and "community" become the subject of discourse, as well as the object of psychic and cultural identifications. For Bhabha, the supplementary or doubled nature of the national sign – in which "the people" are caught between subject and object status – opens a potential critical space to undermine and alter communal values of the cultural dominant, and to think through new political possibilities.

As far as the relations between social formations and racist ideologies go, contradictions, realignments and flows have been some of the principal terms in which social-theoretic debate has unfolded. Generally speaking, the analytical focus has tended to concentrate on transformations in the dynamic relationship between personality, society, and culture – expressed in the form of, say, racist resurgences or fervently nationalist counter-modernizing movements. Many critical social theorists have thus developed powerful accounts of the ways in which racist individuals and cultures may rationalize, repress, project, or disavow dominant cultural representations of biological difference, racial attributes, genetic discriminations, and general moral or ethical categorizations in the production of oppressive social relations. Yet racialized discourse and racist expression is certainly not only at work within political discourses; it is also, and crucially, reproduced within the disciplines and discourses of the academy. That is to say, many intellectual disciplines reflect racist ideas, both in terms of their history and practice. Sander L. Gilman, in "Sigmund Freud and the Epistemology of Race" (chapter 16), demonstrates, for example, that various psychological and psychoanalytic concepts dramatize this normalization of racisms. By looking at the manner in which psychoanalysis has been inextricably bound up with Jewish culture, Gilman traces both the contributions and limitations of Freud's theories for understanding anti-Semitism. Given that our social world is one in which racism is deeply pervasive, it is hardly surprising, suggests Gilman, that racist modes of thought are represented in psychoanalytic theory. But what is surprising is the manner in which Freud's work, in analytical terms, assaults racialized categories and conceptions of subjectivity throughout modernity. For Gilman, as for Freud, racism cannot be explained away as some kind of aberrant irrationality; rather, racist beliefs, attitudes, and emotions operate within the unconscious, and so racist ideology involves the interlocking of psychology and social processes.

Racial prejudices also need to be understood in a broad historical context. In substantial part their roots are interwoven with western modernization, expansionism, and colonialism. In chapter 17, "Masters, Mistresses, Slaves, and the Antinomies of Modernity," Paul Gilroy emphasizes that the development of black slave culture is of fundamental importance to understanding the racial politics of modernity's Enlightenment project. Taking the social-theoretic work of Jürgen Habermas and Marshall Berman as exemplary of the ways in which black political formations are at once included and excluded from the grand narrative of the Enlightenment and its operational principles, Gilroy argues the need to revise the terms of debate over western culture and modernization in the light of the history of the African diaspora.

What follows from all this is that ethnic identity, far from being some biological stamp upon an individual, is bound up with dynamic and changing relations of political domination, social exclusion, religious heritages, and forms of culture. Thus, for many social theorists the question of how to develop antiracist strategies is an issue that touches on much more than just a mere awareness of possible misunderstandings in and between dominant and ethnic or subcultural identities. For, according to Gayatri Chakravorty Spivak, the production of identity and especially the writing of historical identities – always a process of conflicting and contested narratives – is intrinsically askew from its received sign-systems. Misunderstandings, one might say, are built into the analysis of minority histories in contemporary historiography; the struggle for inclusion and representation, says Spivak, shields the "cognitive failure" of all claims to knowledge. In "Subaltern Studies: Deconstructing Historiography" (chapter 18), Spivak turns her attention to the writings of authors connected to *Subaltern Studies*, a group of intellectuals attempting to recover Indian minority histories by writing the subaltern classes (peasants, slaves, women, children) back into the history of nationalism and the nation, and by translating the subaltern's voice into a contemporary political project.[23] Interestingly, Spivak reads the work of this group against the grain of their own theoretical ambitions and political intentions, focusing especially on the slippages and gaps of some core discursive strategies of the group. The attempt to recover a subaltern or peasant consciousness, she asserts, is in fact an attempt to disclose an identity (unified, fractured, or transformable), and to that extent such constructions of historicity are subject to the projections and investments of the elite, the theorist, the historian. By drawing on deconstructive and post-structuralist theorists, especially Derrida, Spivak seeks to define different configurations of subaltern consciousness; indeed, she points out that the effect of the subject can itself be read as subaltern and thus resistant to historicization.

5   Feminism, Gender, and Sexual Difference

Feminism, perhaps more than any other political and theoretical current within contemporary western societies, has profoundly problematized approaches to questions of self, identity, power, economy, culture, knowledge, and justice. Inspired by the re-emergence of the women's movement in the late 1960s, feminist social theorists have developed powerful and productive accounts which locate both women and men within socio-structural relations of gender, as well as the social and political dimensions of women's oppression and the analysis of male domination (or patriarchy). While feminists stress that the social world is a gendered world, such has been the rapid proliferation and diversification of feminist theorizing that there is by no means a consensus about the sources and dynamics of how gender systems are produced, reproduced, and transformed. Indeed, the very diversity of women's personal and political positions in society and representations in culture has been increasingly explored in contemporary feminist theory, from issues of child-rearing arrangements, through the meanings and values of sexual difference, to the denial or suppression of racial and ethnic gendered identities.

In this way, feminism has emerged as an interdisciplinary site of lively controversy in contemporary social theory. Current varieties of feminist social thought are wide-ranging, and include liberal, radical, post-structuralist, postmodernist, post-Marxist, psychoanalytic, and Foucauldian forms – with each carrying quite distinct implications for understandings of theory, politics, and methodology.[24] Against the backdrop of this theoretical complexity, the following questions emerge as central in current feminist social thought. How are gender systems of domination and oppression constituted and reproduced across time and space? How does gender relate to sexuality and sexual practice? How does gender interconnect with other forms of social relations such as class and race? How are relations of difference and otherness established between men and women, and how might these relate to the construction of sexualities, masculinities, femininities? What are the important determinants of the widespread sociopolitical denigration of women and the feminine? How can previously repressed, unarticulated, or denied aspects of femininity be reclaimed for creative social relationships?

Much traditional feminist talk assumed that an appeal to women in general was a sufficient foundational basis upon which to construct a radical theory of sexual politics. The distinction between sex and gender was crucial in this respect, and provided the conceptual underpinnings upon which many in the women's movement argued for new articulations of gender identities and sexual politics. Feminists such as Kate Millett and Ann Oakley challenged popular understandings of biology as fixed and immutable, and instead concentrated on the construction of biological differences in conjunction with the social environment.[25] If the cultural meanings and representations attached to biological differences of sex are changeable, then so too it is possible – and indeed urgent – to promote the reconstruction of the system of gender power which characterizes modern societies. Taken as a whole, however, this unification of women under the sign of a universal male dominance became increasingly implausible. "What was most attractive," writes Terry Lovell, "in radical feminist thought – its insistence that gender domination existed in its own right and was not reducible to any other form of domination, was also a source of difficulty at the level of theory and analysis as well as of politics. In radical feminist writings 'patriarchy' becomes near-universal and so pervasive that important historical and cultural differences in the social construction of gender are lost from sight."[26] In time, it was feminists of color, sex radicals, and lesbian feminists who brought issues of their own gender-specificities and differences to the fore, while other self-styled critical and postmodern feminists attempted to rethink certain normative issues arising from the re-construction of gender for social theory.

It is through a critique of Freud and psychoanalysis, however, that a number of feminist theorists have sought to explore, reassess, and recover aspects of femininity and feminine modes of thought that were either ignored or denied in the women's movement from the late 1960s and early 1970s. From the stand-point of feminist psychoanalysis, the developmental process of creating a sense of gendered self-identity is regarded as intricately interwoven with particular gender systems, and here it is worth asking about the sorts of emotional conflicts between and about identity, gender, power, and autonomy in the constitution of sexual difference. In her pioneering work on the reproduction of mothering within western capitalist societies, Nancy Chodorow attempts to locate the power of the unconscious, and its centrality to social relations, by analyzing mother/daughter and mother/son relationships in chapter 19: "Gender Personality and the Reproduction of Mothering." Chodorow wishes to explain how asymmetrical gendered relations are reproduced across gener-ations through women's mothering.[27] She argues that the decision to become a mother, as well as patterns of mothering typically associated with male and female development, cannot be adequately explained through recourse to socialization theory. By contrast, her theoretical explanation is that ex-clusive female mothering produces social relations split between connected, empathic female identities on the one hand, and isolated, instrumental male identities on the other. From this perspective, masculine identity is built on a denial of connection with the mother, which results in a fragile emotional world, defensively structured by an instrumental relation to the self, other people, and the social world more generally. Female identity and development, by contrast, is grounded in a strong sense of gender, but is limited in capacity for autonomy and individuality. For Chodorow, mothers largely experience their daughters as doubles of themselves, through a narcissistic projection of sameness. It is this projection of sameness, she suggests, that makes differenti-ation problematic for women.

Like Chodorow, the French feminist theorist Luce Irigaray is interested in women's relation to mothering, as well as to their bodies, desires, and psychic experiences.[28] Indeed, much of her work seeks to engender plural, poetical representations of female sexual pleasure through exploring the richness of women's sexual fantasies. In "This Sex Which Is Not One" (chapter 20), Irigaray takes up Lacan's idea that "woman" exists only as a symptom of male fantasy. Deconstructing psychoanalytic oppositions (both Freudian and Lacanian) between masculine activity and feminine passivity, Irigaray argues that a destructive repetition fuels the core gender splittings of western phallocentric culture – between rationality and emotionality, subjectivity and objectivity, domination and submission. In the patriarchal Symbolic Order, she argues, women are condemned to silence, to their current status as man's Other. Objecting to modernist, monolithic versions of gender development, Irigaray elaborates a feminist appreciation, and indeed celebration, of female sexuality.

Rejecting the Lacanian standpoint that femininity circulates as a sign of lack in the Symbolic Order, Irigaray celebrates the plurality of woman's active sexuality – a sexuality of other desires and other pleasures, which are demanding to be spoken. For Irigaray, women's sexual economy is heterogeneous, dispersed, open-ended, multiple.

In some feminist circles, the concept of identity has been greatly debated and criticized in recent years. This has been so to such an extent that many feminists have suggested that appeals to the idea of identity should be set aside altogether. Indeed, for the post-structuralist feminist theorist Judith Butler the very notion of identity has served to constrain the political possibilities for transforming current gender regimes. Indeed traditional feminist appeals to the "identity of women," in her view, have unintentionally served to reinforce a binary gender order which ruthlessly colonizes and controls dispersed identities and fractured subjectivities. Identity for Butler is thus a form of repression – it is part of a covertly paranoid system of gender roles and compulsive heterosexuality. In "Subjects of Sex/Gender/Desire" (chapter 21), Butler interrogates Lacanian and post-Lacanian theoretical accounts of the binary gender order, and attempts to open up a space for seeing gender as a repetitive performance. She argues that individuals model their gender performances after fantasies, imitations, and idealizations of what it means to be a man or woman within current gender regimes. In this view, our gender performances are analyzed as copies, imitations, and repetitions of cultural stereotypes, linguistic conventions, and symbolic forms governing the production of masculinity and femininity. Subverting the repetition of male-dominated gender regimes, says Butler, is the key task of a critical feminist genealogy.

Postmodern society may well prove to represent a twilight for traditional gendered identities and identity-based gender politics, but it is also a beginning for more affirmative identities, sexualities, genders and communities, a genuinely new set of possibilities for gender politics. Yet how might the new era facilitate the further reconstruction and reinvention of sexualities and genders? In "Living with Uncertainty" (chapter 22), Jeffrey Weeks argues that histories of sexual difference and gender diversity are increasingly put under the miscroscope in contemporary culture. Taking the AIDS crisis as a manifestation of widespread social and cultural change, Weeks examines new forms of personal and moral interdependence against a global backdrop of wider opportunities and fears, hopes and dreads, concerning sexual relationships today. We have, and have to have, says Weeks, a much more engaged relationship with changing sexual expectations and human relationships than used to be the case. For we live in a social world where intersubjective bonds and erotic relations have to be made, and constructed afresh each time. This is a gendered world *decentered* in terms of traditional frameworks (witness the decline of till-death-us-do-part marriages), but *recentered* in terms of emotional and sexual intimacy.

Finally, recent feminist debates have also been much concerned with epistemological problems raised by the study of sexuality and gender. In her programmatic essay "Situated Knowledges: The Science Question in Feminism and the Privilege of Partial Perspective" (chapter 23), Donna J. Haraway warns against appeals to traditional doctrines of objectivity for the grounding of feminist knowledge and politics. Modernist doctrines of objective vision, she suggests, have underpinned the deployment of fixed identity categories. Yet there is nothing about being "female," she says, that binds women together politically and ideologically. Instead, Haraway argues for a nonuniversalistic but still transformative version of postmodern feminism. A commitment to fluid positioning and to passionate detachment, she concludes, is essential for feminists to comprehend the multiplex stories of gender and plurality of knowledges at play in the contemporary age.

6   The Modernity/Postmodernity Debate

Today, as we move into the twenty-first century, it is argued by many, we are witnessing the emergence of a new era. Globalization, new communication technologies, the collapse of Communism, the techno-industrialization of war, the privatization of public resources, the advent of universal consumerism: these are just some of the profound institutional transformations which have taken place at the level of both personal life and planetary systems. Such institutional transformations directly underpin arguments within the social sciences that we stand at the opening of a radical political transition, a transition which leads us to bid farewell to an era dominated by industrial capitalism. Gone is the oppressive, repetitive grind of industrial labour – or so some suggest. Instead, industrialization is replaced by the age of the computational microchip. The floating images and narcissistic codes of the mass media come to be seen as that point where technology invades the inner world of the individual subject, the opening of a new post-word era beyond modernity itself.

A baffling variety of terms have arisen in the attempt to describe novel forms of life beyond modernity – including the "information society," "consumer society," "post-industrial society," "post-capitalist society," "postmodernism," and "postmodernity."[29] Some of the debates about a possible historical transition beyond modernity have concentrated upon institutional dynamics, particularly those which see a shift from industrial production to the production of information as the basis for a new form of political power. Other debates, by contrast, have concentrated on more cultural and aesthetic issues, especially in the realms of art, architecture, and mass culture. These controversies have as a common thread, however, the global expansion of social, economic, and political systems of the developed societies. In this connection, the diagnosis of a postmodern social condition – by far the most debated idea arising from these controversies – is often enough represented as involving the end of modernity and the dissolution of Enlightenment culture.

Several contemporary social theorists in particular have come to be identified with the controversial argument that the concept of postmodernity is best deployed as a description of contemporary experience. Jean-François Lyotard, Jean Baudrillard and Fredric Jameson have, notwithstanding differences in argument, become the symbolic bearers of the case for a *radical postmodernism*.[30] Radical postmodernism is a form of social critique which considers modernity dissolved, and which generates new critical terminologies to comprehend the globalized, mediated nature of today's social, cultural, and political world. Other social theorists have questioned the value of such a broad-ranging historical periodization and global diagnosis, contending that it is not really possible to make sense of the debate over modernity and postmodernity in this manner. Rather than viewing the modernity/postmodernity debate in terms of endings, some social theorists have suggested that modernity is becoming radicalized, intensely reflexive, or pushed to its limits. These arguments might be grouped under the banner of *pragmatic postmodernism*, and theorists associated with this approach include David Harvey, Zygmunt Bauman and Seyla Benhabib. Here the political consequences of modernity are understood as entering into an embarrassing contradiction with its programmatic promises of freedom and justice, such that the condition of postmodernity is understood as an ability to reflect back upon certain core assumptions, practices, and illusions of the modern age. It is to an exploration of the contested distinctions between modernism and postmodernism, modernity and postmodernity, that the following discussion will be directed.

The interplay of order and oppression inherent to social regulation, institutionalized at levels from hospitals and schools through to welfare systems and prisons, is plainly one of the main influences involved in the ordering of daily life in modernity, and in charting out the collective search for a foundational, rationally flawless, and aesthetically perfect, social order. The spirit of modernity makes both possible and necessary social control, order and continuity, with the dominance of means over ends, and energy and resources always rushing ahead of needs and objectives. Paradoxically, however, the modernist project for remaking the world according to the measure of rational calculation and design can be viewed as having fallen victim to the very social process used to justify practices of political control and cultural repression. That is to say, modernist attempts to control, regulate, and order society have often increased, rather than alleviated, human suffering. Expressed in such a manner, the dark side of modernity – the Holocaust, Hiroshima and other catastrophes of twentieth-century history – becomes depressingly all too evident. In short, modernity begins to break apart because of the growing crisis of Enlightenment culture and the way in which the iron grip of instrumental rationality comes to haunt society and politics. This can be given powerful connotations at the level of contemporary culture. From the awesome destructive potential of nuclear weapons to the massive risks of ecological catastrophe, the world in which we live today is fraught with dangers and risks, many of which arise directly as a consequence of the modernist drive for progress. It is against this social-historical backcloth that many social theorists have sought to shift the analysis of contemporary culture towards postmodernity and postmodernization.

Defining the postmodern is the controversial terrain addressed by David Harvey in "Postmodernism" (chapter 24). Modernist expectations, hopes, dreams, ideas, and movements, contends Harvey, are increasingly under pressure and undermined in the contemporary global era of multinational economic and cultural transformations. It is less clear, however, if there is any coherence or meaning to the systems of thought which are replacing modernism and modernity. It is increasingly evident, according to Harvey, that there has been a damaging occlusion of the radically different experiences that coexist, collide, and interpenetrate within the "reality" of modernity. In short, the modernist drive to order, control, and regulate society has been at the cost of repressing "other worlds" and "other voices," such as women, blacks, gays, colonized peoples, and the like. Harvey thus considers in particular how the postmodernist appreciation of "otherness," "multiplicity," and "heterogeneity" have been taken up in radical politics, deployed to reconstruct individual values and social relations in both liberatory and oppressive ways.

One kind of analysis which is particularly interesting for the investigation of postmodernity is the analysis of *narratives*. For postmodernity, in so far as it signifies transformations in the condition of knowledge and communication, is associated with problems of social legitimation, cultural representation, and the exercise of power. In Lyotard's major text on the topic, "The Postmodern Condition" (chapter 25), it is suggested "that the status of knowledge is altered as societies enter what is known as the postindustrial age and cultures enter what is known as the postmodern age." What is altered in the shift from the modern to the postmodern, according to Lyotard, is the legitimating role of narrative, whether in its speculative or emancipatory form. The central premise of Lyotard's thesis is that the "grand narratives" of the modern epoch – reason, emancipation, autonomy, and revolution – have lost their credibility. Modernity was a project that sought to enforce its legitimation in advance: to legitimize social development and political order through the promise of collective emancipation and happiness. Yet the stories told to justify the order-building and chaos-conquering deployments of modernist power have been invalidated by the "dark side" of modernity itself. From the Holocaust to the recurring crises of monopoly capitalism, modernity is reflexively undermined by its use of force, coercion, violence. Such a discreditation of modernity, its narratives for doing and redoing, is inevitably bound up with attitudes of suspicion and ambivalence – both of which Lyotard sees as central to the arrival of a postmodern condition.[31]

Much in sympathy with Lyotard's diagnosis of a postmodern condition, the French sociologist Jean Baudrillard argues that the contemporary age heralds the disappearance of the subject, the death of meaning, the fragmentation of the social, the end of Truth. Postmodernity for Baudrillard is a hyperreal world, a world of *simulational excess*, of seduction and pleasure. Simulations are reproductions of objects or events. The social world, he suggests, is now an endless play of mediated signs, of simulated images, which shift and disperse with every moment. As such, modernist dichotomies between reality and appearance, depth and surface, life and art, subject and object, crumble. Baudrillard identifies three historical orders of simulacra: (1) the feudal era, in which a fixed hierarchy of signs of class, status, and social position was established; (2) the industrial era, in which mechanized production made possible the endless reproducibility of objects of exchange; and, (3) the postmodern age, in which simulation comes to constitute the social world, outstripping the real and representation in the process.[32] In the essay in this volume, "The Precession of Simulacra" (chapter 26), Baudrillard analyzes the complex ways in which simulations structure our social practice, taking Disneyland as a key instance of postmodern reality and its reduplication by signs.

From still another perspective, the American Marxist critic Fredric Jameson contends that the concept of postmodernity is best grasped as a means of understanding changes to the cultural space of "late capitalism." In "The Cultural Logic of Late Capitalism" (chapter 27), which has become a classic statement on the modernity/postmodernity debate, Jameson draws connections between the restructuring of space and time and the radicalization of new media technology on the one hand, and the commodifying logic of global capitalism on the other. For Jameson, as for Lyotard and Baudrillard, postmodernity is a cultural condition of seeming disorder, randomness, fragmentation, excess. Drawing from Lacan's Freud, Jameson examines how a flattening of hierarchy, discernment, evaluation, and value in postmodern cultural conditions is accompanied by a breakdown in the psychological capacity of human subjects to map and locate themselves in terms of the broader social network. Dislocations of self and language, desire and discourse are for Jameson at the heart of the distinctive characteristics of postmodernity as a world system. Unlike Lyotard and Baudrillard, however, Jameson's critique of postmodernity as the cultural dominant of late capitalism seeks to preserve some of the utopian hopes and ambitions of modernity in the late modern age.[33] In particular, Jameson argues for an "aesthetics of cognitive mapping" as a strategy for the empowering of agents and institutions operating in the world space of multinational capital.

Analyzing the postmodernist critique of the death of the subject, of the dissolution of grand narratives, and the demise of standards of rationality and knowledge, Seyla Benhabib considers various developments in contemporary debates about gender in "Feminism and The Question of Postmodernism" (chapter 28). Benhabib argues that postmodernism, in its skeptical and deconstructive attitude towards identity politics and normative claims, constitutes an important alliance for contemporary feminism. Yet by focusing on the relativism and negativity of postmodernist theory, Benhabib also draws attention to some important conceptual and political limitations inherent in arguments that elevate notions of heterogeneity, difference, and otherness at the expense of all else. Developing a dialogue between what she calls weak and strong postmodernist claims, Benhabib examines a range of feminist positions and oppositions to recent critiques of the human subject, institutional justice, and knowledge claims.

The postmodernist thesis of the collapse of grand narratives has been greeted by many with a sense of foreboding. For if narratives of rationality, autonomy, justice, and happiness no longer guide everyday life, surely we are destined to drift into a situation in which "anything goes," a world without moral, ethical, or social order. In "Postmodernity, or Living with Ambivalence" (chapter 29), Zygmunt Bauman challenges such a view. Postmodernity, suggests Bauman, may well prove to represent a new beginning, rather than a demise, for the individual in society, for social responsibility, and for ethics. The core of Bauman's analysis lies in a rejection of the idea that the postmodern is a stage of development beyond modernity. Bauman thinks that proclamations about the end of modernity are sociologically naive. "The postmodern celebration of difference and contingency," writes Bauman in this final chapter, "has not displaced the modern lust for uniformity and certainty." His argument is not so much that we have moved beyond modernity as that we stand in a different relationship to the modern era; this is a relationship in which a postmodern organization and conditioning of modernity leads to genuinely new developments within the contemporary institutional order. According to Bauman, postmodernity is modernity coming to terms with its paradoxes; it is modernity becoming reconciled to its own impossibility at the level of cultural ambitions and political dreams – and deciding, for better or for worse, to live with it. Such liberation from the modernist pursuit of order, control, and hierarchy is liberating to the extent that it clears the way for a deeper appreciation of the open-endedness of possible courses of action for individuals and communities; postmodernity thus turns out to be pluralistic and ambivalent at its core. Yet postmodern ambivalence as a phenomenon filters into anxieties which press in on everyone, generating in turn new fears and discontents which increasingly claim the attention of social institutions and political organizations. The political complexities of our present uncertainty is the core topic of Bauman's discussion of the postmodern in this chapter.

About this Book: Concluding Remarks

In this introduction I have sought to portray the contributions of various social theorists in broad strokes, in order to underline the diversity of conceptual approaches to core issues and problems facing the social sciences and humanities today. I have tried to present these theoretical frameworks in the context of some of the central organizing categories of individual and collective transformations currently occuring in the social world. In addressing these categories – the theory of the human subject; social structure and institutional analysis; contemporary critical theory; race, multiculturalism, difference; feminism, gender, and sexual difference; and the modernity/postmodernity debate – I have sought to introduce the reader to a rich and critical field of research.[34] The selection of readings which follows is drawn from a number of leading figures in contemporary intellectual life, who in very different ways attempt to understand the personal and social transformations associated with the development of modern societies, as well as the postmodern conditioning of contemporary culture.

Notes

Editor's Note: An ellipsis has been used whenever material from the original has been omitted. This applies to all chapters.

1   For further discussion of the influence of Freud and psychoanalysis in contemporary social and political theory, see Stephen Frosh, *The Politics of Psychoanalysis* (London: Macmillan, 1987); Anthony Elliott and Stephen Frosh (eds), *Psychoanalysis in Contexts* (London: Routledge, 1995); Anthony Elliott, *Social Theory and Psychoanalysis in Transition: Self and Society from Freud to Kristeva* (Oxford: Blackwell, 1992); Anthony Elliott, *Psychoanalytic Theory: An Introduction* (Oxford: Blackwell, 1994); Joel Whitebook, *Perversion and Utopia: A Study in Psychoanalysis and Critical Theory* (Cambridge, MA: MIT Press, 1995); Anthony Elliott (ed.), *Freud 2000* (Cambridge: Polity Press, 1998).

2   Saussure was Professor of General Linguistics at the University of Geneva, and his *Course in General Linguistics* was posthumously reconstructed from the notes of his students. See Ferdinand de Saussure, *Course in General Linguistics* (London: Fontana, 1974). There are many criticisms made of Saussure's theories, including the important objection that the explication of meaning is isolated from the social environments of language use as well as the psychological processing of signification, representation, affect. For useful discussions of Saussure see Simon Clarke, *The Foundations of Structuralism* (Sussex: Harvester, 1981); Anthony Giddens, *Central Problems in Social Theory* (London: Macmillan, 1979), ch. 1.

3   Saussure, *Course in General Linguistics*, p. 120.

4   Claude Lévi-Strauss, *The Elementary Structures of Kinship* (London: Eyre and Spottiswoode, 1969), p. 493.

5   Roland Barthes's work can be divided between his early writings which fuse semiotics and structuralism and his later statements which might be characterized as literary post-structuralism. A useful anthology is Susan Sontag (ed.), *Barthes: Selected Writings* (London: Fontana, 1983). See also Louis-Jean Calvet, *Roland Barthes: A Biography* (Indiana: University of Indiana Press, 1995).

6   For critical discussions of Lacan's work in relation to social theory see Peter Dews, *Logics of Disintegration* (London: Verso, 1987), ch. 2; Slavoj Žižek, *The Sublime Object of Ideology* (London: Verso, 1989); Anthony Elliott, *Social Theory and Psychoanalysis in Transition* (Oxford: Blackwell, 1992), ch. 4.

7   For overviews of Kristeva's work and its relationship to social theory see John Lechte, *Julia Kristeva* (London: Routledge, 1990); Jon Fletcher and Andrew Benjamin (eds), *Abjection, Melancholia and Love: The Work of Julia Kristeva* (London: Routledge, 1990); Anthony Elliott, *Social Theory and Psychoanalysis in Transition* (Oxford: Blackwell, 1992), ch. 6. See also Toril Moi (ed.), *The Kristeva Reader* (Oxford: Blackwell, 1986).

8   Karl Marx, *The Eighteenth Brumaire of Louis Bonaparte* (New York: International Publishers, 1963), p. 15.

9   See also Wolfgang Schluchter, *Entwicklung des okzidentalen Rationalismus: Eine Analyse von Max Weber Gesellschaftsgeschichte* (Tübingen: Mohr Siebeck, 1979); Richard Munch, "Parsonian Theory Today" in Anthony Giddens and Jonathan Turner (eds), *Social Theory Today* (Cambridge: Polity, 1987), pp. 116–55; and Roland Robertson and Bryan S. Turner, *Talcott Parsons: Theorist of Modernity* (London: Sage, 1991).

10 See, for example, Durkheim, *Suicide: A Study in Sociology* (London: Routledge and Kegan Paul, 1952). For an analysis of Durkheim's tendency to equate structure with constraint see Anthony Giddens, *Capitalism and Modern Social Theory* (Cambridge: Cambridge University Press, 1971).

11 John B. Thompson, *Studies in the Theory of Ideology* (Cambridge: Polity Press, 1984), p. 148.

12 For detailed discussions of Foucault's work in relation to issues of surveillance and domination see David C. Hoy (ed.), *The Foucault Reader* (Oxford: Blackwell, 1986); Mark Poster, *The Mode of Information* (Cambridge: Polity, 1990); David Lyon, *The Electronic Eye: The Rise of Surveillance Society* (Cambridge: Polity, 1994). Useful discussions of Foucault's theory of power are to be found in Peter Dews, *Logics of Disintegration* (London: Verso, 1987); and Lois McNay, *Foucault: A Critical Introduction* (Cambridge: Polity, 1994).

13 For useful introductory overviews and critical appraisals of the writings of Pierre Bourdieu and Anthony Giddens see John B. Thompson, *Studies In The Theory of Ideology* (Cambridge: Polity, 1984), chs 2 and 4; Charles Lemert, *Sociology After The Crisis* (New York: Westview Press, 1991), ch. 7.

14 Luhmann's introduction of the concept of *meaning* as a fundamental category of systems theory has functionalist overtones. He uses the concept to denote reductions in the complexity of social systems. For further discussion, see Thomas McCarthy, *Ideals and Illusions: On Reconstruction and Deconstruction in Contemporary Critical Theory* (Cambridge, MA: MIT Press, 1991), pp. 154–60.

15 See Ulrich Beck, *Risk Society: Towards a New Modernity* (London: Sage, 1992).

16 There are several fine overviews of the work of the first generation of Frankfurt critical theorists available. In particular, see Martin Jay, *The Dialectical Imagination* (Boston: Little, Brown and Company, 1973); David Held, *Introduction to Critical Theory* (London: Hutchinson, 1980); Seyla Benhabib, *Critique, Norm, Utopia: A Study of the Foundations of Critical Theory* (New York: Columbia University Press, 1986).

17 Max Horkheimer and Theodor Adorno, *Dialectic of Enlightenment* (London: Allen Lane, 1970), p. 54.

18 For useful introductory analyses of Habermas's social theory see William Outhwaite, *Habermas: A Critical Introduction* (Cambridge: Polity, 1994), and Thomas McCarthy, *The Critical Theory of Jürgen Habermas* (Cambridge, MA: MIT, 1978). See also the essays in John B. Thompson and David Held (eds), *Habermas: Critical Debates* (London: Macmillan, 1982).

19 On the importance of Habermas's theory of communicative rationality to the rethinking of political action and collective decision-making in contemporary critical theory see Thomas McCarthy, *Ideals and Illusions: On Reconstruction and Deconstruction in Contemporary Critical Theory* (Cambridge, MA: MIT Press, 1991).

20 See Axel Honneth, *The Critique of Power* (Cambridge, MA: MIT, 1991).

21 For critical discussions of Habermas's engagement with Freud and psychoanalysis see Anthony Elliott, *Social Theory and Psychoanalysis in Transition* (Oxford: Blackwell, 1992); Joel Whitebook, *Perversion and Utopia* (Cambridge, MA: MIT,

1995). Honneth draws from the psychoanalytical critical theory of Jessica Benjamin, especially her work on recognition and autonomy developed in *The Bonds of Love* (London: Virago, 1990).

22   There are many fine overviews of the construction and deconstruction of race and ethnicity in social theory; in particular, see David Theo Goldberg, *Racist Culture* (Oxford: Blackwell, 1993); John R. Feagin and Hernan Vera, *White Racism* (London: Routledge, 1995); Avery F. Gordon and Chrisopher Newfield (eds), *Mapping Multiculturalism* (Minneapolis: University of Minnesota Press, 1996); Montserrat Guibernau and John Rex (eds), *The Ethnicity Reader* (Cambridge: Polity, 1997).

23   The Subaltern Studies Collective was founded in 1982 with the aim of deconstructing colonialist and nationalist perspectives in the historiography of colonized countries. For further discussion, see Ranajit Guha (ed.), *A Subaltern Studies Reader: 1986–1995* (Minneapolis: University of Minnesota Press, 1997).

24   For critical discussions of varieties of feminist social theory see Jane Flax, *Thinking Fragments* (Berkeley: University of California Press, 1990), ch. 5; Linda Nicholson (ed.), *Feminism/Postmodernism* (New York: Routledge, 1990); Michéle Barrett and Anne Phillips (ed.), *Destabilizing Theory: Contemporary Feminist Debates* (Cambridge: Polity, 1992); Seyla Benhabib and Drucilla Cornell (eds), *Feminism As Critique* (Cambridge: Polity, 1987); Alice A. Jardine, *Gynesis: Configurations of Woman and Modernity* (Ithaca: Cornell University Press, 1985); Drucilla Cornell, *Beyond Accommodation* (London: Routledge, 1991).

25   See Kate Millett, *Sexual Politics* (London: Hart-Davis, 1971) and Ann Oakley, *Sex, Gender and Society* (London: Temple-Smith, 1972).

26   Terry Lovell, "Feminist Social Theory" in B. Turner (ed.), *The Blackwell Companion to Social Theory* (Oxford: Blackwell, 1996), p. 315.

27   For a detailed account of this thesis see Nancy Chodorow, *The Reproduction of Mothering* (Berkeley: University of California Press, 1978). See also "Nancy J. Chodorow talks to Anthony Elliott," *Free Associations*, Vol. 6, Part 2, No. 38, 1996: 161–73.

28   For a critical discussion of Irigaray's work and its relation to social theory see Margaret Whitford, *Luce Irigaray: Philosophy in the Feminine* (London: Routledge, 1991).

29   The debates over whether western societies are making a basic transition from modernity to postmodernity are highly complex and terminologically dense. For introductions and commentaries on these debates, see Barry Smart, *Modern Conditions, Postmodern Controversies* (London: Routledge, 1991); Scott Lash and Jonathan Friedman (eds), *Modernity and Identity* (Oxford: Blackwell, 1991); Steven Seidman and David Wagner (eds), *Postmodernism and Social Theory* (Oxford: Blackwell, 1991); Linda Nicholson (ed.), *Feminism/Postmodernism* (New York: Routledge, 1990); Steven Seidman (ed.), *The Postmodern Turn* (Cambridge: Cambridge University Press, 1994); Anthony Elliott, *Subject To Ourselves: Social Theory, Psychoanalysis and Postmodernity* (Cambridge: Polity Press, 1996).

30   The analytical distinction that I propose between radical postmodernism and pragmatic postmodernism is intended as a general one. Differences in historical periodization, particularly in terms of whether the modern/postmodern is viewed in terms of repetition or rupture, is of core significance to grasping the ambiguity and controversy that marks this debate. Notwithstanding these reservations, I have suggested these terms as a means to problematize some of the analytical and political assumptions of modernist and postmodernist social theory. For a related

schema, see Charles Lemert, who breaks the debate into "radical modernism," "strategic postmodernism," and "radical postmodernism": *Postmodernism Is Not What You Think* (Oxford: Blackwell, 1997), ch. 2.

31   For a useful discussion of Lyotard's work in relation to social theory, see C. Rojek and B. S. Turner (eds), *The Politics of Jean-François Lyotard* (London: Routledge, 1998).

32   See Jean Baudrillard, *Symbolic Exchange and Death* (London: Sage, 1993). For useful discussions of Baudrillard's social theory see Douglas Kellner, *Jean Baudrillard* (Cambridge: Polity, 1988); Douglas Kellner (ed.), *Baudrillard: A Critical Reader* (Oxford: Blackwell, 1994); Mike Gane, *Baudrillard's Bestiary: Baudrillard and Culture* (London: Routledge, 1991); Mike Gane, *Baudrillard and Critical and Fatal Theory* (London: Routledge, 1991); Mike Gane (ed.), *Baudrillard Live: Selected Interviews* (London: Routledge, 1993).

33   For further discussion, see Sean Homer, *Fredric Jameson: Marxism, Hermeneutics, Postmodernism* (Cambridge: Polity, 1997).

34   Finally, for the reader who wishes to follow further statements on the current state of social theory, I recommend the following books: John B. Thompson, *Studies in the Theory of Ideology* (Cambridge: Polity, 1984); Anthony Giddens and Jonathan Turner (eds), *Social Theory Today* (Cambridge: Polity, 1988); Peter Dews, *Logics of Disintegration: Post-Structuralist Thought and The Claims of Critical Theory* (London: Verso, 1987); Steven Seidman, *Contested Knowledge: Social Theory in the Postmodern Era* (Oxford: Blackwell, 1994); Bryan S. Turner (ed.), *The Blackwell Companion to Social Theory* (Oxford: Blackwell, 1996); Patrick Baert, *Social Theory in the Twentieth Century* (Cambridge: Polity, 1998).

Part I
The Theory of the Subject

1

The Obsolescence of the Freudian Concept of Man

Herbert Marcuse

Some of the basic assumptions of Freudian theory both in their orthodox as well as revisionist development have become obsolescent to the degree to which their object, namely, the "individual" as the embodiment of id, ego, and superego has become obsolescent in the social reality. The evolution of contemporary society has replaced the Freudian model by a social atom whose mental structure no longer exhibits the qualities attributed by Freud to the psychoanalytic object. Psychoanalysis, in its various schools, has continued and spread over large sectors of society, but with the change in its object, the gap between theory and therapy has been widened. Therapy is faced with a situation in which it seems to help the Establishment rather than the individual. The Truth of psychoanalysis is thereby not invalidated; on the contrary, the obsolescence of its object reveals the extent to which progress has been in reality regression. Psychoanalysis thus sheds new light on the politics of advanced industrial society.

This essay outlines the contribution of psychoanalysis to political thought by trying to show the social and political content in the basic psychoanalytic concepts themselves. The psychoanalytic categories do not have to be "related" to social and political conditions – they are themselves social and political categories. Psychoanalysis could become an effective social and political instrument, positive as well as negative, in an administrative as well as critical function, because Freud had discovered the mechanisms of social and political control in the depth dimension of instinctual drives and satisfactions.

It has often been said that Freud's theory depended, for much of its validity, on the existence of Viennese middle class society in the decades preceding the Fascist era – from the turn of the century to the inter-war period. There is a kernel of truth in this facile correlation, but its geographical and historical limits are false. At the time of its maturity, Freud's theory comprehended the past rather than the present – a vanishing rather than a prevalent image of man, a disappearing form of human existence. Freud describes a dynamic mental structure: the life-and-death struggle between antagonistic forces – id and ego, ego and superego, pleasure principle and reality principle, Eros and Thanatos. This struggle is fought out entirely in and by the individual, in and by his body and mind; the analyst acts as the spokesman (silent spokesman!) of *reason* – in the last analysis the individual's *own* reason. He only activates, articulates what is *in* the patient, his mental faculties and capabilities. "The id shall become ego": here is the rationalist, rational program of psychoanalysis – conquest of the unconscious and its "impossible" drives and objectives. It is by virtue and power of his own reason that the individual abandons the uncompromising claims of the pleasure principle and submits to the dictate of the reality principle, that he learns to maintain the precarious balance between Eros and Thanatos – that he learns to eke out a living in a society (Freud says: "civilization") which is *increasingly* incapable of making him happy, that is to say, of satisfying his instinctual drives.

I wish to emphasize two elements in this conception which indicate its roots in social and political conditions which no longer exist. First, Freud presupposes throughout an irreconcilable conflict between the individual and his society. Second, he presupposes individual awareness of this conflict and, in the case of the patient, the vital need for a settlement – both expressed by the inability to function normally in the given society. The conflict has its roots, not merely in the private case history of the patient but also (and primarily!) in the general, universal fate of the individual under the established reality principle: the ontogenetic case history repeats, in a particular form, the phylogenetic history of mankind. The dynamic of the Oedipus situation is not only the hidden mode of every father-son relationship but also the secret of the enduring domination of man by man – of the conquests and failures of civilization. In the Oedipus situation are the individual and instinctual roots of the reality principle which governs society. To a considerable extent, therapy depends on recognition of the internal link between individual and general unhappiness. The successfully analyzed individual remains unhappy, with an unhappy consciousness – but he is cured, "liberated" to the degree to which he recognizes the guilt and the love of the father, the crime and the right of the authorities, his successors, who continue and extend the father's work. Libidinal ties thus continue to insure the individual's submission to his society: he achieves (relative) autonomy within a world of heteronomy.

What are the historical changes that have made this conception obsolete? According to Freud, the fatal conflict between the individual and society is first and foremost experienced and fought out in the confrontation with the father: here, the universal struggle between Eros and Thanatos erupts and determines the development of the individual. And it is the father who enforces the subordination of the pleasure principle to the reality principle; rebellion and the attainment of maturity are stages in the contest with the father. Thus, the primary "socialization" of the individual is the work of the family, as is whatever autonomy the child may achieve – his entire ego develops in a circle and refuge of privacy: becoming oneself with but also *against* the other. The "individual" himself is the living process of *mediation* in which all repression and all liberty are "internalized," made the individual's own doing and undoing.

Now this situation, in which the ego and superego were formed in the struggle with the father as the paradigmatic representative of the reality principle – this situation is historical: it came to an end with the changes in industrial society which took shape in the inter-war period.[1] I enumerate some of the familiar features: transition from free to organized competition, concentration of power in the hands of an omnipresent technical, cultural, and political administration, self-propelling mass production and consumption, subjection of previously private, asocial dimensions of existence to methodical indoctrination, manipulation, control.[2] In order to elucidate the extent to which these changes have undermined the basis of Freudian theory, I wish to emphasize only two interrelated tendencies which affect the social as well as the mental structure.

First, the classical psychoanalytic model, in which the father and the father-dominated family was the agent of mental socialization, is being invalidated by society's direct management of the nascent ego through the mass media, school and sport teams, gangs, etc. Second, this decline in the role of the father follows the decline of the role of private and family enterprise: the son is increasingly less dependent on the father and the family tradition in selecting and finding a job and in earning a living. The socially necessary repressions and the socially necessary behavior are no longer learned – and internalized – in the long struggle with the father[3] – the ego ideal is rather brought to bear on the ego directly and "from outside," *before* the ego is actually formed as the personal and (relatively) autonomous subject of mediation between him*self* and others.

These changes reduce the "living space" and the autonomy of the ego and prepare the ground for the formation of *masses*. The mediation between the self and the other gives way to immediate identification. In the social structure, the individual becomes the conscious and unconscious object of administration and obtains his freedom and satisfaction in his role *as* such an object; in the mental structure, the ego shrinks to such an extent that it seems no longer capable of sustaining itself, as a self, in distinction from id and superego. The multi-dimensional dynamic by which the individual attained and maintained his own balance between autonomy and heteronomy, freedom and repression, pleasure and pain, has given way to a one-dimensional static identification of the individual with the others and with the administered reality principle. In this one-dimensional structure, the space no longer exists in which the mental processes described by Freud can develop; consequently, the object of psychoanalytic therapy is no longer the same, and the social function of psychoanalysis is changed by virtue of the changes in the mental structure – themselves produced and reproduced by the society.

But according to Freud, the basic mental processes and conflicts are not "historical," confined to a specific period and social structure – they are universal, "eternal," and fatal. Then, these processes cannot have disappeared, and these conflicts cannot have been resolved – they must continue to prevail in different forms corresponding to and expressive of the different contents. They do so in the conditions which characterize the new society: in the behavior of the masses and in their relation to their new masters who impose the reality principle, namely, their leaders. The term "leader" here is meant to designate not only the rulers in authoritarian states but also those in totalitarian democracies, and "totalitarian" here is redefined to mean not only terroristic but also pluralistic absorption of all effective opposition by the established society.

Now Freud himself has applied psychoanalysis to conditions where his classical model of ego formation seemed invalid without essential modifications. In his *Group Psychology and the Analysis of the Ego*, psychoanalysis makes the necessary step from individual to collective psychology, to the analysis of the individual as member of the masses, the individual mind as collective mind – a necessary step because from the beginning Freudian theory had encountered the universal in the particular, the general in the individual unhappiness. The analysis of the ego turns into *political* analysis where individuals combine in masses, and where the ego ideal, conscience, and responsibility have been "projected," removed from the realm of the individual psyche and embodied in an external agent. This agent, which thus assumes some of the most important functions of the ego (and superego), is the *leader*. As their collective ego ideal he unifies the individuals by the double tie of identification with him, and among the individuals themselves. The complex mental processes involved in the formation of masses must remain outside the scope of this chapter; only the points will be emphasized which may show whether the obsolescence of the analysis of the ego also extends to Freud's group psychology. According to Freud's group psychology, the ties which bind the individuals into masses are libidinal relationships. They are in their entirety "aim-inhibited" impulses, and they pertain to a weakened and impoverished ego and thus signify a regression to primitive stages of the development in the last analysis to the primal horde.

Freud derives these features from the analysis of two large "artificial" masses which he takes as examples: the Church and the army. The question is whether at least some results of his analysis can be applied to the formation of even larger masses in advanced industrial society. I shall offer a few suggestions in this respect.

The most general and at the same time fundamental element in the formation of masses in developed civilization is, according to Freud, the specific "regression to a primitive mental activity" which relates an advanced civilization back to the prehistoric beginnings – to the primal horde.

Freud enumerates the following features as characteristic of regression in the formation of masses: "dwindling of the conscious individual personality, the focusing of thoughts and feelings into a common direction, the predominance of emotions and of the unconscious mental life, the tendency to the immediate carrying out of intentions as they emerge." These regressive features indicate that the individual has given up his ego ideal and substituted for it the group ideal as embodied in the leader.[4] Now it seems that the regressive traits noted by Freud are indeed observable in the advanced areas of industrial society. The shrinking of the ego, its reduced resistance to others appears in the ways in which the ego holds itself constantly open to the messages imposed from outside. The antenna on every house, the transistor on every beach, the jukebox in every bar or restaurant are as many cries of desperation – not to be left alone, by himself, not to be separated from the Big Ones, not to be condemned to the emptiness or the hatred or the dreams of oneself. And these cries engulf the others, and even those who still have and want an ego of their own are condemned – a huge captive audience, in which the vast majority enjoys the captor.

But the regression of the ego shows forth in even more fateful forms, above all in the weakening of the "critical" mental faculties: consciousness and conscience. (They are interrelated: no conscience without developed knowledge, without recognition of good and evil.) Conscience and personal responsibility decline "objectively" under conditions of total bureaucratization, where it is most difficult to attribute and to allocate autonomy, and where the functioning of the apparatus determines – and overrides – personal autonomy. However, this familiar notion contains a strong ideological element: the term "bureaucracy" covers (as does the term "administration") very different and even conflicting realities: the bureaucracy of domination and exploitation is quite another than that of the "administration of things," planfully directed toward the development and satisfaction of vital individual needs. In the advanced industrial societies, the administration of things still proceeds under the bureaucracy of domination: here, the perfectly rational and progressive transfer of individual functions to the apparatus is accompanied by the irrational transfer of conscience and by the repression of consciousness.

The insights of psychoanalysis go a long way to explaining the frightful ease with which the people submit to the exigencies of total administration, which include total preparation for the fatal end. Freed from the authority of the weak father, released from the child-centered family, well equipped with the ideas and facts of life as transmitted by the mass media, the son (and to a still lesser degree, the daughter) enter a ready-made world in which they have to find their way. Paradoxically, the freedom which they had enjoyed in the progressive, child-centered family turns out to be a liability rather than a blessing: the ego that has grown without much struggle appears as a pretty weak entity, ill equipped to become a self with and against others, to offer effective resistance to the powers that now enforce the reality principle, and which are so very different from father (and mother) – but also so very different from the images purveyed by the mass media. (In the context of Freudian theory, the paradox disappears: in a repressive civilization, the weakening of the father's role and his replacement by external authorities must weaken the libidinal energy in the ego and thus weaken its life instincts.)

The more the autonomous ego becomes superfluous, even retarding and disturbing in the functioning of the administered, technified world, the more does the development of the ego depend on its "power of negation," that is to say, on its ability to build and protect a personal, private realm with its own individual needs and faculties. Yet this ability is impaired on two grounds: the immediate, external socialization of the ego, and the control and management of free time – the massification of privacy. Deprived of its power of negation, the ego, striving to "find identity" in the heteronomous world, either spends itself in the numerous mental and emotional diseases which come to psychological treatment, or the ego submits quickly to the required modes of thought and behaviour, assimilating its self to the others. But the others, in the role of competitors or superiors, evoke instinctual hostility: identification with their ego ideal activates aggressive energy. The externalized ego ideal guides the spending of this energy: it does not drive the conscience as the moral judge of the ego, but rather directs aggression toward the external enemies of the ego ideal. The individuals are thus mentally and instinctually predisposed to accept and to make their own the political and social necessities which demand the permanent mobilization with and against atomic destruction, the organized familiarity with man-made death and disfiguration.

The member of this society apprehends and evaluates all this, not by himself, in terms of his ego and his own ego ideal (his father and the father's images) but through all others and in terms of their common, externalized ego ideal: the National or Supranational Purpose and its constituted spokesmen. The reality principle speaks en masse: not only through the daily and nightly media which coordinate one privacy with that of all others, but also through the kids, the peer groups, the colleagues, the corporation. The ego conscience is theirs; the rest is deviation, or identity crisis, or personal trouble. But the external ego ideal is not imposed by brute force: there is deep-going harmony between outside and inside, for coordination begins long before the conscious stage: the individuals get from outside what they would want by themselves; identification with the collective ego ideal takes place in the child, although the family is no longer the primary agent of socialization. The conditioning in the family rather is a *negative* one: the child learns that *not* the father but the playmates, the neighbours, the leader of the gang, the sport, the screen are the authorities on appropriate mental and physical behaviour. It has been pointed out how this decisive change is connected with the changes in the economic structure: the decline of the individual and family enterprise, of the importance of traditional "inherited" skills and occupations, the need for general education, the increasingly vital and comprehensive function of professional, business, and labor organizations – all this undermined the role of the father – and the psychoanalytic theory of the superego as the heir of the father. In the most advanced sectors of modern society, the citizen is no longer seriously haunted by father images.

These changes seem to invalidate the Freudian interpretation of modern mass society. Freud's conception demands a leader as the unifying agent, and demands transference of the ego ideal to the leader as father image. Moreover, the libidinal ties which bind the members of the masses to the leaders and to each other are supposed to be an "idealistic remodelling of the state of affairs in the primal horde, where all of the sons knew that they were equally persecuted by the primal father, and feared him equally." But the fascist leaders were no "fathers," and the post-fascist and post-Stalinist top leaders do not display the traits of the heirs of the primal father – not by any stretch of "idealizing" imagination. Nor are their citizens all equally persecuted or equally loved: this sort of equality prevails neither in the democratic nor in the authoritarian states. To be sure, Freud envisaged the possibility that "an idea, an abstraction may . . . be substituted for the leader," or that a "common tendency" may serve as substitute, embodied in the figure of a "secondary leader." The National Purpose, or Capitalism, or Communism, or simply Freedom may be such "abstractions"; but they hardly seem to lend themselves to libidinal identification. And we shall certainly be reluctant, in spite of the state of permanent mobilization, to compare contemporary society with an army for which the commander-in-chief would function as the unifying leader. There are, to be sure, enough leaders, and there are top leaders in every state, but none of them seems to fit the image required for Freud's hypothesis. At least in this respect, the attempt at a psychoanalytic theory of the masses appears untenable – here too, the conception is obsolete. We seem to be faced with a reality which was envisaged only at the margin of psychoanalysis – the *vaterlose Gesellschaft* (society without fathers). In such a society, a tremendous release of destructive energy would occur: freed from the instinctual bonds with the father as authority and conscience, aggressiveness would be rampant and lead to the collapse of the group. Evidently this is not (or not yet) our historical situation: we may have a society in which the individuals are no longer tamed and guided by the father images but other and apparently no less effective agents of the reality principle have taken their place. Who are they?

They are no longer identifiable within the conceptual framework of Freud: society has surpassed the stage where psychoanalytic theory could elucidate the ingression of society into the mental structure of the individuals and thus reveal the mechanisms of social control *in* the individuals. The cornerstone of psychoanalysis is the concept that social controls emerge in the struggle between instinctual and social needs, which is a struggle within the ego and against personal authority. Consequently, even the most complex, the most objective, impersonal social and political control must be "embodied" in a *person* – "embodied" not in the sense of a mere analogy or symbol but in a very literal sense: instinctual ties must bind the master to the slave, the chief to the subordinate, the leader to the led, the sovereign to the people.

Now nobody would deny that such ties still exist: the election campaigns provide sufficient evidence, and the hucksters know only too well how to play on these instinctual processes. But it is not the image of the father that is here invoked; the stars and starlets of politics, television, and sports are highly fungible (in fact, the question may be raised whether their costly promotion is not already wasteful even in terms of the Establishment – wasteful to the extent to which the choice is narrowed down to one between equivalents in the same class of goods). Their fungibility indicates that we cannot possibly attribute to them as *persons* or *"personalities"* the vital role which the embodiments of the ego ideal are supposed to play in establishing social cohesion. These star-leaders, together with the innumerable sub-leaders, are in turn functionaries of a higher authority which is no longer embodied in a person: the authority of the prevailing productive apparatus which, once set in motion and moving efficiently in the set direction, engulfs the leaders and the led – without however, eliminating the radical differences between them, that is, between the masters and the servants. This apparatus includes the whole of the physical plant of production and distribution, the technics, technology, and science applied in this process, and the social division of labor sustaining and propelling the process. Naturally, this apparatus is directed and organized by men, but their ends and the means to attain them are determined by the require-ments of maintaining, enlarging, and protecting the apparatus – a loss of autonomy which seems qualitatively different from the dependence on the available "productive forces" characteristic of preceding historical stages. In the corporate system with its vast bureaucracies, individual responsibility is as diffuse and as intertwined with others as is the particular enterprise in the national and international economy. In this diffusion, the ego ideal takes shape which unites the individuals into citizens of the mass-society: overriding the various competing power elites, leaders, and chiefs, it becomes "embodied" in the very tangible laws which move the apparatus and determine the behaviour of the material as well as the human object; the technical code, the moral code, and that of profitable productivity are merged into one effective whole.

But while Freud's theory of leadership as heir of the father–superego seems to collapse in the face of a society of total reification, his thesis still stands according to which all lasting civilized association, if it is not sustained by brute terror, must be held together by some sort of libidinal relationships – mutual identification. Now while an "abstraction" cannot really become the object of libidinal cathexis, a concrete apparatus can become such an object: the example of the automobile may serve as an illustration. But if the automobile (or another machine) is libidinally cathected over and above its use-value as vehicle or place for unsublimated sexual satisfaction, it clearly provides substitute grati-fication – and a rather poor substitute to boot. Consequently, in Freudian terms, we must assume that the direct, objective enforcement of the reality principle, and its imposition on the weakened ego, involve weakening of the life instincts (Eros) and growth of instinctual aggression, of destructive energy. And under the social and political conditions prevailing in the coexisting technological societies today, the aggressive energy thus activated finds its very concrete and *personified* object in the common *enemy* outside the group.

For capitalism, Communism provides the powerful negation of the ego ideal, of the established reality principle itself, and thus provides the powerful impulse of identification and massification in defense of the established reality principle. The ascendancy of aggressive over libidinal energy appears as an essential factor in this form of social and political cohesion. And in this form, the *personal* cathexis is possible which the reified hierarchy of technological society denies to the individuals – it is the enemy as personified target which becomes the object of instinctual cathexis – the "negative" aggressive cathexis. For in the daily intake of information and propaganda, the images of the enemy are made concrete, immediate – human or rather inhuman: it is not so much Communism, a highly complex and "abstract" social system, as the reds, the commies, the comrades, Castro, Stalin, the Chinese, who are threatening – a very personalized power against which the masses form and unite. The enemy is thus not only more concrete than the abstraction which is his reality – he is also more flexible and fungible and can assimilate many familiar hated impersonations, such as pinks, intellectuals, beards, foreigners, Jews, in accordance with the level and interest of the respective social group.

This recourse to psychoanalytic concepts for the interpretation of political conditions in no way invalidates or even minimizes the obvious *rational* explanation. Obviously, the very existence and growth of Communism presents a clear and present danger to the western systems; obviously, the latter must mobilize all available resources, mental as well as physical, in its defense; obviously, in the area of atomic and automation technology, such mobilization destroys the more primitive and personal forms of "socialization" characteristic of the preceding stages. No depth psychology is necessary in order to understand these developments. It does seem necessary, however, in view of the massive spread and absorption of the image of the enemy, and in view of the impact on the mental structure of the people. In other words, psychoanalysis may elucidate, not the political facts, but what they do to those who suffer these facts.

The danger in mass formation which is perhaps least susceptible to control is the quantum of destructive energy activated by this formation. I see no possibility of denying or even minimizing the prevalence of this danger in advanced industrial society. The arms race, with weapons of total annihilation, with the consent of a large part of the people, is only the most conspicuous sign of this mobilization of destructive energy. To be sure, it is mobilized for the preservation and protection of life – but precisely here, the most provocative propositions of Freud reveal their force: all additional release of destructive energy upsets the precarious balance between Eros and Thanatos and reduces the energy of the life instincts in favor of that of the death instinct. The same thesis applies to the use of destructive energy in the struggle with nature. Technical progress is life-protecting and life-enlarging to the degree to which the destructive energy here at work is "contained" and guided by libidinal energy. This ascendancy of Eros in technical progress would become manifest in the progressive alleviation and pacification of the struggle for existence, in the growth of refined erotic needs and satisfaction. In other words, technical progress would be accompanied by a lasting *desublimation* which, far from reverting mankind to anarchic and primitive stages, would bring about a less repressive yet higher stage of civilization.

Now there is, in the advanced technological societies of the West, *indeed a large desublimation* (compared with the preceding stages) in sexual mores and behavior, in the better living, in the accessibility of culture (mass culture is desublimated higher culture). Sexual morality has been greatly liberalized; moreover, sexuality is operative as commercial stimulus, business asset, status symbol. But does this mode of desublimation signify the ascendancy of the life-preserving and life-enhancing Eros over its fatal adversary? Freud's concept of sexuality may provide a clue for the answer.

Central in this concept is the conflict between sexuality (as the force of the pleasure principle) and society (the institution of the reality principle) as necessarily repressive of the uncompromised claims of the primary life instincts. By its innermost force, Eros becomes "demonstration against the herd instinct," "rejection of the group's influence."[5] In the technological desublimation today, the all but opposite tendency seems to prevail. The conflict between pleasure and the reality principle is managed by a controlled liberalization which increases satisfaction with the offerings of society. But in this form of release, libidinal energy changes its social function: to the degree to which sexuality is sanctioned and even encouraged by society (not "officially," of course, but by the mores and behaviour considered as "regular"), it loses the quality which, according to Freud, is its essentially erotic quality, that of freedom from social control. In this sphere was the surreptitious freedom, the dangerous autonomy of the individual under the pleasure principle; its authoritarian restriction by the society bore witness to the depth of the conflict between individual and society, that is, to the extent of the repression of freedom. Now, with the integration of this sphere into the realm of business and entertainment, the repression itself is repressed: society has enlarged, not individual freedom, but its control over the individual. And this growth of social control is achieved, not by terror but by the more or less beneficial productivity and efficiency of the apparatus.

We have here a highly advanced stage of civilization where society subordinates the individuals to its requirements by extending liberty and equality – or, where the reality principle operates through enlarged but controlled *desublimation*. In this new historical form of the reality principle, progress may operate as vehicle of repression. The better and bigger satisfaction is very real, and yet, in Freudian terms, it is *repressive* inasmuch as it diminishes in the individual psyche the sources of the pleasure principle *and* of freedom: the instinctual – and intellectual – resistance against the reality principle. The intellectual resistance too is weakened at its roots: administered satisfaction extends to the realm of higher culture, of the sublimated needs and objectives. One of the essential mechanisms of advanced industrial society is the mass diffusion of art, literature, music, philosophy; they become part of the technical equipment of the daily household and of the daily work world. In this process, they undergo a decisive transformation; they are losing the qualitative difference, namely, the essential dissociation from the established reality principle which was the ground of their liberating function. Now the images and ideas by virtue of which art, literature, and philosophy once indicted and transcended the given reality are integrated into the society, and the power of the reality principle is greatly extended. These tendencies alone would corroborate Freud's hypothesis that repression increases as industrial society advances and extends its material and cultural benefits to a larger part of the underlying population. The beneficiaries are inextricably tied to the multiplying agencies which produce and distribute the benefits while constantly enlarging the giant apparatus required for the defense of these agencies within and outside the national frontiers; the people turn into the object of administration. As long as peace is maintained, it is a benevolent administration indeed. But the enlarged satisfaction includes and increases the satisfaction of aggressive impulses, and the concentrated mobilization of aggressive energy affects the political process, domestic as well as foreign.

The danger signs are there. The relationship between government and the governed, between the administration and its subjects is changing significantly – without a visible change in the well-functioning democratic institutions. The response of the government to the expressed wants and wishes of the people – essential to any functioning democracy – frequently becomes a response to popular extremism: to demands for more militant, more uncompromising, more risky policies, sometimes blatantly irrational and endangering the very existence of civilization. Thus the preservation of democracy, and of civilization itself, seems increasingly to depend on the willingness and ability of the government to *withstand* and to curb aggressive impulses "from below."

To summarize, the political implications of Freudian theory as seen in the preceding discussion are:

1   The sweeping changes in advanced industrial society are accompanied by equally basic changes in the primary mental structure. In the society at large, technical progress and the global coexistence of opposed social systems lead to an obsolescence of the role and autonomy of the economic and political subject. The result is ego formation in and by the masses, which depend on the objective, reified leadership of the technical and political administration. In the mental structure this process is supported by the decline of the father image, the separation of the ego ideal from the ego and its transference to a collective ideal and a mode of desublimation which intensifies social control of libidinal energy.
2   Shrinkage of the ego, and the collectivization of the ego ideal signify a regression to primitive stages of the development, where the accumulated aggression had to be "compensated" by periodic *transgression*. At the present stage such socially sanctioned transgression seems to be replaced by the normalized social and political use of aggressive energy in the state of permanent preparedness.

3   In spite of its perfectly rational justification in terms of technology and international politics, the activation of surplus aggressive energy releases instinctual forces which threaten to undermine the established political institutions. The sanctioning of aggressive energy demanded in the prevailing situation makes for a growth of popular extremism in the masses – a rise of irrational forces which confront their leadership with their claims for satisfaction.

4   By virtue of this constellation, the masses determine continuously the policy of the leadership on which they depend, while the leadership sustains and increases its power in response and reaction to the dependent masses. The formation and mobilization of masses engenders authoritarian rule in democratic form. This is the familiar plebiscitarian trend – Freud has uncovered its instinctual roots in the advance of civilization.

5   These are the repressive tendencies. The masses are not identical with the "people" on whose sovereign rationality a free society was to be established. Today, the chance of freedom depends to a great extent on the power and willingness to oppose mass opinion, to assert unpopular policies, to alter the direction of progress. Psychoanalysis cannot offer political alternatives, but it can contribute to the restoration of private autonomy and rationality. The politics of mass society begin at home, with the shrinking of the ego and its subjection to the collective ideal. Counteracting this trend may also begin at home: psychoanalysis may help the patient to live with a conscience of his own and with his own ego ideal, which may well mean living in refusal and opposition to the Establishment.

Thus psychoanalysis draws its strength from its obsolescence: from its insistence on individual needs and individual potentialities which have become outdated in the social and political development. That which is obsolete is not, by this token, false. If the advancing industrial society and its politics have invalidated the Freudian model of the individual and his relation to society, if they have undermined the power of the ego to dissociate itself from others, to become and remain a self, then the Freudian concepts invoke not only a past left behind but also a future to be recaptured. In his uncompromising denunciation of what a repressive society does to man, in his prediction that, with the progress of civilization, the guilt will grow and death and destruction will ever more effectively threaten the life instincts, Freud has pronounced an indictment which has since been corroborated: by the gas chambers and labor camps, by the torture methods practiced in colonial wars and "police actions," by man's skill and readiness to prepare for life underground. It is not the fault of psychoanalysis if it is without power to stem this development. Nor can it buttress its strength by taking in such fads as Zen Buddhism, existentialism, etc. The truth of psychoanalysis lies in its loyalty to its most provocative hypotheses.

Notes

1   These changes have been described and analyzed in *Studien über Authoritât und Familie* (Paris: Felix Alcan, 1936), a book edited by Max Horkheimer for the Institut für Sozialforschung. See especially the contributions by Max Horkheimer and Erich Fromm.

2   The trends merely mentioned here are treated at length in my book *One-Dimensional Man: Studies in the Ideology of Advanced Industrial Society* (Boston: Beacon, 1964).

3   To be sure, the father continues to enforce the primary diversion of sexuality from the mother, but his authority is no longer fortified and perpetuated by his subsequent educational and economic power.

4   Sigmund Freud, *Group Psychology and the Analysis of the Ego* (New York: Liveright, 1949), p. 91 and p. 103. All subsequent quotations in this chapter refer to the same work and edition.

5   Ibid., p. 121. To be sure, according to Freud, Eros strives to unite living cells into ever-larger units, but this unification would mean, for the human being, the strengthening and transcendence of the Ego rather than its reduction.

2

Language and Speech

Roland Barthes

1 In Linguistics

1.1 *In Saussure* The (dichotomic) concept of *language/speech* is central in Saussure and was certainly a great novelty in relation to earlier linguistics which sought to find the causes of historical changes in the evolution of pronunciation, spontaneous associations and the working of analogy, and was therefore a linguistics of the individual act.[1] In working out this famous dichotomy, Saussure started from the 'multiform and heterogeneous' nature of language, which appears at first sight as an unclassifiable reality,[2] the unity of which cannot be brought to light, since it partakes at the same time of the physical, the physiological, the mental, the individual and the social. Now this disorder disappears if, from this heterogeneous whole, is extracted a purely social object, the systematized set of conventions necessary to communication, indifferent to the *material* of the signals which compose it, and which is a *language (langue)*; as opposed to which *speech (parole)* covers the purely individual part of language (phonation, application of the rules and contingent combinations of signs).

1.2 *The language (langue)* A *language* is therefore, so to speak, language minus speech: it is at the same time a social institution and a system of values. As a social institution, it is by no means an act, and it is not subject to any premeditation. It is the social part of language, the individual cannot by himself either create or modify it; it is essentially a collective contract which one must accept in its entirety if one wishes to communicate. Moreover, this social product is autonomous, like a game with its own rules, for it can be handled only after a period of learning. As a system of values, a language is made up of a certain number of elements, each one of which is at the same time the equivalent of a given quantity of things and a term of a larger function, in which are found, in a differential order, other correlative values: from the point of view of the language, the sign is like a coin[3] which has the value of a certain amount of goods which it allows one to buy, but also has value in relation to other coins, in a greater or lesser degree. The institutional and the systematic aspect are of course connected: it is because a language is a system of contractual values (in part arbitrary, or, more exactly, unmotivated) that it resists the modifications coming from a single individual, and is consequently a social institution.

1.3   Speech (parole)   In contrast to the language, which is both institution and system, *speech* is essentially an individual act of selection and actualization; it is made in the first place of the 'combination thanks to which the speaking subject can use the code of the language with a view to expressing his personal thought' (this extended speech could be called discourse), and secondly by the 'psycho-physical mechanisms which allow him to exteriorize these combinations'. It is certain that phonation, for instance, cannot be confused with the language; neither the institution nor the system are altered if the individual who resorts to them speaks loudly or softly, with slow or rapid delivery, etc. The combinative aspect of speech is of course of capital importance, for it implies that speech is constituted by the recurrence of identical signs: it is because signs are repeated in successive discourses and within one and the same discourse (although they are combined in accordance with the infinite diversity of various people's speech) that each sign becomes an element of the language; and it is because speech is essentially a combinative activity that it corresponds to an individual act and not to a pure creation.

1.4   *The dialectics of language and speech*   Language and speech: each of these two terms of course achieves its full definition only in the dialectical process which unites one to the other: there is no language without speech, and no speech outside language. It is in this exchange that the real linguistic *praxis* is situated, as Merleau-Ponty has pointed out. And V. Brøndal writes, 'A language is a purely abstract entity, a norm which stands above individuals, a set of essential types, which speech actualizes in an infinite variety of ways.'[4] Language and speech are therefore in a relation of reciprocal comprehensiveness. On the one hand, the language is 'the treasure deposited by the practice of speech, in the subjects belonging to the same community' and, since it is a collective summa of individual imprints, it must remain incomplete at the level of each isolated individual: a language does not exist perfectly except in the 'speaking mass'; one cannot handle speech except by drawing on the language. But conversely, a language is possible only starting from speech: historically, speech phenomena always precede language phenomena (it is speech which makes language evolve), and genetically, a language is constituted in the individual through his learning from the environmental speech (one does not teach grammar and vocabulary which are, broadly speaking, the language, to babies). To sum, a language is at the same time the product and the instrument of speech: their relationship is therefore a genuinely dialectical one. It will be noticed (an important fact when we come to semiological prospects) that there could not possibly be (at least according to Saussure) a linguistics of speech, since any speech, as soon as it is grasped as a process of communication, is *already* part of the language: the latter only can be the object of a science. This disposes of two questions at the outset: it is useless to wonder whether speech must be studied *before* the language; the opposite is impossible – one can only study speech straight away inasmuch as it reflects the language (inasmuch as it is 'glottic'). It is just as useless to wonder *at the outset* how to separate the language from speech: this is no preliminary operation, but on the contrary the very essence of linguistic and later semiological investigation: to separate the language from speech means *ipso facto* constituting the problematics of the meaning.

1.5   *In Hjelmslev*   Hjelmslev[5] has not thrown over Saussure's conception of *language/speech*, but he has redistributed its terms in a more formal way. Within the language itself (which is still opposed to the act of speech) Hjelmslev distinguishes three planes: (i) the *schema*, which is the language as pure form (before choosing this term Hjelmslev hesitated between 'system', 'pattern' or 'framework' for this plane): this is Saussure's *langue* in the strictest sense of the word. It might mean, for instance, the French r as defined phonologically by its place in a series of oppositions; (ii) the *norm*, which is the language as material form, after it has been defined by some degree of social realization, but still independent of this realization; it would mean the r in oral French, whichever way it is pronounced (but not that of written French); and, (iii) the *usage*, which is the language as a set of habits prevailing in a given society: this would mean the r as it is pronounced in some regions. The relations of determination between speech, usage, norm and schema are varied: the norm determines usage and speech; usage determines speech but is also determined by it; the schema is determined at the same time by speech, usage and norm. Thus appear (in fact) two fundamental planes: (i) the *schema*, the theory of which merges with that of the form[6] and of the linguistic institution; and, (ii) the group *norm-usage-speech*, the theory of which merges with that of the substance[7] and of the execution. As – according to Hjelmslev – norm is a pure methodical abstraction and speech a single concretion ('a transient document'), we find in the end a new dichotomy *schema/usage*, which replaces the couple *language/speech*. This redistribution by Hjelmslev is not without interest, however: it is a radical formalization of the concept of the language (under the name of *schema*) and eliminates concrete speech in favour of a more social concept: *usage*. This formalization of the language and socialization of speech enables us to put all the 'positive' and 'substantial' elements under the heading of speech, and all the differentiating ones under that of the language, and the advantage of this, as we shall see presently, is to remove one of the contradictions brought about by Saussure's distinction between the language and the speech.

1.6 *Some problems* Whatever its usefulness and its fecundity, this distinction nevertheless brings some problems in its wake. Let us mention only three.

Here is the first: is it possible to identify the language with the code and the speech with the message? This identification is impossible according to Hjelmslev's theory. P. Guiraud refuses it for, he says, the conventions of the code are explicit, and those of the language implicit;[8] but it is certainly acceptable in the Saussurean framework, and A. Martinet takes it up.[9]

We encounter an analogous problem if we reflect on the relations between speech and syntagm.[10] Speech, as we have seen, can be defined (outside the variations of intensity in the phonation) as a (varied) combination of (recurrent) signs; but at the level of the language itself, however, there already exist some fixed syntagms (Saussure cites a compound word like *magnanimus*). The threshold which separates the language from speech may therefore be precarious, since it is here constituted by 'a certain degree of combination'. This leads to the question of an analysis of those fixed syntagms whose nature is nevertheless linguistic (glottic) since they are treated as one by paradigmatic variation (Hjelmslev calls this analysis morpho-syntax). Saussure had noticed this phenomenon of transition: 'there is probably also a whole series of sentences which belong to the language, and which the individual no longer has to combine himself'.[11] If these stereotypes belong to the language and no longer to speech, and if it proves true that numerous semiological systems use them to a great extent, then it is a real *linguistics of the syntagm* that we must expect, which will be used for all strongly stereotyped 'modes of writing'.

Finally, the third problem we shall indicate concerns the relations of the language with relevance (that is to say, with the signifying element proper in the unit). The language and relevance have sometimes been identified (by Trubetzkoy himself), thus thrusting outside the language all the non-relevant elements, that is, the combinative variants. Yet this identification raises a problem, for there are combinative variants (which therefore at first sight are a speech phenomenon) which are nevertheless *imposed,* that is to say, arbitrary: in French, it is required by the language that the *l* should be voiceless after a voiceless consonant (*oncle*) and voiced after a voiced consonant (*ongle*) without these facts leaving the realm of phonetics to belong to that of phonology. We see the theoretical consequences: must we admit that, contrary to Saussure's affirmation ('in the language there are only differences'), elements which are not differentiating can all the same belong to the language (to the institution)? Martinet thinks so; Frei attempts to extricate Saussure from the contradiction by localizing the differences in *subphonemes,* so that, for instance, *p* could not be differentiating in itself, but only, in it, the consonantic, occlusive voiceless labial features, etc. We shall not here take sides on this question; from a semiological point of view, we shall only remember the necessity of accepting the existence of syntagms and variations which are not signifying and are yet 'glottic', that is, belonging to the language. This linguistics, hardly foreseen by Saussure, can assume a great importance wherever fixed syntagms (or stereotypes) are found in abundance, which is probably the case in mass-languages, and every time non-signifying variations form a second-order corpus of signifiers, which is the case in strongly connated languages:[12] the rolled *r* is a mere combinative variant at the denotative level, but in the speech of the theatre, for instance, it signals a country accent and therefore is a part of a code, without which the message of 'ruralness' could not be either emitted or perceived.

1.7 *The idiolect* To finish on the subject of *language/speech* in linguistics, we shall indicate two appended concepts isolated since Saussure's day. The first is that of the *idiolect*.[13] This is 'the language inasmuch as it is spoken by a single individual' (Martinet), or again 'the whole set of habits of a single individual at a given moment' (Ebeling). Jakobson has questioned the interest of this notion: the language is always socialized, even at the individual level, for in speaking to somebody one always tries to speak more or less the other's language, especially as far as the vocabulary is concerned ('private property in the sphere of language does not exist'): so the idiolect would appear to be largely an illusion. We shall nevertheless retain from this notion the idea that it can be useful to designate the following realities: (i) the language of the aphasic who does not understand other people and does not receive a message conforming to his own verbal patterns; this language, then, would be a pure idiolect (Jakobson); (ii) the 'style' of a writer, although this is always pervaded by certain verbal patterns coming from tradition, that is, from the community; and, (iii) finally, we can openly broaden the notion, and define the idiolect as the language of a linguistic community, that is, of a group of persons who all interpret in the same way all linguistic statements: the idiolect would then correspond roughly to what we have attempted to describe elsewhere under the name of 'writing'.[14] We can say in general that the hesitations in defining the concept of idiolect only reflect the need for an intermediate entity between speech and language (as was already proved by the *usage* theory in Hjelmslev), or, if you like, the need for a speech which is already institutionalized but not yet radically open to formalization, as the language is.

1.8 *Duplex structures* If we agree to identify *language/speech* and *code/message*, we must here mention a second appended concept which Jakobson has elaborated under the name of *duplex structures*; we shall do so only briefly, for his exposition of it has been reprinted.[15] We shall merely point out that under the name '*duplex structures*' Jakobson studies certain special cases of the general relation *code/message*: two cases of circularity and two cases of overlapping; (i) reported speech, or messages within a message (M/M): this is the general case of indirect styles; (ii) proper names: the name signifies any person to whom this name is attributed and the circularity of the code is evident (C/C): *John means a person named John*; (iii) cases of autonymy ('*Rat* is a syllable'): the word is here used as its own designation, the message overlaps the code (M/C) – this structure is important, for it covers the 'elucidating interpret-ations', namely, circumlocutions, synonyms and translations from one language into another; and, (iv) the *shifters* are probably the most interesting double structure: the most ready example is that of the personal pronoun (*I*, *thou*) an indicial symbol which unites within itself the conventional and the existential bonds: for it is only by virtue of a conventional rule that *I* represents its object (so that *I* becomes *ego* in Latin, *ich* in German, etc.), but on the other hand, since it designates the person who utters it, it can only refer existentially to the utterance (C/M).

Jakobson reminds us that personal pronouns have long been thought to be the most primitive layer of language (Rumboldt), but that in his view, they point rather to a complex and adult relationship between the code and the message: the personal pronouns are the last elements to be acquired in the child's speech and the first to be lost in aphasia; they are terms of transference which are difficult to handle. The shifter theory seems as yet to have been little exploited; yet it is a priori, very fruitful to observe the code struggling with the message, so to speak (the converse being much more commonplace); perhaps (this is only a working hypothesis) it is on this side, that of the shifters, which are, as we saw, indicial symbols according to Pierce's terminology, that we should seek the semiological definition of the messages which stand on the frontiers of language, notably certain forms of literary discourse.

2 Semiological Prospects

2.1 *The language, speech and the social sciences* The sociological scope of the *language/speech* concept is obvious. The manifest affinity of the language according to Saussure and of Durkheim's conception of a collective consciousness independent of its individual manifestations has been emphasized very early on. A direct influence of Durkheim on Saussure has even been postulated; it has been alleged that Saussure had followed very closely the debate between Durkheim and Tarde and that his conception of the language came from Durkheim while that of speech was a kind of concession to Tarde's idea on the individual element.[16] This hypothesis has lost some of its topicality because linguistics has chiefly developed, in the Saussurean idea of the language, the 'system of values' aspect, which led to acceptance of the necessity for an immanent analysis of the linguistic institution, and this immanence is inimical to sociological research.

Paradoxically, it is not therefore in the realm of sociology that the best development of the notion of *language/speech* will be found; it is in philosophy, with Merleau-Ponty, who was probably one of the first French philosophers to become interested in Saussure. He took up again the Saussurean distinction as an opposition between *speaking speech* (a signifying intention in its nascent state) and *spoken speech* (an 'acquired wealth' of the language which does not recall Saussure's 'treasure').[17] He also broadened the notion by postulating that any *process* presupposes a *system*:[18] thus there has been elaborated an opposition between *event* and *structure* which has become accepted[19] and whose fruitfulness in history is well known.[20]

Saussure's notion has, of course, also been taken over and elaborated in the field of anthropology. The reference to Saussure is too explicit in the whole work of Claude Lévi-Strauss for us to need to insist on it; we shall simply remind the reader of three facts: (i) that the opposition between process and system (speech and language) is found again in a concrete guise in the transition from the exchange of women to the structures of kinship; ii) that for Lévi-Strauss this opposition has an epistemological value: the study of linguistic phenomena is the domain of mechanistic (in Lévi-Strauss's sense of the word, namely, as opposed to 'statistical') and structural interpretation, and the study of speech phenomena is the domain of the theory of probabilities (macrolinguistics);[21] and, (iii) finally, that the *unconscious* character of the language in those who draw on it for their speech, which is explicitly postulated by Saussure,[22] is again found in one of the most original and fruitful contentions of Lévi-Strauss, which states that it is not the contents which are unconscious (this is a criticism of Jung's archetypes) but the forms, that is, the symbolical function.

This idea is akin to that of Lacan, according to whom the libido itself is articulated as a system of significations, from which there follows, or will have to follow, a new type of description of the collective field of imagination, not by means of its 'themes', as has been done until now, but by its forms and its functions. Or let us say, more broadly but more clearly: by its signifiers more than by its signifieds.

It can be seen from these brief indications how rich in extra- or meta-linguistic developments the notion *language/speech* is. We shall therefore postulate that there exists a general category *language/speech*, which embraces all the systems of signs; since there are no better ones, we shall keep the terms *language* and *speech*, even when they are applied to communications whose substance is not verbal.

2.2 *The garment system* We saw that the separation between the language and speech represented the essential feature of linguistic analysis; it would therefore be futile to propose to apply this separation straightaway to systems of objects, images or behaviour patterns which have not yet been studied from a semantic point of view. We can merely, in the case of some of these hypothetical systems, foresee that certain classes of facts will belong to the category of the *language* and others to that of *speech*, and make it immediately clear that in the course of its application to semiology, Saussure's distinction is likely to undergo modifications which it will be precisely our task to note.

Let us take the garment system for instance; it is probably necessary to subdivide it into three different systems, according to which substance is used for communication.

In clothes as *written* about, that is to say described in a fashion magazine by means of articulated language, there is practically no 'speech': the garment which is described never corresponds to an individual handling of the rules of fashion, it is a systematized set of signs and rules: it is a language in its pure state. According to the Saussurean schema, a language without speech would be impossible; what makes the fact acceptable here is, on the one hand, that the language of fashion does not emanate from the 'speaking mass' but from a group which makes the decisions and deliberately elaborates the code, and on the other hand that the abstraction inherent in any language is here material-ized as written language: fashion clothes (as written about) are the language at the level of vestimentary communication and speech at the level of verbal communication.

In clothes as *photographed* (if we suppose, to simplify matters, that there is no duplication by verbal description), the language still issues from the fashion group, but it is no longer given in a wholly abstract form, for a photographed garment is always worn by an individual woman. What is given by the fashion photograph is a semi-formalized state of the garment system: for on the one hand, the language of fashion must here be inferred from a pseudo-real garment, and on the other, the wearer of the garment (the photographed model) is, so to speak, a normative individual, chosen for her canonic gener-ality, and who consequently represents a 'speech' which is fixed and devoid of all combinative freedom.

Finally, in clothes as *worn* (or real clothes), as Trubetzkoy had suggested,[23] we again find the classic distinction between language and speech. The language, in the garment system, is made (i) by the oppositions of pieces, parts of garment and 'details', the variation of which entails a change in meaning (to wear a béret or a bowler hat does not have the same meaning); and, (ii) by the rules which govern the association of the pieces among themselves, either on the length of the body or in depth. Speech, in the garment system, comprises all the phenomena of anomic fabrication (few are still left in our society) or of individual way of wearing (size of the garment, degree of cleanliness or wear, personal quirks, free association of pieces). As for the dialectic which unites here costume (the language) and clothing (speech), it does not resemble that of verbal language; true, clothing always draws on costume (except in the case of eccentricity, which, by the way, also has its signs), but costume, at least today, *precedes* clothing, since it comes from the ready-made industry, that is, from a minority group (although more anonymous than that of haute couture).

2.3 *The food system*   Let us now take another signifying system: food. We shall find there without difficulty Saussure's distinction. The alimentary language is made of (i) rules of exclusion (alimentary taboos); (ii) signifying oppositions of units, the type of which remains to be determined (for instance the type *savoury/sweet*); (iii) rules of association, either simultaneous (at the level of a dish) or successive (at the level of a menu); and, (iv) rituals of use which function, perhaps, as a kind of alimentary *rhetoric*. As for alimentary 'speech', which is very rich, it comprises all the personal (or family) variations of preparation and association (one might consider cookery within one family, which is subject to a number of habits, as an idiolect). The *menu*, for instance, illustrates very well this relationship between the language and speech: any menu is concocted with reference to a structure (which is both national – or regional – and social); but this structure is filled differently according to the days and the users, just as a linguistic 'form' is filled by the free variations and combinations which a speaker needs for a particular message. The relationship between the language and speech would here be fairly similar to that which is found in verbal language: broadly, it is usage, that is to say, a sort of sedimentation of many people's speech, which makes up the alimentary language; however, phenomena of individual innovation can acquire an institutional value within it. What is missing, in any case, contrary to what happened in the garment system, is the action of a deciding group: the alimentary language is evolved only from a broadly collective usage, or from a purely individual speech.

2.4   *The car system, the furniture system*   To bring to a close, somewhat arbitrarily, this question of the prospects opened up by the *language/speech* distinction, we shall mention a few more suggestions concerning two systems of objects, very different, it is true, but which have in common a dependence in each case on a deciding and manufacturing group: cars and furniture. In the car system, the language is made up by a whole set of forms and details, the structure of which is established differentially by comparing the prototypes to each other (independently of the number of their 'copies'); the scope of 'speech' is very narrow because, for a given status of buyer, freedom in choosing a model is very restricted: it can involve only two or three models, and within each model, colour and fittings. But perhaps we should here exchange the notion of cars as *objects* for that of cars as sociological facts; we would then find in the *driving* of cars the variations in usage of the object which usually make up the plane of speech. For the user cannot in this instance have a direct action on the model and combine its units; his freedom of interpretation is found in the usage developed in time and within which the 'forms' issuing from the language must, in order to become actual, be relayed by certain practices.

   Finally, the last system about which we should like to say a word, that of furniture, is also a semantic object: the 'language' is formed both by the oppositions of functionally identical pieces (two types of wardrobe, two types of bed, etc.), each of which, according to its 'style', refers to a different meaning, and by the rules of association of the different units at the level of a room ('furnishing'); the 'speech' is here formed either by the insignificant variations which the user can introduce into one unit (by tinkering with one element, for instance), or by freedom in associating pieces of furniture together.

2.5   *Complex systems*   The most interesting systems, at least among those which belong to the province of mass-communications, are complex systems in which different substances are engaged. In cinema, television and advertising, the senses are subjected to the concerted action of a collection of images, sounds and written words. It will, therefore, be premature to decide, in their case, which facts belong to the language and which belong to speech, on the one hand as long as one has not discovered whether the 'language' of each of these complex systems is original or only compounded of the subsidiary 'languages' which have their places in them, and on the other hand as long as these subsidiary languages have not been analysed (we know the linguistic 'language', but not that of images or that of music).

As for the press, which can be reasonably considered as an autonomous signifying system, even if we confine ourselves to its written elements only, we are still almost entirely ignorant of a linguistic phenomenon which seems to play an essential part in it: connotation, that is, the development of a system of second-order meanings, which are, so to speak, parasitic on the language proper.[24] This second-order system is also a 'language', within which there develop speech-phenomena, idiolects and duplex structures. In the case of such complex or connoted systems (both characteristics are not mutually exclusive), it is therefore no longer possible to predetermine, even in global and hypothetical fashion, what belongs to the language and what belongs to speech.

2.6 *Problems (I) – the origin of the various signifying systems* The semiological extension of the *language/speech* notion brings with it some problems, which of course coincide with the points where the linguistic model can no longer be followed and must be altered. The first problem concerns the origin of the various systems, and thus touches on the very dialectics of language and speech. In the linguistic model, nothing enters the language without having been tried in speech, but conversely no speech is possible (that is, fulfils its function of communication) if it is not drawn from the 'treasure' of the language. This process is still, at least partially, found in a system like that of food, although individual innovations brought into it can become language phenomena. But in most other semiological systems, the language is elaborated not by the 'speaking mass' but by a deciding group. In this sense, it can be held that in most semiological languages, the sign is really and truly 'arbitrary'[25] since it is founded in artificial fashion by a unilateral decision; these in fact are fabricated languages, 'logo-techniques'. The user follows these languages, draws messages (or 'speech') from them but has no part in their elaboration. The deciding group which is at the origin of the system (and of its changes) can be more or less narrow; it can be a highly qualified technocracy (fashion, motor industry); it can also be a more diffuse and anonymous group (the production of standardized furniture, the middle reaches of ready-to-wear). If, however, this artificial character does not alter the institutional nature of the communication and preserves some amount of dialectical play between the system and usage, it is because, in the first place, although imposed on the users, the signifying 'contract' is no less observed by the great majority of them (otherwise the user is *marked* with a certain 'asociability': he can no longer communicate anything except his eccentricity); and because, moreover, languages elaborated as the outcome of a decision are not entirely free ('arbitrary'). They are subject to the determination of the community, at least through the following agencies: (i) when new needs are born, following the development of societies (the move to semi-European clothing in contemporary African countries, the birth of new patterns of quick feeding in industrial and urban societies), for example; (ii) when economic requirements bring about the disappearance or promotion of certain materials (artificial textiles); and, (iii) when ideology limits the invention of forms, subjects it to taboos and reduces, so to speak, the margins of the 'normal'. In a wider sense, we can say that the elaborations of deciding groups, namely the logo-techniques, are themselves only the terms of an ever-widening function, which is the collective field of imagination of the epoch: thus individual innovation is transcended by a sociological determination (from restricted groups), but these sociological determinations refer in turn to a final meaning, which is anthropological.

2.7   Problems (II) – the proportion between 'language' and 'speech' in the various systems   The second problem presented by the semiological extension of the *language/speech* notion is centred on the proportion, in the matter of volume, which can be established between the 'language' and the corresponding 'speech' in any system. In verbal language there is a very great disproportion between the language, which is a finite set of rules, and speech, which comes under the heading of these rules and is practically unlimited in its variety. It can be presumed that the food system still offers an important difference in the volume of each, since within the culinary 'forms', the modalities and combinations in interpretation are numerous. But we have seen that in the car or the furniture system the scope for combinative variations and free associations is small: there is very little margin – at least of the sort which is acknowledged by the institution itself – between the model and its 'execution': these are systems in which 'speech' is poor. In a particular system, that of written fashion, speech is even almost non-existent, so that we are dealing here, paradoxically, with a language without speech (which is possible, as we have seen, only because this language is upheld by linguistic speech).

The fact remains that if it is true that there are languages without speech or with a very restricted speech, we shall have to revise the Saussurean theory which states that a language is nothing but a system of differences (in which case, being entirely negative, it cannot be grasped outside speech), and complete the couple *language/speech* with a third, presignifying element, a matter or substance providing the (necessary) support of signification. In a phrase like *a long or short dress*, the 'dress' is only the support of a variant (*long/short*) which *does* fully belong to the garment language – a distinction which is unknown in ordinary language, in which, since the sound is considered as *immediately* significant, it cannot be decomposed into an inert and a semantic element. This would lead us to recognize in (non-linguistic) semiological systems three (and not two) planes: that of the matter, that of the language and that of the usage. This of course allows us to account for systems without 'execution', since the first element ensures that there is a materiality of the language; and such a modification is all the more plausible since it can be explained genetically: if, in such systems, the 'language' needs a 'matter' (and no longer a 'speech'), it is because unlike that of human language their origin is in general utilitarian, and not signifying.

Notes

1   The Saussurian notions of *langue* and *parole* present to the translator into English notorious difficulties, which their extension in the present work does nothing to alleviate. We have translated *langue* as *'a'* or *'the language'*, except when the coupling with 'speech' makes the meaning clear. *Les paroles,* whether applied to several people or to several semiotic systems, has been translated by various periphrases which we hope do not obscure the identity of meaning. (Trans. note).

2   It should be noted that the first definition of the language (*langue*) is taxonomic: it is a principle of classification.

3   For further reading, see: Roland Barthes, 'Signifier and Signified', *Elements of Semiology,* II.5.I. In *Writing Degree Zero & Elements of Semiology* (London: Jonathan Cape, 1984).

4   *Acta linguistica,* I, I, p. 5.

5   L. Hjelmslev, *Essais Linguistiques* (Copenhagen, 1959), pp. 69ff.

6   Roland Barthes, 'Signifier and Signified', ch. II,I.3.

7   Ibid.

8   'La mécanique de l'analyse quantitative en linguistique'. In *Études de linguistique appliquée,* 2, Didier, p. 37.

9   A. Martinet, *Éléments de linguistique générale* (Armand Colin, 1960), p. 30. *Elements of General Linguistics,* trans. Elizabeth Palmer (London: Faber & Faber, 1964), pp. 33–4.

10   On syntagm, see Roland Barthes, 'Signifier and Signified', ch. III.

11   Saussure, in R. Godel, *Les sources manuscrites du Cours de Linguistique générale* (Droz, Minard, 1957), p. 90.

12   Roland Barthes, 'Signifier and Signified', ch. IV.

13   R. Jakobson, 'Deux aspects du langage et deux types d'aphasies'. In *Essais de Linguistique générale* (Editions de Minuit, 1963), p. 54. This is the second part of *Fundamentals of Language* (R. Jakobson and M. Halle: The Hague, 1956); C. L. Ebeling, *Linguistic Units* (The Hague: Mouton, 1960), p. 9; A Martinet, *A Functional View of Language* (Oxford: Clarendon Press, 1962), p. 105.

14   Roland Barthes, *Writing Degree Zero,* 1984.

15   *Essais de Linguistique générale,* ch. 9. This is a translation of *Shifters, Verbal Categories and the Russian Verb* (Russian Language Project, Department of Slavic Languages and Literature: Harvard University, 1957).

16   W. Doroszewski, 'Langue et Parole', *Odbitka z Prac Filogisznych,* XLV (Warsaw, 1930), pp. 485–97.

17   M. Merleau-Ponty, *Phénoménologie de la Perception,* 1945, p. 229. *Phenomenology of Perception,* trans. Colin Smith (New York: Routledge & Kegan Paul, in conjunction with the Humanities Press, 1962), pp. 196–7.

18   M. Merleau-Ponty, *Eloge de la Philosophie* (Gallimard, 1953).

19   G. Granger, 'Evénement et structure dans les sciences de l'homme'. In *Cahiers de l'Institut de science économique appliquée,* no. 55, May 1957.
20   See F. Braudel, 'Histoire et sciences sociales: la longue durée'. In *Annales,* Oct.–Dec. 1958.
21   See C. Lévi-Strauss, *Anthropologie Structurale,* p. 230. *Structural Anthropology,* trans. Claire Jacobson and Brooke Grundfest Schopf (New York and London: Basic Books, 1963), pp. 208–9; and 'Les mathématiques d'homme', in *Esprit,* Oct. 1956.
22   'There never is any premeditation, or even any meditation, or reflection on forms, outside the act, the occasion of speech, except an unconscious, non-creative activity: that of classifying' (Saussure, in R. Godel, *Les sources manuscrites du Cours de Linguistique générale,* 1957, p. 58).
23   *Principes de Phonologie,* trans. J. Cantineau, 1957 edn, p. 19.
24   Roland Barthes, 'Signifier and Signified', ch. IV.
25   Ibid., ch. II. 4.3.

3

The Mirror Stage as Formative of the Function of the I as Revealed in Psychoanalytic Experience

Jacques Lacan

The conception of the mirror stage that I introduced at our last congress, thirteen years ago, has since become more or less established in the practice of the French group.[1] However, I think it worthwhile to bring it again to your attention, especially today, for the light it sheds on the formation of the *I* as we experience it in psychoanalysis. It is an experience that leads us to oppose any philosophy directly issuing from the *Cogito*.

Some of you may recall that this conception originated in a feature of human behaviour illuminated by a fact of comparative psychology. The child, at an age when he is for a time, however short, outdone by the chimpanzee in instrumental intelligence, can nevertheless already recognize as such his own image in a mirror. This recognition is indicated in the illuminative mimicry of the *Aha-Erlebnis*, which Köhler sees as the expression of situational apperception, an essential stage of the act of intelligence.

This act, far from exhausting itself, as in the case of the monkey, once the image has been mastered and found empty, immediately rebounds in the case of the child in a series of gestures in which he experiences in play the relation between the movements assumed in the image and the reflected environment, and between this virtual complex and the reality it reduplicates – the child's own body, and the persons and things around him.

This event can take place, as we have known since Baldwin, from the age of six months, and its repetition has often made me reflect upon the startling spectacle of the infant in front of the mirror. Unable as yet to walk, or even to stand up, and held tightly as he is by some support, human or artificial (what, in France, we call a *'trotte-bébé'*), he nevertheless overcomes, in a flutter of jubilant activity, the obstructions of his support and, fixing his attitude in a slightly leaning-forward position, in order to hold it in his gaze, brings back an instantaneous aspect of the image.

For me, this activity retains the meaning I have given it up to the age of eighteen months. This meaning discloses a libidinal dynamism, which has hitherto remained problematic, as well as an ontological structure of the human world that accords with my reflections on paranoiac knowledge.

We have only to understand the mirror stage *as an identification*, in the full sense that analysis gives to the term: namely, the transformation that takes place in the subject when he assumes an image – whose predestination to this phase-effect is sufficiently indicated by the use, in analytic theory, of the ancient term *imago*.

This jubilant assumption of his specular image by the child at the *infans* stage, still sunk in his motor incapacity and nursling dependence, would seem to exhibit in an exemplary situation the symbolic matrix in which the *I* is precipitated in a primordial form, before it is objectified in the dialectic of identification with the other, and before language restores to it, in the universal, its function as subject.

This form would have to be called the Ideal-I,[2] if we wished to incorporate it into our usual register, in the sense that it will also be the source of secondary identifications, under which term I would place the functions of libidinal normalization. But the important point is that this form situates the agency of the ego, before its social determination, in a fictional direction, which will always remain irreducible for the individual alone, or rather, which will only rejoin the coming-into-being (*le devenir*) of the subject asymptotically, whatever the success of the dialectical syntheses by which he must resolve as *I* his discordance with his own reality.

The fact is that the total form of the body by which the subject anticipates in a mirage the maturation of his power is given to him only as *Gestalt*, that is to say, in an exteriority in which this form is certainly more constituent than constituted, but in which it appears to him above all in a contrasting size (*un relief de stature*) that fixes it and in a symmetry that inverts it, in contrast with the turbulent movements that the subject feels are animating him. Thus, this *Gestalt* – whose pregnancy should be regarded as bound up with the species, though its motor style remains scarcely recognizable – by these two aspects of its appearance, symbolizes the mental permanence of the *I*, at the same time as it prefigures its alienating destination; it is still pregnant with the correspondences that unite the *I* with the statue in which man projects himself, with the phantoms that dominate him, or with the automaton in which, in an ambiguous relation, the world of his own making tends to find completion.

Indeed, for the *imagos* – whose veiled faces it is our privilege to see in outline in our daily experience and in the penumbra of symbolic efficacity[3] – the mirror-image would seem to be the threshold of the visible world, if we go by the mirror disposition that the *imago of one's own body* presents in hallucinations or dreams, whether it concerns its individual features, or even its infirmities, or its object-projections; or if we observe the role of the mirror apparatus in the appearances of the *double,* in which psychical realities, however heterogeneous, are manifested.

That a *Gestalt* should be capable of formative effects in the organism is attested by a piece of biological experimentation that is itself so alien to the idea of psychical causality that it cannot bring itself to formulate its results in these terms. It nevertheless recognizes that it is a necessary condition for the maturation of the gonad of the female pigeon that it should see another member of its species, of either sex; so sufficient in itself is this condition that the desired effect may be obtained merely by placing the individual within reach of the field of reflection of a mirror. Similarly, in the case of the migratory locust, the transition within a generation from the solitary to the gregarious form can be obtained by exposing the individual, at a certain stage, to the exclusively visual action of a similar image, provided it is animated by movements of a style sufficiently close to that characteristic of the species. Such facts are inscribed in an order of homeomorphic identification that would itself fall within the larger question of the meaning of beauty as both formative and erogenic.

But the facts of mimicry are no less instructive when conceived as cases of heteromorphic identification, in as much as they raise the problem of the signification of space for the living organism – psychological concepts hardly seem less appropriate for shedding light on these matters than ridiculous attempts to reduce them to the supposedly supreme law of adaptation. We have only to recall how Roger Caillois (who was then very young, and still fresh from his breach with the sociological school in which he was trained) illuminated the subject by using the term *'legendary psycastheniu'* to classify morphological mimicry as an obsession with space in its derealizing effect.

I have myself shown in the social dialectic that structures human knowledge as paranoic[4] why human knowledge has greater autonomy than animal knowledge in relation to the field of force of desire, but also why human knowledge is determined in that 'little reality' (*ce peu de réalité*) which the Surrealists, in their restless way, saw as its limitation. These reflections lead me to recognize in the spatial captation manifested in the mirror-stage, even before the social dialectic, the effect in man of an organic insufficiency in his natural reality – in so far as any meaning can be given to the word 'nature'.

I am led, therefore, to regard the function of the mirror-stage as a particular case of the function of the *imago,* which is to establish a relation between the organism and its reality – or, as they say, between the *Innenwelt* and the *Umwelt.*

In man, however, this relation to nature is altered by a certain dehiscence at the heart of the organism, a primordial discord betrayed by the signs of uneasiness and motor unco-ordination of the neo-natal months. The objective notion of the anatomical incompleteness of the pyramidal system and likewise the presence of certain humoral residues of the maternal organism confirm the view I have formulated as the fact of a real *specific prematurity of birth* in man.

It is worth noting, incidentally, that this is a fact recognized as such by embryologists, by the term *foetalization,* which determines the prevalence of the so-called superior apparatus of the neurax, and especially of the cortex, which psycho-surgical operations lead us to regard as the intraorganic mirror.

This development is experienced as a temporal dialectic that decisively projects the formation of the individual into history. The *mirror stage* is a drama whose internal thrust is precipitated from insufficiency to anticipation – and which manufactures for the subject, caught up in the lure of spatial identification, the succession of phantasies that extends from the fragmented body-image to a form of its totality that I shall call orthopaedic – and, lastly, to the assumption of the armour of an alienating identity, which will mark with its rigid structure the subject's entire mental development. Thus, to break out of the circle of the *Innenwelt* into the *Umwelt* generates the inexhaustible quadrature of the ego's verifications.

This fragmented body – which term I have also introduced into our system of theoretical references – usually manifests itself in dreams when the movement of the analysis encounters a certain level of aggressive disintegration in the individual. It then appears in the form of disjointed limbs, or of those organs represented in exoscopy, growing wings and taking up arms for intestinal persecutions – the very same that the visionary Hieronymus Bosch has fixed, for all time, in painting, in their ascent from the fifteenth century to the imaginary zenith of modern man. But this form is even tangibly revealed at the organic level, in the lines of 'fragilization' that define the anatomy of phantasy, as exhibited in the schizoid and spasmodic symptoms of hysteria.

Correlatively, the formation of the *I* is symbolized in dreams by a fortress, or a stadium – its inner arena and enclosure, surrounded by marshes and rubbish-tips, dividing it into two opposed fields of contest where the subject flounders in quest of the lofty, remote inner castle whose form (sometimes juxtaposed in the same scenario) symbolizes the id in a quite startling way. Similarly, on the mental plane, we find realized the structures of fortified works, the metaphor of which arises spontaneously, as if issuing from the symptoms themselves, to designate the mechanisms of obsessional neurosis – inversion, isolation, reduplication, cancellation and displacement.

But if we were to build on these subjective givens alone – however little we free them from the condition of experience that makes us see them as partaking of the nature of a linguistic technique – our theoretical attempts would remain exposed to the charge of projecting themselves into the unthinkable of an absolute subject. This is why I have sought in the present hypothesis, grounded in a conjunction of objective data, the guiding grid for a *method of symbolic reduction*.

It establishes in the *defences of the ego* a genetic order, in accordance with the wish formulated by Miss Anna Freud, in the first part of her great work, and situates (as against a frequently expressed prejudice) hysterical repression and its returns at a more archaic stage than obsessional inversion and its isolating processes, and the latter in turn as preliminary to paranoic alienation, which dates from the deflection of the specular *I* into the social *I*.

This moment in which the mirror-stage comes to an end inaugurates, by the identification with the *imago* of the counterpart and the drama of primordial jealousy (so well brought out by the school of Charlotte Bühler in the phenomenon of infantile *transitivism)*, the dialectic that will henceforth link the *I* to socially elaborated situations.

It is this moment that decisively tips the whole of human knowledge into mediatization through the desire of the other, constitutes its objects in an abstract equivalence by the co-operation of others, and turns the *I* into that apparatus for which every instinctual thrust constitutes a danger, even though it should correspond to a natural maturation – the very normalization of this maturation being henceforth dependent, in man, on a cultural mediation as exemplified, in the case of the sexual object, by the Oedipus complex.

In the light of this conception, the term primary narcissism, by which analytic doctrine designates the libidinal investment characteristic of that moment, reveals in those who invented it the most profound awareness of semantic latencies. But it also throws light on the dynamic opposition between this libido and the sexual libido, which the first analysts tried to define when they invoked destructive and, indeed, death instincts, in order to explain the evident connection between the narcissistic libido and the alienating function of the *I*, the aggressivity it releases in any relation to the other, even in a relation involving the most Samaritan of aid.

In fact, they were encountering that existential negativity whose reality is so vigorously proclaimed by the contemporary philosophy of being and nothingness.

But unfortunately that philosophy grasps negativity only within the limits of a self-sufficiency of consciousness, which, as one of its premises, links to the *méconnaissances* that constitute the ego, the illusion of autonomy to which it entrusts itself. This flight of fancy, for all that it draws, to an unusual extent, on borrowings from psychoanalytic experience, culminates in the pretention of providing an existential psychoanalysis.

At the culmination of the historical effort of a society to refuse to recognize that it has any function other than the utilitarian one, and in the anxiety of the individual confronting the 'concentrational'[5] form of the social bond that seems to arise to crown this effort, existentialism must be judged by the explanations it gives of the subjective impasses that have indeed resulted from it; a freedom that is never more authentic than when it is within the walls of a prison; a demand for commitment, expressing the impotence of a pure consciousness to master any situation; a voyeuristic-sadistic idealization of the sexual relation; a personality that realizes itself only in suicide; a consciousness of the other than can be satisfied only by Hegelian murder.

These propositions are opposed by all our experience, in so far as it teaches us not to regard the ego as centred on the *perception-consciousness system,* or as organized by the 'reality principle' – a principle that is the expression of a scientific prejudice most hostile to the dialectic of knowledge. Our experience shows that we should start instead from the *function of méconnaissance* that characterizes the ego in all its structures, so markedly articulated by Miss Anna

Freud. For, if the *Verneinung* represents the patent form of that function, its effects will, for the most part, remain latent, so long as they are not illuminated by some light reflected on to the level of fatality, which is where the id manifests itself.

We can thus understand the inertia characteristic of the formations of the *I*, and find there the most extensive definition of neurosis just as the captation of the subject by the situation gives us the most general formula for madness, not only the madness that lies behind the walls of asylums but also the madness that deafens the world with its sound and fury.

The sufferings of neurosis and psychosis are for us a schooling in the passions of the soul, just as the beam of the psychoanalytic scales, when we calculate the tilt of its threat to entire communities, provides us with an indication of the deadening of the passions in society.

At this junction of nature and culture, so persistently examined by modern anthropology, psychoanalysis alone recognizes this knot of imaginary servitude that love must always undo again, or sever.

For such a task, we place no trust in altruistic feeling, we who lay bare the aggressivity that underlies the activity of the philanthropist, the idealist, the pedagogue, and even the reformer.

In the recourse of subject to subject that we preserve, psychoanalysis may accompany the patient to the ecstatic limit of the '*Thou art that*', in which is revealed to him the cipher of his mortal destiny, but it is not in our mere power as practitioners to bring him to that point where the real journey begins.

Notes

1   Delivered at the 16th International Congress of Psychoanalysis, Zürich, July 17, 1949.
2   Throughout this article I leave in its peculiarity the translation I have adopted for Freud's *Ideal-Ich* [i.e., 'je-idéal'], without further comment, other than to say that I have not maintained it since.
3   Cf. Claude Lévi-Strauss, *Structural Anthropology*, ch. X.
4   Cf. 'Aggressivity in Psychoanalysis', p. 8. and *Ecrits*, p. 180.
5   '*Concentrationnaire*', an adjective coined after World War II (this article was written in 1949) to describe the life of the concentration camp. In the hands of certain writers it became, by extension, applicable to many aspects of 'modern' life. [Trans.].

4

Revolution in Poetic Language

Julia Kristeva

The Semiotic *Chora* Ordering the Drives

We understand the term 'semiotic' in its Greek sense: $\sigma\eta\mu\epsilon\tilde{\iota}o\nu$ = distinctive mark, trace, index, precursory sign, proof, engraved or written sign, imprint, trace, figuration. This etymological reminder would be a mere archaeological embellishment (and an unconvincing one at that, since the term ultimately encompasses such disparate meanings) were it not for the fact that the pre-ponderant etymological use of the word, the one that implies a *distinctiveness*, allows us to connect it to a precise modality in the signifying process. This modality is the one Freudian psychoanalysis points to in postulating not only the *facilitation* and the structuring *disposition* of drives, but also the so-called *primary processes* which displace and condense both energies and their inscrip-tion. Discrete quantities of energy move through the body of the subject who is not yet constituted as such and, in the course of his development, they are arranged according to the various constraints imposed on this body – always already involved in a semiotic process – by family and social structures. In this way the drives, which are 'energy' charges as well as 'psychical' marks, articu-late what we call a *chora:* a non-expressive totality formed by the drives and their stases in a motility that is as full of movement as it is regulated.

We borrow the term *chora*[1] from Plato's *Timaeus* to denote an essentially mobile and extremely provisional articulation constituted by movements and their ephemeral stases. We differentiate this uncertain and indeterminate *articulation* from a *disposition* that already depends on representation, lends itself to phenomenological spatial intuition and gives rise to a geometry. Although our theoretical description of the *chora* is itself part of the discourse of representation that offers it as evidence, the *chora,* as rupture and articulations

Translated by Margaret Waller.

(rhythm), precedes evidence, verisimilitude, spatiality and temporality. Our discourse – all discourse – moves with and against the *chora* in the sense that it simultaneously depends upon and refuses it. Although the *chora* can be designated and regulated, it can never be definitely posited: as a result, one can situate the *chora* and, if necessary, lend it a topology, but one can never give it axiomatic form.[2]

The *chora* is not yet a position that represents something for someone (i.e., it is not a sign); nor is it a *position* that represents someone for another position (i.e., it is not yet a signifier either); it is, however, generated in order to attain to this signifying position. Neither model nor copy, the *chora* precedes and underlies figuration and thus specularization, and is analogous only to vocal or kinetic rhythm. We must restore this motility's gestural and vocal play (to mention only the aspect relevant to language) on the level of the socialized body in order to remove motility from ontology and amorphousness[3] where Plato confines it in an apparent attempt to conceal it from Democritean rhythm. The theory of the subject proposed by the theory of the unconscious will allow us to read in this rhythmic space, which has no thesis and no position, the process by which signifiance is constituted. Plato himself leads us to such a process when he calls this receptacle or *chora* nourishing and maternal,[4] not yet unified in an ordered whole because deity is absent from it. Though deprived of unity, identity or deity, the *chora* is nevertheless subject to a regulating process [*réglementation*] which is different from that of symbolic law but nevertheless effectuates discontinuities by temporarily articulating them and then starting over, again and again.

The *chora* is a modality of signifiance in which the linguistic sign is not yet articulated as the absence of an object and as the distinction between real and symbolic. We emphasize the regulated aspect of the *chora*: its vocal and gestural organization is subject to what we shall call an objective *ordering* [*ordonnancement*], which is dictated by natural or socio-historical constraints such as the biological difference between the sexes or family structure. We may therefore posit that social organization, always already symbolic, imprints its constraint in a mediated form which organizes the *chora* not according to a *law* (a term we reserve for the symbolic) but through an *ordering*.[5] What is this mediation?

According to a number of psycholinguists, 'concrete operations' precede the acquisition of language, and organize pre-verbal semiotic space according to logical categories, which are thereby shown to precede or transcend language. From their research we shall retain not the principle of an operational state[6] but that of a pre-verbal functional state that governs the connections between the body (in the process of constituting itself as a body proper), objects and the protagonists of family structure.[7] But we shall distinguish this functioning from symbolic operations that depend on language as a sign system – whether the language [*langue*] is vocalized or gestural (as with deaf-mutes). The kinetic functional stage of the *semiotic* precedes the establishment of the sign; it is not, therefore, cognitive in the sense of being assumed by a knowing, already constituted subject. The genesis of the *functions*[8] organizing the semiotic process can be accurately elucidated only within a theory of the subject that does not reduce the subject to one of understanding, but instead opens up within the subject this other scene of pre-symbolic functions. The Kleinian theory expanding upon Freud's positions on the drives will momentarily serve as a guide.

Drives involve pre-Oedipal semiotic functions and energy discharges that connect and orient the body to the mother. We must emphasize that 'drives' are always already ambiguous, simultaneously assimilating and destructive; this dualism, which has been represented as a tetrad[9] or as a double helix, as in the configuration of the DNA and RNA molecule,[10] makes the semiotized body a place of permanent scission. The oral and anal drives, both of which are oriented and structured around the mother's body,[11] dominate this sensorimotor organization. The mother's body is therefore what mediates the symbolic law organizing social relations and becomes the ordering principle of the semiotic *chora*,[12] which is on the path of destruction, aggressivity and death. For although drives have been described as disunited or contradictory structures, simultaneously 'positive' and 'negative', this doubling is said to generate a dominant 'destructive wave' that is the drive's most characteristic trait: Freud notes that the most instinctual drive is the death drive.[13] In this way, the term 'drive' denotes waves of attack against stases, which are themselves constituted by the repetition of these charges; together, charges and stases lead to no identity (not even that of the 'body proper') that could be seen as a result of their functioning. This is to say that the semiotic *chora* is no more than the place where the subject is both generated and negated, the place where his unity succumbs before the process of charges and stases that produce him. We shall call this process of charges and stases a *negativity* to distinguish it from negation, which is the act of a judging subject.

Checked by the constraints of biological and social structures, the drive charge thus undergoes stases. Drive facilitation, temporarily arrested, marks *discontinuities* in what may be called the various material supports [*matériaux*] susceptible to semiotization: voice, gesture, colours. Phonic (later phonemic), kinetic or chromatic units and differences are the marks of these stases in the drives. Connections or *functions* are thereby established between these discrete marks which are based on drives and articulated according to their resemblance or opposition, either by slippage or by condensation. Here we find the principles of metonymy and metaphor indissociable from the drive economy underlying them.

Although we recognize the vital role played by the processes of displacement and condensation in the organization of the semiotic, we must also add to these processes the relations (eventually representable as topological spaces) that connect the zones of the fragmented body to each other and also to 'external' 'objects' and 'subjects', which are not yet constituted as such. This type of relation makes it possible to specify the *semiotic* as a psychosomatic modality of the signifying process; in other words, not a symbolic modality but one articulating (in the largest sense of the word) a continuum: the connections between the glottal and anal sphincters in (rhythmic and intonational) vocal modulations, or those between the sphincters and family protagonists, for example.

All these various processes and relations, anterior to sign and syntax, have just been identified from a genetic perspective as previous and necessary to the acquisition of language, but not identical to language. Theory can 'situate' such processes and relations diachronically within the process of the constitution of the subject precisely because *they function synchronically within the signifying process of the subject himself,* i.e., the subject of *cogitatio.* Only in *dream* logic, however, have they attracted attention, and only in certain signifying practices, such as the *text,* do they dominate the signifying process.

It may be hypothesized that certain semiotic articulations are transmitted through the biological code or physiological 'memory' and thus form the inborn bases of the symbolic function. Indeed, one branch of generative linguistics asserts the principle of innate language universals. As it will become apparent in what follows, however, the *symbolic* – and therefore syntax and all linguistic categories – is a social effect of the relation to the other, established through the objective constraints of biological (including sexual) differences and concrete, historical family structures. Genetic programmings are necessarily semiotic: they include the primary processes such as displacement and condensation, absorption and repulsion, rejection and stasis, all of which function as innate preconditions, 'memorizable' by the species, for language acquisition.

Mallarmé calls attention to the semiotic rhythm within language when he speaks of 'The Mystery in Literature' ['Le Mystère dans les lettres']. Indifferent to language, enigmatic and feminine, this space underlying the written is rhythmic, unfettered, irreducible to its intelligible verbal translation; it is musical, anterior to judgement, but restrained by a single guarantee: syntax. [. . .]

Our positing of the semiotic is obviously inseparable from a theory of the subject that takes into account the Freudian positing of the unconscious. We view the subject in language as decentring the transcendental ego, cutting through it and opening it up to a dialectic in which its syntactic and categorical understanding is merely the liminary moment of the process, which is itself always acted upon by the relation to the other dominated by the death drive and its productive reiteration of the 'signifier'. We will be attempting to formulate the distinction between *semiotic* and *symbolic* within this perspective, which was introduced by Lacanian analysis, but also within the constraints of a practice – the *text* – which is only of secondary interest to psychoanalysis.

The Thetic: Rupture and/or Boundary

We shall distinguish the semiotic (drives and their articulations) from the realm of signification, which is always that of a proposition or judgement, in other words, a realm of *positions*. This positionality, which Husserlian phenom-enology orchestrates through the concepts of *doxa*, *position* and *thesis*, is structured as a break in the signifying process, establishing the *identification* of the subject and its object as preconditions of propositionality. We shall call this break, which produces the positing of signification, a *thetic* phase. All enunci-ation, whether of a word or of a sentence, is thetic. It requires an identification; in other words, the subject must separate from and through his image, from and through his objects. This image and these objects must first be posited in a space that becomes symbolic because it connects the two separated positions, recording them or redistributing them in an open combinatorial system.

The child's first so-called holophrastic enunciations include gesture, the object and vocal emission. Because they are perhaps not yet sentences, generative grammar is not readily equipped to account for them. Nevertheless, they are already thetic in the sense that they separate an object from the subject, and attribute to it a semiotic fragment, which thereby becomes a signifier. That this attribution is either metaphoric or metonymic ('woof-woof' says the dog, and all animals become 'woof-woof') is logically secondary to the fact that it constitutes an *attribution*, which is to say, a positing of identity or difference, and that it represents the nucleus of judgement or proposition. [. . .]

Modern philosophy recognizes that the right to represent the founding *thesis* of signification (sign and/or proposition) devolves upon the transcendental ego. But only since Freud have we been able to raise the question not of the origin of this thesis but rather of the process of its production. To brand the thetic as the foundation of metaphysics is to risk serving as an antechamber for metaphysics – unless, that is, we specify the way the thetic is produced in our view, the Freudian theory of the unconscious and its Lacanian development show, precisely, that thetic signification is a stage attained under certain precise conditions during the signifying process, and that it constitutes the subject without being reduced to this process precisely because it is the threshold of language. Such a standpoint constitutes neither a reduction of the subject to the transcendental ego, nor a denial [*dénégation*] of the thetic phase that establishes signification.

The Mirror and Castration Positing the Subject as Absent from the Signifier

In the development of the subject, such as it has been reconstituted by the theory of the unconscious, we find the thetic phase of the signifying process, around which signification is organized, at two points: the mirror stage and the 'discovery' of castration.

The first, the mirror stage, produces the 'spatial intuition' which is found at the heart of the functioning of signification – in signs and in sentences. From that point on, in order to capture his image unified in a mirror, the child must remain separate from it, his body agitated by the semiotic motility we discussed above, which fragments him more than it unifies him in a representation. According to Lacan, human physiological immaturity, which is due to premature birth, is thus what permits any permanent positing whatsoever and, first and foremost, that of the image itself, as separate, heterogeneous, dehiscent.[14] Captation of the image and the drive investment in this image, which institute primary narcissism, permit the constitution of objects detached from the semiotic *chora*. Lacan maintains, moreover, that the specular image is the 'prototype' for the 'world of objects'.[15] Positing the imaged ego leads to the positing of the object, which is, likewise, separate and signifiable.

Thus the two separations that prepare the way for the sign are set in place. The sign can be conceived as the voice that is projected from the agitated body (from the semiotic *chora*) on to the facing *imago* or on to the object, which simultaneously detach from the surrounding continuity. Indeed, a child's first holophrastic utterances occur at this time, within what are considered the boundaries of the mirror stage (six to eighteen months). On the basis of this positing, which constitutes a *break*, signification becomes established as a digital system with a double articulation combining discrete elements. Language-learning can therefore be thought of as an acute and dramatic confrontation between positing-separating-identifying and the motility of the semiotic *chora*. Separation from the mother's body, the *fort-da* game, anality and orality, all act as a permanent negativity that destroys the image and the isolated object even as it facilitates the articulation of the semiotic network, which will afterwards be necessary in the system of language where it will be more or less integrated as a *signifier*.

Castration puts the finished touches on the process of separation that posits the subject as signifiable, which is to say, separate, always confronted by an other: *imago* in the mirror (signified) and semiotic process (signifier). As the addressee of every demand, the mother occupies the place of alterity. Her replete body, the receptacle and guarantor of demands, takes the place of all narcissistic, hence imaginary, effects and gratifications; she is, in other words, the phallus. The discovery of castration, however, detaches the subject from his dependence on the mother, and the perception of this lack [*manque*] makes the phallic function a symbolic function – *the* symbolic function. This is a decisive moment fraught with consequences: the subject, finding his identity in the symbolic, *separates* from his fusion with the mother, *confines* his *jouissance* to the genital and transfers semiotic motility on to the symbolic order. Thus ends the formation of the thetic phase, which posits the gap between the signifier and the signified as an opening up towards every desire but also every act, including the very *jouissance* that exceeds them.[16]

At this point we would like to emphasize, without going into the details of Lacan's argument, that the phallus totalizes the effects of signifieds as having been produced by the signifier: the phallus is itself a signifier. In other words, the phallus is not given in the utterance but instead refers outside itself to a precondition that makes enunciation possible. For there to be enunciation, the *ego* must be posited in the signified, but it must do so as a function of the *subject* lacking in the signifier; a system of finite positions (signification) can only function when it is supported by a subject and on the condition that this subject is a want-to-be [*manque à être*].[17] Signification exists precisely because there is no subject in signification. The gap between the imaged ego and drive motility, between the mother and the demand made on her, is precisely the break that establishes what Lacan calls the place of the Other as the place of the 'signifier'. The subject is hidden 'by an ever purer signifier',[18] this want-to-be confers on an *other* the role of containing the possibility of signification; and this other, who is no longer the mother (from whom the child ultimately separates through the mirror stage and castration), presents itself as the place of the signifier that Lacan will call 'the Other'.

Is this to say, then, that such a theoretical undertaking transcendentalizes semiotic motility, setting it up as a transcendental signifier? In our view, this transformation of semiotic motility serves to remove it from its auto-erotic and maternal enclosure and, by introducing the signifier/signified break, allows it to produce signification. By the same token, signification itself appears as a stage of the signifying process – not so much its base as its boundary. Signification is placed 'under the sign of the pre-conscious'.[19] Ultimately, this signifier/signified transformation, constitutive of language, is seen as being indebted to, induced and imposed by the social realm. Dependence on the mother is severed, and transformed into a symbolic relation to an other, the constitution of the Other is indispensable for communicating with an other. In this way, the signifier/signified break is synonymous with social sanction: 'the first social censorship'.

Thus we view the thetic phase – the positing of the *imago*, castration and the positing of semiotic motility – as the place of the Other, as the precondition for signification, i.e., the precondition for the positing of language. The thetic phase marks a threshold between two heterogeneous realms: the semiotic and the symbolic. The second includes part of the first and their scission is thereafter marked by the break between signifier and signified. *Symbolic* would seem an appropriate term for this always split unification that is produced by a rupture and is impossible without it. Its etymology makes it particularly pertinent. The σύμβοϰον is a sign of recognition: an 'object' split in two and the parts separated, but, as eyelids do, σύμβοϰον brings together the two edges of that fissure. As a result, the 'symbol' is any joining, any bringing together that is a contract – one that either follows hostilities or presupposes them – and, finally, any exchange, including an exchange of hostility.

Not only is symbolic, thetic unity divided (into signifier and signified), but this division is itself the result of a break that put a heterogeneous functioning in the position of signifier. This functioning is the instinctual semiotic, preceding meaning and signification, mobile, amorphous, but already regulated, which we have attempted to represent through references to child psychoanalysis (particularly at the pre-Oedipal stage) and the theory of drives. In the speaking subject, fantasies articulate this irruption of drives within the realm of the signifier; they disrupt the signifier and shift the metonymy of desire, which acts within the place of the Other, on to a *jouissance* that divests the object and turns back towards the auto-erotic body. That language is a defensive construction reveals its ambiguity – the death drive underlying it. If language, constituted as symbolic through narcissistic, specular, imaginary investment, protects the body from the attack of drives by making it a place – the place of the signifier – in which the body can signify itself through positions; and if, therefore, language, in the service of the death drive, is a pocket of narcissism towards which this drive may be directed, then fantasies remind us, if we had ever forgotten, of the insistent presence of drive heterogeneity.[20]

All poetic 'distortions' of the signifying chain and the structure of signification may be considered in this light: they yield under the attack of the 'residues of first symbolizations' (Lacan), in other words, those drives that the thetic phase was not able to sublate [*relever, aufheben*] by linking them into signifier and signified. As a consequence, any disturbance of the 'social censorship' – that of the signifier/signified break – attests, perhaps first and foremost, to an influx of the death drive, which no signifier, no mirror, no other and no mother could ever contain. In 'artistic' practices the semiotic – the precondition of the symbolic – is revealed as that which also destroys the symbolic, and this revelation allows us to presume something about its functioning.

Psychoanalysts acknowledge that the pre-Oedipal stages Melanie Klein discusses are 'analytically unthinkable' but not inoperative, and, furthermore, that the relation of the subject to the signifier is established and language-learning is completed only in the pre-genital stages that are set in place by the retroaction of the Oedipus complex (which itself brings about initial genital maturation).[21] Thereafter, the supposedly characteristic functioning of the pre-Oedipal stages appears only in the complete, post-genital handling of language, which presupposes, as we have seen, a decisive imposition of the phallic. In other words, the subject must be firmly posited by castration so that drive attacks against the thetic will not give way to fantasy or to psychosis but will instead lead to a 'second-degree thetic', i.e., a resumption of the functioning characteristic of the semiotic *chora* within the signifying device of language. This is precisely what artistic practices, and notably poetic language, demonstrate.

Starting from and (logically and chronologically) after the phallic position and the castration that underlies it – in other words, after the Oedipus complex and especially after the regulation of genitality by the retroactive effect of the Oedipus complex in puberty – the semiotic *chora* can be read not as a failure of the thetic but instead as its very precondition. Neurotics and psychotics are defined as such by their relationship to what we are calling the thetic. We now see why, in treating them, psychoanalysis can only conceive of semiotic motility as a disturbance of language and/or of the order of the signifier. Conversely, the refusal of the thetic phase and an attempt to hypostasize semiotic motility as autonomous from the thetic – capable of doing without it or unaware of it – can be seen as a resistance to psychoanalysis. Some therefore even contend that one can find in poetry the unfolding of this refusal of the thetic, something like a direct transcription of the genetic code – as if practice were possible without the thetic and as if a text, in order to hold together as a text, did not require a completion [*finition*], a structuration, a kind of total-ization of semiotic motility. This completion constitutes a synthesis that requires the thesis of language in order to come about, and the semiotic pulver-izes it only to make it a new device – for us, this is precisely what distinguishes a text as *signifying-practice* from the 'drifting-into-non-sense' [*dérive*] that characterizes neurotic discourse. The distinction cannot be erased unless one puts oneself outside 'monumental history' in a transcendence which often proves to be one of the reactionary forces combining that history's discrete blocks.[22]

In this way, only the subject, for whom the thetic is not a repression of the semiotic *chora* but instead a position either taken on or undergone, can call into question the thetic so that a new disposition may be articulated. Castration must have been a problem, a trauma, a drama, so that the semiotic can return through the symbolic position it brings about. This is the crux of the matter: both the completion of the Oedipus complex and its reactivation in puberty are needed for the *Aufhebung* of the semiotic in the symbolic to give rise to a signi-fying *practice* that has a socio-historical function (and is not just a self-analytical discourse, a substitute for the analyst's couch). At the same time, however, this completion of the Oedipal stage and the genitality it gives rise to should not repress the semiotic, for such a repression is what sets up metalanguage and the 'pure signifier'. No pure signifier can effect the *Aufhebung* (in the Hegelian sense) of the semiotic without leaving a remainder, and anyone who would believe this myth need only question his fascination or boredom with a given poem, painting or piece of music. As a traversable boundary, the thetic is completely different from an imaginary castration that must be evaded in order to return to the maternal *chora*. It is clearly distinct as well from a castration imposed once and for all, perpetuating the well-ordered signifier and positing it as sacred and unalterable within the enclosure of the Other.[23]

Notes

1 The term '*chora*' has recently been criticized for its ontological essence by Jacques Derrida, *Positions*, annot. and trans. Alan Bass (Chicago: University of Chicago Press, 1981), pp. 75 and 106, n. 39.

2 Plato emphasizes that the receptacle (ὑποδοχεῖον), which is also called space (χώρα) *vis-à-vis* reason, is necessary – but not divine since it is unstable, uncertain, ever changing and becoming; it is even unnameable, improbable, bastard: 'Space, which is everlasting, not admitting destruction; providing a situation for all things that come into being but itself apprehended without the senses by a sort of bastard reasoning, and hardly an object of belief. This, indeed, is that which we look upon as in a dream and say that anything that is must needs be in some place and occupy some room . . .' (*Timaeus*, trans. Francis M. Cornford, 52a–52b). Is the receptacle a 'thing' or a mode of language? Plato's hesitation between the two gives the

receptacle an even more uncertain status. It is one of the elements that antedate not only the *universe* but also *names* and even *syllables*. 'We speak . . . positing them as original principles, elements (as it were, letters) of the universe; whereas one who has ever so little intelligence should not rank them in this analogy even so low as syllables' (ibid., 48b). 'It is hard to say, with respect to any one of these, which we ought to call really water rather than fire, or indeed which we should call by any given name rather than by all the names together or by each severally, so as to use language in a sound and trustworthy way . . . Since, then, in this way no one of these things ever makes its appearance as the *same* thing, which of them can we steadfastly affirm to be this – whatever it may be – and not something else, without blushing for ourselves? It cannot be done' (ibid., 49b–d).

3   There is a fundamental ambiguity: on the one hand, the receptacle is mobile and even contradictory, without unity, separable and divisible: pre-syllable, pre-word. Yet, on the other hand, because this separability and divisibility antecede numbers and forms, the space or receptacle is called *amorphous*: thus its suggested rhythmicity will in a certain sense be erased, for how can one think an articulation of what is not yet singular but is nevertheless necessary? All we may say of it, then, to make it intelligible, is that it is amorphous but that it 'is of such and such a quality', not even an index or something in particular ('this' or 'that'). Once named, it immediately becomes a container that takes the place of infinitely repeatable separability. This amounts to saying that this repeated separability is 'ontologized' the moment a *name* or a *word* replaces it, making it intelligible. 'Are we talking idly whenever we say that there is such a thing as an intelligible Form of anything? Is this nothing more than a word?' (ibid., 51c). Is the Platonic *chora* the 'nominability' of rhythm (of repeated separation)?

Why then borrow an ontologized term in order to designate an articulation that antecedes positing? First, the Platonic term makes explicit an insurmountable problem for discourse: once it has been named, that functioning, even if it is presymbolic, is brought back into a symbolic position. All discourse can do is differentiate, by means of a 'bastard reasoning', the receptacle from the motility, which, by contrast, is not posited as being 'a *certain* something' ['une *telle*']. Secondly, this motility is the precondition for symbolicity, heterogeneous to it, yet indispensable. Therefore what needs to be done is to try to differentiate, always through a 'bastard reasoning', the specific arrangements of this motility, without seeing them as recipients of accidental singularities, or a *Being* always posited in itself, or a projection of the *One*. Moreover, Plato invites us to differentiate in this fashion when he describes this motility, while gathering it into the receiving membrane. 'But because it was filled with powers that were neither alike nor evenly balanced, there was no equipoise in any region of it, but it was everywhere swayed unevenly and shaken by these things and by its motion shook them in turn. And they, being thus moved, were perpetually being separated and carried in different directions, just as when things are shaken and winnowed by means of winnowing baskets and other instruments for cleaning corn . . . it separated the most unlike kinds farthest apart from one another, and thrust the most alike closest together: whereby the different kinds came to have different regions, even before the ordered whole consisting of them came to be . . . but were altogether in such a condition as we should expect for anything when deity is absent from it' (ibid., 52d–53b). Indefinite 'conjunctions' and 'disjunctions' (functioning, devoid of Meaning), the *chora* is governed by a necessity that is not God's law.

4   The Platonic space or receptacle is a mother and wet nurse: 'Indeed we may fittingly compare the Recipient to a mother, the model to a father, and the nature that arises between them to their offspring' (ibid., 50d); 'Now the wet nurse of Becoming was made watery and fiery, received the characters of earth and air, and was qualified by all the other affections that go with these . . .' (ibid., 52d; translation modified).

5   'Law', which derives etymologically from *lex*, necessarily implies the act of judgement whose role in safeguarding society was first developed by the Roman law courts. 'Ordering', on the other hand, is closer to the series 'rule', 'norm' (from the Greek [γνώμων] meaning 'discerning' [adj.], 'carpenter's square' [noun]), etc., which implies a numerical or geometrical necessity. On normativity in linguistics, see Alain Rey, 'Usages, jugements et prescriptions linguistiques', *Langue Francaise*, 16, Dec. 1972, p. 5. But the temporary ordering of the *chora* is not yet even a rule: the arsenal of geometry is posterior to the *chora's* motility; it fixes the *chora* in place and reduces it.

6   Operations are, rather, an act of the subject of understanding. [Hans G. Furth, in *Piaget and Knowledge: theoretical foundations* (Englewood Cliffs, NJ; Prentice-Hall, 1969), offers the following definition of 'concrete operations': 'characteristic of the first stage of operational intelligence. A concrete operation implies underlying general Systems or "groupings" such as classification, seriation, number. Its applicability is limited to objects considered as real (concrete)' (p. 260) – Trans.]

7   Piaget stresses that the roots of sensorimotor operations precede language and that the acquisition of thought is due to the symbolic function, which, for him, is a notion separate from that of language *per se*. See Jean Piaget, 'Language and symbolic operations', in *Piaget and Knowledge,* pp. 121–30.

8   By 'function' we mean a dependent variable determined each time the independent variables with which it is associated are determined. For our purposes, a function is what links stases within the process of semiotic facilitation.

9   Such a position has been formulated by Lipot Szondi, *Experimental Diagnostic of Drives,* trans. Gertrude Aull (New York: Grune & Stratton, 1952).

10   See James D. Watson, *The Double Helix: a personal account of the discovery of the structure of DNA* (London: Weidenfeld & Nicolson, 1968).

11   Throughout her writings, Melanie Klein emphasizes the 'pre-Oedipal' phase, i.e., a period of the subject's development that precedes the 'discovery' of castration and the positing of the superego, which itself is a subject to (paternal) Law. The processes she describes for this phase correspond, *but on a genetic level,* to what we call the semiotic, as opposed to the symbolic, which underlies and conditions the semiotic. Significantly, these pre-Oedipal processes are organized through projection on to the mother's body, for girls as well as for boys: 'at this stage of development children of both sexes believe that it is the body of their mother which contains all that is desirable, especially their father's penis', *The Psychoanalysis of Children,* trans. Alix Strachey (London: Hogarth Press, 1932), p. 269. Our own view of this stage is as follows: Without 'believing' or 'desiring' any 'object' whatsoever, the subject is in the process of constituting himself *vis-à-vis* a non-object. He is in the process of separating from this non-object so as to make that non-object 'one' and posit himself as 'other': the mother's body is the not-yet-one that the believing and desiring subject will image as a 'receptacle'.

12   As for what situates the mother in symbolic space, we find the phallus again (see Jacques Lacan, 'La relation d'objet et les structures freudiennes', *Bulletin de*

Psychologie, April 1957, pp. 426–30), represented by the mother's father, i.e., the subject's maternal grandfather (see Marie-Claire Boons, 'Le meurtre du Père chez Freud', *L'Inconscient,* 5, Jan.–March 1968, pp. 101–29).

13   Though disputed and inconsistent, the Freudian theory of drives is of interest here because of the predominance Freud gives to the death drive in both 'living matter' and the 'human being'. The death drive is transversal to identity and tends to disperse narcissisms whose constitution ensures the link between structures and, by extension, life. But at the same time and conversely, narcissism and pleasure are only temporary positions from which the death drive blazes new paths [*se fraye de nouveaux passages*]. Narcissism and pleasure are therefore inveiglings and realizations of the death drive. The semiotic *chora,* converting drive discharges into stases, can be thought of both as a delaying of the death drive and as a possible realization of this drive, which tends to return to a homeostatic state. This hypothesis is consistent with the following remark: 'at the beginning of mental life', writes Freud, 'the struggle for pleasure was far more intense than later but not so unrestricted: it had to submit to frequent interruptions', *Beyond the Pleasure Principle,* in James Strachey (ed.), *The Standard Edition of the Works of Sigmund Freud* (London: Hogarth Press and the Institute of Psychoanalysis, 1953), vol. XVIII, p. 63.

14   'The fact is that the total form of the body by which the subject anticipates in a mirage the maturation of his power is given to him only as *Gestalt,* that is to say, in an exteriority in which this form is certainly more constituent than constituted, but in which it appears to him above all in a contrasting size (*un relief de stature*) that fixes it and in a symmetry that inverts it, in contrast with the turbulent movements that the subject feels are animating him.' Lacan, 'The mirror stage as formative of the function of the I', in *Ecrits: a selection*, trans. Alan Sheridan (New York: Norton, 1977), p. 2.

15   'The subversion of the subject and the dialectic of desire in the Freudian unconscious', *Ecrits: a selection,* p. 319.

16   In Lacan's terminology, castration and the phallus are defined as 'position', 'localization' and 'presence': 'We know that the unconscious castration complex has the function of a knot: . . . (2) in a regulation of the development that gives its *ratio* to this first role: namely, the *installation* in the subject of an unconscious *position* without which he would be unable to identity himself with the ideal type of his sex . . .' ('The signification of the phallus', *Ecrits: a selection,* p. 281; emphasis added). 'We know that in this term Freud specifies the first genital maturation: on the one hand, it would seem to be characterized by the imaginary dominance of the phallic attribute and by masturbatory *jouissance* and, on the other, it *localizes* this *jouissance* for the woman in the clitoris, which is thus raised to the function of the phallus' (p. 282; emphasis added). '[The phallus] is the signifier intended to *designate* as a whole the effects of the signified, in that the signifier conditions them by its *presence* as a signifier' (p. 285; emphasis added).

17   Lacan himself has suggested the term 'want-to-be' for his neologism (*manque à être*). Other proposed translations include 'want-of-being' (Leon S. Roudiez, personal communication) and 'constitutitive lack' (Jeffrey Mehlman, 'The "floating signifier": from Lévi-Strauss to Lacan', *Yale French Studies,* 48, 1972, p. 37). – Trans.

18   Lacan, *Ecrits: a selection,* p. 299.

19   Ibid.

20   Our definition of language as deriving from the death drive finds confirmation in Lacan: 'From the approach that we have indicated, the reader should recognize in

the metaphor of the return to the inanimate (which Freud attaches to every living body) that margin beyond life that language gives to the human being by virtue of the fact that he speaks, and which is precisely that in which such a being places in the position of a signifier, not only those parts of his body that are exchangeable, but this body itself' ('The subversion of the subject and the dialectic of desire in the Freudian unconscious', *Ecrits: a selection,* p. 301). We would add that the symbolism of magic is based on language's capacity to store up the death drive by taking it out of the body. Lévi-Strauss suggests this when he writes that 'the relationship between monster and disease is internal to [the patient's] mind, whether conscious or unconscious: It is a relationship between symbol and thing symbolized, or, to use the terminology of linguists, between signifier and signified. The shaman provides the sick woman with a *language,* by means of which unexpressed and otherwise inexpressible psychic states can be immediately expressed. And it is the transition to this verbal expression – at the same time making it possible to undergo in an ordered and intelligible form a real experience that would otherwise be chaotic and inexpressible – which induces the release of the physiological process, that is, the reorganization, in a favourable direction, of the process to which the sick woman is subjected.' ('The effectiveness of symbols', in *Structural Anthropology,* pp. 1978; translation modified.)

21 See Lacan, 'On a question preliminary to any possible treatment of psychosis', in *Ecrits: a selection,* p. 197.

22 'The theory of textual writing's history may be termed "monumental history" in so far as it serves as a "ground" ['*fait fond*'] in a literal way, in relation to a "cursive", figural (teleological) history which has served at once to constitute and dissimulate a written/exterior space ... Writing "that recognizes the rupture" is therefore irreducible to the classical (representational) concept of "written text": what it writes is never more than one part of itself. It makes the rupture the intersection of two sets (two irreconcilable states of language)'. (Philippe Sollers, 'Program', in David Hayman (ed.), *Writing and the Experience of Limits,* trans. Philip Barnard and David Hayman (New York: Columbia University Press, 1983), p. 7. Our reading of Lautréamont and Mallarmé will attempt to follow these principles, see *La Révolution du langage poétique,* (Paris: Seuil, 1974), pp. 361–609. [This is the first of many references to the latter portion of *La Révolution du langage poétique,* which has not been translated – trans.].

23 Indeed, even Lacanian theory, although it establishes the signifier as absolute master, makes a distinction between two modalities of the signifier represented by the two levels of the 'completed graph' (*Ecrits: a selection,* p. 314). On the one hand, the *signifier* as 'signifier's treasure', as distinct from the *code,* 'for it is not that the univocal correspondence of a sign with something is preserved in it, but that the signifier is constituted only from a synchronic and enumerable collection of elements in which each is sustained only by the principle of its opposition to each of the others' (p. 304). Drives function within this 'treasure of the signifiers' (p. 314), which is also called a signifying 'battery'. But from that level on, and even beforehand, the subject submits to the signifier, which is also shown as a 'punctuation in which the signification is constituted as finished product' (p. 304). In this way the path from the treasure to punctuation forms a 'previous site of the pure subject of the signifier', which is not yet, however, the true place [*lieu*] of the Other. On that level, the psychotic 'dance' unfolds, the 'pretence' [*feinte*] that 'is satisfied with that previous Other', accounted for by game theory. The fact remains that this

previous site does not exhaust the question of signification because the subject is not constituted from the code that lies in the Other, but rather from the message emitted by the Other. Only when the Other is distinguished from all other partners, unfolding as signifier and signified – and, as a result, articulating himself within an always already sentential signification and thus transmitting messages – only then are the preconditions for language ('speech') present.

At this second stage, the signifier is not just a 'treasure' or a 'battery' but a *place* [lieu]: 'But it is clear that Speech begins only with the passage from "pretence" to the order of the signifier, and that the signifier requires another locus – the locus of the Other, the Other witness, the witness Other than any of the partners – for the Speech that it supports to be capable of lying, that is to say, of presenting itself as Truth' (p. 305). Only from this point will the ego start to take on various configurations. What seems problematic about this arrangement, or in any case what we believe needs further development, is the way in which the 'battery', the 'treasure' of the signifier, functions. In our opinion, game theory cannot completely account for this functioning, nor can a signification be articulated until an alterity is *distinctly posited* as such. One cannot speak of the 'signifier' before the positing or the thesis of the Other, the articulation of which begins only with the mirror stage. But what of the previous processes that are not yet 'a site', but a *functioning*? The thetic phase will establish this functioning, as a signifying *order* (though it will not stop it) and will return in this order.

5

The Individual and Representation

Cornelius Castoriadis

The Sense of Autonomy – the Individual

If autonomy is at the centre of the objectives and at the crossroads of the paths of the revolutionary project, this term must be specified and clarified. We shall attempt to clarify it first on the level where it is easiest to grasp: in relation to the individual, and shall then move to the level which is of particular interest to us here, the collective level. We shall try to understand what an autonomous individual is – and what an autonomous or unalienated society is.

Freud proposed as a maxim of psychoanalysis: 'Where Id was, Ego shall come to be' (*Wo Es war, soll Ich werden*). *Ego* is here, as an initial approximation, consciousness in general. The *Id*, which properly speaking is the origin and the place of drives ('instincts'), must be taken in this context as representing the unconscious in the broadest sense. *Ego*, consciousness and will, must take the place of the dark forces which, 'in me', dominate, act for me – 'act me' as G. Groddeck said.[1] These forces are not simply – are not so much, but we shall return to this later – pure instincts, libido or death instinct. What is at issue is instead their interminable, phantasmatic and fantastic alchemy, and along with this, and in particular, the unconscious forces of formation and repression, the super-ego and the unconscious Self. It is necessary, straightaway, to interpret this sentence. Ego must take the place of Id – this can mean neither the suppression of drives, nor the elimination or the absorption of the unconscious. It is a matter of taking their place as an *agency of decision.* Autonomy would then be consciousness's rule over the unconscious. Without prejudice to the new depth dimension revealed by Freud, this is the programme proposed by philosophical reflection on the individual for the past 25 centuries, at once the assumption and the outcome of ethics as it has been viewed by Plato and the Stoics, Spinoza or Kant. (It is of immense importance in itself, but not for this discussion, that Freud proposes an effective way to attain what, for philosophers, had remained an 'ideal' accessible through abstract knowledge).[2] If to autonomy, that is to self-legislation or self-regulation, one opposes heteronomy, that is legislation or regulation by another, then autonomy is my law opposed to the regulation by the unconscious, which is another law, the law of another, other than myself.

In what sense can we say that the regulation by the unconscious is the law of another? Of what other? Of a literal other, not of another, unknown 'Self' but of another *in* me. As Jacques Lacan says, 'The unconscious is the discourse of the Other'; it is to a great extent the depository of intentions, desires, investments, demands, expectations – significations to which the individual has been exposed from the moment of conception and even before, as these stem from those who engendered and raised him or her.[3] Autonomy then appears as: my discourse must take the place of the discourse of the Other, of a foreign discourse that is in me, ruling over me: speaking through myself. This clarification immediately indicates the *social* dimension of the problem (little matter that the Other in question at the start is the 'narrow' parental other; through a series of obvious connections, the parental couple finally refers to society as a whole and to its history).

What, however, is this discourse of the Other – no longer as to its origin but as to its quality? And up to what point can it be eliminated?

The essential characteristic of the discourse of the Other, from the point of view that interests us here, is its relation to the *imaginary*. It has to do with the fact that, ruled by this discourse, the subject takes himself or herself to be something he or she is not (or is not necessarily) and that for him or her, others and the entire world undergo a corresponding misrepresentation. The subject does not express himself or herself but is expressed by someone, and therefore exists as a part of another's world (certainly misrepresented in its turn). The subject is ruled by an imaginary, lived as even more real than the real, yet not known as such, precisely *because* it is not known as such. What is essential to heteronomy – or to alienation in the general sense of the term – on the level of the individual, is the domination of an autonomized imaginary which has assumed the function of defining for the subject both reality and desire. The 'repression of drives' as such, the conflict between the 'pleasure principle' and the 'reality principle' do not constitute individual alienation, which is finally the almost unlimited reign of a principle of *de*-reality. The important conflict in this respect is not that between drives and reality (if this conflict sufficed as a pathogenic cause, there would never have been a single, even approximative resolution of the Oedipus complex from the beginning of time, and never would a man and a woman have walked upon the earth). The important conflict is that between drives and reality, on the one hand, and the imaginary development within the subject, on the other.

The *Id* in Freud's adage therefore is to be understood as signifying essentially this function of the unconscious which invests imaginary reality, autonomizes it, and confers on it the power of decision – the content of this imaginary being related to the discourse of the Other ('repetition' but also amplified transformation of this discourse).

It is where this function of the unconscious was, and along with it the discourse of the Other which fuels it, that Ego is to come to be. This means that my discourse is to take the place of the discourse of the Other. But what is my discourse? What is a discourse that is mine?

A discourse that is mine is a discourse that has negated the discourse of the Other, that has negated it not necessarily in its content, but inasmuch as it is the discourse of the Other. In other words, a discourse that, by making clear both the origin and the sense of this discourse, has negated it or affirmed it in awareness of the state of affairs, by referring its sense to that which is constituted as the subject's own truth – as my own truth.

If in this interpretation Freud's adage were taken in an absolute sense, it would propose an inaccessible objective. Never will my discourse be wholly mine in the sense defined above. Obviously, I could never begin everything all over again, even if only to ratify what already happened. This is also because – and we shall return to this later – the notion of the subject's own truth is itself much more a problem than a solution.

This is just as true of the relation to the imaginary function of the unconscious. How can we conceive of a subject that would have entirely absorbed the imaginative function, how could we dry up this spring in the depths of ourselves from which flow both alienating phantasies and free creation truer than truth, unreal deliria and surreal poems, this eternally new beginning and ground of all things, without which nothing would have a ground, how can we eliminate what is at the base of, or in any case what is inextricably bound up with what makes us human beings – our symbolic function, which presupposes our capacity to see and to think in a thing something which it is not?

Inasmuch as we do not want to make Freud's maxim a mere regulative idea defined in reference to an impossible state – and thus a new mystification – another sense had to be given to it. It must be understood as referring not to an attained state but to an active situation; not to an ideal person who has become a pure Ego once and for all, who would proffer a discourse all its own, who would never produce phantasies, but to a real person who would be unceasingly involved in the movement of taking up again what had been acquired, the discourse of the Other, who is capable of uncovering phantasies as phantasies and who, finally, never allows them to rule – unless he or she is so willing. This is not a simple 'tending towards', it is actually a situation, definable in terms of characteristics which mark a radical separation between it and the state of heteronomy. These characteristics do not consist in an 'awareness' achieved once and for all, but in *another relation* between the conscious and the unconscious, between lucidity and the function of the imaginary, in *another attitude* of the subject with respect to himself or herself, in a profound modification of the activity-passivity mix, of the sign under which this takes place, of the respective place of the two elements that compose it. How little it is a question in all this of a power grab by consciousness in the strict sense is shown in the fact that Freud's proposition can be completed by its inverse. 'Where Ego is, Id must spring forth' (*Wo Ich bin, soll Es auftauchen*). Desire, drives – whether it be Eros or Thanatos – this is me, too, and these have to be brought not only to consciousness but to expression and to existence.[4] An autonomous subject is one that knows itself to be justified in concluding: this is indeed true, and: this is indeed my desire.

Autonomy is therefore not a clarification without remainder nor is it the total elimination of the discourse of the Other unrecognized as such. It is the establishment of another relation between the discourse of the Other and the subject's discourse. The total elimination of the discourse of the Other unrecognized as such is an unhistorical state. The weight of the discourse of the Other unrecognized as such can be seen even in those who have made the most radical attempts to pursue the interrogation and the critique of tacit presuppositions to the end – whether this be Plato, Descartes, Kant, Marx or Freud himself. However, there are indeed those who – like Plato and Freud – never *gave up* this pursuit, and there are those who stopped and who, as a result, at times became alienated to their own discourse which became other. There is the continuous and continually actualizable possibility of regarding, objectifying, setting at a distance, detaching and finally transforming the discourse of the Other into the discourse of the subject.

But just what is this subject? This third term of Freud's sentence, which is to come where Id was, is certainly not the point-like ego of the 'I think'. It is not the subject as pure activity, possessing no constraints, no inertia, this will o' the wisp of subjectivist philosophers, this flame unencumbered by any physical support, ties or nourishment. This activity of the subject who is 'working on itself', encounters as its object the wealth of contents (the discourse of the Other) with which it has never finished. And, without this object, it simply is not at all. The subject is also activity, but this activity is acting on some thing, otherwise it is nothing. It is therefore codetermined by what it gives itself as an object. But this aspect of mutual 'inhering in' belonging to the subject and the object – intentionality, the fact that the subject exists only to the extent that it posits an object – is only an initial, relatively superficial determination, it is what carries the subject into the world, it is what continually puts the subject in the street. There is another determination, one that does not concern the orientation of the intentional fibres of the subject, but their very material, which carries the world into the subject and introduces the street into what the subject may take to be its own den. For the active subject, which is a *subject* of . . . , which convokes before itself, posits, objectifies, looks at and sets at a distance, what is it – is it a pure gaze, the naked capacity for evoking something, setting it at a distance, a spark outside of time, non-dimensionality? No, it is a gaze *and* the support for this gaze, thought *and* the support for this thought, it is activity *and* the acting body – the material body and the metaphorical body. A gaze in which there is not already something that has itself been looked at can see nothing; a thought in which there is not something that has been thought about can think of nothing. What we have been calling *support* here is not simply the biological support; it is the fact that *content, no matter which, is always already present* and that it is not a residue, a scoria, something that encumbers or an indifferent material but the *efficient condition for the subject's activity*. This support, this content belongs neither simply to the subject nor simply to the other (or to the world). It is the produced and productive union of the self and the other (or of the world). In the subject *as subject* we find the non-subject, and all the traps it falls into, have been dug out by subjectivist philosophy itself for having forgotten this fundamental truth. In the subject there is, to be sure, as one of its moments 'that which can never become an object', inalienable freedom, the always present possibility of redirecting the gaze, of abstracting from any particular content, of bracketing everything, including oneself, except inasmuch as the self has this capacity that springs forth as presence and absolute proximity at the very moment it places itself at a distance from itself. However, this moment is abstract, empty; it never has and never will produce anything other than the silent and useless self-evidence of the *cogito sum*, the immediate certainty of existing as a thinking substance, which cannot legitimately express itself through language. For once even unpronounced speech makes a first opening, the world and others infiltrate from every direction, consciousness is overwhelmed by the torrent of meanings, which come, so to speak, not from the outside but from the inside. It is only through the world that one can think the world. Once thought is the thought of something, the content re-emerges, not only in what is to be thought but in that by means of which it is thought (*darin, wodurch es gedacht wird*). Without this content, in the place of the subject one would find no more than its ghost. And in this content, there is always to be found, directly or indirectly, the other and others. The other is just as fully present in the form as in the fact of discourse, as the demand for confrontation and for truth (which obviously does not mean that truth is confused with the agreement of opinions). Finally, and it is only apparently far removed from our discussion to recall that the support for this union of the subject and the non-subject in the subject, the point of connection between the self and the other, is the body, that 'material' structure heavy with virtual meaning. The body, which is not alienation – this would be meaningless – but participation in the world and in sense, attachment and mobility, preconstitution of a universe of significations before any reflexive thought.

It is because it 'forgets' this concrete structure of the subject that traditional philosophy, the narcissism of consciousness fascinated by its own naked forms, reduces to the level of the conditions of servitude both the other and corporeality. And it is because it wants to base itself on the pure freedom of a fictive subject that it condemns itself to rediscover the alienation of the actual subject as an insoluble problem. In the same way, wanting to base itself on exhaustive rationality, it must constantly run up against the impossible reality of an irreducibly irrational element. This is how it finally ends up being an irrational and alienated undertaking; all the more irrational as it seeks, digs out, and purifies unendingly the conditions for its rationality; all the more alienated as it unceasingly affirms its naked freedom, whereas this freedom is at once incontestable and useless.

The subject in question is, therefore, not the abstract moment of philosophical subjectivity; it is the actual subject traversed through and through by the world and by others. The Ego of autonomy is not the absolute Self, the monad cleaning and polishing its external-internal surface in order to eliminate the impurities resulting from contact with others. It is the active and lucid agency that constantly reorganizes its contents, through the help of these same contents, that produces by means of a material and in relation to needs and ideas, all of which are themselves mixtures of what it has already found there before it and what it has produced itself.

In this connection too, it cannot be a matter of entirely eliminating the discourse of the other – not only because this is an unending task, but because the other is in each case present in the activity that 'eliminates' him. And this is why there can never exist any truth that would be the 'subject's own' in any absolute sense. The subject's own truth is always participation in a truth that surpasses him, a truth rooted in him and that finally roots him in society and in history, even as the subject realizes his autonomy. [. . .]

The Question of the Origin of Representation

The essential part of Freud's work consisted, perhaps, in the discovery of the imaginary element in the psyche – in revealing the most profound dimensions of what I am calling here the radical imagination. But one could just as well say that a large part of his work aims at, or ineluctably leads to, reducing, covering over or concealing anew this very role. In the positivist atmosphere surrounding him, and which influenced him profoundly and definitively – behind which, obviously, lies traditional metaphysics, determined-being, causes that have become forces, ends that have become 'principles' – Freud began by seeking 'real' factors that would account for the history of the psyche, its organization, and, finally, even its being. We are familiar with his initial belief in the positive reality of the event corresponding to the traumatic memory of neurotics; then, the reversal of this opinion brought about by the impossibility of believing in the 'reality' of the vast number of the seduction scenes of a child by an adult recounted by patients; the search for the primal scene as a real event, finally abandoned but only regretfully and over strong resistance, in the case of the *Wolf-man*; and, finally, when ontogenesis was unable to deliver real material as the necessary and sufficient support, if not the cause, of phantasy, the recourse (how paradoxical and how intrinsically contradictory!) to phylogenesis in the theoretical hope of a 'positive' verification of his theses on the psyche.

The essential role of the imagination, although it is neither recognized or even named, in fact appears in Freud by means of the central importance of phantasy in the psyche and the *relative* independence and autonomy of phantasizing. Phantasizing is discovered as an unexpungible component of deep psychic life. But how was one to account for its relation to the other components of this life, of the origin of its content, and of the source of its power?

The drive (*Trieb*) can be manifested in the psyche only by means of a representation; the psyche submits the drive to the obligation of a delegation through representation (*Vorstellungsrepräsentanz des Triebes*); also, undoubtedly, to that of the 'delegation through affect', but this is a different problem. What is the origin of this representation, and what can its content be, in particular: why is it *this specific* content?

Paradoxes arise as soon as we approach these questions.

Representation can be formed only in and through the psyche; this assertion, moreover, is redundant, for the psyche *is* that very thing, the emergence of representations accompanied by an affect and inserted into an intentional process. This representation, Freud explicitly affirms, can be formed only on the instructions of the drive – which at the start, however, has no representative (delegate) in the psyche and so finds itself condemned to silence. An initial bridge must be postulated between the 'soul' and the 'body'; the first representative core must be found to be constituted, to conform to, or better to relate to the demands of the drive as the mediation between the soul and the body before any canonical procedure of mediation has been established. To be sure, we can say that the first delegation of the drive in the psyche is the affect, in particular that of displeasure. But we can find nothing in an affect, whether of pleasure or of unpleasure, that could account for the form or the content of a representation; at most the affect could induce the 'finality' or the 'orientation' of the representative process. It is therefore necessary to postulate (even if this is only implicitly) that the psyche is the capacity to produce an 'initial' representation, the capacity of putting into image or making an image (*Bildung* and *Einbildung*). This may appear self-evident. But this image-making must at the same time relate to a drive, at a time when nothing ensures this relation. This may well be the point of condensation and accumulation for all the mysteries of the 'bonding' between the soul and the body.

Where does the psyche get the elements – the material *and* the organization – for this representation? The paradoxes we encounter here are by no means proper to Freud alone; they have a venerable tradition in philosophy. If the psyche produces everything out of itself, if it is sheer and total production of its own representations with respect to their form (organization) and to their content, we can wonder how and why it should ever meet anything other than itself and its own products. And, if we say that it borrows the elements of representation from the 'real', then we are advancing an assertion that is meaningless (how can one borrow something from someone that he does not possess? The real cannot be at one and the same time real and the real representation of the real in the real); we are also obliterating what will be a constant vector in Freudian thought: the 'impression' (*Eindruck*, to use the Kantian term), that by means of which the 'real' announces itself in the psyche, becomes an element in the representation only in relation to a psychical elaboration that can produce, depending on the subject and the moment, the most divergent and most unexpected results. The 'gradualist' attempt to solve the problem is here, just as it is everywhere else, simply a way of sidestepping it: impressions are held to be elaborated, at each stage, in a 'richer' and more 'developed' manner, in relation to the totality of previous 'experience'. But already the 'first stage' of the constitution of this experience presupposes the psyche's capacity to organize into an *experience*, however rudimentary, what would otherwise remain a chaos of internal and external impressions. There is no doubt that this capacity of organization undergoes a vast development in and through the history of the subject; but how could it undergo this if it were not, at some minimal yet essential degree, already present at the start? The very postulate of the gradualist thesis, namely that this capacity is refined in relation to and through the feedback of its 'products', presupposes an initial producer of an initial product.

There is no possibility of understanding the problematic of representation if we seek the origin of representation outside of representation itself. The psyche is, to be sure, 'the receptivity of impressions', the capacity of being-affected-by. . . ; but it is also, and more importantly (for without this the receptivity of impressions would produce nothing) the emergence of representation as an irreducible and unique mode of being and as the organization of something in and through its figuration, its 'being put into images'. The psyche is a *forming*, which exists in and through *what* it forms and *how* it forms; it is *Bildung* and *Einbildung* – formation and imagination – it is the radical imagination that makes a 'first' representation arise out of a nothingness of representation, that is to say, *out of nothing*.

Psychical life can exist only if the psyche has this original capacity to make representations arise, and, 'at the start', a 'first' representation which must, in a certain manner, contain within itself the possibility of organizing all representations – something that is formed and forming, a figure that would be the seed of the schemata of figuration; hence, in as embryonic a form as one may like, the organizing elements of the psychical world that will later develop, with decisive additions coming from outside but which are, nevertheless, received and elaborated in accordance with the requirements posited by the original representation.

This necessity, which is inherent in the Freudian problematic, is not made explicit there. It is even covered over due to the deep motivations that prevented Freud from thematizing the question of the imagination as such. Contained potentially within his thought, it is in fact hidden in Freud and in many of his successors by a second problematic, that of phantasies and of derived imaginary formations.

It is obviously in phantasy and in similar formations that the imagination in action presents itself to observation and clinical study. And if we concentrate on the analysis and interpretation of phantasies provided by clinical material, we shall always, by definition, be dealing with derived products; the constitution of these products involves the entire range of psychical functions. We would then see in phantasmatization (and in the imagination) no more than late modes of operation which could never be understood in their *raison d'être*, their organization and their content except through recourse to other functions and factors. Thus Freud will write that phantasying (*phantasieren*) is reduced to what occurs 'after the reality principle has been established' and that, before this, simply 'whatever was thought of (wished for) [that is to say, the represented] was simply presented in a hallucinatory manner': 'With the introduction of the reality principle one species of thought-activity was split off; it was kept free from reality-testing and remained subordinate to the pleasure principle alone. This activity is *phantasying*, which begins already in children's play, and later, continued as *day-dreaming*, abandons dependence on real objects.' Before this phase, when the state of psychic tranquillity is disturbed by the demands of internal needs, 'whatever was thought of (wished for) was simply presented in a hallucinatory manner, just as still happens today with our dream-thoughts every night'. 'Thought' signifies here, as so often in Freud, 'represented'.[5] This shift is possible only if one neglects to investigate further into the signification of this 'hallucinatory manner' and its dream equivalence. It may, however, be explained, if not justified, in terms of the apparent and paradoxical reference to the 'real' implied by the term 'hallucination': both in general and in the cases cited by Freud, the hallucination borrows its elements from the 'real', and the primary hallucination *par excellence* is, for Freud, the one that palliates the absence of the mother's breast, by positing its image as 'real'. This is the model – that is, the model of the product of the imagination which, under the pressure of drive (or even of need, as Freud says in the text quoted above) covers over a 'deficiency' with the reproduction of the representation (posed as equivalent to perception) of a scene of satisfaction which has an antecedent in 'real' perception – that has always been used subsequently to conceive of the question of the phantasy, however 'primal' it may have been termed, and of the imagination. One might, nonetheless, have wondered just what is and of what is made the 'state of psychical tranquility' to which Freud refers, and what is the representation that accompanies it. For if this is a *psychical* state, it also necessarily exists as a *representation*; its breaking apart by 'internal need' is the calling into question of this representation and, in being restored with the help of an activity of representation (whether hallucinatory or not), the aim of the psyche must betray the *status quo ante* to which it wishes to return. [. . .]

If, as Laplanche and Pontalis correctly remind us, 'far from seeking to base the phantasy on drives, Freud instead made the play of drive forces depend on prior phantasmatic structures',[6] then one must admit that originary phantasmatization, what I term the radical imagination, pre-exists and presides over every organization of drives, even the most primitive one, that it is the condition for the drive to attain psychical existence, that the drive borrows 'at the start' its 'delegation by representation', its *Vorstellungsrepräsentanz* from a backdrop of primal representation (*Ur-vorstellung*). But, if this is the case, then it is not sufficient to say that 'the emergence of the phantasy . . . (can be found) by tying it to the appearance of auto-eroticism'.[7] For what is generally meant by auto-eroticism, what Freud is referring to in the *Three Essays*,[8] anyway, is still a secondary formation, presupposing the child's capacity 'to form a total idea of the person to whom the organ that is giving him satisfaction belongs' and the 'loss of the object', tied to a manifest corporeal activity. There is, however, something quite different, something at an infinitesimal and infinite distance from the latter, which Freud later in the context of the theory of narcissism brought to light and which he never gave up. This is what could be called originary auto-eroticism or primary narcissism, the fact that the 'first object of the libido is the undifferentiated Id-Ego', that 'to begin with, the child does not distinguish between the breast and its own body; when the breast has to be separated from the body and shifted to the "outside". . . , it carries with it as an "object" a part of the original narcissistic libidinal cathexis'.[9] So it is not the case that one 'must assume a reflexive form (seeing oneself) in the drives that, according to Freud, would be primordial'.[10] Rather, the 'reflexive' form – an improper term, as we shall see – of the libido *is*, if we follow Freud, its primordial form. This originary narcissistic cathexis or investment is necessarily *representation* as well (otherwise it would not be psychical) and it can then be nothing other than a 'representation' (unimaginable and unrepresentable for us) of the *Self*. If, as Laplanche and Pontalis aptly remark, one must 'look' for this primordial degree precisely where the subject no longer situates itself in the various terms of 'phantasy', this is for the simple reason that the originary psychical subject *is this* primordial 'phantasy': at once the representation and the investment of a Self that is All. This is why the subject is not this or that thing *in* the phantasy – nor will it be this or that in the unconscious phantasies that will occur later, inasmuch as these fully obey the rules of the primary process.

This same difficulty in distinguishing among the various formations as they offer themselves, mixed together on the level of phenomena, the different strata of their constitution and that to which each stratum refers as a mode of being and a mode of organization, reappears when we consider social imaginary significations. Freud will thus speak of 'wish-compensating phantasies' in connection with cultural formations such as religion, art, and so on.[11] More generally speaking, the psychoanalytic conception of social phenomena will tend to assimilate them to compensations, coverings, defences, etc.; this is correct at a certain level or in relation to a certain order of these formations. But these compensations, coverings or defences have meaning and the capacity to exist only on the basis of the institution of society, as the already signifying condition of every developed signification, which could borrow neither its mode of being nor its content from any source outside itself, which is a 'response' to the requirement for signification posited by the social-historical, a response which must *also* provide for the possibility and the actuality of meaning for the social individuals that it institutes and produces.

Forgetting this difference imposes a confusion on the conceptions which – just as popular interpretations stretching back to times immemorial[12] do – attempt to construe imaginary formations as a 'response' to a situation (of the subject or of society) which would already clearly be defined outside of any imaginary component, on the basis of 'real' (or 'structural') givens. When they do not aim at interpreting the *content* of *secondary* and *derived* formations, these conceptions can exist only by covering over essential questions. First of all, even when it is a question of secondary formations, why is it that the prevalent mode of response by the subject (or by society) is situated in the imaginary, and how can an imaginary formation 'respond' to a real need or to a 'structural' necessity – namely, a logical one? Next, how can the 'triggering' situation, however it may be defined, come to *signify* something for the subject (or for society) in a way that will provoke or induce a 'response'? Finally, where does the subject (or society) get the elements of this response? These conceptions are the only ones to be represented in contemporary psychoanalytic literature – just as in sociological literature the homologous ones are almost the only ones to be found. The various versions all share a common postulate: the whole psychical elaboration, regardless of the elements it 'borrows' right and left and the laws governing it, finds its starting point in the necessity for the subject to fill in, cover over, stitch up a void, a lack, a gap which is considered consubstantial to the subject itself. Little matter the way in which this gap is defined: as the insurmountable refusal of the unconscious to give up Oedipal desire (this obviously refers to relatively late formations and posits the gap as conditioned by an 'outside', a division corresponding to the split into consciousness and the unconscious); as a difference between the satisfaction sought and the satisfaction obtained; the quest for an initial lost object which, by definition, can never reach its conclusion; the split implied in the very structure of the subject. In all these cases, the function imputed to the imaginary is that of replacing, patching together, covering over what is necessarily a gaping hole, a split, a lack in the subject's being.

How is it, then, that this lack comes into being as a *lack for a subject?* The subject, it is said, is this very thing – desire; and desire is sustained only by the lack of its object.

This apparently innocent tautology, however, that one can only desire in as much as one does not possess something,[13] becomes here the instrument of a paralogism. Desire is sustained only by the lack of a *desired* object. How can we speak of an object that is lacking if the psyche has not first posited this object as desirable? How can an object be desirable if it has not been invested (cathected), and how can it be invested if it has never been 'present' in any way? Desire is certainly always the desire of a missing object (or one that could be missing) but the missing object is constituted as such by the relation to desire. Lack as such, whether 'real' or otherwise, constitutes nothing at all, and every subject bathes in a non-denumerable infinity of 'lacks'. One should therefore posit at least the following connection: the subject emerges by positing itself as desiring a given object, which is to say, by positing at the same time a given object as desirable for it. The subject would then constitute itself as a desiring subject by constituting in the same stroke the object as a desirable object. But can we simply stop here and consider this moment as the 'first' one, as inaugurating the subject? Only if we renounce asking the essential question: under what conditions can an object be constituted by the psyche as an object of desire (aside from the trivial condition that it must be 'lacking')? In other words, under what conditions can a lack, a loss or a difference *exist* for the psyche – and be that very thing, lack, loss, difference? More than this: under what conditions can this lack, loss or difference be, in every instance, *other*, be 'constituted' in another way by this or that other subject?

It is futile to attempt to reduce these conditions to characteristics of the 'object' as such, or to characteristics of the subject as a living being, correlative and coordinated to the former. The 'missing object' – which is typically and generally speaking, the breast – is the same everywhere and always. It is also the same, for instance, for all mammals; but if certain 'desiring machines' are calves, all calves are not 'desiring machines'. The correlation, coordination and preadequation of the 'object' to the subject as a living being refers, of course, to something that the subject as a living being cannot be unaware of or neglect, and grants to certain objects are given an important privilege; this translates the subject's insertion in an organization that already exists, posited before him and independently of him. This organization, however, is that of the first natural stratum, and all this concerns the subject as a simple living being, that is as animal human being. This insertion of the subject as a living being and of certain objects in a chain that translates the biological-corporeal reality of the subject, which *is* this very reality says nothing yet, as such, about the psychical world. Obviously, what the psyche brings into being is not dictated by this biological-corporeal reality, for then it would always and everywhere be the same; nor is this done in 'absolute freedom' in relation to this reality, which can neither be ignored nor manipulated in any totally arbitrary way (even this affirmation has to be made with certain reservations: an anorexic infant *makes* himself die, his psyche is stronger than his biological regulatory system).

It is this original and irreducible relation of the psyche to the biological-corporeal reality of the subject that is intended by the Freudian idea of *anaclisis* (*Anlehnung*),[14] which contains much more than simply positing these two extreme and abstract limits: that psychical working out is neither dictated by biological organization nor absolutely free with respect to it. What the idea of *anaclisis*, of leaning on, states is: in the first place, there can be no oral instinct without mouth and breast, no anal instinct without an anus – *and* the existence of the mouth and the breast, or of the anus, still says nothing about the oral instinct in general, the anal instinct in general, about what becomes of them in a given culture, even less, what becomes of them in a given individual. But *more importantly*, in the second place: the existence of the mouth and breast, or of the anus, is not a mere 'external condition', without which there would be no oral or anal instinct, or more generally, no psychical functioning as we know it – in the same way as it is clear that without oxygen in the atmosphere or the circulatory system there would be no psyche, no phantasies or sublimation. Oxygen contributes nothing to phantasies, it 'allows them to exist'. The mouth-breast, or the anus, have to be 'taken into account' by the psyche and, what is more, they support and induce. Support and induce what, exactly? Here again, the radical powerlessness of traditional thought, of inherited logic-ontology, is evident as soon as we move outside of the areas in relation to which this thought has been developed. Mouth and breast, like the anus and faeces, like the penis or vagina are neither causes nor means, and certainly not 'signifiers' in some univocal relation to a signified which would always and everywhere be the same, *nor even* the *same* for the *same* subject. We must learn to think otherwise; we have to understand that the idea of anaclisis, of leaning on, is just as original and irreducible as the idea of cause or the idea of symbolizing. The privileged somatic data will always be taken up again by the psyche, psychical working out will have to 'take them into account', they will leave their mark on it – but which mark and in what manner cannot be reflected in the identitary frame of reference of determinacy. For the creativity of the psyche enters in here as radical imagination, as the emergence of representation (phantasying) and the alteration of representation, thereby rendering absurd the idea that the breast or the anus are the 'cause' of a phantasy as well as the idea that the oral or the anal can be assigned once and for all to a universal and complete determination-determinacy.

Notes

1   G. Groddeck, *The Book of the It*, trans. V. M. E. Collins (London: Vision Press, 1950; New York: Vintage Books, 1961).

2   '. . . the nucleus of our being, but it is not so much that Freud commands us to seek it as so many others before him have with the empty adage "know thyself" – as to reconsider the ways that lead to it, and which he shows us.' Jacques Lacan, *Écrits: a selection* (London: Tavistock Publications, 1977), pp. 173–4.

3   See Jacques Lacan (1961), 'Remarques sur le rapport de D. Lagache'. In *Psychoanalyse*, 6, p. 116.

4   'An ethic announces itself . . . through the advent not of fear but of desire.' Jacques Lacan, *Écrits* (Paris: Le Seuil, 1966), p. 684.

5   Sigmund Freud (1911), 'Formulations on the Two Principles of Mental Functioning'. In *Gesammelte Werke*, vol. VIII, p. 234; *The Standard Edition of the Complete Psychological Works of Sigmund Freud*, vol. XII, p. 219. The derivation of 'thought' on the basis of representation is clearly formulated, ibid., *G.W.*, vol. VIII, p. 23; *S.E.*, vol. XII, p. 221.

6   This is already the case in writings as early as 'Draft N'. *S.E.*, vol. I, pp. 254–7; cf. also *G.W.*, vol. X, p. 294; *S.E.*, vol. XIV, p. 196 or *G.W.*, vol. XII, p. 156; *S.E.*, vol. XVII, p. 120.

7   Jean Laplanche and J.-B. Pontalis (1964), 'Fantasme originaire, fantasmes des origines, origine du fantasme'. In *Les Temps Moderne*, no. 215, April, p. 1865.

8   *G.W.*, vol. V, p. 123; *S.E.*, vol. VII, p. 222.

9   *G.W.*, vol. XVII, p. 115.

10 J. Laplanche and J.-B. Pontalis, 'Fantasme originaire . . .' p. 1867.

11 See, for example: 'Das Interesse an der Psychoanalyse'. In *G.W.*, vol. VIII, p. 416; *S.E.*, vol. XIII, p. 186: '. . . the neuroses themselves have turned out to be attempts to find *individual* solutions for the problems of compensating for unsatisfied wishes, while institutions seek to provide *social* solutions for these same problems'

(italicized in the text). The expression *Wunschkompensatorische Phantasien,* desire or wish compensating phantasies, returns often in Freud's writings.

12 'A starving man dreams of bread,' says a Greek proverb.
13 Plato in the *Symposium* (200 c–e) stated more correctly that one can desire something one does not lack in the sense that one wishes to continue possessing it.
14 This term has been translated here, as often as possible, by *leaning on* [Trans.].

Part II
Social Structure and Institutional Analysis

6

The Means of Correct Training

Michel Foucault

At the beginning of the seventeenth century, Walhausen spoke of 'strict discipline' as an art of correct training. The chief function of the disciplinary power is to 'train', rather than to select and to levy; or, no doubt, to train in order to levy and select all the more. It does not link forces together in order to reduce them; it seeks to bind them together in such a way as to multiply and use them. Instead of bending all its subjects into a single uniform mass, it separates, analyses, differentiates, carries its procedures of decomposition to the point of necessary and sufficient single units. It 'trains' the moving, confused, useless multitudes of bodies and forces into a multiplicity of individual elements – small, separate cells, organic autonomies, genetic identities and continuities, combinatory segments. Discipline 'makes' individuals; it is the specific technique of a power that regards individuals both as objects and as instruments of its exercise. It is not a triumphant power, which because of its own excess can pride itself on its omnipotence; it is a modest, suspicious power, which functions as a calculated, but permanent economy. These are humble modalities, minor procedures, as compared with the majestic rituals of sovereignty or the great apparatuses of the state. And it is precisely they that were gradually to invade the major forms, altering their mechanisms and imposing their procedures. The legal apparatus was not to escape this scarcely secret invasion. The success of disciplinary power derives no doubt from the use of simple instruments; hierarchical observation, normalizing judgement and their combination in a procedure that is specific to it, the examination.

Hierarchical Observation

The exercise of discipline presupposes a mechanism that coerces by means of observation; an apparatus in which the techniques that make it possible to see induce effects of power, and in which, conversely, the means of coercion make those on whom they are applied clearly visible. Slowly, in the course of the classical age, we see the construction of those 'observatories' of human multiplicity for which the history of the sciences has so little good to say. Side by side with the major technology of the telescope, the lens and the light beam, which were an integral part of the new physics and cosmology, there were the minor techniques of multiple and intersecting observations, of eyes that must see without being seen; using techniques of subjection and methods of exploitation, an obscure art of light and the visible was secretly preparing a new knowledge of man.

These 'observatories' had an almost ideal model: the military camp – the short-lived, artificial city, built and reshaped almost at will; the seat of a power that must be all the stronger, but also all the more discreet, all the more effective and on the alert in that it is exercised over armed men. In the perfect camp, all power would be exercised solely through exact observation; each gaze would form a part of the overall functioning of power. The old, traditional square plan was considerably refined in innumerable new projects. The geometry of the paths, the number and distribution of the tents, the orientation of their entrances, the disposition of files and ranks were exactly defined; the network of gazes that supervised one another was laid down: [. . .] The camp is the diagram of a power that acts by means of general visibility. For a long time this model of the camp or at least its underlying principle was found in urban development, in the construction of working-class housing estates, hospitals, asylums, prisons, schools: the spatial 'nesting' of hierarchized surveillance. The principle was one of 'embedding' ('encastrement'). The camp was to the rather shameful art of surveillance what the dark room was to the great science of optics.

A whole problematic then develops: that of an architecture that is no longer built simply to be seen (as with the ostentation of palaces), or to observe the external space (cf. the geometry of fortresses), but to permit an internal, articulated and detailed control – to render visible those who are inside it; in more general terms, an architecture that would operate to transform individuals: to act on those it shelters, to provide a hold on their conduct, to carry the effects of power right to them, to make it possible to know them, to alter them. Stones can make people docile and knowable. The old simple schema of confinement and enclosure – thick walls, a heavy gate that prevents entering or leaving – began to be replaced by the calculation of openings, of filled and empty spaces, passages and transparencies. [. . .]

The perfect disciplinary apparatus would make it possible for a single gaze to see everything constantly. A central point would be both the source of light illuminating everything, and a locus of convergence for everything that must be known: a perfect eye that nothing would escape and a centre towards which all gazes would be turned. [. . .]

But, the disciplinary gaze did, in fact, need relays. The pyramid was able to fulfil, more efficiently than the circle, two requirements: to be complete enough to form an uninterrupted network – consequently the possibility of multiplying its levels, and of distributing them over the entire surface to be supervised – and yet to be discreet enough not to weigh down with an inert mass on the activity to be disciplined, and not to act as a brake or an obstacle to it; to be integrated into the disciplinary mechanism as a function that increases its possible effects. It had to be broken down into smaller elements, but in order to increase its productive function: specify the surveillance and make it functional.

This was the problem of the great workshops and factories, in which a new type of surveillance was organized. It was different from the one practised in the regimes of the manufactories, which had been carried out from the outside by inspectors, entrusted with the task of applying the regulations; what was now needed was an intense, continuous supervision; it ran right through the labour process; it did not bear – or not only – on production (the nature and quantity of raw materials, the type of instruments used, the dimensions and quality of the products); it also took into account the activity of the men, their skill, the way they set about their tasks, their promptness, their zeal, their behaviour. But it was also different from the domestic supervision of the master present beside his workers and apprentices; for it was carried out by clerks, supervisors and foremen. As the machinery of production became larger and more complex, as the number of workers and the division of labour increased, supervision became ever more necessary and more difficult. It became a special function, which had nevertheless to form an integral part of the production process, to run parallel to it throughout its entire length. A specialized personnel became indispensable, constantly present and distinct from the workers. [. . .]

Hierarchized, continuous and functional surveillance may not be one of the great technical 'inventions' of the eighteenth century, but its insidious extension owed its importance to the mechanisms of power that it brought with it. By means of such surveillance, disciplinary power became an 'integrated' system, linked from the inside to the economy and to the aims of the mechanism in which it was practised. It was also organized as a multiple, automatic and anonymous power; for although surveillance rests on individuals, its functioning is that of a network of relations from top to bottom, but also to a certain extent from bottom to top and laterally; this network 'holds' the whole together and traverses it in its entirety with effects of power that derive from one another: supervisors, perpetually supervised. The power in the hierarchized surveillance of the disciplines is not possessed as a thing, or transferred as a property; it functions like a piece of machinery. And, although it is true that its pyramidal organization gives it a 'head', it is the apparatus as a whole that produces 'power' and distributes individuals in this permanent and continuous field. This enables the disciplinary power to be both absolutely indiscreet, since it is everywhere and always alert, since by its very principle it leaves no zone of shade and constantly supervises the very individuals who are entrusted with the task of supervising; and absolutely 'discreet', for it functions permanently and largely in silence. Discipline makes possible the operation of a relational power that sustains itself by its own mechanism and which, for the spectacle of public events, substitutes the uninterrupted play of calculated gazes. Thanks to the techniques of surveillance, the 'physics' of power, the hold over the body, operate according to the laws of optics and mechanics, according to a whole play of spaces, lines, screens, beams, degrees and without recourse, in principle at least, to excess, force or violence. It is a power that seems all the less 'corporal' in that it is more subtly 'physical'.

Normalizing Judgement

1   At the heart of all disciplinary systems functions a small penal mechanism. It enjoys a kind of judicial privilege with its own laws, its specific offences, its particular forms of judgement. The disciplines established an 'infra-penality'; they partitioned an area that the laws had left empty; they defined and repressed a mass of behaviour that the relative indifference of the great systems of punishment had allowed to escape. [. . .] The workshop, the school, the army were subject to a whole micro-penality of time (latenesses, absences, interruptions of tasks), of activity (inattention, negligence, lack of zeal), of behaviour (impoliteness, disobedience), of speech (idle chatter, insolence), of the body ('incorrect' attitudes, irregular gestures, lack of cleanliness), of sexuality (impurity, indecency). At the same time, by way of punishment, a whole series of subtle procedures was used, from light physical punishment to minor deprivations and petty humiliations. It was a question both of making the slightest departures from correct behaviour subject to punishment, and of giving a punitive function to the apparently indifferent elements of the disciplinary apparatus: so that, if necessary, everything might serve to punish the slightest thing; each subject find himself caught in a punishable, punishing universality. [. . .]
2   But discipline brought with it a specific way of punishing that was not only a small-scale model of the court. What is specific to the disciplinary penality is non-observance, that which does not measure up to the rule, that which departs from it. The whole indefinite domain of the non-conforming is punishable: the soldier commits an 'offence' whenever he does not reach the level required; a pupil's 'offence' is not only a minor infraction, but also an inability to carry out his tasks. [. . .]
   The order that the disciplinary punishments must enforce is of a mixed nature: it is an 'artificial' order, explicitly laid down by a law, a programme, a set of regulations. But it is also an order defined by natural and observable processes: the duration of an apprenticeship, the time taken to perform an exercise, the level of aptitude refer to a regularity that is also a rule. The children of the Christian Schools must never be placed in a 'lesson' of which they are not yet capable, for this would expose them to the danger of being unable to learn anything; yet the duration of each stage is fixed by regulation and a pupil who at the end of three examinations has been unable to pass into the higher

order must be placed, well in evidence, on the bench of the 'ignorant'. In a disciplinary regime punishment involves a double juridico-natural reference.

3   Disciplinary punishment has the function of reducing gaps. It must therefore be essentially *corrective*. In addition to punishments borrowed directly from the judicial model (fines, flogging, solitary confinement), the disciplinary systems favour punishments that are exercise – intensified, multiplied forms of training, several times repeated: the regulations of 1766 for the infantry laid down that lance-corporals 'who show some negligence or lack of willingness will be reduced to the rank of private', and they will be able to rise to their former rank only after new exercises and a new examination. [. . .] Disciplinary punishment is, in the main, isomorphic with obligation itself; it is not so much the vengeance of an outraged law as its repetition, its reduplicated insistence. So much so that the corrective effect expected of it involves only incidentally expiation and repentance; it is obtained directly through the mechanics of a training. To punish is to exercise.

4   In discipline, punishment is only one element of a double system: gratification-punishment. And it is this system that operates in the process of training and correction [. . .] [which] makes possible a number of operations characteristic of disciplinary penality. First, the definition of behaviour and performance on the basis of the two opposed values of good and evil; instead of the simple division of the prohibition, as practised in penal justice, we have a distribution between a positive pole and a negative pole; all behaviour falls in the field between good and bad marks, good and bad points. [. . .] What we have here is a transposition of the system of indulgences. And by the play of this quantification, this circulation of awards and debits, thanks to the continuous calculation of plus and minus points, the disciplinary apparatuses hierarchized the 'good' and the 'bad' subjects in relation to one another. Through this micro-economy of a perpetual penality operates a differentiation that is not one of acts, but of individuals themselves, of their nature, their potentialities, their level or their value. By assessing acts with precision, discipline judges individuals 'in truth'; the penality that it implements is integrated into the cycle of knowledge of individuals.

5   The distribution according to ranks or grade has a double role: it marks the gaps, hierarchizes qualities, skills and aptitudes; but it also punishes and rewards. It is the penal functioning of setting in order and the ordinal character of judging. Discipline rewards simply by the play of awards, thus making it possible to attain higher ranks and places; it punishes by reversing this process. Rank in itself serves as a reward or punishment. [. . .]

In short, the art of punishing, in the regime of disciplinary power, is aimed neither at expiation, nor even precisely at repression. It brings five quite distinct operations into play: it refers individual actions to a whole that is at once a field of comparison, a space of differentiation and the principle of a rule to be followed. It differentiates individuals from one another, in terms of the following overall rule: that the rule be made to function as a minimal threshold, as an average to be respected or as an optimum towards which one must move. It measures in quantitative terms and hierarchizes in terms of value the abilities, the level, the 'nature' of individuals. It introduces, through this 'value-giving' measure, the constraint of a conformity that must be achieved. Lastly, it traces the limit that will define difference in relation to all other differences the external frontier of the abnormal. The perpetual penality that traverses all points and supervises every instant in the disciplinary institutions compares, differentiates, hierarchizes, homogenizes, excludes. In short, it *normalizes*.

It is opposed, therefore, term by term, to a judicial penalty whose essential function is to refer, not to a set of observable phenomena, but to a corpus of laws and texts that must be remembered; that operates not by differentiating individuals, but by specifying acts according to a number of general categories; not by hierarchizing, but quite simply by bringing into play the binary opposition of the permitted and the forbidden; not by homogenizing, but by operating the division, acquired once and for all, of condemnation. The disciplinary mechanisms secreted a 'penality of the norm', which is irreducible in its principles and functioning to the traditional penality of the law. The minor court that seems to sit permanently in the buildings of discipline, and which sometimes assumes the theatrical form of the great legal apparatus, must not mislead us: it does not bring, except for a few formal remnants, the mechanisms of criminal justice to the web of everyday existence', or at least that is not its essential role; the disciplines created – drawing on a whole series of very ancient procedures – a new functioning of punishment, and it was this that gradually invested the great external apparatus that it seemed to reproduce in either a modest or an ironic way. The juridico-anthropological functioning revealed in the whole history of modern penality did not originate in the superimposition of the human sciences on criminal justice and in the requirements proper to this new rationality or to the humanism that it appeared to bring with it; it originated in the disciplinary technique that operated these new mechanisms of normalizing judgement.

The power of the Norm appears through the disciplines. Is this the new law of modern society? Let us say rather that, since the eighteenth century, it has joined other powers – the Law, the Word (*Parole*) and the Text, Tradition – imposing new delimitations upon them. The Normal is established as a principle of coercion in teaching with the introduction of a standardized education and the establishment of the *écoles normales* (teachers' training colleges); it is established in the effort to organize a national medical profession and a hospital system capable of operating general norms of health; it is established in the standardization of industrial processes and products. Like surveillance and with it, normalization becomes one of the great instruments of power at the end of the classical age. For the marks that once indicated status, privilege and affiliation were increasingly replaced – or at least supplemented – by a whole range of degrees of normality indicating membership of a homogeneous social body but also playing a part in classification, hierarchization and the distribution of rank. In a sense, the power of normalization imposes homogeneity; but it individualizes by making it possible to measure gaps, to determine levels, to fix specialities and to render the differences useful by fitting them one to another. It is easy to understand how the power of the norm functions within a system of formal equality, since within a homogeneity that is the rule the norm introduces, as a useful imperative and as a result of measurement, all the shading of individual differences.

The Examination

The examination combines the techniques of an observing hierarchy and those of a normalizing judgement. It is a normalizing gaze, a surveillance that makes it possible to qualify, to classify and to punish. It establishes over individuals a visibility through which one differentiates them and judges them. That is why, in all the mechanisms of discipline, the examination is highly ritualized. In it are combined the ceremony of power and the form of the experiment, the deployment of force and the establishment of truth. At the heart of the procedures of discipline, it manifests the subjection of those who are perceived as objects and the objectification of those who are subjected. The superimposition of the power relations and knowledge relations assumes in the examination all its visible brilliance. It is yet another innovation of the classical age that the historians of science have left unexplored. People write the history of experiments on those born blind, on wolf-children or those under hypnosis. But who will write the more general, more fluid, but also more determinant history of the 'examination' – its rituals, its methods, its characters and their roles, its play of questions and answers, its systems of marking and classification? For in this slender technique are to be found a whole domain of knowledge, a whole type of power. One often speaks of the ideology that the human 'sciences' bring with them, in either discreet or prolix manner. But does their very technology, this tiny operational schema that has become so widespread (from psychiatry to pedagogy, from the diagnosis of diseases to the hiring of labour), this familiar method of the examination, implement, within a single mechanism, power relations that make it possible to extract and constitute knowledge? It is not simply at the level of consciousness, of representations and in what one thinks one knows, but at the level of what makes possible the knowledge that is transformed into political investment. [. . .]

The examination introduced a whole mechanism that linked to a certain type of the formation of knowledge a certain form of the exercise of power.

1   *The examination transformed the economy of visibility into the exercise of power.* Traditionally, power was what was seen, what was shown and what was manifested and, paradoxically, found the principle of its force in the movement by which it deployed that force. Those on whom it was exercised could remain in the shade; they received light only from that portion of power that was

conceded to them, or from the reflection of it that for a moment they carried. Disciplinary power, on the other hand, is exercised through its invisibility; at the same time it imposes on those whom it subjects to a principle of compulsory visibility. In discipline, it is the subjects who have to be seen. Their visibility assures the hold of the power that is exercised over them. It is the fact of being constantly seen, of being able always to be seen, that maintains the disciplined individual in his subjection. And the examination is the technique by which power, instead of emitting the signs of its potency, instead of imposing its mark on its subjects, holds them in a mechanism of objectification. In this space of domination, disciplinary power manifests its potency, essentially by arranging objects. The examination is, as it were, the ceremony of this objectification.

Hitherto the role of the political ceremony had been to give rise to the excessive, yet regulated manifestation of power; it was a spectacular expression of potency, an 'expenditure', exaggerated and coded, in which power renewed its vigour. It was always more or less related to the triumph. The solemn appearance of the sovereign brought with it something of the consecration, the coronation, the return from victory; even the funeral ceremony took place with all the spectacle of power deployed. Discipline, however, had its own type of ceremony. It was not the triumph, but the review, the 'parade', an ostentatious form of the examination. In it the 'subjects' were presented as 'objects' to the observation of a power that was manifested only by its gaze. They did not receive directly the image of the sovereign power; they only felt its effects – in replica, as it were – on their bodies, which had become precisely legible and docile. [. . .]

2   *The examination also introduces individuality into the field of documentation*. The examination leaves behind it a whole meticulous archive constituted in terms of bodies and days. The examination that places individuals in a field of surveillance also situates them in a network of writing; it engages them in a whole mass of documents that capture and fix them. The procedures of examination were accompanied at the same time by a system of intense registration and of documentary accumulation. A 'power of writing' was constituted as an essential part in the mechanisms of discipline. On many points, it was modelled on the traditional methods of administrative documentation, though with particular techniques and important innovations. Some concerned methods of identification, signalling or description. This was the problem in the army, where it was necessary to track down deserters, avoid repeating enrolments, correct fictitious 'information' presented by officers, know the services and value of each individual, establish with certainty the balance-sheet of those who had disappeared or died. It was the problem of the hospitals, where it was necessary to recognise patients, expel shammers, follow the evolution of diseases, study the effectiveness of treatments, map similar cases and the beginnings of epidemics. It was the problem of the teaching establishments, where one had to define the aptitude of each individual, situate his level and his abilities, indicate the possible use that might be made of them. [. . .]

Hence the formation of a whole series of codes of disciplinary individuality that made it possible to transcribe, by means of homogenization the individual features established by the examination: the physical code of signalling, the medical code of symptoms, the educational or military code of conduct or performance. These codes were still very crude, both in quality and quantity, but they marked a first stage in the 'formalization' of the individual within power relations.

The other innovations of disciplinary writing concerned the correlation of these elements, the accumulation of documents, their seriation, the organization of comparative fields making it possible to classify, to form categories, to determine averages, to fix norms. The hospitals of the eighteenth century, in particular, were great laboratories for scriptuary and documentary methods. The keeping of registers, their specification, the modes of transcription from one to the other, their circulation during visits, their comparison during regular meetings of doctors and administrators, the transmission of their data to centralizing bodies (either at the hospital or at the central office of the poor-houses), the accountancy of diseases, cures, deaths, at the level of a hospital, a town and even of the nation as a whole formed an integral part of the process by which hospitals were subjected to the disciplinary regime. Among the fundamental conditions of a good medical 'discipline', in both senses of the word, one must include the procedures of writing that made it possible to integrate individual data into cumulative systems in such a way that they were not lost; so to arrange things that an individual could be located in the general register and that, conversely, each datum of the individual examination might affect overall calculations.

Thanks to the whole apparatus of writing that accompanied it, the examination opened up two correlative possibilities: firstly, the constitution of the individual as a describable, analysable object, not in order to reduce him to 'specific' features, as did the naturalists in relation to living beings, but in order to maintain him in his individual features, in his particular evolution, in his own aptitudes or abilities, under the gaze of a permanent corpus of knowledge; and, secondly, the constitution of a comparative system that made possible the measurement of overall phenomena, the description of groups, the characterization of collective facts, the calculation of the gaps between individuals, their distribution in a given 'population'. [. . .]

3   *The examination, surrounded by all its documentary techniques, makes each individual a 'case'*: a case which at one and the same time constitutes an object for a branch of knowledge and a hold for a branch of power. The case is no longer, as in casuistry or jurisprudence, a set of circumstances defining an act and capable of modifying the application of a rule; it is the individual as he may be described, judged, measured, compared with others, in his very individuality; and it is also the individual who has to be trained or corrected, classified, normalized, excluded, etc.

For a long time ordinary individuality – the everyday individuality of everybody – remained below the threshold of description. To be looked at, observed, described in detail, followed from day to day by an uninterrupted writing was a privilege. The chronicle of a man, the account of his life, his historiography, written as he lived out his life formed part of the rituals of his power. The disciplinary methods reversed this relation, lowered the threshold of describable individuality and made of this description a means of control and a method of domination. It is no longer a monument for future memory, but a document for possible use. And this new describability is all the more marked in that the disciplinary framework is a strict one: the child, the patient, the madman, the prisoner, were to become, with increasing ease from the eighteenth century, and according to a curve which is that of the mechanisms of discipline, the object of individual descriptions and biographical accounts. This turning of real lives into writing is no longer a procedure of heroization; it functions as a procedure of objectification and subjection. The carefully collated life of mental patients or delinquents belongs, as did the chronicle of kings or the adventures of the great popular bandits, to a certain political function of writing; but in a quite different technique of power.

The examination as the fixing, at once ritual and 'scientific', of individual differences, as the pinning down of each individual in his own particularity (in contrast with the ceremony in which status, birth, privilege, function are manifested with all the spectacle of their marks) clearly indicates the appearance of a new modality of power in which each individual receives as his status his own individuality, and in which he is linked by his status to the features, the measurements, the gaps, the 'marks' that characterize him and make him a 'case'.

   Finally, the examination is at the centre of the procedures that constitute the individual as effect and object of power, as effect and object of knowledge. It is the examination which, by combining hierarchical surveillance and normalizing judgement, assures the great disciplinary functions of distribution and classification, maximum extraction of forces and time, continuous genetic accumulation, optimum combination of aptitudes and, thereby, the fabrication of cellular, organic, genetic and combinatory individuality. With it are ritualized those disciplines that may be characterized in a word by saying that they are a modality of power for which individual difference is relevant.

7

Structures, *Habitus*, Practices

Pierre Bourdieu

Objectivism constitutes the social world as a spectacle offered to an observer who takes up a 'point of view' on the action and who, putting into the object the principles of his relation to the object, proceeds as if it were intended solely for knowledge and as if all the interactions within it were purely symbolic exchanges. This viewpoint is the one taken from high positions in the social structure, from which the social world is seen as a representation (as the word is used in idealist philosophy, but also as in painting) or a performance (in the theatrical or musical sense), and practices are seen as no more than the acting-out of roles, the playing of scores or the implementation of plans. The theory of practice as practice insists, contrary to positivist materialism, that the objects of knowledge are constructed, not passively recorded, and, contrary to intellectualist idealism, that the principle of this construction is the system of structured, structuring dispositions, the *habitus*, which is constituted in practice and is always oriented towards practical functions. It is possible to step down from the sovereign viewpoint from which objectivist idealism orders the world, as Marx demands in the *Theses on Feuerbach*, but without having to abandon to it the 'active aspect' of apprehension of the world by reducing knowledge to a mere recording. To do this, one has to situate oneself *within* 'real activity as such', that is, in the practical relation to the world, the pre-occupied, active presence in the world through which the world imposes its presence, with its urgencies, its things to be done and said, things made to be said, which directly govern words and deeds without ever unfolding as a spectacle. One has to escape from the realism of the structure, to which objectivism, a necessary stage in breaking with primary experience and constructing the objective relationships, necessarily leads when it hypostatizes these relations by treating them as realities already constituted outside of the history of the group – without falling back into subjectivism, which is quite incapable of giving an account of the necessity of the social world. To do this, one has to return to practice, the site of the dialectic of the *opus operatum* and the *modus operandi;* of the objectified products and the incorporated products of historical practice; of structures and *habitus*. [. . .]

The conditionings associated with a particular class of conditions of existence produce *habitus*, systems of durable, transposable dispositions, structured structures predisposed to function as structuring structures, that is, as principles which generate and organize practices and representations that can be objectively adapted to their outcomes without presupposing a conscious aiming at ends or an express mastery of the operations necessary in order to attain them. Objectively 'regulated' and 'regular' without being in any way the product of obedience to rules, they can be collectively orchestrated without being the product of the organizing action of a conductor.

It is, of course, never ruled out that the responses of the *habitus* may be accompanied by a strategic calculation tending to perform in a conscious mode the operation that the *habitus* performs quite differently, namely an estimation of chances presupposing transformation of the past effect into an expected objective. But these responses are first defined, without any calculation, in relation to objective potentialities, immediately inscribed in the present, things to do or not to do, things to say or not to say, in relation to a probable, 'upcoming' future (*un à venir*), which – in contrast to the future seen as 'absolute possibility' (*absolute Möglichkeit*) in Hegel's (or Sartre's) sense, projected by the pure project of a 'negative freedom' – puts itself forward with an urgency and a claim to existence that excludes all deliberation. Stimuli do not exist for practice in their objective truth, as conditional, conventional triggers, acting only on condition that they encounter agents conditioned to recognize them. The practical world that is constituted in the relationship with the *habitus*, acting as a system of cognitive and motivating structures, is a world of already realized ends – procedures to follow, paths to take – and of objects endowed with a 'permanent teleological character', in Husserl's phrase, for example, tools or institutions. This is because the regularities inherent in an arbitrary condition ('arbitrary' in Saussure's and Mauss' sense) tend to appear as necessary, even natural, since they are the basis of the schemes of perception and appreciation through which they are apprehended.

If a very close correlation is regularly observed between the scientifically constructed objective probabilities (for example, the chances of access to a particular good) and agents' subjective aspirations ('motivations' and 'needs'), this is not because agents consciously adjust their aspirations to an exact evaluation of their chances of success, like a gambler organizing his stakes on the basis of perfect information about his chances of winning. In reality, the dispositions durably inculcated by the possibilities and impossibilities, freedoms and necessities, opportunities and prohibitions inscribed in the objective conditions (which science apprehends through statistical regularities such as the probabilities objectively attached to a group or class) generate dispositions objectively compatible with these conditions and in a sense pre-adapted to their demands. The most improbable practices are therefore excluded, as unthinkable, by a kind of immediate submission to order that inclines agents to make a virtue of necessity, that is, to refuse what is anyway denied and to will the inevitable. The very conditions of production of the *habitus*, a virtue made of necessity, mean that the anticipations it generates tend to ignore the restriction to which the validity of calculation of probabilities is subordinated, namely that the experimental conditions should not have been modified. Unlike scientific estimations, which are corrected after each experiment according to rigorous rules of calculation, the anticipations of the *habitus*, practical hypotheses based on past experience, give disproportionate weight to early experiences. Through the economic and social necessity that they bring to bear on the relatively autonomous world of the domestic economy and family relations, or more precisely, through the specifically familial manifestations of this external necessity (forms of the division of labour between the sexes, household objects, modes of consumption, parent–child relations, etc.), the structures characterizing a determinate class of conditions of existence produce the structures of the *habitus*, which in their turn are the basis of the perception and appreciation of all subsequent experiences.

The *habitus*, a product of history, produces individual and collective practices – more history – in accordance with the schemes generated by history. It ensures the active presence of past experiences which, deposited in each organism in the form of schemes of perception, thought and action, tend to guarantee the 'correctness' of practices and their constancy over time, more reliably than all formal rules and explicit norms. This system of dispositions – a present past that tends to perpetuate itself into the future by reactivation in similarly structured practices, an internal law through which the law of external necessities, irreducible to immediate constraints, is constantly exerted – is the principle of the continuity and regularity which objectivism sees in social practices without being able to account for it; and also of the regulated transformations that cannot be explained either by the extrinsic, instantaneous determinisms of mechanistic sociologism or by the purely internal but equally instantaneous determination of spontaneist subjectivism. Overriding the spurious opposition between the forces inscribed in an earlier state of the system outside the body, and the internal forces arising instantaneously as motivations springing from free will, the internal dispositions – the internalization of externality – enable the external forces to exert themselves, but in accordance with the specific logic of the organisms in which they are incorporated, i.e. in a durable, systematic and non-mechanical way. As an acquired system of generative schemes, the *habitus* makes possible the free production of all the thoughts, perceptions and actions inherent in the particular conditions of its production – and only those. Through the *habitus*, the structure of which it is the product governs practice, not along the paths of a mechanical determinism, but within the constraints and limits initially set on its inventions. This infinite yet strictly limited generative capacity is difficult to understand only so long as one remains locked in the usual antinomies – which the concept of the *habitus* aims to transcend – of determinism and freedom, conditioning and creativity, consciousness and the unconscious, or the individual and society. Because the *habitus* is an infinite capacity for generating products – thoughts, perceptions, expressions and actions – whose limits are set by the historically and socially situated conditions of its production, the conditioned and conditional freedom it provides is as remote from creation of unpredictable novelty as it is from simple mechanical reproduction of the original conditioning.

Nothing is more misleading than the illusion created by hindsight in which all the traces of a life, such as the works of an artist or the events at a biography, appear as the realization of an essence that seems to preexist them. Just as a mature artistic style is not contained, like a seed, in an original inspiration but is continuously defined and redefined in the dialectic between the objectifying intention and the already objectified intention, so too the unity of meaning which, after the event, may seem to have preceded the acts and works announcing the final significance, retrospectively transforming the various stages of the temporal series into mere preparatory sketches, is constituted through the confrontation between questions that only exist in and for a mind armed with a particular type of schemes and the solutions obtained through application of these same schemes. The genesis of a system of works or practices generated by the same *habitus* (or homologous *habitus*, such as those that underlie the unity of the lifestyle of a group or a class) cannot be described either as the autonomous development of a unique and always self-identical essence, or as a continuous creation of novelty, because it arises from the necessary yet unpredictable confrontation between the *habitus* and an event that can exercise a pertinent incitement on the *habitus* only if the latter snatches it from the contingency of the accidental and constitutes it as a problem by applying to it the very principles of its solution; and also because the *habitus*, like every 'art of inventing', is what makes it possible to produce an infinite number of practices that are relatively unpredictable (like the corresponding situations) but also limited in their diversity. In short, being the product of a particular class of objective regularities, the *habitus* tends to generate all the 'reasonable', 'common-sense' behaviours (and only these) which are possible within the limits of these regularities, and which are likely to be positively sanctioned because they are objectively adjusted to the logic characteristic of a particular field, whose objective future they anticipate. At the same time, 'without violence, art or argument', it tends to exclude all 'extravagances' ('not for the likes of us'), that is, all the behaviours that would be negatively sanctioned because they are incompatible with the objective conditions.

Because they tend to reproduce the regularities immanent in the conditions in which their generative principle was produced while adjusting to the demands inscribed as objective potentialities in the situation as defined by the cognitive and motivating structures that constitute the *habitus*, practices cannot be deduced either from the present conditions which may seem to have provoked them or from the past conditions which have produced the *habitus*, the durable principle of their production. They can therefore only be accounted for by relating the social conditions in which the *habitus* that generated them was constituted, to the social conditions in which it is implemented, that is, through the scientific work of performing the interrelationship of these two states of the social world that the *habitus* performs, while concealing it, in and through practice. The 'unconscious', which enables one to dispense with this interrelating, is never anything other than the forgetting of history which history itself produces by realizing the objective structures that it generates in the quasi-natures of *habitus*. [. . .]

The *habitus* – embodied history, internalized as a second nature and so forgotten as history – is the active presence of the whole past of which it is the product. As such, it is what gives practices their relative autonomy with respect to external determinations of the immediate present. This autonomy is that of the past, enacted and acting, which, functioning as accumulated capital, produces history on the basis of history and so ensures the permanence in change that makes the individual agent a world within the world. The *habitus* is a spontaneity without consciousness or will, opposed as much to the mechanical necessity of things without history in mechanistic theories as it is to the reflexive freedom of subjects 'without inertia' in rationalist theories.

Thus the dualistic vision that recognizes only the self-transparent act of consciousness or the externally determined thing has to give way to the real logic of action, which brings together two objectifications of history, objectification in bodies and objectification in institutions or, which amounts to the same thing, two states of capital, objectified and incorporated, through which a distance is set up from necessity and its urgencies. This logic is seen in paradigmatic form in the dialectic of expressive dispositions and instituted means of expression (morphological, syntactic and lexical instruments, literary genres, etc.) which is observed in the intentionless invention of regulated improvisation. Endlessly overtaken by his own words, with which he maintains a relation of 'carry and be carried', as Nicolai Hartmann put it, the virtuoso finds in his discourse the triggers for his discourse, which goes along like a train laying its own rails. In other words, being produced by a *modus operandi* which is not consciously mastered, the discourse contains an 'objective intention', as the Scholastics put it, which outruns the conscious intentions of its apparent author and constantly offers new pertinent stimuli to the *modus operandi* of which it is the product and which functions as a kind of 'spiritual automaton'. If witticisms strike as much by their unpredictability as by their retrospective necessity, the reason is that the *trouvaille* that brings to light long buried resources presupposes a *habitus* that so perfectly possesses the objectively available means of expression that it is possessed by them, so much so that it asserts its freedom from them by realizing the rarest of the possibilities that they necessarily imply. The dialectic of the meaning of the language and the 'sayings of the tribe' is a particular and particularly significant case of the dialectic between *habitus* and institutions, that is, between two modes of objectification of past history, in which there is constantly created a history that inevitably appears, like witticisms, as both original and inevitable.

This durably installed generative principle of regulated improvisations is a practical sense which reactivates the sense objectified in institutions. Produced by the work of inculcation and appropriation that is needed in order for objective structures, the products of collective history, to be reproduced in the form of the durable, adjusted dispositions that are the condition of their functioning, the *habitus*, which is constituted in the course of an individual history, imposing its particular logic on incorporation, and through which agents partake of the history objectified in institutions, is what makes it possible to inhabit institutions, to appropriate them practically, and so to keep them in activity, continuously pulling them from the state of dead letters, reviving the sense deposited in them, but at the same time imposing the revisions and transformations that reactivation entails. Or rather, the *habitus* is what enables the institution to attain full realization: it is through the capacity for incorporation, which exploits the body's readiness to take seriously the performative magic of the social, that the king, the banker or the priest are hereditary monarchy, financial capitalism or the Church made flesh. Property appropriates its owner, embodying itself in the form of a structure generating practices perfectly conforming with its logic and its demands. If one is justified in saying, with Marx, that 'the lord of an entailed estate, the first-born son, belongs to the land', that 'it inherits him', or that the 'persons' of capitalists are the 'personification' of capital, this is because the purely social and quasi-magical process of socialization, which is inaugurated by the act of marking that institutes an individual as an eldest son, an heir, a successor, a Christian, or simply as a man (as opposed to a woman), with all the corresponding privileges and obligations, and which is prolonged, strengthened and confirmed by social treatments that tend to transform instituted difference into natural distinction, produces quite real effects, durably inscribed in the body and in belief. An institution, even an economy, is complete and fully viable only if it is durably objectified not only in things, that is, in the logic, transcending individual agents, of a particular field, but also in bodies, in durable dispositions to recognize and comply with the demands immanent in the field.

In so far – and only in so far – as *habitus* are the incorporation of the same history, or more concretely, of the same history objectified in *habitus* and structures, the practices they generate are mutually intelligible and immediately adjusted to the structures, and also objectively concerted and endowed with an objective meaning that is at once unitary and systematic, transcending subjective intentions and conscious projects, whether individual or collective. One of the fundamental effects of the harmony between practical sense and objectified meaning (*sens*) is the production of a common-sense world, whose immediate self-evidence is accompanied by the objectivity provided by consensus on the meaning of practices and the world, in other words the harmonization of the agents' experiences and the constant reinforcement each of them receives from expression – individual or collective (in festivals, for example), improvised or programmed (commonplaces, sayings) – of similar or identical experiences. [. . .]

The objective homogenizing of group or class *habitus* that results from homogeneity of conditions of existence is what enables practices to be objectively harmonized without any calculation or conscious reference to a norm and mutually adjusted in the absence of any direct interaction or, *a fortiori*, explicit co-ordination. The interaction itself owes its form to the objective structures that have produced the dispositions of the interacting agents, which continue to assign them their relative positions in the interaction and elsewhere. 'Imagine,' Leibniz suggests,[1] 'two clocks or watches in perfect agreement as to the time. This may occur in one of three ways. The first consists in mutual influence; the second is to appoint a skilful workman to correct them and synchronize constantly; the third is to construct these two clocks with such art and precision that one can be assured of their subsequent agreement.' So long as one ignores the true principle of the conductorless orchestration which gives regularity, unity and systematicity to practices even in the absence of any spontaneous or imposed organization of individual projects, one is condemned to the naive artificialism that recognizes no other unifying principle than conscious co-ordination. The practices of the members of the same group or, in a differentiated society, the same class, are always more and better harmonized than the agents know or wish, because, as Leibniz again says, 'following only (his) own laws', each 'nonetheless agrees with the other'. The habitus is precisely this immanent law, *lex insita*, inscribed in bodies by identical histories, which is the precondition not only for the co-ordination of practices but also for practices of co-ordination. The corrections and adjustments the agents themselves consciously carry out presuppose mastery of a common code; and undertakings of collective mobilization cannot succeed without a minimum of concordance between the *habitus* of the mobilizing agents (prophet, leader, etc.) and the dispositions of those who recognize themselves in their practices or words, and, above all, without the inclination towards grouping that springs from the spontaneous orchestration of dispositions. [. . .]

Sociology treats as identical all biological individuals who, being the products of the same objective conditions, have the same *habitus*. A social class (in-itself) – a class of identical or similar conditions of existence and conditionings – is at the same time a class of biological individuals having the same *habitus*, understood as a system of dispositions common to all products of the same conditionings. Though it is impossible for all (or even two) members of the same class to have had the same experiences, in the same order, it is certain that each member of the same class is more likely than any member of another class to have been confronted with the situations most frequent for members of that class. Through the always convergent experiences that give a social environment its physiognomy, with its 'closed doors', 'dead ends' and 'limited prospects', the objective structures that sociology apprehends in the form of probabilities of access to goods, services and powers, inculcate the 'art of assessing likelihoods', as Leibniz put it, of anticipating the objective future, in short, the 'sense of reality', or realities, which is perhaps the best-concealed principle of their efficacy.

To define the relationship between class *habitus* and individual *habitus* (which is inseparable from the organic individuality that is immediately given to immediate perception – *intuitus personae* – and socially designated and recognized – name, legal identity, etc.), class (or group) *habitus*, that is, the individual habitus in so far as it expresses or reflects the class (or group), could be regarded as a subjective but non-individual system of internalized structures, common schemes of perception, conception and action, which are the precondition of all objectification and apperception; and the objective co-ordination of practices and the sharing of a world-view could be founded on the perfect impersonality and interchangeability of singular practices and views. But this would amount to regarding all the practices or representations produced in accordance with identical schemes as impersonal and inter-changeable, like individual intuitions of space which, according to Kant, reflect none of the particularities of the empirical ego. In fact, the singular *habitus* of members of the same class are united in a relationship of homology, that is, of diversity within homogeneity reflecting the diversity within homo-geneity characteristic of their social conditions of production. Each individual system of dispositions is a structural variant of the others, expressing the singularity of its position within the class and its trajectory. 'Personal' style, the particular stamp marking all the products of the same *habitus*, whether practices or works, is never more than a deviation in relation to the style of a period or class, so that it relates back to the common style not only by its conformity – like Phidias, who, for Hegel, had no 'manner' – but also by the difference that makes the 'manner'.

The principle of the differences between individual *habitus* lies in the singularity of their social trajectories, to which there correspond series of chronologically ordered determinations that are mutually irreducible to one another. The *habitus* which, at every moment, structures new experiences in accordance with the structures produced by past experiences, which are modified by the new experiences within the limits defined by their power of selection, brings about a unique integration, dominated by the earliest ex-periences, of the experiences statistically common to members of the same class. Early experiences have particular weight because the *habitus* tends to ensure its own constancy and its defence against change through the selection it makes within new information by rejecting information capable of calling into question its accumulated information, if exposed to it accidentally or by force, and especially by avoiding exposure to such information. One only has to think, for example, of homogamy, the paradigm of all the 'choices' through which the *habitus* tends to favour experiences likely to reinforce it (or the empirically confirmed fact that people tend to talk about politics with those who have the same opinions). Through the systematic 'choices' it makes among the places, events and people that might be frequented, the *habitus* tends to protect itself from crises and critical challenges by providing itself with a milieu to which it is as pre-adapted as possible, that is, a relatively constant universe of situations tending to reinforce its dispositions by offering the market most favourable to its products. And once again it is the most paradoxical property of the *habitus*, the unchosen principle of all 'choices', that yields the solution to the paradox of the information needed in order to avoid information. The schemes of perception and appreciation of the *habitus* which are the basis of all the avoidance strategies are largely the product of a non-conscious, unwilled avoidance, whether it results automatically from the conditions of existence (for example, spatial segregation) or has been produced by a strategic intention (such as avoidance of 'bad company' or 'unsuitable books') originating from adults themselves formed in the same conditions.

Even when they look like the realization of explicit ends, the strategies produced by the *habitus* and enabling agents to cope with unforeseen and constantly changing situations are only apparently determined by the future. If they seem to be oriented by anticipation of their own consequences, thereby encouraging the finalist illusion, this is because, always tending to reproduce the objective structures that produced them, they are determined by the past conditions of production of their principle of production, that is, by the already realized outcome of identical or interchangeable past practices, which co-incides with their own outcome only to the extent that the structures within which they function are identical to or homologous with the objective structures of which they are the product. Thus, for example, in the interaction between two agents or groups of agents endowed with the same *habitus* (say A and B), everything takes place as if the actions of each of them (say a_1 for A) were organized by reference to the reactions which they call forth from any agent possessing the same *habitus* (say b_1 for B). They therefore objectively imply anticipation of the reaction which these reactions in turn call forth (a_2, A's reaction to b_1). But the teleological description, the only one appropriate to a 'rational actor' possessing perfect information as to the preferences and competences of the other actors, in which each action has the purpose of making possible the reaction to the reaction it induces (individual A performs an action a_1, a gift for example, in order to make individual B produce action b_1, so that he can then perform action a_1, a stepped-up gift), is quite as naive as the mechanistic description that presents the action and the riposte as so many steps in a sequence of programmed actions produced by a mechanical apparatus. [. . .]

The *habitus* contains the solution to the paradoxes of objective meaning without subjective intention. It is the source of these strings of 'moves' which are objectively organized as strategies without being the product of a genuine strategic intention – which would presuppose at least that they be apprehended as one among other possible strategies. If each stage in the sequence of ordered and oriented actions that constitute objective strategies can appear to be de-termined by anticipation of the future, and in particular, of its own consequences (which is what justifies the use of the concept of strategy), it is because the practices that are generated by the *habitus* and are governed by the past conditions of production of their generative principle are adapted in advance to the objective conditions whenever the conditions in which the *habitus* functions have remained identical, or similar, to the conditions in which it was constituted. Perfectly and immediately successful adjustment to the objective conditions provides the most complete illusion of finality, or – which amounts to the same thing – of self-regulating mechanism.

The presence of the past in this kind of false anticipation of the future performed by the *habitus* is, paradoxically, most clearly seen when the sense of the probable future is belied and when dispositions ill-adjusted to the objective chances because of a hysteresis effect (Marx's favourite example of this was Don Quixote) are negatively sanctioned because the environment they actually encounter is too different from the one to which they are objectively adjusted. In fact the persistence of the effects of primary conditioning, in the form of the *habitus*, accounts equally well for cases in which dispositions function out of phase and practices are objectively ill-adapted to the present conditions because they are objectively adjusted to conditions that no longer obtain. The tendency of groups to persist in their ways, due *inter alia* to the fact that they are composed of individuals with durable dispositions that can outlive the economic and social conditions in which they were produced, can be the source of misadaptation as well as adaptation, revolt as well as resignation.

One only has to consider other possible forms of the relationship between dispositions and conditions to see that the pre-adjustment of the *habitus* to the objective conditions is a 'particular case of the possible' and so avoid unconsciously universalizing the model of the near-circular relationship of near-perfect reproduction, which is completely valid only when the conditions of production of the *habitus* and the conditions of its functioning are identical or homothetic. In this particular case, the dispositions durably inculcated by the objective conditions and by a pedagogic action that is tendentially adjusted to these conditions, tend to generate practices objectively compatible with these conditions and expectations pre-adapted to their objective demands (*amor fati*). As a consequence, they tend, without any rational calculation or conscious estimation of the chances of success, to ensure immediate correspondence between the *a priori* or *ex ante* probability conferred on an event (whether or not accompanied by subjective experiences such as hopes, expectation, fears, etc.) and the *a posteriori* or *ex post* probability that can be established on the basis of past experience. They thus make it possible to understand why economic models based on the (tacit) premise of a 'relationship of intelligible causality', as Max Weber calls it, between generic ('typical') chances 'objectively existing as an average' and 'subjective expectations', or, for example, between investment or the propensity to invest and the rate of return expected or really obtained in the past, fairly exactly account for practices which do not arise from knowledge of the objective chances.

By pointing out that rational action, 'judiciously' oriented according to what is 'objectively valid', is what 'would have happened if the actors had had knowledge of all the circumstances and all the participants' intentions',[2] that is, of what is 'valid in the eyes of the scientist', who alone is able to calculate the system of objective chances to which perfectly informed action would have to be adjusted, Weber shows clearly that the pure model of rational action cannot be regarded as an anthropological description of practice. This is not only because real agents only very exceptionally possess the complete information, and the skill to appreciate it, that rational action would presuppose. Apart from rare cases which bring together the economic and cultural conditions for rational action oriented by knowledge of the profits that can be obtained in the different markets, practices depend not on the average chances of profit, an abstract and unreal notion, but on the specific chances that a singular agent or class of agents possesses by virtue of its capital, this being understood, in this respect, as a means of appropriation of the chances theoretically available to all. [. . .]

Only in imaginary experience (in the folk tale, for example), which neutralizes the sense of social realities, does the social world take the form of a universe of possibles equally possible for any possible subject. Agents shape their aspirations according to concrete indices of the accessible and the inaccessible, of what is and is not 'for us', a division as fundamental and as fundamentally recognized as that between the sacred and the profane. The preemptive rights on the future that are defined by law and by the monopolistic right to certain possibles that it confers are merely the explicitly guaranteed form of the whole set of appropriated chances through which the power relations of the present project themselves into the future, from where they govern present dispositions, especially those towards the future. In fact, a given agent's practical relation to the future, which governs his present practice, is defined in the relationship between, on the one hand, his *habitus* with its temporal structures and dispositions towards the future, constituted in the course of a particular relationship to a particular universe of probabilities, and on the other hand a certain state of the chances objectively offered to him by the social world. The relation to what is possible is a relation to power; and the sense of the probable future is constituted in the prolonged relationship with a world structured according to the categories of the possible (for us) and the impossible (for us), of what is appropriated in advance by and for others and what one can reasonably expect for oneself. The *habitus* is the principle of a selective perception of the indices tending to confirm and reinforce it rather than transform it, a matrix generating responses adapted in advance to all objective conditions identical to or homologous with the (past) conditions of its production; it adjusts itself to a probable future which it anticipates and helps to bring about because it reads it directly in the present of the presumed world, the only one it can ever know. It is thus the basis of what Marx calls 'effective demand' (as opposed to 'demand without effect', based on need and desire), a realistic relation to what is possible, founded on and therefore limited by power. This disposition, always marked by its (social) conditions of acquisition and realization, tends to adjust to the objective chances of satisfying need or desire, inclining agents to 'cut their coats according to their cloth', and so to become the accomplices of the processes that tend to make the probable a reality.

Notes

1   G. W. Leibniz, *Second éclaircissement du systéme de la communication des substances*, in his *Œuvres philosophiques*, vol II, ed. P. Janet (Paris: Landrange, 1866), p. 548.
2   Max Weber, *Economy and Society* (New York: Bedminster, 1968), vol. I, p. 6.

8

Elements of the Theory of Structuration

Anthony Giddens

In offering a preliminary exposition of the main concepts of structuration theory it will be useful to begin from the divisions which have separated functionalism (including systems theory) and structuralism on the one hand from hermeneutics and the various forms of 'interpretative sociology' on the other.[1] Functionalism and structuralism have some notable similarities, in spite of the otherwise marked contrasts that exist between them. Both tend to express a naturalistic standpoint, and both are inclined towards objectivism. Functionalist thought, from Comte onwards, has looked particularly towards biology as the science providing the closest and most compatible model for social science. Biology has been taken to provide a guide to conceptualizing the structure and the functioning of social systems and to analysing processes of evolution via mechanisms of adaptation. Structuralist thought, especially in the writings of Lévi-Strauss, has been hostile to evolutionism and free from biological analogies. Here the homology between social and natural science is primarily a cognitive one in so far as each is supposed to express similar features of the overall constitution of mind. Both structuralism and functionalism strongly emphasize the pre-eminence of the social whole over its individual parts (i.e., its constituent actors, human subjects).

In hermeneutic traditions of thought, of course, the social and natural sciences are regarded as radically discrepant. Hermeneutics has been the home of that 'humanism' to which structuralists have been so strongly and persistently opposed. In hermeneutic thought, such as presented by Dilthey, the gulf between subject and social object is at its widest. Subjectivity is the preconstituted centre of the experience of culture and history and as such provides the basic foundation of the social or human sciences. Outside the realm of subjective experience, and alien to it, lies the material world, governed by impersonal relations of cause and effect. Whereas for those schools of thought which tend towards naturalism subjectivity has been regarded as something of a mystery, or almost a residual phenomenon, for hermeneutics it is the world of nature which is opaque – which, unlike human activity, can be grasped only from the outside. In interpretative sociologies, action and meaning are accorded primacy in the explication of human conduct; structural concepts are not notably prominent, and there is not much talk of constraint. For functionalism and structuralism, however, structure (in the divergent senses attributed to that concept) has primacy over action, and the constraining qualities of structure are strongly accentuated.

The differences between these perspectives on social science have often been taken to be epistemological, whereas they are in fact also ontological. What is at issue is how the concepts of action, meaning and subjectivity should be specified and how they might relate to notions of structure and constraint. If interpretative sociologies are founded, as it were, upon an imperialism of the subject, functionalism and structuralism propose an imperialism of the social object. One of my principal ambitions in the formulation of structuration theory is to put an end to each of these empire-building endeavours. The basic domain of study of the social sciences, according to the theory of structuration, is neither the experience of the individual actor, nor the existence of any form of societal totality, but social practices ordered across space and time. Human social activities, like some self-reproducing items in nature, are recursive. That is to say, they are not brought into being by social actors but continually re-created by them via the very means whereby they express themselves as actors. In and through their activities agents reproduce the conditions that make these activities possible. However, the sort of 'knowledgeability' displayed in nature, in the form of coded programmes, is distant from the cognitive skills displayed by human agents. It is in the conceptualizing of human knowledgeability and its involvement in action that I seek to appropriate some of the major contributions of interpretative sociologies. In structuration theory a hermeneutic starting-point is accepted in so far as it is acknowledged that the description of human activities demands a familiarity with the forms of life expressed in those activities. [. . .]

Structure, Structuration

Let me now move to the core of structuration theory: the concepts of 'structure', 'system' and 'duality of structure'. The notion of structure (or 'social structure'), of course, is very prominent in the writings of most functionalist authors and has lent its name to the traditions of 'structuralism'. But in neither instance is this conceptualized in a fashion best suited to the demands of social theory. Functionalist authors and their critics have given much more attention to the idea of 'function' than to that of 'structure', and consequently the latter has tended to be used as a received notion. But there can be no doubt about how 'structure' is usually understood by functionalists and, indeed, by the vast majority of social analysts – as some kind of 'patterning' of social relations or social phenomena. This is often naively conceived of in terms of visual imagery, akin to the skeleton or morphology of an organism or to the girders of a building. Such conceptions are closely connected to the dualism of subject and social object: 'structure' here appears as 'external' to human action, as a source of constraint on the free initiative of the independently constituted subject. As conceptualized in structuralist and post-structuralist thought, on the other hand, the notion of structure is more interesting. Here it is characteristically thought of not as a patterning of presences but as an intersection of presence and absence; underlying codes have to be inferred from surface manifestations.

   These two ideas of structure might seem at first sight to have nothing to do with one another, but in fact each relates to important aspects of the structuring of social relations, aspects which, in the theory of structuration, are grasped by recognizing a differentiation between the concepts of 'structure' and 'system'. In analysing social relations we have to acknowledge both a syntagmatic dimension, the patterning of social relations in time–space involving the reproduction of situated practices, and a paradigmatic dimension, involving a virtual order of 'modes of structuring' recursively implicated in such reproduction. In structuralist traditions there is usually ambiguity over whether structures refer to a matrix of admissible transformations within a set or to rules of transformation governing the matrix. I treat structure, in its most elemental meaning at least, as referring to such rules (and resources). It is misleading, however, to speak of 'rules of transformation' because all rules are inherently transformational. Structure thus refers, in social analysis, to the structuring properties allowing the 'binding' of time–space in social systems, the properties which make it possible for discernibly similar social practices to exist across varying spans of time and space and which lend them 'systemic' form. To say that structure is a 'virtual order' of transformative relations means that social systems, as reproduced social practices, do not have 'structures' but rather exhibit 'structural properties' and that structure exists, as time–space presence, only in its instantiations in such practices and as memory traces orienting the conduct of knowledgeable human agents. This does not prevent us from conceiving of structural properties as hierarchically organized in terms of the time–space extension of the practices they recursively organize. The most deeply embedded structural properties, implicated in the reproduction of societal totalities, I call *structural principles*. Those practices which have the greatest time–space extension within such totalities can be referred to as *institutions*.

   To speak of structure as 'rules' and resources, and of structures as isolable sets of rules and resources, runs a distinct risk of misinterpretation because of certain dominant uses of 'rules' in the philosophical literature.

1   Rules are often thought of in connection with games, as formalized prescriptions. The rules implicated in the reproduction of social systems are not generally like this. Even those which are codified as laws are characteristically

subject to a far greater diversity of contestations than the rules of games. Although the use of the rules of games such as chess, etc. as prototypical of the rule-governed properties of social systems is frequently associated with Wittgenstein, more relevant is what Wittgenstein has to say about children's play as exemplifying the routines of social life.

2   Rules are frequently treated in the singular, as if they could be related to specific instances or pieces of conduct. But this is highly misleading if regarded as analogous to the operation of social life, in which practices are sustained in conjunction with more or less loosely organized sets.

3   Rules cannot be conceptualized apart from resources, which refer to the modes whereby transformative relations are actually incorporated into the production and reproduction of social practices. Structural properties thus express forms of *domination* and *power*.

4   Rules imply 'methodical procedures' of social interaction, as Garfinkel in particular has made clear. Rules typically intersect with practices in the con-textuality of situated encounters: the range of 'ad hoc' considerations which he identifies are chronically involved with the instantiation of rules and are fundamental to the form of those rules. Every competent social actor, it should be added, is *ipso facto* a social theorist on the level of discursive consciousness and a 'methodological specialist' on the levels of both discursive and practical consciousness.

5   Rules have two aspects to them, and it is essential to distinguish these conceptually, since a number of philosophical writers (such as Winch) have tended to conflate them. Rules relate on the one hand to the constitution of *meaning*, and on the other to the *sanctioning* of modes of social conduct.

I have introduced the above usage of 'structure' to help break with the fixed or mechanical character which the term tends to have in orthodox sociological usage. The concepts of system and structuration do much of the work that 'structure' is ordinarily called upon to perform. In proposing a usage of 'structure' that might appear at first sight to be remote from conventional interpretations of the term, I do not mean to hold that looser versions be abandoned altogether. 'Society', 'culture' and a range of other forms of sociological terminology can have double usages that are embarrassing only in contexts where a difference is made in the nature of the statements employing them. Similarly, I see no particular objection to speaking of 'class structure', 'the structure of the industrialized societies' and so on, where these terms are meant to indicate in a general way relevant institutional features of a society or range of societies.

One of the main propositions of structuration theory is that the rules and resources drawn upon in the production and reproduction of social action are at the same time the means of system reproduction (the duality of structure). But how is one to interpret such a claim? In what sense is it the case that when I go about my daily affairs my activities incorporate and reproduce, say, the overall institutions of modern capitalism? What rules are being invoked here in any case? Consider the following possible instances of what rules are:

1   'The rule defining checkmate in chess is . . .';
2   A formula: $an = n^2 + n-1$;
3   'As a rule R gets up at 6.00 every day';
4   'It is a rule that all workers must clock in at 8.00 a.m.'

Many other examples could of course be offered, but these will serve in the present context. In usage (3) 'rule' is more or less equivalent to habit or routine. The sense of 'rule' here is fairly weak, since it does not usually presuppose some sort of underlying precept that the individual is following or any sanction which applies to backup that precept; it is simply something that the person habitually does. Habit is part of routine, and I shall strongly emphasize the importance of routine in social life. 'Rules', as I understand them certainly impinge upon numerous aspects of routine practice, but a routine practice is not as such a rule.

Cases (1) and (4) have seemed to many to represent two types of rule, constitutive and regulative. To explain the rule governing checkmate in chess is to say something about what goes into the very making of chess as a game. The rule that workers must clock in at a certain hour, on the other hand, does not help define what work is; it specifies how work is to be carried on. As Searle puts it, regulative rules can usually be paraphrased in the form 'Do X', or 'If Y, do X.' Some constitutive rules will have this character, but most will have the form 'X counts as Y', or 'X counts as Y in context C'.[2] That there is something suspect in this distinction, as referring to two types of rule, is indicated by the etymological clumsiness of the term 'regulative rule'. After all, the word 'regulative' already implies 'rule': its dictionary definition is 'control by rules'. I would say of (1) and (4) that they express two aspects of rules rather than two variant types of rule. (1) is certainly part of what chess is, but for those who play chess it has sanctioning or 'regulative' properties; it refers to aspects of play that must be observed. But (4) also has constitutive aspects. It does not perhaps enter into the definition of what 'work' is, but it does enter into that of a concept like 'industrial bureaucracy'. What (1) and (4) direct our attention to are two aspects of rules: their role in the constitution of meaning, and their close connection with sanctions.

Usage (2) might seem the least promising as a way of conceptualizing 'rule' that has any relation to 'structure'. In fact, I shall argue, it is the most germane of all of them. I do not mean to say that social life can be reduced to a set of mathematical principles, which is very far from what I have in mind. I mean that it is in the nature of formulae that we can best discover what is the most analytically effective sense of 'rule' in social theory. The formula $an = n^2 + n-1$ is from Wittgenstein's example of number games.[3] One person writes down a sequence of numbers; a second works out the formula supplying the numbers which follow. What is a formula of this kind, and what is it to understand one? To understand the formula is not to utter it. For someone could utter it and not understand the series; alternatively, it is possible to understand the series without being able to give verbal expression to the formula. Understanding is not a mental process accompanying the solving of the puzzle that the sequence of numbers presents – at least, it is not a mental process in the sense in which the hearing of a tune or a spoken sentence is. It is simply being able to apply the formula in the right context and way in order to continue the series.

A formula is a generalizable procedure – generalizable because it applies over a range of contexts and occasions, a procedure because it allows for the methodical continuation of an established sequence. Are linguistic rules like this? I think they are – much more than they are like the sorts of rule of which Chomsky speaks. And this seems also consonant with Wittgenstein's arguments, or a possible construal of them at any rate. Wittgenstein remarks, 'To understand a language means to be a master of a technique.'[4] This can be read to mean that language use is primarily methodological and that rules of language are methodically applied procedures implicated in the practical activities of day-to-day life. This aspect of language is very important, although not often given much prominence by most followers of Wittgenstein. Rules which are 'stated', as (1) and (4) above, are interpretations of activity as well as relating to specific sorts of activities: all codified rules take this form, since they give verbal expression to what is supposed to be done. But rules are procedures of action, aspects of *praxis*. It is by reference to this that Wittgenstein resolves what he first of all sets up as a 'paradox' of rules and rule-following. This is that no course of action can be said to be guided by a rule because every course of action can be made to accord with that rule. However, if such is the case, it is also true that every course of action can be made to conflict with it. There is a misunderstanding here, a confusing of the interpretation or verbal expression of a rule with following the rule.[5]

Let us regard the rules of social life, then, as techniques or generalizable procedures applied in the enactment/reproduction of social practices. Formulated rules – those that are given verbal expression as canons of law, bureaucratic rules, rules of games and so on – are thus codified interpretations of rules rather than rules as such. They should be taken not as exemplifying rules in general but as specific types of formulated rule, which, by virtue of their overt formulation, take on various specific qualities.[6]

So far these considerations offer only a preliminary approach to the problem. How do formulae relate to the practices in which social actors engage and what kinds of formulae are we most interested in for general purposes of social analysis? As regards the first part of the question, we can say that awareness of social rules, expressed first and foremost in practical consciousness, is the very core of that 'knowledgeability' which specifically characterizes human agents. As social actors, all human beings are highly 'learned' in respect of knowledge which they possess and apply in the production and reproduction of day-to-day social encounters; the vast bulk of such knowledge is practical rather than theoretical in character. As Schutz and many others have pointed out, actors employ typified schemes (formulae) in the course of their daily activities to negotiate routinely the situations of social life. Knowledge of procedure, or mastery of the techniques of 'doing' social activity, is by definition methodological. That is to say, such knowledge does not specify all the situations which an actor might meet with, nor could it do so; rather, it provides for the generalized capacity to respond to and influence an indeterminate range of social circumstances.

Those types of rule which are of most significance for social theory are locked into the reproduction of institutionalized practices, that is, practices most deeply sedimented in time–space.[7] The main characteristics of rules relevant to general questions of social analysis can be described as follows:

intensive	tacit	informal	weakly sanctioned
:	:	:	
shallow	discursive	formalized	strongly sanctioned

By rules that are intensive in nature, I mean formulae that are constantly invoked in the course of day-to-day activities, that enter into the structuring of much of the texture of everyday life. Rules of language are of this character. But so also, for example, are the procedures utilized by actors in organizing turn-taking in conversations or in interaction. They may be contrasted with rules which, although perhaps wide in scope, have only a superficial impact upon much of the texture of social life. The contrast is an important one, if only because it is commonly taken for granted among social analysts that the more abstract rules – e.g., codified law – are the most influential in the structuring of social activity. I would propose, however, that many seemingly trivial procedures followed in daily life have a more profound influence upon the generality of social conduct. The remaining categories should be more or less self-explanatory. Most of the rules implicated in the production and reproduction of social practices are only tacitly grasped by actors: they know how to 'go on'. *The discursive formulation of a rule is already an interpretation of it*, and, as I have noted, may in and of itself alter the form of its application. Among rules that are not just discursively formulated but are formally codified, the type case is that of laws. Laws, of course, are among the most strongly sanctioned types of social rules and in modern societies have formally prescribed gradations of retribution. However, it would be a serious mistake to underestimate the strength of informally applied sanctions in respect of a variety of mundane daily practices. Whatever else Garfinkel's 'experiments with trust' might be thought to demonstrate they do show the extraordinarily compelling force with which apparently minor features of conversational response are invested.[8]

The structuring qualities of rules can be studied in respect, first of all, of the forming, sustaining, termination and reforming of encounters. Although a dazzling variety of procedures and tactics are used by agents in the constitution and reconstitution of encounters, probably particularly significant are those involved in the sustaining of ontological security. Garfinkel's 'experiments' are certainly relevant in this respect. They indicate that the prescriptions involved in the structuring of daily interaction are much more fixed and constraining than might appear from the ease with which they are ordinarily followed. This is surely because the deviant responses or acts that Garfinkel instructed his 'experimenters' to perform disturbed the sense of ontological security of the 'subjects' by undermining the intelligibility of discourse. Breaking or ignoring rules is not, of course, the only way in which the constitutive and sanctioning properties of intensively invoked rules can be studied. But there is no doubt that Garfinkel has helped to disclose a remarkably rich field of study – performing the 'sociologist's alchemy', the 'transmutation of any patch of ordinary social activity into an illuminating publication'.[9]

I distinguish 'structure' as a generic term from 'structures' in the plural and both from the 'structural properties of social systems'.[10] 'Structure' refers not only to rules implicated in the production and reproduction of social systems but also to resources (about which I have so far not said much but will do so shortly). As ordinarily used in the social sciences, 'structure' tends to be employed with the more enduring aspects of social systems in mind, and I do not want to lose this connotation. The most important aspects of structure are rules and resources recursively involved in institutions. Institutions by definition are the more enduring features of social life. In speaking of the structural properties of social systems I mean their institutionalized features, giving 'solidity' across time and space. I use the concept of 'structures' to get at relations of transformation and mediation which are the 'circuit switches' underlying observed conditions of system reproduction.

Let me now answer the question I originally posed: in what manner can it be said that the conduct of individual actors reproduces the structural properties of larger collectivities? The question is both easier and more difficult to answer than it appears. On a logical level, the answer to it is nothing more than a truism. That is to say, while the continued existence of large collectivities or societies evidently does not depend upon the activities of any particular individual, such collectivities or societies manifestly would cease to be if all the agents involved disappeared. On a substantive level, the answer to the question depends upon issues yet to be broached – those concerning the mechanisms of integration of different types of societal totality. It is always the case that the day-to-day activity of social actors draws upon and reproduces structural features of wider social systems. But 'societies' – as I shall make clear – are not necessarily unified collectivities. 'Social reproduction' must not be equated with the consolidation of social cohesion. The location of actors and of collectivities in different sectors or regions of more encompassing social systems strongly influences the impact of even their habitual conduct upon the integration of societal totalities. Here we reach the limits of linguistic examples which might be used to illustrate the concept of the duality of structure. Considerable illumination of problems of social analysis can be derived from studying the recursive qualities of speech and language. When I produce a grammatical utterance, I draw upon the same syntactical rules as those that utterance helps to produce. But I speak the 'same' language as the other speakers in my language community; we all share the same rules and linguistic practices, give or take a range of relatively minor variations. Such is not necessarily the case with the structural properties of social systems in general. But this is not a problem to do with the concept of the duality of structure as such. It is to do with how social systems, especially 'societies', should be conceptualized.

The Duality of Structure

Structure(s)	System(s)	Structuration
Rules and resources, or sets of transformation relations, organized as properties of social systems	Reproduced relations between actors or collectivities, organized as regular social practices	Conditions governing the continuity or transmutation of structures, and therefore the reproduction of social systems

Let me summarize the argument thus far. Structure, as recursively organized sets of rules and resources, is out of time and space, save in its instantiations and co-ordination as memory traces, and is marked by an 'absence of the subject'. The social systems in which structure is recursively implicated, on the contrary, comprise the situated activities of human agents, reproduced across time and space. Analysing the structuration of social systems means studying the modes in which such systems, grounded in the knowledgeable activities of situated actors who draw upon rules and resources in the diversity of action contexts, are produced and reproduced in interaction. Crucial to the idea of structuration is the theorem of the duality of structure, which is logically implied in the arguments portrayed above. The constitution of agents and structures are not two independently given sets of phenomena, a dualism, but represent a duality. According to the notion of the duality of structure, the structural properties of social systems are both medium and outcome of the practices they recursively organize. Structure is not 'external' to individuals: as memory traces, and as instantiated in social practices, it is in a certain sense more 'internal' than exterior to their activities in a Durkheimian sense. Structure is not to be equated with constraint but is always both constraining and enabling. This of course does not prevent the structured properties of social systems from stretching away, in time and space, beyond the control of any individual actors. Nor does it compromise the possibility that actors' own theories of the social systems which they help to constitute and reconstitute in their activities may reify those systems. The reification of social relations, or the discursive 'naturalization' of the historically contingent circumstances and products of human action, is one of the main dimensions of ideology in social life.[11]

Even the crudest forms of reified thought, however, leave untouched the fundamental significance of the knowledgeability of human actors. For knowledgeability is founded less upon discursive than practical consciousness. The knowledge of social conventions, of oneself and of other human beings, presumed in being able to 'go on' in the diversity of contexts of social life is detailed and dazzling. All competent members of society are vastly skilled in the practical accomplishments of social activities and are expert 'sociologists'. The knowledge they possess is not incidental to the persistent patterning of social life but is integral to it. This stress is absolutely essential if the mistakes of functionalism and structuralism are to be avoided, mistakes which, suppressing or discounting agents' reasons – the rationalization of action as chronically involved in the structuration of social practices – look for the origins of their activities in phenomena of which these agents are ignorant.[12] But it is equally important to avoid tumbling into the opposing error of hermeneutic approaches and of various versions of phenomenology, which tend to regard society as the plastic creation of human subjects. Each of these is an illegitimate form of reduction, deriving from a failure adequately to conceptualize the duality of structure. According to structuration theory, the moment of the production of action is also one of reproduction in the contexts of the day-to-day enactment of social life. This is so even during the most violent upheavals or most radical forms of social change. It is not accurate to see the structural properties of social systems as 'social products' because this tends to imply that preconstituted actors somehow come together to create them.[13] In reproducing structural properties to repeat a phrase used earlier, agents also reproduce the conditions that make such action possible. Structure has no existence independent of the knowledge that agents have about what they do in their day-to-day activity. Human agents always know what they are doing on the level of discursive consciousness under some description. However, what they do may be quite unfamiliar under other descriptions, and they may know little of the ramified consequences of the activities in which they engage.

The duality of structure is always the main grounding of continuities in social reproduction across time–space. It in turn presupposes the reflexive monitoring of agents in, and as constituting, the *durée* of daily social activity. But human knowledgeability is always bounded. The flow of action continually produces consequences which are unintended by actors, and these unintended consequences also may form unacknowledged conditions of action in a feedback fashion. Human history is created by intentional activities but it is not an intended project; it persistently eludes efforts to bring it under conscious direction. However, such attempts are continuously made by human beings, who operate under the threat and the promise of the circumstance that they are the only creatures who make their 'history' in cognizance of that fact.

The theorizing of human beings about their action means that just as social theory was not an invention of professional social theorists, so the ideas produced by those theorists inevitably tend to feed back into social life itself. One aspect of this is the attempt to monitor, and thereby control, highly generalized conditions of system reproduction – a phenomenon of massive importance in the contemporary world. To grasp such monitored processes of reproduction conceptually, we have to make certain distinctions relevant to what social systems 'are' as reproduced practices in interaction settings. The relations implied or actualized in social systems are, of course, widely variable in terms of their degree of 'looseness' and permeability. But, this being accepted, we can recognize two levels in respect of the means whereby some elements of 'systemness' is achieved in interaction. One is that generally prominent in functionalism, as referred to earlier, where independence is conceived of as a homeostatic process akin to mechanisms of self-regulation operating within an organism. There can be no objection to this as long as it is acknowledged that the 'looseness' of most social systems makes the organic parallel a very remote one and that this relatively 'mechanized' mode of system reproduction is not the only one found in human societies. Homeostatic system reproduction in human society can be regarded as involving the operation of causal loops, in which a range of unintended consequences of action feed back to reconstitute the initiating circumstances. But in many contexts of social life there occur processes of selective 'information filtering' whereby strategically placed actors seek reflexively to regulate the overall conditions of system reproduction either to keep things as they are or to change them.[14]

The distinction between homeostatic causal loops and reflexive self-regulation in system reproduction must be complemented by one further, and final, one: that between social and system integration.[15] 'Integration' may be understood as involving reciprocity of practices (of autonomy and dependence) between actors or collectivities.[16] Social integration then means systemness on the level of face-to-face interaction. System integration refers to connections with those who are physically absent in time or space. The mechanisms of system integration certainly presuppose those of social integration, but such mechanisms are also distinct in some key respects from those involved in relations of co-presence.

Social Integration	System Integration
Reciprocity between actors in contexts of co-presence	Reciprocity between actors or collectivities across extended time–space

Notes

1   For more detailed discussions of the basic concepts of structuration theory, the reader should turn to A. Giddens, *New Rules of Sociological Method* (London: Hutchinson, 1976), esp. chs 2 and 3; *Central Problems in Social Theory* (London:

Hutchinson, 1977); and *A Contemporary Critique of Historical Materialism* (London: Macmillan, 1981) chs 1 and 2.

2   John R. Searle, *Speech Acts* (Cambridge: Cambridge University Press, 1969), pp. 34–5.

3   Ludwig Wittgenstein, *Philosophical Investigations* (Oxford: Blackwell, 1972), p. 59.

4   Ibid., p. 81.

5   Ibid.

6   Ibid.

7   Giddens, *Central Problems in Social Theory*, pp. 80ff.

8   Harold Garfinkel, 'A conception of, and experiments with, "trust" as a condition of stable concerted actions'. In O. J. Harvey, *Motivation and Social Interaction* (New York: Ronald Press, 1963).

9   Erving Goffman, *Frame Analysis* (New York: Harper, 1974), p. 5.

10 In *New Rules of Sociological Method* I had not appreciated the need to distinguish 'structure' from 'structures' and used the latter term too casually as synonymous with the former.

11 Giddens, *Central Problems in Social Theory*, pp. 195–6.

12 Cf. Roy Bhaskar, *The Possibility of Naturalism* (Brighton: Harvester, 1979), ch. 2.

13 Ibid., p. 48.

14 Cf. ibid., pp. 78–9. There I distinguished three levels of 'systemness' which here, for purposes of simplification, are reduced to two.

15 This distinction was introduced into the literature by David Lockwood who, however, deployed it rather differently from the way I do: David Lockwood, 'Social integration and system integration'. In George Zollschan and W. Hirsch. *Explorations in Social Change* (London: Routledge, 1964).

16 My formulation of the concept of 'system integration' in *Central Problems in Social Theory*, p. 77, was ambiguous. I did not make it clear whether the separation of social from system integration depended upon a distinction between co-presence and absence in social relations, or between the ties linking actors as contrasted with those linking collectivities. As I use it now, the notion refers to the first of these two sets of contrasts, but they are in any case closely overlapping, so the fault was not too consequential.

9

Society Turns Back upon Itself

Alain Touraine

Beyond Function

Human societies cannot be sufficiently defined by their rules and the instruments by which they function.

They act upon their own functioning, either to modify it or to transcend it.

1 First, by *applied experience,* or in other words by politics. The norms that govern social interactions are not intangible; they are in large part the result of decisions and in consequence can be modified as the result of a change in the relations of force or influence between actors, and also as the result of modification occurring in the environment.

Modern analyses of organization and decision making have greatly extended our knowledge of society's internal and external exchanges and consequently of the temporary and partial character of its norms, which are the products of interaction and transactions.

As a political actor society no longer resembles an organism ensuring its stability by homeostasis; it is constantly modifying its activities and its organization by adaptation.

2 Second, by what I term *historicity.* Human society cannot be reduced to an organism always reproducing itself immutably, dependent for any transformation in itself upon mutations brought about by internal or external events. Its capability is not limited to adapting itself to a changing environment and is constantly modifying the rules by which it functions.

It also has the capability of positing, beside the order of its activities, the order of its representations. It possesses a symbolic capacity that enables it to construct a system of *knowledge* together with technical tools which it can use to intervene in its own functioning.

But we must go further. This capacity for acting upon itself, this non-coincidence of society with its own rules of functioning, must be much more than just the creation of the order of words beside the order of things. This "double" of society must also have means of action, of intervention in the material functioning of society, and therefore means of *investment*. Lastly, this distance between society and itself is also apprehended by social consciousness. A tragic and arrogant apprehension, because it is simultaneously apprehension of a wrenching asunder and of a dominion. Inventor of knowledge, agent of investment, creator of an *image of creativity* that I term a *cultural model*, society produces itself, imposes a meaning on its practices, *turns back upon itself*. It does not exist solely in nature; it does not possess a history only; it possesses historicity, which is the capacity to produce its own social and cultural field, its own historical environment.

Society produces itself. This cannot mean that it creates the conditions of its existence starting from an idea. For where would this idea come from, and how could it be conceived of other than as a metasocial warrant for social organization–divine providence, human nature, idea, march of history? But nor can it mean that these representations and these orientations have been formed on the basis of a material experience that could be defined independently of them.

We must not search here for any first cause. Labor is a state of the forces of production determined by historicity, that is to say by a model of knowledge, by a type of accumulation, and by an image of creativity or cultural model; but these components of historicity always appear as a distancing of society from itself and from the reproduction of its functioning. The specific characteristic of human society is precisely this distance between the totality of the activities that define a society's functioning and the system of meaning that simultaneously determines it and is formed on the basis of it, in a circle that will only appear vicious if one is looking for a first cause, and which on the contrary defines the particularity of society as a system when compared to other concrete systems.

To sum up, a certain historicity expresses itself through certain characteristics of the social organization, a level of productivity, a capacity for growth, and a technical division of labor. It is on the basis of this organization of labor that accumulation makes it possible to emerge from the economic cycle and that the cultural model occupies the gap formed between historicity and functioning. Historicity is always linked to a material situation; it gives it meaning, informs it.

One must reject equally both the idea that the forms of social life are determined by a material situation, such as the state of technology, and also the contrary idea that society imposes culture upon nature, writes civilization on the virgin page of an untamed natural world.

Historicity is neither idea nor material situation; it is the specific characteristic of social action, which constitutes its experience through the meaning it gives to it.

Human activity, on all levels of technical development, is the organization of a technical environment and not integration into a natural whole. From first hunter to missile builder, man is the producer of techniques. Analysis must start from this action, which is simultaneously instrumental, economic, and ideological, to use terms that are at the same time in everyday use yet laden with obscurities; which is a model of knowledge, accumulation, and cultural model, to use the terms I shall employ here, referring to the organization of a field of experience, the setting aside of a proportion of the resources available for consumption, and an image of creativity.

Historicity is not transcendence; it is not that which escapes from society conceived of as a system. On the contrary, it is that which makes it possible to conceive of society as a system, but without having to reduce it to another and less complex type. Through historicity activity becomes meaning and meaning once more becomes practice.

It is this double movement, up toward historicity and – even more important – down from it, through the system of historical action, society's institutions and organizations, that will constitute one of the two central themes of this book. The second is an investigation of the forms of social interaction linked with historicity and with the production of society by society itself: class relations.

It is a mistake to criticize the functionalist sociologies of integration and values by confronting them with the history of societies or by the forces of conflict and change with them. One runs a great risk of being forced back into presociological interpretations.

I do not blame functionalist sociology for having represented society as a system; that is its great positive contribution. Its error was to conceive that system in accordance with mechanistic or organistic images so inadequate that they simultaneously force one back to an evolutionist vision, inherited from nineteenth-century liberal and positivist optimism, impregnated with the most unacceptable kind of idealism and ethnocentrism.

The Components of Historicity:
Knowledge, Accumulation, Cultural Model

1   Serge Moscovici has pointed out with some force that society is not in opposition to nature and that it is consequently false to distinguish between the natural order and social values, between the body and the soul of social activity. Nature is a cultural definition of matter. Thus we ought not to speak of nature but of "states of nature," which is to say, of *systems of knowledge.*

This work of knowledge is never identifiable with economic activity. Production and consumption are economic categories that always pertain to a study of exchanges. But any system of labor also includes the intervention of "natural forces," of an activity of knowledge. Science, for example, is not an economic element, does not in itself have a price, because it does not produce goods but, rather, endows society with a nature, as religious thought did in another type of society.

This first component of historicity, the model of knowledge, is at the same time the most fundamental and the one that will play the most limited role in our analysis of society. It is fundamental because it manifests most directly the human capacity to create through knowledge an image of the world and social relations and an image of the nonsocial.

Before coming to any particular piece of sociological analysis we encounter the primary fact that human language orders a universe organized by technique, thus permitting the turning back of experience on itself that enables man – and man alone – to have a history, in other words, to produce not only his changing but his situation itself. However, the fundamental role of this component also makes it dependent. It does not govern the orientations of social and cultural action or the forms of accumulation and relations of production directly. Itself a force of production par excellence, it appears both at the very beginning and at the very end of the analysis: a set of means and technical operations on the one hand, and on the other a sign of society's distance in relation to its own functioning.

2   This separation between the two orders of phenomena lumped together under the name of work is not conceivable without a recognition of the economic forms of historicity. The existence of work on work presupposes a process of *accumulation.*

One part of the consumable product is set aside and invested in works that bear the stamp of the cultural model. The closer one comes to industrialized societies the more this accumulation is identifiable with productive investment. Whereas, on the other hand, in societies with a weak historicity, with only a slight capability of action upon themselves, the uses to which the accumulated resources are put are not directly productive: temples and priests, castles and courts absorb the surplus withdrawn from consumption. But accumulation always has economic uses, since those who control it, even if their central role is a religious or political one, are filling a role essential to production. The greater the amount of accumulation the greater the extent to which it transforms the conditions of production. When it is small, the surplus collected is set aside from economic activity and used for the realization of major constructions or works. On the other hand, an important share of the resources accumulated in an industrialized society is used to transform the conditions of labor directly and *to produce labor,* which is the role of technology. Investment modifies the organization of work and thus its productivity.

3   A society is not adequately defined by the state of its productive forces; such a definition ought to be derived from the relations between its activity and its capability of acting on that activity. This distance is apprehended culturally: every society is oriented by this apprehension of creativity, which I term its *cultural model.* In a society with a strong historicity, which is to say one in which the production of labor exercises a strong control over the production of wealth, this apprehension of creativity is *practical*: science is recognized as creativity, as the force directly transforming the state of nature. In a society with a weak historicity, on the other hand, creativity is apprehended only abstractly, not as *praxis* but as *logos,* as a metasocial order. This cultural model is not a representation of the model of knowledge but of the distance between the production

and the reproduction of work, and thus of society's capability of acting upon itself.

I therefore use the phrase "cultural model" in a very specific sense, not in order to describe such and such an orientation or observable value within a society, but to define, within a conceptual system, that essential aspect of historicity by means of which the society "reflects" upon itself by apprehending its own capability of action in a way that defines the field of social relations and what I shall call the system of historical action. Let me say right away, however, that even when historicity is most completely controlled by the ruling class, the cultural model is not reducible to the dominant ideology. Ideology pertains to specific actors; *the cultural model pertains to a type of society as totality*; it contributes to a definition of the field of social relations. The actors, however much opposed to each other they may be, interact and enter into conflict within a cultural model.

All this shows that a cultural model cannot be situated other than qualitatively in relation to other cultural models. Each cultural model contributes to the definition of a type of society, not to that of a specific collectivity.

This cultural model is not a system of values. It entails no judgment as to what is socially good or bad. It defines a cultural field. Let one example suffice: to recognize science as the contemporary form of creativity does not in itself entail any judgment on the positive or negative aspects of a society dominated by science. One may say with equal justification either that science creates plenty or that it is threatening humanity with total destruction. It is in this sense that science is not a social value, that it does not distinguish positive conduct from negative conduct.

The orientations of historical action do not constitute principles enthroned at the center of society and directly defining forms of social organization, because society is not an actor, a sovereign, a legislator. They define the thematic of a society, not its government.

Society Torn Apart

The fact that a society produces itself and is not reducible to its functioning leads directly to the existence of opposing social classes and the conflict between them.

It is not society *as a whole* that turns back upon itself in order to orient itself. It is always utopian to think that a collectivity transforms *itself*, is capable of simultaneously acting in accordance with certain forms and transcending them, of providing for investment as well as for consumption.

The class that manages society's accumulation, its model of knowledge, and its cultural model is the society's *ruling class*. This class identifies itself with the society's historicity. But since it is no more than one part of society, it is therefore also identifying historicity with its private interests, confusing the cultural model with its own ideology. The ruled class reacts to this domination both defensively, by insisting on its own social and cultural identity, and offensively, by contesting the power of the ruling class, by appealing to the very historicity that the ruling class is appropriating. It is therefore clear that the orientations of historicity do not by themselves determine rules of conduct, because between them we find interposed the class conflict and the nature of social domination. The orientations of historical action are the "stake" in the class struggle. Which means both that they are not the ideology of the ruling class and that they are not independent of class relations, which otherwise would be no more than a mode of social stratification.

Class relations are linked to forces of production, to a state of economic activity and technical division of labor; but they are more than this: *they are the expression of historical action itself in terms of social actors,* the expression of society's capacity to act upon itself by its investment of the resources accumulated in activities selected by a cultural model.

But it is the state of class relations that governs the mechanisms of decision in a society, and thus too the formation of the rules that in their turn govern social organization, thereby enabling us to reject any sociology of values.

The main lines of class relations need to be indicated here.

We cannot present the ruling class as purely creative, as the class that makes it possible to step aside from routine and the defense of immediate interests in order to tackle long-term projects, general ideas, complex strategies. That would obviously ignore the fact that the ruling class defends private interests and privileges and, even more important, the fact that it dominates the lower classes, the workers. But nor can one reduce accumulation to a class relation, that of exploiter and exploited. In particular, the closer one approaches to the industrialized societies the more productivity of work is defined not by individual work alone or even that of the team, but by the forms of organization, of the overall programming of production, and by the application of science, technology, and mathematics to economic activity. A simple observation, but one that prevents us from presenting labor relations as simply a confrontation between worker-producer and profit taker.

The essential thing is to recognize that the always present, always essential relation of domination to exploitation is not separable – if we are to understand the functioning of society as the conduct of actors – from society's relation to its historicity. It is not enough to say that the ruling class performs the task of developing the forces of production. For to say that is stating a material fact but telling us nothing about its social significance. But if we try to see what lies beneath it, we discover the tug the ruling class exerts on the whole of society toward a particular type of historicity.

Of the three components of historicity, accumulation is the one that makes possible the wrenching away of historicity from activity, the distancing of society from its own functioning. The mode of knowledge posits the fact of society's noncoincidence with its being: beside those shackling activities governed by the requirements of the collectivity's survival and its adaptation to the environment from which it draws its subsistence, it sets the world of the image (to use the word adopted by Kenneth Boulding in *The Image: Knowledge and Life in Society*, University of Michigan Press, 1956). Accumulation gives a material content to this distancing.

Economic activity is not reducible to the production–consumption cycle; what is subtracted from that cycle is used in the service of society's transcendence of itself, whether it be a transcendence toward the future, a process of growth, or a transcendence directed toward a principle of order and unity, either of a religious or of a political type.

It is now easier to see what historicity is.

In order to define it, must we make a hypothesis about the orientations of human action? Must we set up an image of a man drawn by his will to creation, his desire for enrichment, or more generally still by a need to work? It is normal that there should emerge a favored image of man in every society, a type of hero. But this very fact, which would become less clear on closer examination, shows plainly that it cannot constitute a principle of explanation, since these human types change from one era and one society to another. To speak of human nature in this sense is a roundabout way either of introducing an ideology or of describing certain aspects of one society. If we try to explain society by means of social conducts, then we condemn ourselves to the inability to produce anything but interpretations of society, since we have introduced at the outset that which must be explained.

But it is equally impossible to look upon social situations as material "facts," when by their very definition they are sets of conducts and of social relations, in other words, of actions.

For the sociologist, to posit an opposition between the network of social relations and the priority of "material" activities – the activities of production and reproduction of individual and collective existence – can have no meaning. Such an idea belongs merely to historicist thought; whether one posits over and above society the development of the mind or the priority of "natural" needs and the activities intended to satisfy them, one is still explaining society by the nonsocial; it is obvious that this method is as unacceptable today as it was when Durkheim condemned it.

We must also eliminate other, less crude concepts of society that equally omit all recourse to the concept of actions.

We cannot consider a society as an organism endowed with balancing mechanisms that is able to transform itself in the direction of a growing complexity simply under the influence of external stimuli. Even less can we consider it as a being endowed with a sort of built-in code that will modify itself as a result of mutations occurring during its transmission, change then being the result of individual actions sanctioned by their efficacy, their material success, and reacting on the social code to transform it. We are bound to recognize that human collectivities are systems defined in their specific and essential characteristics not by their code of functioning but by their capacity to be oriented by a cultural model.

What I term historicity is thus the particular nature of social systems which, above and beyond their reproduction combined with any accidents that might make them change, and also beyond their possibilities for trial-and-error and adaptation, have the capacity to act upon themselves through the intermediary of a set of cultural and social orientations.

All societies are at the same time activities and a "reflection" upon those activities, which in its turn governs the orientations of social action, the mechanisms of decision and the modalities of functioning in concrete societies.

Their capacity to modify their relation with the environment is manifested in a model of knowledge, in a type of accumulation, and in a cultural model that together constitute historicity. This latter governs a system of orientations that controls the systems of functioning and adaptation. The content of historicity depends upon the society's type of activity, on its labor, but transforms that activity into culture and into social organization.

Society governs its activity by the molding of knowledge, by accumulation, by awareness of creativity, so that all aspects of its organization become at the same time means in the service of that production of society by itself. Social organization as such is not exclusive to the human species but mankind is the only species that possesses sufficient symbolic capability to produce the sense – both meaning and direction – of its experience; the only one for which nature is culture, creation, and normative orientation, in the name of which triad its organization is organized, transformed, and, I repeat, produced.

Human societies are open systems not only capable of modifying their goals, but also possessed of the capacity to create normatively oriented conducts, to produce and to destroy their social order.

This capacity does not entirely define social life. Society functions on three levels: *it produces itself, but it also adapts itself and consumes itself*. And these three levels I shall term in this chapter: *the field of historicity*, *the institutional system*, and *the social organization*. But if historicity must be the central theme of sociology, that is because only human societies possess such a capacity of self-transformation, which is linked to the human being's symbolic capacity, in other words to his ability to act upon his relation to his environment and upon his social organization.

It is possible that a society might lose its historicity, that it might sink into mere reproduction or divide itself totally into a mass and an elite; it is also possible that it could cease to be capable of adaptation, in other words that it might reduce itself wholly to its political system, to the strategies of its members and to its own strategy with regard to other societies. A human society can be a system of historicity; it is not driven along as though in spite of itself by a force running through it, by the march of history or some transhistoric essence. Historicity is neither a type of conduct nor an impersonal force; it is the production of society by society.

The evolutionist philosophies of history which made use of notions of force and energy must be completely replaced by the study of historic action, in other words of the elements whose interrelations define the action of society's self-transformation. There is no question of introducing a theory of social change at this point; it is neither convention nor convenience that has made social change the theme of this book's final chapter. A society's historicity is not the process that causes it to pass from state T to state $T + 1$. It is a concept strictly defined *within a synchronic analysis*. A society constitutes in terms of its resources an image that is not a representation but a set of schemas of cultural and social orientations that mold the collective experience: model of knowledge, type of accumulation, cultural model. This historicity is realized in a system of historical action and in class relations, in a political system and in forms of social organization.

Rather than placing a society in history, we are talking about placing historicity in the heart of society as the organizing principle of a field of practices and relations. Thus, not only is an analysis of change inappropriate, but, further, in many ways this approach makes such an analysis more difficult, since it cannot then be undertaken other than on the basis of research into the tensions and non-coincidences between the historicity of a society and the nature of the forms of social practice that are informed by it while at the same time escaping from it as concrete, complex, "historical" social unities. Change cannot be understood except on the basis of the opposition between structure and event.

Historicity, as the foundation of social structure, is neither an idea nor a material force. It is useless to ask oneself whether it falls into the category of economics, politics, or ideology. Those terms themselves merely produce confusion, or, even worse, refer back to a separation between subject and object absolutely incompatible with the task of sociology, which is to study social action. For social action is at once labor and consciousness, practice and orientation, mechanisms and finalities, all always inseparable.

Tensions and Conflicts

Having placed the theme of historicity at the outset of this analysis, I had better also take precautions against possible misunderstandings. Certainly, I have no intention of intoning a hymn of praise to the creative power of man, governing and ordering an untamed nature and led by his own inspiration, the impulse of his soul, or divine grace, beyond the everydayness of the world.

Such a vision of things – which can take less crude forms – expresses the presociological thought that cannot be transcended until the moment society discovers that it in fact possesses virtually unlimited power over itself. By separating society's soul from its body, this vision is presupposing that the existence of that soul has a warrant in some essence – Man, God, History – and that social facts have no meaning other than the actor's intention and internal life, which impose themselves upon an inert nature. When one disencumbers oneself from all recourse to idealist notions, then nature ceases to be either savage or paradisiac; it is simply a set of natural systems, open or closed, functioning in accordance with laws which it is the business of science to discover.

The further we move away from an abstract humanism, the vaster the field of these natural systems within human existence reveals itself to be. Hence the steady extension of the natural sciences. But we cannot separate this recognition of "human nature" from the formulation of the specific characteristics of society and the human species. Man molds his environment and his social organization; he does not insert himself into an ecological whole; he organizes that whole on the basis of his own transforming activity.

In a word, he has a history. It is this capacity to produce his own transformation that I call historicity, and which is at the same time activity and self-consciousness, work of knowledge and cultural model. This historicity does not give form to the formless; on the contrary, it is linked to existing natural systems: the biological being, including the human mind, the interpersonal relations through which personality is formed, and the forms of sociability. Corresponding to each state of historicity there is a certain "nature" that is its complement and its opposite, but it is not in historicity's power to determine the characteristics of the natural systems that organize the activity on the basis of which historicity is formed, and which it in its turn governs.

All reflection on historicity should shed light on the close bond between two apparently opposed ideas whose complementarity must be understood.

First, the relation between social activity and historicity is *circular*. Historicity comes into being on the basis of a state of collective activity: its content is determined by the form of that activity. In the other direction, social organization always results from the dominion of sociocultural orientations and class relations – themselves governed by historicity – over resources and sets of means.

Why should this be called a vicious circle? On the contrary, it is a question of positing the most elementary condition of all for the existence of any sociological analysis. Once that circle is broken, idealism will flood in. Historicity is not an idea but a concept introduced with the sole purpose of destroying, root and branch, all appeal to any metasocial warrant for social order. Society is what it makes itself be on the basis of what it is, and not on the basis of principles or values that cannot be anything, for the sociologist, but ideologies pertaining to particular actors.

Second, this interdependence of activity and historicity, of work and of work upon work, creates *tension* and is *distancing*. Hence the emphasis I put upon providing a sociology of historicity, an actionalist sociology, in opposition to current work inspired by functionalism, even though the latter no longer appears today as anything more than a somewhat vague orientation, lacking the academic power it had at the time when I first began my fight against it.

It is a constant tendency of sociology, often in the name of empiricism, to accept the social order as being neutral and to see each individual occupying his place within it, entering into relations with others, in order to realize a series of exchanges within that order in conformity with the rules of the social game. The actor carries his status and his role around with him, just as the laborer wears on his coveralls the name of his firm, which is taken to be his group and therefore his social being. It is a naively conservative sociology in consequence, one that examines with the minutest attention how society functions while taking pains at least equally great to avoid asking itself *what* is functioning.

Society viewed in its historicity, and consequently social actors too, as participants in that historicity, cannot be defined by their content but, primarily, by the gap, *the distance,* separating the production of society by itself from the reproduction of its activity. This means in the first place that analysis of society is not built up directly around the content of historicity but around the tension between historicity and the natural systems mobilized by social activity. We shall encounter this fundamental tension, in changing forms, at every level of society, and its recognition imposes a critical procedure diametrically opposed to that of positivism.

This means in turn that no actor is alone the bearer of this tension. It is *a system of social interactions* or class relations that constitutes the unity of action within which this tension manifests itself. It is impossible to single out each individual's place, or to insert each individual in a proper place, because society is not a game in which there are pawns that have rights and are subject to constraints. Social relations govern the relations between historicity and society's functioning. And in parallel to this, as I have already pointed out, the most fundamental social interactions of all, class relations, cannot be understood except as historicity at work.

One might wonder at this point what mark historicity stamps upon the social actors. My analysis of *social movements* will answer this question in essence, since such movements are the confrontation of agents of the social classes seeking control over historicity and over the mode of society's production of itself. This is a theme that corresponds to the circularity of activity and historicity that I have recognized as being one of the faces of the sociology of historicity.

What is there that corresponds in the same way to its other face, to the recognition of tension and rending? The ultimate mark of participation in historicity is the distance that remains between the actor and the roles he plays, not only in social exchanges of all kinds, but even within social movements, insofar as these latter have no concrete existence unless they are also political – or even military – organizations and units.

Instead of the call to *liberty* referring to some human essence beyond all social determinisms, a procedure both unacceptable and incomprehensible to the sociologist, instead of liberty being no more than the uncertainty lying at the intersection of a number of independent series, liberty is transcendence toward a historicity that no actor ever has the right to appropriate completely, that no form of social organization, no system of political decision making, no system of class relations can totally exhaust, because they are all stages of historicity's redescent toward the functioning of society.

Transcendence and not possession. The moment the actor identifies himself with historicity he is confusing it with an organization, which may be without social consequences if that confusion is perpetrated merely by an individual actor enclosed within a personal utopia, but which produces the most dramatic effects when the holder of a power, reversing the movement of analysis, identifies historicity with order and identifies himself with that now sanctified order.

10

The Concept of Society

Niklas Luhmann

I

If one considers sciences such as biology, psychology or sociology from the distance of an uninvolved observer one might conclude that biology has to do with life, psychology with the soul or consciousness, and sociology with society. A closer look makes it apparent, however, that these disciplines have characteristic difficulties with concepts intended to designate the unity of their object. The concept of autopoiesis is addressed directly to this problem. It was originally introduced by Humberto Maturana with respect to life,[1] but it may well be applicable to consciousness and to society. It is, however, a concept which plays almost no role in the daily business of these disciplines, so that we are left with the question "why is there this particular problem of designating the unity of the object of these disciplines by a scientific concept?"

It is therefore not surprising that sociology also has difficulties in designating the unity of its object. Should we say "social"? But the concept is too nice, too friendly, too warmhearted. What about the unsocial, crime, Durkheim's anomie? We could try the concept of society, and in fact what we find in other disciplines or in public discourse is the habit of counting sociology among the social sciences. But if one looks for a concept of society then the difficulties really begin. The word is used. One looks in vain, however, for a concept which designates the intended object with an accuracy sufficient for theoretical purposes.

Originally there may have been historical reasons for this abstention. When sociology started to organize itself as an academic discipline at the end of the last century the concept of society was already available but had been stamped by its own history and thus was problematic, even unusable some considered,

Translated by David Roberts.

for the purposes of the new discipline. Either the concept functioned as the component of a distinction: state and society or society and community, which caused what it was supposed to designate to disappear into the difference – or should I say into the fold? Or it was misused for political ideas and consequently ideologically disputed. If one did not want to follow "formal sociology" by doing without the term completely, then it needed to be given precision against its own history. This, however, never really succeeded.

Well, those were the problems of our honored classics. They are not ours. If sociology is still afraid of this hurdle there must be other reasons at work. It seems to me that we can speak of "obstacles épistémologiques" in exactly the sense Gaston Bachelard intended by this concept.[2] There are certain advantages in traditional expectations in relation to the concept which cannot be replaced (or only with difficulty, only in the context of a completely new paradigm).

I would like to indicate what I consider the three most important of these obstacles:

1   The first concerns the assumption that society consists of human beings or of relations between human beings. I call this the humanist prejudice. But how is it to be understood? Does society consist of arms and legs, thoughts and enzymes? Does the barber cut society's hair? Does it sometimes need insulin? What kind of operation characterizes society if the chemistry of the cell is as much part of it as the alchemy of unconscious repression? Obviously the humanist deliberately clings to conceptual blurring. But then one must ask: why? The theorist becomes the patient himself.

2   The second prejudice which blocks conceptual development consists in the presumption of a territorial multiplicity of societies. China is one, Brazil another, Paraguay is one and so too then is Uruguay. All efforts at accurate delimitation have failed, whether they rely on state organization or on language, culture, tradition. Of course there are evident differences between living conditions in these territories but such differences have to be explained as differences within society and not presumed as differences between societies. Or does sociology want to let geography solve its central problem?

3   The third prejudice is of an epistemological nature. It is the result of the distinction between subject and object. The epistemology which was dominant in our century thought of subject and object (like thought and being, cognition and object) as separate and considered observation and description of the world as extra as possible; indeed, cognition was only recognized as such when every circular interlocking with its object was avoided. Only subjects have the privilege of self-reference. Things are how they are.

Society, however, is quite evidently a self-describing object. Theories of society are theories in society about society. If this is epistemologically forbidden there can be no adequate concept of society. In other words: the concept of society has to be formed autologically. It must contain itself in itself. Outside of sociology this is a common occurrence. The concept of autologic – which is itself an autological concept – derives from linguistics. Names like Wittgenstein or Heinz von Foerster, George Spencer Brown or Gotthard Günther testify to the currency of this insight. The linguistic turn in philosophy makes it inescapable. Equally Quine's call for a naturalized epistemology. Why then should sociology show itself resistant when its object makes its relevance particularly clear. Perhaps for this very reason! Perhaps sociology knows it too well – or too critically – to feel comfortable in it. If that is the case then sociology must be encouraged. It does not have to end in affirmation, consensus, conformism. On the contrary: the theological prototype of the observer of the system in the system is the Devil! Or Perseus, who decapitated Medusa with that ease and indirectness presented so beautifully by Italo Calvino in his *Lezioni Americane*.[3]

Trying to keep one's head above water by means of micro-empirical research is certainly not sufficient, nor is it sufficient, as in Frankfurt, to cultivate fear of contact, to persist in resolute resignation or to attack everyone who does not believe in the utopia of a normatively paid up rationality. The problem is rather a problem of theory design. Developments in interdisciplinary or trans-disciplinary fields such as cognitive sciences or cybernetics, systems theory, evolution theory, information theory offer sufficient stimuli to make the attempt worthwhile.

II

For this attempt I propose that we start from the concept of system. That does not say much yet, as this concept is used in very different senses. A first precision, which immediately leads to unfamiliar territory, consists of under-standing system not as a particular type of *object* but as a particular distinction – namely that between system and environment. This has to be grasped exactly. To this end I take the conceptual scheme with which George Spencer Brown introduces his *Laws of Form*.[4] A system is the form of a distinction, possesses therefore two sides: the system (as the inside of the form) and the environment (as the outside of the form). Only the *two* sides together constitute the distinc-tion, constitute the form, constitute the concept. The environment is thus for this form just as important, just as indispensable as the system itself. As distinc-tion the form is closed: "Distinction is perfect continence" in Spencer Brown's words.[5] That is to say: everything which can be observed and described with this distinction belongs either to the system or to the environment. Certain peculiarities make themselves apparent. Does the unity of the system belong to the system or to the environment? And where do you find the boundary of the form? The boundary between system and environment separates the two sides of the form, marks the unity of the form and is for this reason not to be found on either side of the form. The boundary exists only as an instruction to cross it – whether from inside to outside or from outside to inside.

Let us put these difficult questions to one side for the moment. They cannot be dealt with on the level of development of a theory of such low complexity.

Instead let us take up the question of how form, of how the difference between system and environment is produced. The conceptual schema of Spencer Brown's calculus of form presupposes time, works with time, explains itself through time – similar to Hegel's logic.

Here I have chosen the concept of production (or poiesis as distinct from praxis) deliberately, since it presupposes distinction as form and asserts that a work can be produced even if the producer cannot produce all the necessary causes himself. This fits, as can readily be seen, the distinction between system and environment. The system disposes over internal and external causes for the production of its product, and it can use the internal causes in such a way that there results sufficient possibilities of combining external and internal causes.

The work which is produced, however, is the system itself, or more exactly, the form of the system, the difference between system and environment. This is exactly what the concept of autopoiesis is intended to designate. It is explicitly set against a possible concept of autopraxis. It is not a question of self-satisfying activities like smoking, swimming, chatting, reasoning. The concept of autopoiesis, then, necessarily leads on to the difficult and often misunderstood concept of the *operative closure of the system.* Applied to production it of course does not mean causal isolation, autarchy, cognitive solipsism, as opponents have often supposed. It is rather the necessary consequence of the trivial (conceptually tautological) fact that no system can operate outside of its boundaries. This leads to the conclusion – which forms the first stage of a clarification of the concept of society – that we are dealing here (that is, if we want to use the form-concept of system) with an *operatively closed autopoietic system.*

On this level of abstraction it is not immediately clear what that means. It means that we have placed ourselves on the other side of those epistemological obstacles which appeared so problematic, since operative closure excludes human beings as well as countries from the system of society. And it includes instead operations of self-observation and of self-description. The humanists and geographers can draw comfort, however, from the fact that the environment is an indispensable component of the distinction. It belongs to the form of the system. Excluding human beings as living and conscious systems and countries with their geographic and demographic particularities from society does not mean that they are lost to theory. They simply are not to be found where they were previously thought to be – with disastrous consequences for the development of theory. They are to be found not in society but in its environment.

III

The most important piece of work on the concept of society remains to be done. It is posed by the question "which is the operation which produces the system of society and, we must add, produces it from its products, that is, reproduces it?"

It must be a precisely identified manner of operating. If, to be safe, one names many operations – such as thought and action, structure formation and processes – the desired unity disappears in the pallor and insipidity of "and". ("Ands" should be forbidden in the technical requirements of theory construction.) We have to take risks in determining the manner of operation by which society produces and reproduces itself. Otherwise the concept loses all contours.

My proposal is that we make the concept of communication the basis and thereby switch sociological theory from the concept of action to the concept of system. This enables us to present the social system as an operatively closed system consisting only of its own operations reproduced by communications from communications. With the concept of action external references can hardly be avoided. An action requires, since it must be attributed, reference to socially constituted complexes: a subject, an individual, for all practical purposes even a living body, that is, a place in space. Only with the help of the concept of communication can we think of a social system as an autopoietic system, which consists only of elements, namely communications, which produce and reproduce it through the network of precisely these elements, that is, through communication.

The theoretical decisions for a conception of society as an autopoietic system and for the characterization of the operation which reproduces the system as communication thus belong together. They are mutually conditioning. This means in turn that the concept of communication becomes a decisive factor in determining the concept of society. According to the way communication is defined, so too is society – definition understood here in the exact sense of the determination of boundaries. In other words, theory construction must be carried out with two eyes, one directed to the concept of society, the other to the concept of communication. Only thus does it gain the necessary sharpness of focus.

The concept of communication is already altered by this constellation. One cannot reduce it to communicative action and register the participation of others, either as mere effect of this action or as normative implication in Habermas's sense. Nor can communication be comprehended as transmission of information from one place to another. Such conceptions presuppose in one form or another carriers of the events, who are not themselves constituted by communication. The combination systems theory/communications theory requires on the contrary a concept of communication which allows us to say that all communication is produced only by communication – of course in an environment which enables and tolerates it.

Here we can utilize a distinction going back to antiquity and customary since Karl Bühler. I reformulate it as the distinction between information, communicative act (Mitteilung) and understanding. A communication only comes about when these three aspects can be synthesized. As opposed to simple perceptions of behavior, understanding must be based on a distinction between the communicative act and information. This is our starting point. Without such a primary distinction no communication can come about. If this precondition is satisfied, and that is necessarily the case with the use of language, further communication can occupy itself with itself. It is now, and only now, rich and complex enough for that. It can occupy itself with the information or with the reasons why just this is said here and now; or with the difficulties of understanding the meaning of the communication or finally with the next step: whether the proffered meaning is to be accepted or rejected. The distinction between information, communicative act, and understanding is therefore a distinction which produces distinctions, which, once made, keep the system going. And communication is nothing other than that operation which comes out of such transformation of distinctions into distinctions.

It is important to bear in mind that the individual communicative event is completed by understanding. This does not yet decide the question, whether what is understood forms the basis of further communication or not. That may be the case – or not. Communications can be accepted or rejected. Any other conception would have the absurd consequence that rejected communications were not actually communications. This is the reason why it is false to impute to communications an inherent, quasi-teleological tendency to consensus. If that were the case, everything would already have been over long ago and the world as silent as it once was. Communication, however, does not exhaust itself, it produces rather, by means of self-provocation as it were, at every step a bifurcation of acceptance and rejection. Every communicative event closes and opens the system. And only thanks to this bifurcation can there also be history, whose course depends on which path is taken: the yes-path or the no-path.

IV

If this concept of communication is accepted, then all the customary epistemological obstacles of customary social theory are dissolved in one go; and their place is taken by problems which are better suited to theoretically informed scientific research.

On this basis it is clear that concrete human beings are not a part of society but a part of its environment. Equally it would make little sense to say that society consists of "relations" between human beings. The concept of communication contains a very much more precise proposal (and possibly reconstructs what normal sociologists mean when they speak of "relations"). It is not sufficient for instance that someone sees or hears someone else – unless he observes his behavior with the aid of the distinction between information and communicative act. To speak or write about somebody is not sufficient to establish this relation to him as a social relation. Only communication itself is a social operation.

The concept of territorial boundaries is equally dispensable and with it the assumption of a multiplicity of regional societies. The meaning that space and boundaries have in space arises from their communicative use but communication itself does not have a place-in-space. It may be dependent through its material substratum on spatial conditions. But whereas spatial conditions are one of the most important, even the only means of expression of social order for animal societies, the significance of spatial conditions for the evolution of socio-cultural society has diminished as a result of language, writing, and telecommunications to such an extent that we must assume that in present conditions communication determines the remaining meaning of space and not inversely that space enables and limits the possibility of communication.

Finally, the concept of communication brings out clearly that society is a self-observing and a self-describing system. Even simple communication is only possible in a recursive network of earlier and later communications. Such a network can become its own theme, can inform itself about its own communication, can doubt information, refuse acceptance, give norms to reliable or non-reliable information etc. – as long as this occurs in the operative form of communication. This makes a double state of affairs evident: that society is a self-observing and describing system and that it can use its own manner of operation and must use it in order to carry out such self-referential operations. And this applies also to science and also to sociology. All communications about society are conditioned by society. There is no external observer with any even partially adequate competence. Although, of course, each individual consciousness can think about what it considers society to be, each immune system can observe itself with respect to illnesses which only arise on the basis of the social life of human beings etc.

We can now determine the concept of society as an intermediary result. Society is the comprehensive system of all communications, which reproduce themselves autopoietically through the recursive network of communications which produce new (and always other) communications. The emergence of such a system includes communications, since they are only internally capable of continuation. And it excludes everything else. The reproduction of such a system thus requires the capacity to discriminate between system and environment. Communications can recognize communications and distinguish them from other states of affairs, which belong to the environment in the sense that one can certainly communicate about them but not with them.

This leads to the question: "what changes when we use this concept? What becomes visible or invisible if we observe with the aid of the form thereby given? Or even, if I may employ a formulation from Italo Calvino's *Lezioni Americane*: does this concept offer us access 'alla totalita del dicibile e del non decibile'?[6]"

To start, we lose the possibility of making statements about "man" (in the singular). This appears to discomfort many. But if it is the case that "man" has only been with us since the eighteenth century, there are good reasons for saying: forget it! He belongs to an age of transition in which it was not yet possible to describe modern society adequately, and where instead one had to take refuge in illusions about the future in order to preserve the hope of an improvable unity by means of the semantic association of "society," "the future" and "man." This projection of an imaginary man (or even worse, of an image of man) had to give up determining man through his difference to minerals, plants, and animals. It presented itself as a concept without a counter concept, that is to say: with the high probability of a moral burden through the distinction good men/bad men.

If this can be sacrificed – with a light or a heavy heart according to the strength of the need to be good: what has been gained by proposing instead a differential concept, that is, a form of the concept of society which compels us to distribute everything between system and environment and to avoid statements about the unity of the difference?

I want to discuss this question with reference to three examples – language, the relation between individual and society, and rationality.

V

As regards language, a system-theoretical concept of society suggests that we give up the notion that language is a system. However much linguists in the wake of Saussure cling to this notion because it appears to ensure the academic self-sufficiency of their discipline, one can hardly comprehend both language and society as system. The degree of overlap would be too great without leading to a congruence of the concepts, since there is also non-linguistic communication. The relation between the two systems would remain unclear. Linguists, of course, can take pleasure in the thought that they are not sociologists. The differentiation of disciplines is not, however, a sufficient answer to such questions of substance.

If the concept of system is no longer to be applied to language, this, of course, does not mean that the phenomenon of language loses significance. The contrary is true. The empty place in theory can be filled in a different way with the aid of the concept of structural coupling. This concept was introduced by Humberto Maturana and its purpose is to designate how operatively closed autopoietic systems can maintain themselves in an environment, which on the one hand is the precondition of the autopoiesis of the system but on the other does not intervene in this autopoiesis.[7] The problem, which is solved by this concept, consists in this, that the system can only be determined through its own structures and indeed only through structures which it constructs and can alter through its own operations; at the same time it cannot be disputed that this kind of operative autonomy presupposes a cooperation, an accommodation on the part of the environment. Life does not exist in just any physical or chemical environmental conditions, even if the world cannot determine where the hare runs. As Maturana puts it, structural couplings stand in an orthogonal relation to the autopoiesis of the system. They contribute no operations with the capacity to reproduce the system itself, that is to say in our case: no communications. They stimulate the system, however, to irritations, they disturb the system in a manner which is then given an internal form with which the system can work. We could think here of Piaget's conceptual pair assimilation/accommodation or also of the way in which functionalist psychology speaks of generalized expectations and disappointment of expectations.

Applied to communication, we can say with the help of this concept that as a result of its striking characteristics language serves the structural coupling of communication and consciousness. Language keeps communication and consciousness, hence also society and individual, separate. A thought can never *be* communication just as communication can never be a thought. In the recursive network of its own operations communication always has different preceding and following events to the sequence in the field of attention of an individual consciousness. There is no overlap on the operative level. We are dealing with two different operatively closed systems. What is decisive is that *despite this* language is able to couple the systems and precisely in their *different* manner of operation. Language achieves this through its artificial noticeability in the acoustic medium of noises and then in the optical medium of written signs. It can fascinate and center consciousness and at the same time reproduce communication. Accordingly its function does not lie in the mediation of references to the external world but solely in structural coupling.

This, however, is only the one side of its achievement. Like all structural couplings language has an inclusive and an exclusive effect. It increases the irritability of consciousness through communication and the irritability of society through consciousness, which transforms internal states into language and into understanding or non-understanding. This means at the same time that *other* sources of irritation are *excluded* for the system of society, that is, language isolates society from almost all environmental events of a physical, chemical, or living nature with the sole exception of irritation through impulses of consciousness. Just as the brain is almost completely isolated from everything that occurs in the environment by the extremely small physical capacity for resonance of eye and ear, so too the system of society is almost completely isolated from everything that occurs in the world – with a small range of stimuli which are channelled through consciousness. What applies to the brain also applies to society: this almost complete isolation is the condition of operative closure with the possibility of the construction of high internal complexity.

VI

These reflections already take us into the vicinity of the question of the relation between individual and society. Let me first recall the corresponding epistemological obstacle: sociology cannot really comprehend the individual as part of society but it cannot separate itself from this notion. Sociology has been wrestling with this problem ever since it became an academic discipline. By contrast the concept of society presented here proceeds from a complete separation of individual and society. And my thesis is that on this basis a theoretical programme is possible which takes the individual seriously.

To put it in the harshest form: the "participation" of the individual in society is excluded. There is no communication between individual and society, since communication is always an internal operation of the social system. Society can never reach beyond itself with its own operations and take hold of the individual; it can only reproduce with its own operations its own operations. Society cannot operate outside its own boundaries – that ought to be easily understandable (but why is it not accepted?). The same applies in turn for life and the individual consciousness. Here too the system-reproducing operations remain in the system. No thought can leave the consciousness which it reproduces. And should not we add: fortunately? For what would happen and how would I be able to develop individuality if *others* with *their* thoughts could move *mine?* And how are we to imagine society as the hypnosis of all by all?

Of course it is possible for the individual to have his own conception of society. And above all it is possible for communication to use persons as addressees and as themes. But then we should speak of persons in the strict ancient sense and not of individuals (human beings, consciousness, subjects, etc.). The names and forenames used in communication have not the least similarity with what they designate. Nobody is "I". As little as the word apple is an apple.

Taking individuality seriously means comprehending individuals as the product of their own activity, as self-referential historical machines, which determine with each auto-operation the starting condition for further operations and are able to do this *only* through their *own* operations.

There is thus no normative integration of individuals into society. There are, in other words, no norms from which one can diverge if one wants to. And there is no consensus, if that is understood to mean that the empirical circumstances, in which individuals find themselves, somehow concur. There are only corresponding observational schemata in which an observer self-determines the observation that behavior agrees or diverges from a norm. And this observer can also be a communicating system – a court, the mass media, etc. If we want to ask what the basis in reality of norms or of imputed consensus is, then we must observe an observer; and if we give up accepting God as the observer of the world, then there are several other possibilities.

Only if one accepts the theory in all its radicality is it possible to see what the complimentary concept of structural coupling achieves. It explains why despite this operative closure things do not occur randomly in the world. Structural couplings ensure the cumulation of certain, and the exclusion of other, irritations. From this there arise trends in the self-determination of structures which depend on the particular irritations with which they have to deal. Organisms are adapted to the gravitational pull of the earth, often in a quite specific fashion. A whale crushes its own internal organs through its pure weight if it is not in water but beached. A human child, which is constantly exposed to the strange sounds which function as speech, learns to speak. Every society socializes individuals on the other side of its structural couplings, and as society, it is exactly adjusted to doing this. Language is binarily coded with the possibility of divergent behavior. Society places in this fashion (completely uncontrollable) individuals in an optional schema. It concedes as freedom what it cannot in any case alter: and this in such a sharply schematized form that communication about yes and no, about conforming or non-conforming behavior can be continued however the individual decides. We recognize here in evolutionary terms extremely improbable, highly selective arrangements: the separation and connection of systems, of freedom and order.

VII

Freedom and order – they were the terms of the problem (or the "variables") of the last convincing concept of rationality brought forth by Europe. The liberal credo could be formulated in a manner akin to Leibniz: as much freedom as possible with as much order as necessary. Since then there have only been products of disintegration, whether in the form of distinguishing several concepts of rationality without determining rationality as such (Weber, Habermas), whether in the form of the distinction between rationality and irrationality which acknowledges the justification of both sides of the distinction – but again: without indicating what is the nature of the assertion of this distinction; or to put it differently, what is designated by its form. To this corresponds the evaporation of the concept of reason: a quality of living human creatures has become an only approximately attainable – in the literal sense – utopian ideal.

It is not readily apparent whether a systems-theoretical concept of society could help us to escape this dilemma at all or how. In any case there is no way back to the old European rational continuum of being and thought or of nature and action, whereby rationality lay exactly in the convergence of the two sides, that is, thought corresponded in its own fashion to being or action in its own fashion to nature. All the same we note in distinctions such as being/thought and nature/action a peculiar asymmetry which seems to conceal, from a present perspective, the structure of rationality. If we are to assume that thought should correspond *in its own being* to being and action *in its own nature* to nature, then it is clear that the distinction appears again on one of its two sides in thought or in action. George Spencer Brown calls the operation which realizes such a structure, a re-entry of form in the form – or the re-entry of the distinction in what it has distinguished.[8] The context of the calculus of form in which this occurs suggests we should think of the dissolution of a paradox, namely the paradox of the use of a distinction which cannot distinguish itself. Whatever the case, with the help of this active (but not violent) interpretation of the old European conceptuality of rationality we can pose the question, whether it must remain tied to anthropological (or humanistic) concepts like thought and action or whether we cannot at least detach the figure of re-entry. This is a step which is easy for systems theory since it determines the form of the system through the (asymmetrical) distinction between system and environment.

Such re-entry is inescapable not only for systems of consciousness but also for the system of society. The operatively accomplished differentiation between system and environment returns in the system as the distinction between self-reference and external reference. Communication can only occur if the system avoids confusion between its own operation and about what is communicated. The communicative act and information must be distinguished and remain distinct, otherwise no communication will occur. The system operates by means of the continual reproduction of the difference between self-reference and external reference. That *is* its autopoiesis. That alone ensures its operative closure. Correspondingly, consciousness externalizes continually and in each operation what its brain, the organ of self-observation of the states of its organism, suggests. Consciousness *must* equally distinguish continually between self-reference and external reference and observe itself-in-distinction-from-the-environment by means of this distinction. Precisely because operative interventions in the environment are impossible, self-observation by means of this distinction is the compelling condition of the autopoiesis of the system; and this applies as much to society as to consciousness.

If we are looking for a conceptuality which would replace the cosmological rationality of the old world, this is where we should have to start. The result, however, would be an operatively induced "as it is" – rationality, quite unideal and without an option for non-rational operations. It would amount to no more than the continual internally reproduced double orientation to what the system identifies as itself and as environment. This would be the rationality of a first order observer. We only arrive at a more demanding conceptuality on the level of second order observation. This presupposes that the system observes itself during the execution of re-entry. It must accordingly take the distinction self-reference/external reference as its basis and carry this distinction over into its self-reference. It must be clearly aware not only that the differentiation of the system from the rest of the world (which then becomes environment) is accomplished through its own operations and could not come about without this Münchhausen-like self-activity. It must also be aware that the distinction between self-reference and external reference, which is thereby made possible, is a distinction of its own and requires operations of its own. Self-reference/external reference re-enters the difference into what it has distinguished. It is the difference through which the system assures its own unity. With this insight the world becomes a construction, whichever distinction forms it. Indisputably the world is now reality, since the distinguishing and constructing operations have already been accomplished; and indisputably the world is now construction, for without a splitting through a distinction, which can be applied in very different ways (different for each system), there would be nothing to see. We thus find ourselves in a situation which philosophers like Fichte and Derrida have used in order to drive philosophy to despair. If we want to see ourselves as successors to the old European conceptuality, rationality can only be comprehended from this situation. But how?

The best known way out is to insist on an external reference. Or, what amounts to the same thing: to switch to meta-levels. We can adduce Russell, Tarski, Gödel here. Fundamentally, however, that is still thinking in terms of a theology of grace. As far as I can see, as a non-philosopher, even more exact analysis of the so-called problem of reference has only decomposed this problem. Think only of Quine's critique of logical empiricism and its assumption that reference, truth, and meaning (ens et verum et bonum?) converge. We have already drawn the conclusion: the *problem of reference* must be replaced by the *distinction* between self-reference and external reference – by a distinction, which, like enzymes in cells, is at the same time product and code of the corresponding operations of the system. All the same, if we conceive of society as that system which is above all confronted with expectations of rationality, then the way out through externalizing or through meta-levels (Gödelization) is anyway unusable. For where would there be a higher level or an external world which could have a redemptive or conditioning effect?

Does this lead to the conclusion that society finally is that system against which all rationality has to prove itself rational?

I must content myself with posing this question and, as at an auction, wait for other offers.

Notes

1   See Humberto R. Maturana, *Erkennen: Die Organisation und Verköperung von Wirklichkeit* (Braunschweig, 1982).

2   Gaston Bachelard, *Le formation de l'esprit scientifique: Contribution à une psychoanalyse de la connaisance objective* (Paris, 1938).

3   Italo Calvino, *Lezioni Americane* (Milan, 1988), p. 6ff.

4   George Spencer Brown (1969), *Laws of Form* (New York, 1979).

5   Ibid., p. 1.

6   Italo Calvino, *Lezioni Americane*, p. 72. Cf. also Nikias Luhmann and Peter Fuchs. *Reden und Schweigen* (Frankfurt, 1989).

7   "The human kind" of the eighteenth century still had this meaning, whereas "humankind" according to the directives of American copy-editors serves today to avoid the sexist expression "mankind".

8   Humberto R. Maturana, *Erkennen: Die Organisation und Verköperung von Wirklichkeit*, pp. 143ff., 243ff.

9   See George Spencer Brown, *Laws of Form*, pp. 56 ff., 69ff.

11

Individualization and "Precarious Freedoms": Perspectives and Controversies of a Subject-orientated Sociology

Ulrich Beck and Elisabeth Beck-Gernsheim

What Does 'Individualization of Lifestyles' Mean?

'Only the day before yesterday, only four years ago, a grand experiment for humanity, that had lasted forty years, came to an end here.' These words were spoken in Luther's town of Wittenberg by Friedrich Schorlemmer at the end of 1993.

> Seventeen million Germans lived in the walled province in enforced collectivization. A one-party state was seen as the highest form of freedom, individualization was damned as subjectivism. A risk-taking approach to the future was rejected in the name of 'scientific' optimism. The 'victors of history' were to set the norms and strive towards a unitary society (the socialist community). Human beings, understood as ceaselessly active communal creatures, were fed on the safe goal of communism, which was guaranteed by scientific laws. People were not allowed to decide anything because there was nothing left to decide, because history had already decided everything 'up there'. But they did not need to decide, either . . .
>
> Now, in freedom, they may and must decide for themselves; all the existing institutions have collapsed, all the old certainties are gone. . . The joy of freedom is at the same time a falling into a void. Now let everyone look after himself. What are the rules? Who's in charge? Those who have, and know how to increase what they have. Seventeen million people have reached this point, but

the West's caravan moves on, calling to us: 'Come with us. We know the way. We know the goal. We don't know any way. We don't know any goal. What is certain? That everything's uncertain, precarious. Enjoy our lack of ties as freedom.'[1]

The development in China is different, yet in many ways similar. There, too, the collective system that provided a guaranteed income, the 'iron rice-bowl', is breaking down. Earlier, people had hardly any scope for choice in private or professional life, but the minimal safety net of Communism offered them state-subsidized accommodation, training and health care. It is this state care from the cradle to the grave, tied to the work collective in the factory or on the land, that is now disintegrating. Its place is being taken by contracts linking income and job security to ability and performance. People are now expected to take their lives into their own hands and to pay a market price for services they receive. 'The constant refrain among urban Chinese is that they can no longer keep up with the quickened pace of life. They are confused by shifting values and outlooks on such fundamentals as careers, marriage and family relations'.[2]

Whatever we consider – God, nature, truth, science, technology, morality, love, marriage – modern life is turning them all into 'precarious freedoms'. All metaphysics and transcendence, all necessity and certainty is being replaced by artistry. In the most public and the most private ways we are becoming – helplessly – high-wire dancers in the circus tent. And many of us fall. Not only in the West, but in the countries that have abruptly opened their doors to Western ways of life. People in the former GDR, in Poland, Russia or China, are caught up in a dramatic 'plunge into modernity'.

Such examples, seemingly remote to citizens of the old Federal German Republic, point nevertheless to a dynamic that is familiar to us, too. Schorlemmer's address contains the catchword 'individualization'. This concept implies a group of social developments and experiences characterized, above all, by two meanings. In intellectual debate as in reality these meanings constantly intersect and overlap (which, hardly surprisingly, has given rise to a whole series of misunderstandings and controversies). On one hand, individualization means the *dis*integration of previously existing social forms – for example, the increasing fragility of such categories as class and social status, gender roles, family, neighbourhood, etc. Or, as in the case of the GDR and other states of the Eastern Bloc, it means the collapse of state-sanctioned normal biographies, frames of reference, role models. Wherever such tendencies towards disintegrations show themselves the question also arises: which new modes of life are coming into being where the old ones, ordained by religion, tradition or the state, are breaking down?

The answer points to the second aspect of individualization. It is, simply, that in modern societies new demands, controls and constraints are being imposed on individuals. Through the job market, the welfare state and institutions, people are tied into a network of regulations, conditions, provisos. From pension rights to insurance protection, from educational grants to tax rates: all these are institutional reference points marking out the horizon within which modern thinking, planning and action must take place.

Individualization in this sense, therefore, certainly does not mean an 'un-fettered logic of action, juggling in a virtually empty space'; nor does it mean mere 'subjectivity', an attitude which refuses to see that 'beneath the surface of life is a highly efficient, densely-woven institutional society'.[3] On the contrary, the space in which modern subjects deploy their options is anything but a non-social sphere. The density of regulations informing modern society is well known, even notorious (from the MOT test and the tax return to the laws governing the sorting of refuse). In its overall effect it is a work of art of labyrinthine complexity, which accompanies us literally from the cradle to the grave.

The decisive feature of these modern regulations or guidelines is that, far more than earlier, individuals must, in part, supply them for themselves, import them into their biographies through their own actions. This has much to do with the fact that traditional guidelines often contained severe restric-tions or even prohibitions on action (such as the ban on marriage, in pre-industrial societies, which prevented members of non-property-owning groups from marrying; or the travel restrictions and the recent obstructions to marriage in the Eastern Bloc states, which forbade contact with the 'class enemy'). By contrast, the institutional pressures in modern Western society tend rather to be offers of services or incentives to action – take, for example, the welfare state, with its unemployment benefit, student grants or mortgage relief. To simplify: one was born into traditional society and its preconditions (such as social estate and religion). For modern social advantages one has to *do* something, to make an active effort. One has to win, know how, to assert oneself in the competition for limited resources – and not only once, but day after day.

The normal biography thus becomes the 'elective biography', the 'reflexive biography', the 'do-it-yourself biography'.[4] This does not necessarily happen by choice, nor does it necessarily succeed. The do-it-yourself biography is always a 'risk biography', indeed a 'tightrope biography', a state of permanent (partly overt, partly concealed) endangerment. The façade of prosperity, consumption, glitter can often mask the nearby precipice. The wrong choice of career or just the wrong field, compounded by the downward spiral of private misfortune, divorce, illness, the repossessed home – all this is called merely bad luck. Such cases bring into the open what was always secretly on the cards: the do-it-yourself biography can swiftly become the breakdown biography. The pre-ordained, unquestioned, often enforced ties of earlier times are replaced by the principle: 'until further notice'. [. . .]

Perspectives and Controversies of an Individual-orientated Sociology

All sociology splits into two opposed views of the same thing. The social dimension can be regarded either from the standpoint of *individuals* or from that of the *whole* (society, state, the common good, class, group, organization, etc.).[5] Both standpoints are founded on the structure of social action, which can be analysed either in terms of the agents or in terms of the social structure. However, that both standpoints are equally possible, equally necessary or equally original does not mean that they are equally valuable or have equal rights; still less does it mean that they are identical. Rather, each of these viewpoints relativizes, criticizes the other (subtly, but with abundant consequences): anyone who analyses society from the standpoint of the individual does not accept its form at a particular time as a preordained, unalterable datum, but calls it into question. Here, sociological thought is not far from the 'art of mistrust', to use a formulation of Peter Berger,[6] adapted from Nietzsche. Indeed, it tends to 'destabilize' existing power relationships, as Zygmunt Bauman, for example, puts it.[7] By contrast, where the so-called 'operational requirements' of society (or subdivisions of it) provide the framework of reference, they are often presented to the outside world simply as the inner happiness of the ego. To apply this happiness there are funnels – known as 'duties' – and institutions for pouring it through these funnels, for purposes of intimidation: schools, courts, marriages, organizations, etc.

The prevailing sociology has usually made things easy for itself by cutting off the questions that arise here with the strict injunction, backed up by thick volumes, that individuals can only be or become individuals within society. In this way they continually repress the idea: what would happen if these individuals wanted a different society, or even a different type of society?

The old sociology, still well-endowed with university chairs, is armed against this idea: the general interest, congealed as structure, is condensed and glorified as Parsonian 'functional pre-requisites'. From such prerequisites – as from a cornucopia of secularized ethical duties – pour forth 'role patterns', 'functions', 'demands', 'subsystems', equally remote from God and the earth, divorced from action and yet its pre-condition, which are to be applied as a standard to the confusion and refractoriness of individuals, to yield judgements such as 'normal', 'deviant', 'erroneous' and 'absurd'.

Accordingly, the 'individualistic' perspective on society has up to now been usually dismissed as presumptuous and self-contradictory. There is talk – using an up-to-date idiom – of 'demand inflation' and the 'ego society'. The decay of values is deplored, while it is forgotten that such decay is as old as Socrates. The GDR – up to now – has had exemplary experience of the inverse question and has foundered on it: what happens to institutions without individuals? What does it mean when individuals withdraw their assent from the institutional elite? The same question was urgently posed in Italy in 1993 (and in France, Sweden, Finland, Germany, the USA, etc.) and the answer was the same: the political systems tremble. Where the functionalist viewpoint, based on system theory, is dominant, a 'subject-orientated' sociology often appears not only deviant but subversive. For it can sometimes reveal that the party and institutional elites are riders without horses.

Nor is it true, of course, that both conceptions of the social order are incomplete in themselves and need to supplement each other. But before such a need for harmony smooths over a conflict which has not yet been fought out openly, it should be pointed out here that for some centuries the view of the totality has suppressed that of individuals. In view of this it is time to turn the tables and ask what kind of society comes into being *after* the demise of the great political camps and the party-political consensus.

In other words: the two points of view remain until further notice incompatible; they are even becoming, through a modernization which is setting individuals and their demands and dilemmas *free*, more and more irreconcilable, and are giving rise to antithetical explanations, methods, theories and intellectual traditions.

It will be objected that this is not a meaningful antithesis. Entities which presuppose each other analytically, individuals and society, cannot be described as a social conflict. Moreover, both viewpoints lay claim to both viewpoints. He who embraces the 'whole' (of society) – the functionality of social formations – in his field of vision, self-evidently claims to include the standpoint of individuals as well. If necessary, this is presented as the morally correct standpoint that must be asserted against the false self-consciousness of individuals in their own well-understood interests. Whereas, conversely, every variant of subject- or individual-orientated sociology naturally also offers statements and explanations about the intrinsic reality of social formations and systems, their structure, stage-management, etc.

The antithesis between the individual- and system-based viewpoints should be understood as a historical development. If, in traditional, pre-industrial societies, we can still – perhaps – assume a fairly balanced relationship between the two frames of reference, this pre-stabilized harmony breaks down with the unfolding of modernity. This is the central theme of sociology in Emile Durkheim and Georg Simmel. But both still assume that it is possible to integrate individualized society, as it were transcendentally, through values. Such a possibility, however, became more unrealistic the more individuals were released from classical forms of integration in groups, including family and class. What is emerging today can be called, with Hans Magnus Enzensberger, 'the average exoticism of everyday life':

> It is most obvious in the provinces. Market towns in Lower Bavaria, villages in the Eifel Hills, small towns in Holstein are populated by figures no one could have dreamed of only thirty years ago. For example, golf-playing butchers, wives imported from Thailand, counter-intelligence agents with allotments, Turkish Mullahs, women chemists in Nicaragua committees, vagrants driving Mercedes, autonomists with organic gardens, weapons-collecting tax officials, peacock-breeding smallholders, militant lesbians, Tamil ice-cream sellers, classics scholars

in commodity futures trading, mercenaries on home leave, extremist animal-rights activists, cocaine dealers with solariums, dominas with clients in top management, computer freaks commuting between Californian data banks and nature reserves in Hesse, carpenters who supply golden doors to Saudi Arabia, art forgers, Karl May researchers, bodyguards, jazz experts, euthanasists and porno producers. Into the shoes of the village idiots and the oddballs, of the eccentrics and the queer fish, has stepped the average deviationist, who no longer stands out at all from millions like him.[8]

Under such conditions, institutions are founded on antiquated images of individuals and their social situations. To avoid endangering their own power, the administrators of these institutions maintain the status quo at all costs (supported by a sociology operating with the old conceptual stereotypes). An amusing consequence of this is that the political class regards the individuals 'out there' as no less stupid and brazen than the society of individuals considers the political class. The question as to which of them is right can – in principle – be easily decided. The idea that only the party elite and the bureaucratic apparatus knows what is what and that everyone else is imbecilic is one that characterized the Soviet Union – until it collapsed.

'This society', Enzensberger writes of the German Federal Republic, is no longer capable of being disappointed. It registered very early, very quickly what's going on in Bonn. The way the parties present themselves also contributes to this cynical view. The politicians try to compensate for the loss of their authority, the erosion of power and trust, by a huge expenditure on advertising. But these wasteful battles are counter-productive. The message is tautologous and empty. They always say only one thing, which is, 'I am I' or 'We are we'. The zero statement is the preferred form of self-presentation. That naturally confirms people's belief that no ideas can be expected from this caste . . . When the posters say: 'It's Germany's future', then everyone knows that these are empty words, at most it's about the future of the milk subsidy to farmers, of the health insurance contributions or benefits . . . The Federal Republic is relatively stable and relatively successful not because of, but despite being ruled by the people who grin down from the election posters.[9]

The theory of individualization takes sides in political debate in two ways: first, it elaborates a frame of reference which allows the subject area – the conflicts between individuals and society – to be analysed from the standpoint of individuals. Secondly, the theory shows how, as modern society develops further, it is becoming questionable to assume that collective units of meaning and action exist. System theories, which assume an existence and reproduction of the social independence of the actions and thoughts of individuals, are thereby losing reality content. To exaggerate slightly: system theory is turning into a system *metaphysics* which obstructs the view of the virulent social and political process whereby, in all spheres of activity, the content, goals, foundations and structures of the 'social' are having to be renegotiated, reinvented and reconstructed.[10]

A sociology which confronts the viewpoint serving the survival of institutions with the viewpoint of individuals is a largely undeveloped area of the discipline. Almost all sociology, through a 'congenital bias', is based on a negation of individuality and the individual. The social has almost always been conceived in terms of tribes, religions, classes, associations, and above all, recently, of social systems. The individuals were the interchangeable element, the product of circumstances, the character's masks, the subjective factor, the environment of the systems, in short: the indefinable. Sociology's credo, to which it owes its professional identity, states over and over again that the individual is the *illusion* of individuals who are denied insight into the social conditions and conditionality of their lives.

The works of world literature, the great narratives and dramas that have held the epochs in thrall, are variations of this doctrine of the higher reality and dignity of the general, social dimension, the indivisible unit of which – as the term *individere* itself implies – is the individual. But is a science of *individere* actually possible? Is not a 'sociology of the individual' (unless it contents itself with the social history of that concept, in the context of discourse theory) a self-contradiction, a pig with wings, a disguised appeal for sociology to abolish itself?

One does not need to go to the opposite extreme to see that many of the main concepts of sociology are on a war footing with the basic idea of individualization theory: that traditional contexts are being broken up, reconnected, recast; are becoming in all cases decidable, decision-dependent, in need of justification. Where this historical development is asserting itself, the viewpoints from 'above' and 'below', from the social whole and from the individual, are diverging. At the same time, the questions stirred up by system theory's perspective are still in force, and even take on increased importance as they become more unmanageable. Take, for example, the declining birthrate, which can only be deciphered if seen against the background of the changed wishes, hopes and life-plans of men and women. On the level of society as a whole, it brings with it a whole string of secondary consequences and questions (education policy, labour market management, pensions, local planning, immigration policy, etc.). Individuals, their preferences and aversions, are becoming the interference factor, that which is simply incalculable, a constant source of irritation, because they upset all calculations – education quotas, study plans, pension calculations, etc. Among politicians and administrators, and the academic experts who prepare their texts, this heightens the suspicion of irrationality, since it keeps turning the current legal, administrative and computing formulae into waste-paper. Where hitherto-accepted assumptions are found wanting, the clamour about 'mood democracy' and the 'elbow society' begins. Norms and moral standards are set. But the tidal wave of new life-designs, of do-it-yourself and tightrope biographies, cannot be either held back or understood in this way. The scurrying of the individualized lifestyles, elaborated in the personal trial-and-error process (between training, retraining, unemployment and career, between hopes of love, divorce, new dreams of happiness), is un-amenable to the need for standardization of bureaucratized political science and sociology.

No-one denies that important matters are thought about and initiated by these disciplines, too. But what was previously regarded as background noise to be neglected, is now being seen, more and more undeniably, as the basic situation. The frame of reference of institutionalized state politics and administration on one hand, and that of individuals trying to hold together their biography fragments on the other, are breaking apart and then colliding antagonistically in opposed conceptions of 'public welfare', 'quality of life', 'future viability', 'justice', 'progress'. A rift is opening between the images of society prevalent in politics and institutions, and those arising from the situations of individuals struggling for viable ways of living.

In this tension-laden field, sociology must re-think its concepts and its research routines. In the face of Enzensberger's 'average exoticism of everyday life', together with what is now formulated with scholarly caution as the 'pluralization of lifestyles', old classifications and schemata are becoming as ideologically suspect as they are necessary to the institutional actors. Take, for example, the studies which 'prove' that the increasingly numerous non-marital partnerships are really pre-conjugal communities, and that post-conjugal communities are actually only a preliminary form of the next marriage, so that marriage can be proclaimed the transcendental victor throughout all this turbulence. Such consolations have their market and their grateful customers: the turmoils of individualization, their message runs, are a storm in surviving marriage's teacup.

This confirms the old adage that the echo coming back out of the wood is the same as the shout that went into it. Anyone who 'maritalizes' alternative ways of living should not be surprised if he sees marriages wherever he looks. But this is a prime example of blind empiricism. Even methodical brilliance that is able to avoid calling its categorical framework into question, becomes a second-hand bookshop stocked with standard social groups, which only exist as an ideal: though as such they are very much alive.[11]

Prospect: How Can Highly Individualized Societies Be Integrated?

Individualization has a double face: 'precarious freedoms'. Expressed in the old, wrong terms, emancipation and anomie form together, through their political chemistry, an explosive mixture. The consequences and questions erupting in all parts of society are correspondingly deep-reaching and nerve-deadening; they increasingly alarm the public and preoccupy social scientists. To mention only a few: how do children grow up when there are fewer and fewer clear guidelines and responsibilities in families? Can connections be made with the growing tendency towards violence among young people? Is the age of mass products and mass consumption coming to an end with the pluralization of lifestyles, and must the economy and industry adapt themselves to products and product fashions that can be combined individually, with corresponding methods of production?

Is it possible, at all, for a society in the drifting sand of individualization to be registered statistically and analysed sociologically? Is there any remaining basic unit of the social, whether the household, the family, or the commune? How could such units be defined and made operational? How should the various political spheres – for example local politics, traffic policy, environmental policy, family policy, welfare policy – react to the diversification and transitoriness of needs and situations? How must social work (and its educational content) change when poverty is divided up and, as it were, distributed laterally among biographies? What architecture, what spatial planning, what educational planning does a society need under the pressure of individualization? Has the end come for the big parties and the big associations, or are they just starting a new stage of their history?

Behind all these irritating questions, a basic question is making itself more and more clearly heard: is it still at all possible to integrate highly individualized societies? As is shown by the rebirth of nationalism, of ethnic differences and conflicts in Europe, there is a strong temptation to react to these challenges with the classical instruments of encapsulation against 'aliens': which means turning back the wheels of social modernization. No doubt, the acceptance of violence against foreigners in the streets (for example) may indeed be explained in this way. In Germany as in other western European states an uprising against the 1970s and 1980s is in progress, a *Kulturkampf* of the two modernities. Old certainties, just now grown fragile, are again proclaimed – from everyday life to politics, from the family to the economy and the concept of progress. The highly individualized, find-out-for-yourself society is to be replaced by an inwardly heterogeneous society outwardly consolidated into a fortress – and the demarcation against 'foreigners' fits in with this calculation.

To put the matter ironically: since man can no longer, 'unfortunately', deny the right of women to vote; since women's desire for education can only with difficulty be held in check, since everything that might be useful in this regard proves awkward, a perhaps quite serviceable alternative route is being taken – not quite consciously but not quite unconsciously either. It involves achieving the same goals through the dramaturgy of violence and nationalism. Here the breach of the taboo on right-wing extremist violence has a reason little regarded up to now: the counter-revolt, pent up in the West too, against the individualization, feminization and ecologization of everyday life. Quite incidentally, violence reinstates the priorities of orthodox industrial society – economic growth, the faith in technology, the nuclear family, the gender hierarchy – banishing the tiresome spirits of permanent questioning; or seeming to do so.

But nailing down the status quo or even doing a backwards *salto mortale* cannot, at the end of the twentieth century, provide a basis of legitimacy. The same is true of the three ways of integrating highly industrialized societies that are mentioned again and again in the debate. They, too, are becoming uncertain, fragile, unable to function in the longer term.

The first is the possibility of what might be called a transcendental consensus, an integration through values, which was the driving force of classical sociology from Durkheim to Parsons. Opposing this today is the realization that the diversification of cultural perceptions and the connections people have to make for themselves eat away the very foundations on which value-communities can feed and constantly renew themselves.

Others, secondly, contrast to this integration through values an integration founded on joint material interests. If an avowal of common values (which, of course, always has a narrowing, repressive side) is no longer possible, it is replaced in highly developed society by the share in prosperity that is felt by broad sections of the population, binding them into the society. According to this theory, the cohesion of the old Federal Republic rested primarily on the growing 'economic cake', whereas the new, enlarged republic – where recession, shortage and poverty are starting to take control – faces severe tests. But even disregarding this topical development, the basic assumption is itself questionable. To hope that only material interests and institutional dependence (consumption, job market, welfare state, pensions) create cohesion, is to confuse the problem with the solution, making a virtue (desired by theory) out of the necessity of disintegrating groups and group-allegiances.

Thirdly, national consciousness, too, is no longer able to provide a basis for stable integration. This is not only shown by the polarizations generated by the 'national project'. It is also, René König wrote as early as 1979, 'much too abstract in relation to real and very tangible fissures';[12] it is simply no longer able to reach and bind these splits. In other words, with the mobilization of ethnic identities, it is precisely national integration which breaks down:

> This can be called a 'relapse into the middle ages', and the disintegration of the existing large societies into separate, opposed local powers can be seen as the decay of the old 'nations' – a process which has been a reality in some parts of the old and new worlds for some time now. Here, the old path from alliances to empires is reversed; the great empires sometimes split up into federative formations, or the individual parts split off along lines determined by political, ethnic or other factors.[13]

So what is left? In conclusion, we would like, at least, to indicate the possibility of a different kind of integration and to put it forward for discussion. To summarize our basic idea: highly individualized societies can only be bound together – if at all – first, through a clear understanding of precisely this situation; and secondly, if people can be successfully mobilized and motivated for the challenges present at the centre of their lives (unemployment, destruction of nature, etc.). Where the old sociality is 'evaporating', society must be reinvented. Integration therefore becomes possible if no attempt is made to arrest and push back the break-out of individuals. It can happen if we make conscious use of this situation, and try to forge new, politically open, creative forms of bond and alliance. The question of whether we still have the strength, the imagination – and the time – for this 'invention of the political' is, to be sure, a matter of life and death.[14]

In one of his last major essays, König sketched a positively utopian role for sociology in this connection. He believed it could contribute to integration through enabling the highly complex society to reflect and observe itself creatively and methodically. He criticized the 'ruling class of today' in the strongest terms because it had 'lived entirely on a legitimacy borrowed from old elites and had added nothing of its own'. In this situation, König goes on, 'sociology could make this highly complex thematic context transparent . . . Admittedly, integration could not then be achieved on the institutional level' – either ethnically, socially, economically or through state nationalism. 'To an extent, it can only be implemented "in thought".' Therefore, it could be achieved 'only within the framework of a new philosophy, which no longer revolved around "being" and "becoming", but around the chances for human beings under the conditions that have been described'.[15]

What König proposes is in fact very topical – an integration to be attained 'in thought', in the struggle for new existential foundations for industrial civilization. Post-traditional societies threatening the cohesion of this civilization can only become integrable – if at all – through the experiment of their self-interpretation, self-observation, self-opening, self-discovery, indeed, their self-invention. Their future, their ability to have and shape a future, is the measure of their integration. Whether they can succeed in this is, of course, questionable. Perhaps it will turn out that individualization and integration are in fact mutually exclusive. And sociology – is it really able to make an intellectual contribution to pluralist societies? Or will it remain stuck in its routines, obliterating the big outlines of change and challenge with its minute calculations of developmental trends?

In his novel *The Man without Qualities*,[16] Robert Musil distinguishes between a sense for reality and a sense for possibility. He defines the latter as 'the capacity to think how everything could "just as easily" be, and to attach no more importance to what is than to what is not'. Someone who sees possible truths, Musil goes on, has, 'at least in the opinion of their devotees . . . something positively divine, a fiery, soaring quality, a constructive will . . . that does not shrink from reality but treats it, on the contrary, as a mission and an invention . . . Since his ideas . . . are nothing else than as yet unborn realities, he too of course has a sense of reality; but it is a sense of possible reality. . .'.[17] Undoubtedly, sociology, too, ought to develop such a sense of possible reality – but that is another matter.

Notes

1 Friedrich Schorlemmer, 'Der Befund ist nicht alles'. Contribution to debate on *Bindungsverlust und Zukunftsangst in der Risikogesellschaft*, 30 October 1993, in Halle; manuscript, p. 1.

2 Lena H. Sun, 'Freedom has a Price, Chinese Discover'. *International Herald Tribune*, 14 June 1993. p. 5.

3 Respectively, this is how Ilona Ostner and Peter Roy ('Späte Heirat – Ergebnis Biographisch Unterschiedlicher Erfahrungen mit "Cash" und "Care"'. Project proposal to Deutsche Forschungsgemeinschaft (DFG), (Bremen, 1991), p. 18) and Karl Ulrich Mayer ('Soziale Ungleichheit und Lebensläufe'. In Bern Giesen and Claus Leggewie (eds), *Experiment Vereinigung* (Berlin, 1991), p. 88.) understand individualization. For a summary of the debate on individualization, see Ulrich Beck, 'The Debate on the "Individualization Theory"', in Today's Sociology in Germany'. In Bernhard Schäfers (ed.), *Sociology in Germany – Development, Institutionalization, Theoretical Disputes* (Opladen: Leske Verlag, 1994).

4 Ronald Hitzler (*Kleine Lebenswelten – Ein Bietrag zum Verstehen von Kultur.* (Opladen: Westdeutscher Verlag, 1988) writes about 'do-it-yourself biography' (*Bastelbiographie*); Anthony Giddens (*Self-Identity and Modernity* London: Polity, 1991) writes about 'reflexive biography'; Katrin Ley ('Von der Normal – zur Wahlbiographie'. In Kohli and Robert (eds), *Biographie und Soziale Wirklichkeit.* (Stuttgart: Metzler, 1984), pp. 239–60.) deals with 'elective biography' (*Wahlbiographie*).

5 Karl Martin Bolte, 'Subjektorientierte Soziologie – Plädoyer für eine Forschungsperspektive.' In Bolte and Treutner (eds), *Subjektorientierte Arbeits – und Berufssociologie* (Frankfurt/M: Campus, 1983), pp. 12–36.

6 Peter L. Berger, *Einladung zur Soziologie* (Munich: Deutsche Taschenbuch Verlag, 1977), p. 40.

7 Zygmunt Bauman, *Thinking Sociologically* (Oxford: Blackwell; Cambridge MA, 1991), p. 17.

8 Hans Magnus Enzensberger, *Mediocrity and Delusion. Collected Diversions*, trans. Martin Chalmers (London: Verso, 1992), p. 179.

9 Ibid., pp. 143, 138.

10 Cf. the theory of reflexive modernization in Ulrich Beck, *Die Erfindung des Politischen* (Frankfurt: Suhrkamp, 1993), esp. ch. III; and U. Beck, A. Giddens and S. Lash, *Reflexive Modernization – Politics, Tradition and Aesthetics in the Modern Social Order* (Cambridge: Polity Press, 1994).

11 The pragmatic, *a priori* method of mass-data sociology is worth noting: quantitative methods presuppose pre-formed categories and concepts (even if they are nominally de-activated). However, a society which is individualizing itself eludes these standardizations imposed by research method (which is already giving rise to unmanageable complications in the introduction of flexible working time and work contracts, for example). It is therefore difficult for a sociology proud of its technical virtuosity to jump over its own shadow and address questions of a self-individualizing society. But at the same time it becomes clear, here again, how woefully sociology has so far neglected the question of what kind of sociological empiricism, of scholarly and social self-observation, is appropriate to a society

caught in the draught and sand-drift of individualization. Cf. U. Beck and J. Allmendinger, *Individualisierung und die Erhebung Sozialer Ungleichheit* (Munich: DFG research project, 1993).

12   René König, 'Gesellschaftliches Bewusstsein und Sociologie'. In Günther Lüschen (ed.), *Deutsche Soziologie seit 1945,* special edition 21, 1979. p. 364.

13   Ibid., p. 364.

14   Ulrich Beck (1993), *Die Erfindung des Politischen*. For the English translation, Ulrich Beck, *The Reinvention of Politics* (Polity, 1996).

15   René König, 'Gesellschaflisches Bewusstein und Sociologie', p. 367. See also, Bernhard Peters, *Die integration moderner Gesellschaften* (Frankfurt/M: Suhrkamp, 1993).

16   Robert Musil, *The Man without Qualities* (London: Secker and Warburg, 1961).

17   Ibid., p. 12.

Part III
Contemporary Critical Theory

12

The Uncoupling of System and Lifeworld

Jürgen Habermas

The provisional concept of society proposed here is radically different in one respect from the Parsonian concept: the mature Parsons reinterpreted the structural components of the lifeworld – culture, society, personality – as action systems constituting environments for one another. Without much ado, he subsumed the concept of the lifeworld gained from an action-theoretical perspective under systems-theoretical concepts. As we shall see below, the structural components of the lifeworld become subsystems of a general system of action, to which the physical substratum of the lifeworld is reckoned along with the "behavior system." The proposal I am advancing here, by contrast, attempts to take into account the methodological differences between the internalist and the externalist viewpoints connected with the two conceptual strategies.

From the participant perspective of members of a lifeworld it looks as if sociology with a systems-theoretical orientation considers only one of the three components of the lifeworld, namely, the institutional system, for which culture and personality merely constitute complementary environments. From the observer perspective of systems theory, on the other hand, it looks as if life-world analysis confines itself to one societal subsystem specialized in maintaining structural patterns (pattern maintenance); in this view, the components of the lifeworld are merely internal differentiations of this subsystem which specifies the parameters of societal self-maintenance. It is already evident on methodological grounds that a systems theory of society cannot be self-sufficient. The structures of the lifeworld, with their own inner logic placing internal constraints on system maintenance, have to be gotten at by a hermeneutic approach that picks up on members' pretheoretical knowledge. Furthermore, the objective conditions under which the systems-theoretical objectification of the lifeworld becomes necessary have themselves only arisen in the course of social evolution. And this calls for a type of explanation that does not already move within the system perspective.

I understand social evolution as a second-order process of differentiation: system and lifeworld are differentiated in the sense that the complexity of the one and the rationality of the other grow. But it is not only qua system and qua lifeworld that they are differentiated; they get differentiated from one another at the same time. It has become conventional for sociologists to distinguish the stages of social evolution as tribal societies, traditional societies, or societies organized around a state, and modern societies (where the economic system has been differentiated out). From the system perspective, these stages are marked by the appearance of new systemic mechanisms and corresponding levels of complexity. On this plane of analysis, the uncoupling of system and lifeworld is depicted in such a way that the lifeworld, which is at first co-extensive with a scarcely differentiated social system, gets cut down more and more to one subsystem among others. In the process, system mechanisms get further and further detached from the social structures through which social integration takes place. As we shall see, modern societies attain a level of system differentiation at which increasingly autonomous organizations are connected with one another via delinguistified media of communication: these systemic mechanisms – for example, money – steer a social intercourse that has been largely disconnected from norms and values, above all in those sub-systems of purposive rational economic and administrative action that, on Weber's diagnosis, have become independent of their moral-political foundations.

At the same time, the lifeworld remains the subsystem that defines the pattern of the social system as a whole. Thus, systemic mechanisms need to be anchored in the lifeworld: they have to be institutionalized. This institutionalization of new levels of system differentiation can also be perceived from the internal perspective of the lifeworld. Whereas system differentiation in tribal societies only leads to the increasing complexity of pregiven kinship systems, at higher levels of integration new social structures take shape, namely, the state and media-steered subsystems. In societies with a low degree of differentiation, systemic interconnections are tightly interwoven with mechanisms of social integration; in modern societies they are consolidated and objectified into norm-free structures. Members behave toward formally organized action systems, steered via processes of exchange and power, as toward a block of quasi-natural reality; within these media-steered subsystems society congeals into a second nature. Actors have always been able to sheer off from an orientation to mutual understanding, adopt a strategic attitude, and objectify normative contexts into something in the objective world, but in modern societies, economic and bureaucratic spheres emerge in which social relations are regulated only via money and power. Norm-conformative attitudes and identity-forming social memberships are neither necessary nor possible in these spheres; they are made peripheral instead. [. . .]

In subsystems differentiated out via steering media, systemic mechanisms create their own, norm-free social structures jutting out from the lifeworld. These structures do, of course, remain linked with everyday communicative practice via basic institutions of civil or public law. We cannot directly infer from the mere fact that system and social integration have been largely uncoupled to linear dependency in one direction or the other. Both are conceivable: the institutions that anchor steering mechanisms such as power and money in the lifeworld could serve as channels *either* for the influence of the lifeworld on formally organized domains of action *or*, conversely, for the influence of the system on communicatively structured contexts of action. In the one case, they function as an institutional framework that subjects system maintenance to the normative restrictions of the lifeworld, in the other, as a base that subordinates the life-world to the systemic constraints of material reproduction and thereby "mediatizes" it.

In theories of the state and of society, both models have been played through. Modern natural law theories neglected the inner logic of a functionally stabilized civil society in relation to the state; the classics of political economy were concerned to show that systemic imperatives were fundamentally in harmony with the basic norms of a polity guaranteeing freedom and justice. Marx destroyed this practically very important illusion; he showed that the laws of capitalist commodity production have the latent function of sustaining a structure that makes a mockery of bourgeois ideals. The lifeworld of the capitalist carrier strata, which was expounded in rational natural law and in the ideals of bourgeois thought generally, was devalued by Marx to a socio-cultural superstructure. In his picture of base and superstructure he is also raising the methodological demand that we exchange the internal perspective of the lifeworld for an observer's perspective, so that we might grasp the systemic imperatives of an independent economy as they act upon the bourgeois lifeworld *a tergo*. In his view, only in a socialist society could the spell cast upon the lifeworld by the system be broken, could the dependence of the superstructure on the base be lifted.

In one way, the most recent systems functionalism is an heir-successor to Marxism, which it radicalizes and defuses at the same time. On the one hand, systems theory adopts the view that the systemic constraints of material production, which it understands as imperatives of self-maintenance of the general social system, reach right through the symbolic structures of the lifeworld. On the other hand, it removes the critical sting from the base-superstructure thesis by reinterpreting what was intended to be an empirical diagnosis as a prior analytical distinction. Marx took over from bourgeois social theory a presupposition that we found again in Durkheim: it is not a matter of indifference to a society whether and to what extent forms of social integration dependent on consensus are repressed and replaced by anonymous forms of system integrative sociation. A theoretical approach that presents the lifeworld merely as one of several anonymously steered subsystems undercuts this distinction. Systems theory treats accomplishments of social and system integration as functionally equivalent and thus deprives itself of the standard of communicative rationality. And without that standard, increases in complexity achieved *at the expense* of a rationalized lifeworld cannot be identified *as costs*. Systems theory lacks the analytic means to pursue the question that Marx (also) built into his base-superstructure metaphor and Weber renewed in his own way by inquiring into the paradox of societal rationalization. For us, this question takes on the form of whether the rationalization of the lifeworld does not become paradoxical with the transition to modern societies. The rationalization of the lifeworld makes possible the emergence and growth of subsystems whose independent imperatives turn back destructively upon the lifeworld itself.

I shall now take a closer look at the conceptual means by which this hypothesis might be given a more exact formulation. The assumption regarding a "mediatization" of the lifeworld refers to "interference" phenomena that arise when system and lifeworld have become differentiated from one another to such an extent that they can exert mutual influence upon one another. The mediatization of the lifeworld takes effect on and with the structures of the lifeworld; it is not one of those processes that are available as themes *within* the lifeworld, and thus it cannot be read off from the intuitive knowledge of members. On the other hand, it is also inaccessible from an external, systemstheoretical perspective. Although it comes about counterintuitively and cannot easily be perceived from the internal perspective of the lifeworld, there are indications of it in the formal conditions of communicative action.

The uncoupling of system integration and social integration means at first only a differentiation between two types of action coordination, one coming about through the consensus of those involved, the other through functional interconnections of action. System-integrative mechanisms attach to the effects of action. As they work through action orientations in a subjectively inconspicuous fashion, they may leave the socially integrative contexts of action which they are parasitically utilizing structurally unaltered – it is this sort of intermeshing of system with social integration that we postulated for the development level of tribal societies. Things are different when system integration intervenes in the very forms of social integration. In this case, too, we have to do with latent functional interconnections, but the subjective inconspicuousness of systemic constraints that *instrumentalize* a communicatively structured lifeworld takes on the character of deception, of objectively false consciousness. The effects of the system on the lifeworld, which change the structure of contexts of action in socially integrated groups, have to remain hidden. The reproductive constraints that instrumentalize a lifeworld without weakening the illusion of its self-sufficiency have to hide, so to speak, in the pores of communicative action. This gives rise to a *structural violence* that, without becoming manifest as such, takes hold of the forms of intersubjectivity of possible understanding. Structural violence is exercised by way of systemic restrictions on communication; distortion is anchored in the formal conditions of communicative action in such a way that the interrelation of the objective, social, and subjective worlds gets prejudged for participants in a typical fashion. In analogy to the cognitive a priori of Lukács' "forms of objectivity," I shall introduce the concept of a *form of understanding* [*Verständigungsform*].

Lukács defined forms of objectivity as principles that, through the societal totality, preform the encounters of individuals with objective nature, normative reality, and their own subjective nature. He speaks of a priori forms of objectivity because, operating within the framework of the philosophy of the subject, he starts from the basic relation of a knowing and acting subject to the domain of perceptible and manipulable objects. After the change of paradigm introduced by the theory of communication, the formal properties of the intersubjectivity of possible understanding can take the place of the conditions of the objectivity of possible experience. A form of mutual understanding represents a compromise between the general structures of communicative action and reproductive constraints unavailable as themes within a given lifeworld. Historically variable forms of understanding are, as it were, the sectional planes that result when systemic constraints of material reproduction inconspicuously intervene in the forms of social integration and thereby mediatize the lifeworld.

I shall now (a) illustrate the concept of a form of understanding with those civilizations in which religious-metaphysical worldviews take on ideological functions, in order (b) to gain an analytic perspective on the hypothetical sequence of forms of mutual understanding.

(*a*) In societies organized around a state, a need for legitimation arises that, for structural reasons, could not yet exist in tribal societies. In societies organized through kinship, the institutional system is anchored ritually, that is, in a practice that is interpreted by mythical narratives and that stabilizes its normative validity all by itself. By contrast, the authority of the laws in which a general political order is articulated has to be guaranteed, in the first instance, by the ruler's power of sanction. But political domination has socially integrating power only insofar as disposition over means of sanction does not rest on naked repression, but on the authority of an office anchored in turn in a legal order. For this reason, laws need to be intersubjectively recognized by citizens; they have to be legitimated as right and proper. This leaves culture with the task of supplying reasons why an existing political order deserves to be recognized. Whereas mythical narratives interpret and make comprehensible a ritual practice of which they themselves are part, religious and metaphysical worldviews of prophetic origin have the form of doctrines that can be worked up intellectually and that explain and justify an existing political order in terms of the world-order they explicate.[1]

The need for legitimation that arises, for structural reasons, in civilizations is especially precarious. If one compares the ancient civilizations with even strongly hierarchized tribal societies, one finds an unmistakable increase in social inequality. In the framework of state organization, units with different structures can be functionally specified. Once the organization of social labor is uncoupled from kinship relations, resources can be more easily mobilized and more effectively combined. But this expansion of material reproduction is gained at the price of transforming the stratified kinship system into a strati-fied class society. What presents itself from a system perspective as an integration of society at the level of an expanded material reproduction, means, from the perspective of social integration, an increase in social inequality, wholesale economic exploitation, and the juridically cloaked repression of dependent classes. The history of penal law provides unmistakable indicators of the high degree of repression required in all ancient civilizations. Social movements that can be analyzed as class struggles – although they were not carried on as such – pose a threat to social integration. For this reason, the func-tions of exploitation and repression fulfilled by rulers and ruling classes in the systemic nexus of material reproduction have to be kept latent as far as possible. Worldviews have to become ideologically efficacious. [. . .]

At first glance, it strikes one as puzzling that ideological interpretations of the world and society could be sustained *against all appearances* of barbaric injustice. The constraints of material reproduction could not have reached so effectively and relentlessly through the class-specific lifeworlds of civilizations if cultural traditions had not been immunized against dissonant experiences. I would explain this unassailability by the systemic restrictions placed on communi-cation. Although religious-metaphysical worldviews exerted a strong attraction on intellectual strata; although they provoked the hermeneutic efforts of many generations of teachers, theologians, educated persons, preachers, mandarins, bureaucrats, citizens, and the like; although they were reshaped by argumentation, given a dogmatic form, systematized and ration-alized in terms of their own motifs, the basic religious and metaphysical concepts lay at a level of undifferentiated validity claims where the rationality potential of speech remains more tightly bound than in the profane practice of everyday life, which had not been worked through intellectually. Owing to the fusion of ontic, normative, and expressive aspects of validity, and to the culti-cally rooted fixation of a corresponding belief attitude, the basic concepts that carried, as it were, the legitimation load of ideologically effective worldviews were immunized against objections already within the cognitive reach of everyday communication. The immunization could succeed when an institu-tional separation between the sacred and the profane realms of action ensured that traditional foundations were not taken up "in the wrong place"; within the domain of the sacred, communication remained *systematically restricted* due to the lack of differentiation between spheres of validity, that is, *as a result of the formal conditions of possible understanding.*[2]

The mode of legitimation in civilizations is thus based on a form of under-standing that systemically limits possibilities of communication owing to its failure to differentiate sufficiently among the various validity claims. Earlier we placed mythical, religious-metaphysical, and modern worldviews in a hier-archy, according to the degree of decentration of the world-understandings they make possible. Analogously, we can order action orientations, and the realms of action they define, according to the degree of differentiation of validity aspects, and in this way we can get at the relative a priori of the form of understanding dominant at a given time and place. These *forms of the inter-subjectivity of mutual understanding* do not reflect the structures of dominant worldviews in any symmetrical manner, for established interpretive systems do not pervade all areas of action with the same intensity. As we have seen, in civilizations the immunizing power of the form of understanding derives from a peculiar, structurally describable differential between two realms of action: in comparison to profane action orientations, sacred ones enjoy a greater authority, even though validity spheres are less differentiated and the potential for rationality is less developed in sacred than in profane domains of action.

(*b*) With a systematic investigation of forms of understanding in mind, I shall distinguish four domains of action: (1) the domain of cultic practice; (2) the domain in which religious systems of interpretation have the power directly to orient everyday practice; and finally the profane domains in which the cultural shock of knowledge is utilized for (3) communication and (4) purposive activity, without the structures of the worldview directly taking effect in action orientations.

Since I regard (1) and (2) as belonging to the sacred realm of action, I can avoid difficulties that result from Durkheim's oversimplified division.

Magical practices carried on by individuals outside of the cultic community should not be demoted, as Durkheim proposed they should, to the profane realm. Everyday practice is permeated throughout with ceremonies that cannot be understood in utilitarian terms. It is better not to limit the sacred realm of action to cultic practice, but to extend it to the class of actions based on religious patterns of interpretation.[3]

Furthermore, there are internal relations between the structures of world-views and the kinds of cultic actions: to myth there corresponds a *ritual* practice (and sacrificial actions) of tribal members; to religious-metaphysical world-views a *sacramental* practice (and prayers) of the congregation; to the religion of culture [*Bildungsreligion*] of the early modern period, finally, a *contemplative* presentation of auratic works of art. Along this path, cultic practice gets "disenchanted," in Weber's sense; it loses the character of compelling the gods to some end, and it is less and less carried on in the consciousness that a divine power can be *forced* to do something.[4]

Within the realm of profane action I shall distinguish between communicative and purposive activity; I shall assume that these two *aspects* can be distinguished even when corresponding *types* of action (not to mention *domains* of action defined by these types) have not yet been differentiated. The distinction between communicative and purposive activity is not relevant to the sacred realm. In my view, there is no point in contrasting religious cults and magical practices from this perspective.[5]

The next step would be to place the practices in different domains of action in a developmental-logical order according to the degree to which aspects of validity have been differentiated from one another. At one end of the scale stands ritual practice, at the other end the practice of argumentation. If we further consider that between the sacred and the profane domains there are differentials in authority and rationality – and in the opposite directions – we then have the points of view relevant to ordering the forms of understanding in a systematic sequence. The following schema (figure 12.1) represents four forms of mutual understanding ordered along the line of a progressive unfettering of the rationality potential inherent in communicative action. The areas (1–2) and (3–4) stand for the form of understanding in archaic societies, the areas (5–6) and (7–8) for that in civilizations, the areas (9–10) and (11–12) for that in early modern societies.

Taking the archaic form of understanding as an example, I shall next give a somewhat more detailed account of the contrasting directions of the differentials in authority and rationality between the sacred and the profane domains of action. Following that I shall comment more briefly on the forms of understanding typical of civilizations (5–8) and of early modern societies (9–12).

(*ad* 1 and 2) We find ritualized behavior already in vertebrate societies; in the transitional field between primate hordes and paleolithic societies, social integration was probably routed primarily through those strongly ritualized modes of behavior we counted above as symbolically mediated interaction. Only with the transformation of primitive systems of calls into grammatically regulated, propositionally differentiated speech was the sociocultural starting point reached at which ritualized *behavior* changed into ritualized *action*; language opened up, so to speak, an interior view of rites. From this point on, we no longer have to be content with *describing* ritualized behavior in terms of its observable features and hypothesized functions; we can try to *understand* rituals – insofar as they have maintained a residual existence and have become known to us through field studies.

A modern observer is struck by the extremely irrational character of ritual practices. The aspects of action that we cannot help but keep apart today are merged in one and the same act. The element of purposive activity comes out in the fact that ritual practices are supposed magically to bring about states in the world; the element of normatively regulated action is noticeable in the quality of obligation that emanates from the ritually conjured, at once attracting and terrifying, powers; the element of expressive action is especially clear in the standardized expressions of feeling in ritual ceremonies; finally an assertoric aspect is also present inasmuch as ritual practice serves to represent and reproduce exemplary events or mythically narrated original scenes.

Ritual practice is, of course, already part of a sociocultural form of life in which a higher form of communication has emerged with grammatical speech. Language (in the strict sense) breaks up the unity of teleological, normative, expressive, and cognitive aspects of action. Yet mythical thought shields ritual practice from the tendencies toward decomposition that appear at the level of language (with the differentiation between action oriented to mutual understanding and to success, and the transformation of adaptive behavior into purposive activity). Myth holds the same aspects together on the plane of

Domains of action / Differentiation of validity spheres	Sacred		Profane	
	Cultic practice	World-views that steer practice	Communication	Purposive activity
Confusion of relations of validity and effectiveness: performative-instrumental attitude	1. Rite (institutionalization of social solidarity)	2. Myth	—	—
Differentiation between relations of validity and effectiveness: orientation to success vs. to mutual understanding	5. Sacrament/prayer (institutionalization of paths to salvation and knowledge)	6. Religious and metaphysical world-views	3. Communicative action bound to particular contexts and with a holistic orientation to validity	4. Purposive activity as a task-oriented element of roles (utilization of technical innovations)
Differentiation of specific validity claims at the level of action: objectivating vs. norm-conformative vs. expressive attitudes	9. Contemplative presentation of auratic art (institutionalization of the enjoyment of art)	10. Religious ethics of conviction, rational natural law, civil religion	7. Normatively regulated communicative action with an argumentative handling of truth claims	8. Purposive activity organized through legitimate power (utilization of specialized practical–professional knowledge)
Differentiation of specific validity claims at the level of discourse: communicative action vs. discourse	—	—	11. Normatively unbound communicative action with institutionalized criticism	12. Purposive activity as ethically neutral purposive-rational action (utilization of scientific technologies and strategies)

Figure 12.1 Forms of mutual understanding

interpretation that are fused together in ritual on the plane of practice. An interpretation of the world that confuses internal relations of meaning with external relations among things, validity with empirical efficacy, can protect ritual practice against rips in the fabric woven from communicative and purposive activity indistinguishably. This explains its coexistence with profane contexts of cooperation in which goal-oriented actions are effectively coordinated within the framework of kinship roles. The experience gained in everyday practice is worked up in myth and connected with narrative explanations of the orders of the world and of society. In this regard, myth bridges over the two domains of action.

We can see in the formal structures of the relevant action orientations that there is a rationality differential between sacred and profane domains. At the heart of the sacred realm is ritual practice, which stands or falls with the interweaving of purposive activity and communication, of orientations to success with orientations to mutual understanding. It is stabilized by a mythical understanding of the world that, while it develops in narrative form, that is, at the level of grammatical speech, nonetheless exhibits similar categorical structures. In the basic categories of myth, relations on validity are still confused with relations of effectiveness. On the other hand, the mythical worldview is opened to the flow of experience from the realm of profane action. Everyday practice already rests on a difference between aspects of validity and reality.

(*ad* 3 and 4) It is above all in the areas of production and warfare that cooperation based on a division of labor develops and requires action oriented to success. From the standpoint of developmental history as well, efficacy is the earliest aspect of the rationality of action. As long as truth claims could barely be isolated on the level of communicative action, the "know-how" invested in technical and strategic rules could not yet take the form of explicit knowledge. In contrast to magic, the profane practice of everyday life already calls for differentiating between orientations to success and to mutual understanding. However, within communicative action the claims to truth, to truthfulness, and to rightness likely flowed together in a whole that was first broken up in a methodical fashion when, with the advent of writing, a stratum of literati arose who learned to produce and process texts.

The normative scope of communicative action was relatively narrowly restricted by particularistic kinship relations. Under the aspect of fulfilling standardized tasks, goal-directed cooperative actions remained embedded in a communicative practice that itself served to fulfill narrowly circumscribed social expectations. These expectations issued from a social structure regarded as part of a mythically explained and ritually secured world-order. The mythical system of interpretation closed the circuit between profane and sacred domains.

(*ad* 5 and 6) When a holistic concept of validity was constituted, internal relations of meaning could be differentiated from external relations among things, though it was still not possible to discriminate among the various aspects of validity. As Weber has shown, it is at this stage that religious and metaphysical worldviews arise. Their basic concepts proved to be resistant to every attempt to separate off the aspects of the true, the good, and the perfect. Corresponding to such worldviews is a sacramental practice with forms of prayer or exercises and with demagicalized communication between the individual believer and the divine being. These worldviews are more or less dichotomous in structure; they set up a "world beyond" and leave a demythologized "this world" or a desocialized "world of appearances" to a disenchanted everyday practice. In the realm of profane action, structures take shape that break up the holistic concept of validity.

(*ad* 7 and 8) On the level of communicative action, the syndrome of validity claims breaks up. Participants no longer only differentiate between orientations to success and to mutual understanding, but between the different basic pragmatic attitudes as well. A polity with a state and conventional legal institutions has to rely on obedience to the law, that is, on a norm-conforming attitude toward legitimate order. The citizens of the state must be able to distinguish this attitude – in everyday actions as well – from an objectivating attitude toward external nature and an expressive attitude *vis-à-vis* their own inner nature. At this stage, communicative action can free itself from particularistic contexts, but it stays in the space marked out by solid traditional norms. An argumentative treatment of texts also makes participants aware of the differences between communicative action and discourse. But specific validity claims are differentiated only on the plane of action. There are not yet forms of argumentation tailored to specific aspects of validity.[6]

Purposive activity also attains a higher level of rationality. When truth claims can be isolated, it becomes possible to see the internal connection between the efficiency of action oriented to success and the truth of empirical statements, and to make sure of technical know-how. Thus practical professional knowledge can assume objective shape and be transmitted through teaching. Purposive activity gets detached from unspecific age and sex roles. To the extent that social labor is organized via legitimate power, special activities can define occupational roles.

(*ad* 9 and 10) That validity claims are not yet fully differentiated at this stage can be seen in the cultural tradition of the early modern period. Independent cultural value spheres do take shape, but to begin with only science is institutionalized in an unambiguous fashion, that is, under the aspect of exactly one validity claim. An autonomous art retains its aura and the enjoyment of art its contemplative character; both features derive from its cultic origins. An ethics of conviction remains tied to the context of religious traditions, however subjectivized; postconventional legal representations are still coupled with truth claims in rational natural law and form the nucleus of what Robert Bellah has called "civil religion." Thus, although art, morality and law are already differentiated value spheres, they do not get wholly disengaged from the sacred domain so long as the internal development of each does not proceed unambiguously under precisely one specific aspect of validity. On the other hand, the forms of modern religiosity give up basic dogmatic claims. They destroy the metaphysical-religious "world beyond" and no longer dichotomously contrast this profane world to Transcendence, or the world of appearances to the reality of an underlying *Essence*. In domains of profane action, structures can take shape that are defined by an unrestricted differentiation of validity claims on the levels of action *and* argumentation.

(*ad* 11 and 12) It is here that discourse becomes relevant for profane spheres of action, too. In everyday communication, participants can keep apart not only different basic pragmatic attitudes, but also the levels of action and discourse. Domains of action normed by positive law with post-traditional legal institutions, presuppose that participants are in a position to shift from naively performing actions to reflectively engaging in argumentation. To the extent that the hypothetical discussion of normative validity claims is institutionalized, the critical potential of speech can be brought to bear on existing institutions. Legitimate orders still appear to communicatively acting subjects as something normative, but this normativity has a different quality insofar as institutions are no longer legitimated per se through religious and metaphysical worldviews.

Purposive activity is freed from normative contexts in a more radicalized sense. Up to this point, action oriented to success remained linked with norms of action and embedded in communicative action within the framework of a task-oriented system of social cooperation. But with the legal institutionalization of the monetary medium, success-oriented action steered by egocentric calculations of utility loses its connection to action oriented by mutual understanding. This strategic action, which is disengaged from the mechanism of reaching understanding and calls for an objectivating attitude even in regard to interpersonal relations, is promoted to the model for methodically dealing with a scientifically objectivated nature. In the instrumental sphere, purposive activity gets free of normative restrictions to the extent that it becomes linked to flows of information from the scientific system.

The two areas on the left in the bottom row of figure 12.1 have been left empty because, with the development of modern societies, the sacred domain has largely disintegrated, or at least has lost its structure-forming significance. At the level of completely differentiated validity spheres, art sheds its cultic background, just as morality and law detach themselves from their religions and metaphysical background. With this *secularization of bourgeois culture*, the cultural value spheres separate off sharply from one another and develop according to the standards of the inner logics specific to the different validity claims. Culture loses just those formal properties that enabled it to take on ideological functions. Insofar as these tendencies – schematically indicated here – actually do establish themselves in developed modern societies, the structural force of system imperatives intervening in the forms of social integration can no longer hide behind the rationality differential between sacred and profane domains. The modern form of understanding is too transparent to provide a niche for this structural violence by means of inconspicuous restrictions on communication. Under these conditions it is to be expected that the competition between forms of system and social integration would become more visible than previously. In the end, systemic mechanisms suppress forms of social integration even in those areas where a consensus-dependent co-ordination of action cannot be replaced, that is, where the symbolic reproduction of the lifeworld is at stake. In these areas, the *mediatization* of the lifeworld assumes the form of a *colonization*.

Notes

1   N. Eisenstadt, "Cultural Traditions and Political Dynamics: The Origins and Modes of Ideological Politics." *British Journal of Sociology* 32, 1981, p. 155ff.
2   M. Bloch also uses a communications-theoretical approach to explain the ideological functions that actions passed down from the period of tribal society can take on in class societies. The formalism according to which ritual practices can assume such functions may be characterized in terms of restrictions on communication. M. Bloch, "The Disconnection of Power and Rank as a Process." In S. Friedman and M. J. Rowland (eds), *The Evolution of Social Systems* (London, 1977); and idem, "The Past and Present in the Present." *Man*, 13, 1978, p. 278ff.
3   See, for example, L. Mair, *An Introduction to Social Anthropology* (rev. edn), (Oxford, 1972), p. 229.
4   On the contrast between ritual and sacramental practice, see Mary Douglas, *Natural Symbols* (London, 1973), p. 281.
5   L. Mair, *An Introduction to Social Anthropology*, p. 229.
6   Strictly speaking, not even the philosophical discourse of Greek philosophy was specialized about the isolated validity claim of propositional truth.

13

Patterns of Intersubjective Recognition: Love, Rights and Solidarity

Axel Honneth

In order to avoid having to speak of 'love' only in the restricted sense that the concept has acquired since Romanticism's revaluation of intimate sexual relationships, it is initially advisable to follow a usage that is as neutral as possible.[1] Love relationships are to be understood here as referring to primary relationships insofar as they – on the model of friendships, parent-child relationships, as well as erotic relationships between lovers – are constituted by strong emotional attachments among a small number of people. [. . .]

This way of speaking of primary affectional relationships as depending on a precarious balance between independence and attachment is much the same as the approach taken, as part of an attempt to determine the causes of pathological disorders, by psychoanalytic object-relations theory. With the turn in psychoanalysis to interactions in early childhood, affectional attachment to other persons is revealed to be a process whose success is dependent on the mutual maintenance of a tension between symbiotic self-sacrifice and individual self-assertion. For this reason, the research tradition of object-relations theory is especially well suited to rendering love intelligible as the interactive relationship that forms the basis for a particular pattern of reciprocal recognition.

In object-relations theory, conclusions are drawn, on the basis of the therapeutic analysis of relational pathologies, as to the conditions that can lead to a successful form of emotional attachment to other persons. Of course, before psychoanalysis could be brought to this sort of concentration on the interpersonal aspects of human action, a series of theoretical impulses were required, which were able to put into question the orthodox conception of how the child's instinctual life develops.[2] For Freud and his followers, the child's interaction partners were initially significant only to the degree to which they acted as the objects of libidinal charges stemming from the intrapsychic conflict between unconscious instinctual demands and gradually emerging ego-controls. Beyond this merely intermediate, secondary role, only the mother was granted the independent status of a significant other, because the threatened loss of the mother in the phase of psychological helplessness of the infant was considered to be the cause of all more mature varieties of anxiety.[3] Since this established a picture of the psychological development of children in which their relations to other persons were viewed merely as a function of the unfolding of libidinal instincts, the empirical studies of René Spitz were enough to raise the first doubts about this approach. For what his observations showed was that the withdrawal of maternal care also led to severe disturbances in the behaviour of the infant in cases in which otherwise all of its physical needs were taken care of.[4] As Morris Eagle has shown in his overview, *Recent Developments in Psychoanalysis*,[5] this first indication of the independent significance of emotional bonds for early childhood development was supported and strengthened by a series of further results from psychological research. Experimental investigations in ethology were able to demonstrate that the attachment of baby primates to their so-called substitute mothers cannot stem from an experience of the satisfaction of instincts but rather from the experience of 'comfort'.[6] The path-breaking studies by John Bowlby led to the conclusion that human infants develop an active willingness to produce interpersonal proximity, which provides the basis for all later forms of affectional bonds.[7] And Daniel Stern, inspired largely by the research of Spitz and Bowlby, has been able to provide convincing evidence for a conception of the interaction between 'mother' and child as a highly complex process, in which both participants acquire, through practice, the capacity for the shared experience of emotions and perceptions.[8]

All of this must have been extremely unsettling for psychoanalysis, or at least for those parts of the psychoanalytical world – as could be found in Britain and the USA after the war – that were still receptive to the results of research. For, contrary to the Freudian structural model of the ego and the id, the evidence seemed to point to the lasting significance of very early, prelinguistic inter-active experiences. If the socialization process was predominantly dependent on experiences that children have in their first interpersonal relationships, then one could no longer maintain the orthodox idea that psychological development occurred as a sequence of organizational forms of 'monological' relations between libidinal drives and ego-capacity. Instead, the conceptual framework of psychoanalysis was in need of a fundamental extension along the separate dimension of the social interactions in which, through emotional relationships to other persons, children learn to see themselves as independent subjects. Finally, this theoretical conclusion was supported on the therapeutic side by the discovery that a growing number of patients suffered from mental illnesses that could not be traced back to intrapsychic conflicts between ego and id components but rather only to interpersonal disturbances in the process of the child's detachment. As they appeared in symptoms of borderline disorders or narcissism, these pathologies forced therapists to draw on explanatory approaches that accorded independent significance to the mutual bonds between children and significant others and that were thus incompatible with orthodox ideas.

Object-relations theory represents the first attempt at a conceptual response to the various challenges just outlined. It systematically takes into account the increased insight into the psychological status of interactive experiences in early childhood by supplementing the organization of libidinal drives with affective relationships to other persons as a second component of the maturational process. But what makes object-relations theory seem especially well suited to the purposes of a phenomenology of recognition relations is not the intersubjectivist extension of the psychoanalytic framework of explanation as such. Rather, it can convincingly portray love as a particular form of recognition only owing to the specific way in which it makes the success of affectional bonds dependent on the capacity, acquired in early childhood, to strike a balance between symbiosis and self-assertion. The path to this central insight, in which the intuitions of the young Hegel are confirmed to a surprising degree, was prepared by the English psychoanalyst Donald W. Winnicott. Since then, drawing on his writings, Jessica Benjamin has developed a first attempt at a psychoanalytic interpretation of the love relationship as a process of mutual recognition.

Winnicott wrote from the perspective of a psychoanalytically oriented paediatrician attempting, in the context of treating mental behavioural disorders, to gain an understanding of the 'good-enough' conditions for the socialization of young children.[9] What separates him from the approach found in the orthodox tradition of psychoanalysis is an insight that can easily be fitted into the theoretical framework constructed by Hegel and Mead. In the first months of life, infants are so dependent on the practical extension of their behaviour via the care they receive that it is a misleading abstraction on the part of psychoanalytic research to study the infant in isolation from all significant others, as an independent object of inquiry.[10] The care with which the 'mother' keeps the newborn baby alive is not added to the child's behaviour as something secondary but is rather merged with the child in such a way that one can plausibly assume that every human life begins with a phase of undifferentiated intersubjectivity, that is, of symbiosis. For Winnicott, this involves more than what Freudian theory describes under the heading of 'primary narcissism'. Not only does the infant hallucinate that all 'maternal' care flows from the infant's own omnipotence, but the 'mother' also comes to perceive, conversely, all of her child's reactions to be part and parcel of one single cycle of action. This initial, mutually experienced behavioural unit, for which the concept 'primary intersubjectivity' has established itself,[11] raises the central question that occupied Winnicott during his life: how are we to conceive of the interactional process by which 'mother' and child are able to detach themselves from a state of undifferentiated oneness in such a way that, in the end, they learn to accept and love each other as independent persons? Even just the formulation of the question indicates that Winnicott conceived the child's maturational process from the start as a task that can only be accomplished collectively, through the intersubjective interplay of 'mother' and child. Since both subjects are initially included in the state of symbiotic oneness in virtue of their active accomplishments, they must, as it were, learn from each other how to differentiate themselves as independent entities. Accordingly, the concepts that Winnicott uses to characterize the individual phases of this maturational process are always at the same time descriptions not merely of the psychological situation of one participant – the child – but rather of each of the states of the relationship between the 'mother' and the child. The progress that the child's development must make if it is to lead to a psychologically healthy personality is read off changes in the structure of a system of interactions and not off transformations in the organization of individual drive potential. To designate the first phase – that is, the relationship of symbiotic togetherness that begins immediately after birth – Winnicott generally introduces the category of 'absolute dependency'.[12] Here, both partners to interaction are entirely dependent on each other for the satisfaction of their needs and are incapable of individually demarcating themselves from each other. On the other hand, because the 'mother' identified herself projectively with the baby in the course of the pregnancy, she experiences the infant's helpless neediness as a lack of her own sensitivity. For this reason, her emotional attention is so completely devoted to the child that she learns to adapt her care and concern, as if out of an inner urge, to the infant's changing (and yet, as it were, empathically experienced) requirements. Corresponding to this precarious dependence of the 'mother' – whom Winnicott assumes to need the protective recognition of a third party[13] – there is, on the other hand, the utter helplessness of the infant, who is unable to articulate his or her physical and emotional needs communicatively. During the first months of life, the child is incapable of differentiating between self and environment, and moves within a horizon of experience, the continuity of which can only be assured by the supplemental assistance of a partner in interaction. To the extent that vitally necessary qualities of this undifferentiated experiential world include not only the release of instinctual tensions but also the provision of tender comfort, infants are helplessly dependent on the 'mother' to provide them with love by 'holding' them in the necessary ways. It is only in the protective space of 'being held' that infants can learn to coordinate their sensory and motor experiences around a single centre and thereby to develop a body-scheme. Because the activity of 'holding' is so extraordinarily significant for child development, Winnicott occasionally refers to the state of being merged as the 'holding phase'.[14]

Since, in this phase of symbiotic unity 'mother' and child are mutually dependent on each other, they are also only able to end this phase once each of them has been able to acquire a bit of new-found independence. For the 'mother', this emancipatory shift begins at the moment in which she can once again expand her social field of attention, as her primary, bodily identification with the infant begins to disperse. The resumption of an everyday routine and the renewed openness to family and friends forces her to deny the child immediate gratification of the child's needs – which she still spontaneously intuits – in that she increasingly leaves the child alone for long periods of time. Corresponding to the 'mother's' 'graduated de-adaptation',[15] there is an intellectual development, on the part of the infant, in which the expansion of conditioned reflexes is accompanied by the capacity for cognitive differentiation between self and environment. At six months, on average, the child begins to interpret acoustic and optical signals as clues to the future satisfaction of needs, so that the child is slowly able to endure the temporary absence of the 'mother'. In thereby experiencing, for the first time, the 'mother' as something in the world that is outside of his or her omnipotent control, the child simultaneously begins to become aware of his or her dependence. The infant leaves the phase of 'absolute dependence', because the dependence on the 'mother' enters his or her field of view in such a way that the child now learns to orient personal impulses toward specific aspects of her care. This new stage of interaction, which Winnicott labels 'relative dependence',[16] encompasses all of the decisive steps in the development of the child's capacity to form attachments. For this reason, he devoted the largest and most instructive part of his analyses to these steps. These analyses depict the emergence, in the relation between mother and child, of the 'being oneself in another' that represents the model for all more mature forms of love.

For the child, once the 'mother' regains her autonomy and can no longer always be at the child's disposal, a process of disillusionment sets in, thereby generating a major and difficult challenge. The person who, until this point, had been imagined to be part of the child's subjective world has gradually slipped out of the child's omnipotent control, and the child must begin to come to a 'recognition of [the object] as an entity in its own right'.[17] The child is able to accomplish this task to the extent to which his or her social environment allows for the implementation of two psychological mechanisms, which together help the child work through this new experience emotionally. Winnicott addressed the first of these two mechanisms under the keyword 'destruction'. The second is presented within the context of his concept of 'transitional phenomena'.

In response to the gradually acquired awareness of a resistant reality, the infant soon begins to act aggressively, primarily towards the 'mother', who is now perceived by the child to be independent herself. As if to rebel against the loss of omnipotence, the infant attempts to destroy her body – which, until then, had been experienced as a source of pleasure – by hitting, biting, and kicking it. In earlier interpretive approaches, these outbursts of aggression were usually linked causally to the frustrations that inevitably set in with the experience of losing omnipotent control. For Winnicott, by contrast, they represent inherently purposive acts, by which the infant unconsciously tests out whether the affectively charged object does, in fact, belong to a reality that is beyond influence and, in that sense, 'objective'. If the 'mother' survives these destructive attacks without taking revenge, the child has thereby, in a manner of speaking, actively placed himself or herself into a world in which he or she exists alongside other subjects.[18] In this sense, the child's destructive, injurious acts do not represent the expression of an attempt to cope negatively with frustration, but rather comprise the constructive means by which the child can come to recognize the 'mother', unambivalently, as 'an entity in its own right'. If she survived the infant's destructive experiments as a person capable of resistance – indeed, if she, through her refusals, even provided the child with occasion for fits of temper – then the child will, by integrating its aggressive impulses, become able to love her. In the bond that has now been formed, the child is able to reconcile its (still symbiotically supported) devotion to the 'mother' with the experience of standing on its own:

> The mother is needed over this time and she is needed because of her survival value. She is an environment-mother and at the same time an object-mother, the object of excited loving. In this latter role she is repeatedly destroyed or damaged. The child gradually comes to integrate these two aspects of the mother and to be able to love and to be affectionate with the surviving mother at the same time.[19]

If we thus conceive the child's first process of detachment as the result of aggressive behavioural expressions, then there seems to be good reason to follow Jessica Benjamin's suggestion and introduce the Hegelian 'struggle for recognition' here as an instructive explanatory model.[20] For it is indeed only in the attempt to destroy his or her 'mother' – that is, in the form of a struggle – that the child realizes that he or she is dependent on the loving care of an independently existing person with claims of her own. But for the 'mother', in turn, this means that she too must first learn to accept the independence of the child if she wants to 'survive' these destructive attacks in the context of her reestablished sphere of activity. What the aggressively charged situation demands of her, in fact, is that she understand the destructive wish-fantasies of her child as something that goes against her own interests and thus as something that can be ascribed to the child alone, as an already independent person. If, in the way just sketched, a first step of mutual demarcation is successfully taken, then mother and child can acknowledge their dependence on each other's love without having to merge symbiotically.

In a supplementary part of his analyses, Winnicott then claims that the child's capacity to strike a balance, in this early form, between independence and symbiosis varies with the degree of distortion in the development of a second coping mechanism. He presents this with the help of the concept of 'transitional objects'. The empirical phenomenon that Winnicott has in mind here consists in the strong tendency of children a few months in age to form highly affectively charged relationships to objects in their physical environment. Such objects – be it part of a toy, the corner of a pillow, or the child's own thumb – are treated as an exclusive possession, sometimes tenderly loved, sometimes passionately abused. For Winnicott, the key to explaining the function of these transitional objects is the fact that the child's partners to inter-action also situate the objects in a domain of reality, with regard to which the question of fiction or reality becomes unimportant. As if by tacit agreement, they are transferred to an 'intermediate' realm, where it is up to the participants to decide whether to view it as belonging to an inner world of mere halluci-nations or to the empirical world of objective facts:

> Of the transitional object it can be said that it is a matter of agreement between us and the baby that we will never ask the question: 'Did you conceive of this or was it presented to you from without?' The important point is that no decision on this point is expected. The question is not to be formulated.[21]

If one takes into consideration the developmental phase in which the discovery of these intermediate objects of significance occurs, then there are grounds for supposing that they represent surrogates for the 'mother', who has just been lost to external reality. Because they are ontologically ambiguous in nature, the child can actively use them to keep omnipotence fantasies alive, even after the experience of separation, and can simultaneously use them to creatively probe reality. In this playful yet reality-checking manner of utiliza-tion, it also becomes apparent that the function of transitional objects cannot be restricted to the symbiotic appropriation of the role of the 'mother' as experi-enced in the state of merging. The child relates to the objects he or she has selected not only with symbiotic tenderness but also with repeated attacks of rage and attempts to destroy it. Winnicott believes that one can conclude from this that, in the case of transitional objects, one is dealing with ontological links, as it were, that mediate between the primary experience of being merged and the awareness of separateness. In the playful interaction with these affectively charged objects, the child repeatedly attempts to bridge, symbolically, the painful gap between inner and outer reality. The fact that this coincides with the emergence of intersubjectively accepted illusions allows Winnicott to go even one step further and to arrive at a thesis with consequences both far-reaching and difficult to assess. Because this ontological, mediating sphere arises as the solution to a task that people continue to face throughout their lives, it is the psychological origin of all adult interests *vis-à-vis* cultural objectivations. Not without a sense for sharpening the speculative point of the matter, Winnicott writes:

> It is assumed here that the task of reality-acceptance is never completed, that no human being is free from the strain of relating inner and outer reality, and that relief from this strain is provided by an intermediate area of experience . . . which is not challenged (arts, religion, etc.). This intermediate area is in direct continuity with the play area of the small child who is 'lost' in play.[22]

This last phrase also offers a clue as to why the concept of 'transitional objects' is to be understood as a direct extension of Winnicott's interpretation of love in terms of a theory of recognition. According to him, the child is capable of being 'lost' in interaction with the chosen object only if, after the separation from the symbiotically experienced 'mother', the child can generate enough trust in the continuity of her care that he or she is able, under the protection of a felt intersubjectivity, to be alone in a carefree manner. The child's creativity – indeed, the human faculty of imagination in general – presupposes a 'capacity to be alone', which itself can arise only out of a basic confidence in the care of a loved one.[23] From this perspective, far-reaching insights emerge into the connection between creativity and recognition, which are of no further interest to us here. Of central importance, however, for the attempt to reconstruct love as a particular relationship of recognition is Winnicott's claim that the ability to be alone is dependent on the child's trust in the continuity of the 'mother's' care. The thesis thus outlined provides some insight into the type of relation-to-self that one can develop when one knows oneself to be loved by a person that one experiences as independent and for whom one, in turn, feels affection or love.

If the 'mother' managed to pass the child's unconscious test by enduring the aggressive attacks without withdrawing her love in revenge, she now belongs, from the perspective of the child, to a painfully accepted external world. As has been said, the child must now become aware, for the first time, of his or her dependence on the 'mother's' care. If the 'mother's' love is lasting and reliable, the child can simultaneously develop, under the umbrella of her intersubjective reliability, a sense of confidence in the social provision of the needs he or she has and, via the psychological path this opens up, a basic 'capacity to be alone' gradually unfolds in the child. Winnicott traces the young child's ability to be alone – in the sense of beginning to discover, without anxiety, his or her 'own personal life' – back to the experience of the 'continued existence of a reliable mother':[24] only to the extent to which there is 'a good object in the psychic reality of the individual'[25] can he or she become responsive to inner impulses and pursue them in an open, creative way, without fear of being abandoned.

The shift of focus to that part of one's own self that Mead called the 'I' thus presupposes that one trusts the loved person to maintain his or her affection, even when one's own attention is withdrawn. But this certainty is, for its part, just the outwardly oriented side of a mature confidence that one's own needs will lastingly be met by the other because one is of unique value to the other. To this extent, the 'capacity to be alone' is the practical expression of a form of individual relation-to-self, similar to what Erikson conceived of under the title of 'trust'. In becoming sure of the 'mother's' love, young children come to trust themselves, which makes it possible for them to be alone without anxiety.

In one of his typically cryptic asides, Winnicott claims that this communicatively protected ability to be alone is 'the stuff of which friendship is made'.[26] What he is evidently getting at here is the idea that every strong emotional bond between people opens up the possibility of both parties relating to themselves in a relaxed manner, oblivious to their particular situation, much like an infant who can rely on his or her 'mother's' emotional care. This suggestion can be understood as an invitation to identify, in the successful relationship between 'mother' and child, a pattern of interaction whose mature reappearance in adult life is an indication of successful affectional bonds to other people. In this way, we put ourselves methodologically in a position to draw conclusions from the maturational processes of early childhood about the communicative structure that makes love a special relationship of mutual recognition.

We can then proceed from the hypothesis that all love relationships are driven by the unconscious recollection of the original experience of merging that characterized the first months of life for 'mother' and child. The inner state of symbiotic oneness so radically shapes the experiential scheme of complete satisfaction that it keeps alive, behind the back of the subject and throughout the subject's life, the desire to be merged with another person. Of course, this desire for merging can only become a feeling of love once, in the unavoidable experience of separation, it has been disappointed in such a way that it hence- forth includes the recognition of the other as an independent person. Only a refracted symbiosis enables the emergence of a productive interpersonal balance between the boundary-establishment and boundary-dissolution that, for Winnicott, belongs to the structure of a relationship that has matured through mutual disillusionment. There, the capacity to be alone constitutes the subject-based pole of an intersubjective tension, whose opposing pole is the capacity for boundary-dissolving merging with the other. The act of boundary- dissolution, in which subjects experience themselves to be reconciled with one another, can take a wide variety of forms, depending on the type of bond. In friendships, it may be the shared experience of an unselfconscious conversation or an utterly unforced moment together. In erotic relationships, it is the sexual union in which one knows oneself to be reconciled with the other without difference. But in each case, the process of merging obtains its very condition of possibility solely from the opposite experience of encountering the other as someone who is continually re-establishing his or her boundary. It is only because the assurance of care gives the person who is loved the strength to open up to himself or herself in a relaxed relation-to-self that he or she can become an independent subject with whom oneness can be experienced as a mutual dissolution of boundries. To this extent, the form of recognition found in love, which Hegel had described as 'being oneself in another', represents not an intersubjective state so much as a communicative arc suspended between the experience of being able to be alone and the experience of being merged; 'ego- relatedness' and symbiosis here represent mutually required counterweights that, taken together, make it possible for each to be at home in the other.

These conclusions lose some of their speculative character when we consider Jessica Benjamin's psychoanalytical research, in which she has studied patho- logical disorders of the love relationship. She too makes use of object-relations theory in order, on the basis of findings regarding the successful course of the separation of 'mother' and child, to draw conclusions about the structure of interaction essential to a successful bond between adults. But what primarily concerns her in this connection are the dynamics of the disorders of the love relationship that are clinically termed 'masochism' and 'sadism'.[27] It then turns out that one of the advantages of the concept of love found in the theory of recognition – as developed here, following Winnicott – is that it makes it possible to grasp failures of this sort in systematic terms, as one-sidedness in the direction of one of the two poles of the balance of recognition. In pathological cases, the reciprocity of the intersubjectively suspended arc is destroyed by the fact that one of the subjects involved is no longer able to detach himself or herself either from the state of egocentric independence or from that of symbiotic dependence. As Benjamin is able to show, these types of one-sidedness interrupt the continual exchange between ego-relatedness and boundary-dissolution, in that they replace it with a rigid scheme of mutual supplementation. The symbiotically sustained dependence of one partner is then ultimately just the complement to the aggressively tinged omnipotence fantasies upon which the other partner is fixated.[28] For Benjamin, there is of course no doubt but that these distortions of the balance of recognition are to be traced back to psychological disturbances, the cause of which lies in the abortive development of the child's detachment from the 'mother'. To support her position here, she can draw on therapeutic findings such as those presented by Otto F. Kernberg in his psychoanalytic study of the 'pathologies of love life'.[29]

What is of interest here, of course, are not the details of this type of genetic deduction but rather the fact that the basic objects of study here are relational disorders that can be assessed within the categories of mutual recognition. For if it is, in fact, possible to derive a criterion for what counts as a disorder, with regard to affectional bonds, from the idea of the unsuccessful reciprocity of certain tensely balanced states, then this also demonstrates, in turn, the empirical appropriateness of a concept of love conceived in terms of a theory of recognition.

From a therapeutic angle, the possibility of reinterpreting the clinical material on relational pathologies in terms of a structural one-sidedness in the balance of recognition supports the idea that, ideally speaking, the love relationship represents a symbiosis refracted by recognition. Accordingly, every prominent model of an instrumentally one-sided relational constellation – to which the love relationship in general is reduced in Sartre's phenomenological analysis[30] – can be seen as a psychoanalytically explicable deviation from a defensible ideal of interaction. Moreover, because this relationship of recognition prepares the ground for a type of relation-to-self in which subjects mutually acquire basic confidence in themselves, it is both conceptually and genetically prior to every other form of reciprocal recognition. This fundamental level of emotional confidence – not only in the experience of needs and feelings, but also in their expression – which the intersubjective experience of love helps to bring about, constitutes the psychological precondition for the development of all further attitudes of self-respect.[31]

Notes

1   On this, see Niklas Luhmann, *Love as Passion: The Codification of Intimacy*, trans. Jeremy Gaines and Doris L. Jones (Cambridge, MA: Harvard University Press, 1986), ch. 13.

2   See the outstanding overview by Morris N. Eagle, in *Recent Developments in Psychoanalysis: A Critical Evaluation* (New York: McGraw-Hill, 1989). See further J. R. Greenberg and Stephen A. Mitchell, *Object Relations in Psychoanalytic Theory* (Cambridge, MA: Harvard University Press, 1983).

3   Sigmund Freud, *Inhibitions, Symptoms, and Anxiety*, trans. Alix Strachey (New York: Norton, 1959).

4   René A. Spitz, *The First Year of Life: A Psychoanalytic Study of Normal and Deviant Development of Object Relations* in collaboration with W. Godfrey Cobliner (New York: International Universities Press, 1965), esp. ch. 14.

5   Morris N. Eagle (1989), *Recent Developments in Psychoanalysis: A Critical Evaluation*, ch. 2.

6   H. F. Harlow (1958), 'The nature of love'. In *American Psychologist* 13, pp. 673ff.

7   John Bowlby, *Attachment and Loss*, vol. 1: *Attachment* (London: Hogarth Press and the Institute of Psychoanalysis, 1969).

8   Daniel Stern, *The First Relationship: Mother and Infant* (London: Open Books, 1977). I have followed object-relations theorists here in using the term 'mother' to refer to a social role that traditionally has been – but need not be – fulfilled primarily by women. To emphasize the status of this concept as a technical term, it has been placed in quotation marks.

9   I refer in the following to: Donald W. Winnicott, *The Maturational Processes and the Facilitating Environment: Studies in the Theory of Emotional Development* (London: Hogarth Press and the Institute of Psychoanalysis, 1965); *Playing and Reality* (London: Tavistock, 1971). For a succinct account of Winnicott's particular role within psychoanalysis, see J. R. Greenberg and Stephen A. Mitchell, *Object Relations in Psychoanalytic Theory*, ch. 7.

10 Donald W. Winnicott, 'The theory of the parent-infant relationship' (1965), *Maturational Processes and the facilitating Environment*, pp. 37–55.

11 See, for example: Couym Trevorthen, 'Communication and cooperation in early infancy: a description of primary intersubjectivity'. In Margaret Bullowa (ed.), *Before Speech: The Beginning of Interpersonal Communication* (Cambridge: Cambridge University Press, 1979), pp. 321ff; and 'The foundations of intersubjectivity: development of interpersonal and cooperative understanding of infants'. In D. R. Olson (ed.), *The Social Foundations of Language and Thought: Essays in Honor of Jerome S. Bruner* (New York: Norton, 1980), pp. 316ff.

12 Donald W. Winnicott (1965), 'From dependence towards independence in the development of the individual', *The Maturation Processes and the Facilitating Environment*, pp. 83–92.

13 Donald W. Winnicott (1965), *The Maturation Processes and the Facilitating Environment*, p. 52.

14 Ibid., pp. 44–5.

15 Donald W. Winnicott (1965), *The Maturation Processes and the Facilitating Environment*, p. 87.

16 Ibid., pp. 87–9.

17 Donald W. Winnicott (1971), 'The use of an object and relating through identifications', *Playing and Reality*, pp. 86–94.

18 See esp. ibid., pp. 104ff.; see with regard to this complex also Marianne Schreiber, 'Kann der Mensch Verantwortung für seine Aggressivität ubernehmen? Aspekte aus der Psychologie D. W. Winnicotts und Melanie Kleins'. In Alfred Schöpf (ed.), *Aggression und Gewalt: Anthropologisch-Wissenschaftliche Beiträge* (Würzburg: Königshausen & Neumann, 1983), pp. 155ff.

19 Donald W. Winnicott (1965), 'Morals and education', *The Maturational Processes and the Facilitating Environment*, pp. 95–105.

20 Jessica Benjamin, *The Bonds of Love: Psychoanalysis, Feminism, and the Problem of Domination* (New York: Pantheon, 1988), esp. pp. 36ff.

21 Donald W. Winnicott (1971), 'Transitional objects and transitional phenomena', *Playing and Reality*, pp. 1–25.

22 Ibid., p. 13.

23 Donald W. Winnicott (1971), 'Playing: creative activity and the search of the self', ibid., pp. 53–64, esp. pp. 54–6; see also (1965) 'The capacity to be alone', pp. 29–36.

24 Ibid., p. 33.

25 Ibid., p. 32.

26 Ibid., p. 33.

27 Jessica Benjamin (1988), esp. ch. 2.

28 Ibid., pp. 65ff.

29 Otto F. Kernberg, *Object-relations Theory and Clinical Psychoanalysis* (New York: Jason Aronson, 1984), chs 7 and 8.

30 See Jean-Paul Sartre, *Being and Nothingness: An Essay on Phenomenological Ontology*, trans. Hazel E. Barnes (New York: Washington Square Press, 1966), Part III, ch. 3, pp. 441–526.

31 On self-confidence as the result of the experience of love, see inter alia, John Bowlby, *The Making and Breaking of Affectional Bonds* (London: Tavistock, 1979), ch. 6; Erik H. Erikson, *Identity and the Life Cycle* (New York: Norton, 1980), pp. 57–67; less fertile, despite its promising title, is Nathaniel Branden's *The Psychology of Self-Esteem* (Los Angeles: Nash, 1969). Chapter 9 of the book carries the title 'Self-esteem and romantic love', but it remains utterly unclear in both its categories and its conception of the phenomenon. Paul Gilbert, by contrast, has recently made an important philosophical contribution to the analysis of primary relationships such as love and friendship in his *Human Relationships: A Philosophical Introduction* (Oxford: Blackwell, 1991), inter alia chs 2 and 4; in addition, for a recent psychoanalytically oriented presentation of love as a relational pattern, see Martin S. Bergmann, *The Anatomy of Loving* (New York: Columbia University Press, 1987), esp. Part II, pp. 141ff.

14

Truth, Semblance, Reconciliation: Adorno's Aesthetic Redemption of Modernity

Albrecht Wellmer

We can now try to decode Adorno's concept of the truth of art, at least up to a certain point.[1] Like Koppe, I proceed on the basis that we can only speak of the truth of art if we already know what is meant by truth independently of this specific context.[2] I should like to take Habermas's pragmatic differentiation of the everyday concept of truth as my starting point. In Koppe's terms, what we are dealing with here is a distinction between 'apophantic' truth, 'endeetic' truth (truthfulness), and moral and practical truth. These three concepts of truth represent the dimensions of validity for everyday speech, and thus a preconception of 'truth' which is available to every speaker. If we proceed on the basis of an *everyday* concept of truth that is differentiated in this way, then the concept of the truth of art seems at first to take on an enigmatic character. It transpires, however, that art is *involved* in questions of truth in a peculiar and complex way: not only does art open up the experience of reality, and correct and expand it; it is also the case that aesthetic 'validity' (i.e. the 'rightness' of a work of art) *touches on* questions of truth, truthfulness, and moral and practical correctness in an intricate fashion without being attributable to any one of the three dimensions of truth, or even to all three together. We might therefore suppose that the 'truth of art' can only be defended, if at all, as a phenomenon of interference between the various dimensions of truth.

Now in his way, Adorno also emphasized the moment of interference between various dimensions of truth in his discussion of the truth of art; this is apparent in his notion of an interconnection between the mimetic-expressive and the rational moments in the work of art, as well as in his construction of the relationship between truth, semblance and reconciliation. The interpretation of the truth of art as a phenomenon of interference between various dimensions of truth thus represents in the first instance merely a reformulation in terms of linguistic pragmatics of one of Adorno's central ideas. The question of the consequences resulting from this reformulation is therefore of greater importance than the reformulation itself. Some of these consequences have already been adumbrated above, at the point where I drew a distinction between a 'functional' and a 'substantial' relation between the work of art and 'reconciliation' and emphasized the *practical* character of aesthetic cognition in this connection. If we apply this to [the] analysis of Adorno's concept of the truth of art, then what we are doing is separating two aspects of this concept of the truth of art which Adorno integrates dialectically, namely 'truth$_1$' (aesthetic rightness) and 'truth$_2$' (objective truth). This is not intended to mean that aesthetic rightness (*Stimmigkeit*) has nothing to do with aesthetic truth, but rather that aesthetic rightness does not in itself *mean* reconciliation. The substantialization of the relation between the work of art and reconciliation means that, for Adorno, this relation becomes a central moment of the truth *content* of art. For this reason, Adorno is only able to conceive of the act of appropriating the truth of art in terms of a transformation of aesthetic experience into philosophical insight. For Adorno, the attempt to decipher the truth content that is encoded in the work of art is nothing other than the attempt to retrieve the truth of art, which would otherwise be lost, by putting it into words. *What* is retrieved by conceptual articulation in this way, however, is the polemical and utopian concept of art as such, the relation of art to reconciliation as something that can be known. It is a truth *about* art, and not the truth content of any individual work of art. For Adorno, the two planes of analysing the *concept* of art on the one hand and appropriating the specific, concrete truth of art on the other coincide; and it is only because this is so that he is bound to conceive of aesthetic cognition as philosophical insight, and of the truth of art as philosophical truth. In this way it is the apophantic dimension of the truth of art which ultimately comes to dominate the picture: Adorno's aesthetics becomes an apophantic aesthetic of truth.

The interpretation of the truth of art, in terms of a pragmatic philosophy of language, as a phenomenon of interference between the various dimensions of truth clearly carries a greater significance than a mere reformulation of Adorno's insights. For only now does it become possible to arrive at a conceptual distinction between the truth content of works of art and their relation to reconciliation. Between these two poles of the relation of art to truth, which are dialectically integrated in Adorno, the receiving subject enters the picture as a mediating instance. But in the process, the sense in which we speak of the truth content of works of art must itself also change. In view of what was said earlier it is reasonable to suppose that the truth of art will have more to do with a *potential* for truth in works of art than with truth in the literal sense. The truth content of works of art would then be the epitome of the potential effects of works of art that are *relevant* to the truth, or of their potential for *disclosing* truth. Such an interpretation of the truth of art as the epitome of *effects* relevant to the truth admittedly remains unsatisfactory as long as we are not in a position to

say what it is about aesthetic products that makes them *bearers* of truth potential. In other words we would still have to explain the connection between
aesthetic *validity* (*Stimmigkeit*) and the truth of art.

Since no philosopher from Kant to Adorno has been able to clarify entirely
the complex relationship between beauty and truth, the prospects for re-
constructing this central element of Adorno's aesthetics in terms of a pragmatic
philosophy of language are admittedly not very bright. I think it is nevertheless
possible to indicate a direction in which we might look for a solution to this
problem.

I would formulate the problem like this. There is something about art which
leads us to view works of art themselves – or at least many of them – as vehicles
of truth-*claims*; and these claims to *truth* that are made by works of art are
connected with their *aesthetic* claim to validity. In what follows I shall confine
myself to the discussion of apophantic and endeetic truth, i.e. to the apophantic
and endeetic 'truth-claims' of art.

Let us take as our starting-point the intuitive core of the apophantic concept
of the truth of art, which might be characterized by means of such metaphors
as the 'disclosing', 'revealing' or 'showing' of reality. The idea is that art
'discloses', 'reveals' or 'shows' reality in an outstanding fashion. Such
metaphors are interesting because they are, in certain aesthetic contexts, as
unavoidable as they are notoriously misleading. They are unavoidable because
reality can only be shown, and not put into words. They are misleading
because, in the case of art, *what* shows itself can only be shown (in this way) *in
the medium of showing*, which is to say in the work of art itself as something
sensually present; it cannot show itself as an aesthetically unmediated
presence. Therefore what shows itself in the work of art can only be recognized
as something showing itself on the basis of a familiarity with it which did not
before have the character of perceptual evidence. It is as if a mirror had the
capacity to show the 'true' face of human beings: we should only be able to
know *that* it was their *true* face on the basis of a familiarity with them which
only assumed the form of an unveiled sensual presence when the image of
them appeared in the mirror. We can only recognize the 'essence' which
appears in the apparition if we already *know* it as something which does
not appear.

With the help of the metaphors of 'appearing' and 'being shown' we can
clarify the connection between aesthetic validity and the capacity of the
beautiful to disclose reality, even if we cannot clarify the connection between
aesthetic validity and *truth*. In an aesthetic construct (in the traditional sort, at
least) every detail is important; just as a minute alteration of the facial features
would change the expression of a face, so too would the reality that is shown
in an aesthetic construct be altered if the sensual configuration of that construct
were changed. Alternatively we might say that an aesthetic construct is more
or less appropriate, more or less faithful, more or less 'authentic' in making
manifest what appears in it. It may not be a simple matter, of course, to decide
whether reality has been made manifest in an adequate fashion. Or rather, if

the intuitive judgements are controversial, then the corresponding (aesthetic) discussions might be endless.

Such aesthetic discussions are concerned with the correct understanding, the correct perception of the aesthetic phenomenon. They refer back to the aesthetic experience itself, both correcting and expanding it. The aesthetic sense of 'rightness' must, in the final analysis, be *perceived*; and in so far as the aesthetic rightness is connected with the showing of reality, the work of art must also be perceived *as* a reality being shown in the medium of showing, and reality must be *recognized* as showing itself. It must be recognized not in the sense of the truth of a statement, but in the sense that a face is recognized, only with this difference: when we 'recognize' reality in an aesthetic experience (and for Adorno the gesture of showing embodied in the work of art is represented by the expression 'that's how it is'), then what we have known diffusely, experienced vaguely and apprehended implicitly acquires the firm outlines of a sensual experience for the first time. What was always present in diffuse fashion, at a pre-conscious or sub-conscious level, comes together into the manifestation of an image, something which can be 'grasped' – or to use a semantically related term, which can be *'comprehended'*. To put it another way, the uncomprehended experience is illuminated by becoming condensed into an experience of a higher order: experience becomes experienceable.

So far I have been using a Platonic model, as it were, in which 'being acquainted with something' has an ontological precedence over the 'recognizing' of it. But art clearly works in *both* directions: art also *transforms* our experience of the thing we are acquainted with, so that it only becomes the thing we recognize *in retrospect*. Art does not merely disclose reality, it also opens our eyes. This opening of eyes (and ears), this transformation of perception, is the healing of a partial blindness (and deafness), of an incapacity to perceive and experience reality in the way that we learn to perceive and experience it through the medium of aesthetic experience. We might say that in modernist art, this moment of the *transformation* of perception through aesthetic experience becomes increasingly dominant.

Now, what has all this to do with aesthetic *truth*? Clearly the temptation to expand the concept of truth into the realm of aesthetics is based on the power of beauty to disclose reality. This power *manifests* itself in those *effects* of art which are relevant to questions of truth; at the same time it *confronts* us as an aesthetic *validity*-claim. In the light of what we have said so far it is possible to explain in what sense we can speak of a truth-*claim* which corresponds to the truth-*potential* of works of art, and which is inseparable from an *aesthetic* validity-claim. It is evidently not possible to explain what this truth-claim is by reference to an apophantic concept of the truth of art; when we tried to capture this concept in metaphorical terms it eluded our grasp. But we can try, as M. Seel has suggested,[3] to understand the connection between aesthetic validity-claim and truth-claim by reference to the structure of aesthetic discourse, which is a realm in which the question of the 'authenticity' of 'representation' is dealt with at the same time as the question of aesthetic rightness. Aesthetic discourse is the mediating instance between the apophantic metaphors from which we started out, and questions of aesthetic rightness. That is why we can only understand the truth-*claim* of art if we start by looking at the complex relationship of interdependency between the various dimensions of truth in aesthetic discourse. In any dispute over the truth or falsehood of aesthetic constructs which is also to be a dispute over the aesthetic quality of those constructs, the participants have to bring their own experience to bear on the discussion. However, their own experience can only be mobilized for discussion and transformed into arguments within the three dimensions of truth, truthfulness, and moral and practical rightness *simultaneously*. Both the truth-*potential* and the truth-*claim* of art can thus only be explained with recourse to the complex relationship of interdependency between the various dimensions of truth in the living experience of individuals, or in the formation and transformation of attitudes, modes of perception, and interpretations.

Truth can thus only be ascribed to art in a metaphorical sense. But this metaphorical ascription has a firm basis in the relationship between aesthetic validity and the truth-potential of works of art. If we pursue this idea further, we can see that the interweaving of the various dimensions of truth in the *effects* of art and in aesthetic discourse can be related to the metaphorical interweaving of the dimensions of truth in the work of art itself. For it is no coincidence that the metaphors of 'showing' and 'revealing' can be easily linked to those of 'saying' and 'expressing'. Reality is manifested in art, to borrow a phrase from F. Koppe, in a 'mode of being affected'; the processes of 'revealing' and 'expressing' are intermeshed. As something that speaks, as something expressive, art converts what has been diffusely experienced into the presence of a sensual phenomenon; as something that reveals, it becomes eloquent and expressive. Which is why it would also be possible to see the immanent utopia of aesthetic semblance in the overwhelming experience that it can be said, and that – as Adorno once put it – art 'objectifies the ephemeral, thus citing it into permanence'[4]. In so far as the metaphors of 'saying' and 'expressing' dominate the way we think about art, we shall tend to explain what is authentic in a work of art, not in concepts of apophantic truth, but in terms of endeetic truthfulness; this is the tendency I notice in Habermas and – up to a point – in Koppe. But both attempts at an explanation, whether on the basis of apophantic truth or of endeetic truthfulness, share a common weakness in that they have to interpret the work of art by analogy with a special type of speech-act. In a work of art, however, the artist does not (literally) *say* something; and the authenticity of a construct is therefore not decided by the question whether the artist was being truthful. It is rather the other way around: the truthfulness of the artist, in so far as we can speak of it at all, is *shown* by the authenticity of the construct. Neither truth *nor* truthfulness can be ascribed to the work of art in a *non-metaphorical* sense if we are understanding 'truth' and 'truthfulness' in terms of a pragmatically differentiated everyday concept of truth. The *metaphorical* interweaving of truth and truthfulness – and even of normative correctness – in the work of art is, on the contrary, something which we can only explain by the fact that the work of art, as a symbolical construct that carries an *aesthetic* validity-claim, is at the same time the object of an *aesthetic experience* that refers back to our ordinary experience in which the three dimensions of truth are interwoven in a *non-metaphorical* sense.

If we reconstruct the concept of the truth of art in the way that has been indicated here, then it is also possible to combine Kantian insights with motifs of an aesthetic of truth. In his critical account of the aesthetics of truth,[5] R. Bubner has tried to *oppose* Kant's concept of beauty to the aesthetics of truth. I do not believe that this presentation of the matter in terms of stark alternatives is convincing, as indeed is already indicated in Kant's aesthetic by the transition from the analysis of beauty to a theory of the beautiful in art. Kant's idea of characterizing the experience of beauty in terms of an indefinite and free interplay of imagination and understanding is certainly irreconcilable with an apophantic aesthetics of truth, because the free play of the *faculties* is precisely *not* supposed to become fixed as a determinate relationship between concept and intuition. But precisely the *expansion* of the faculties which results from the pleasurable and free interplay of imaginative and intellectual-reflexive moments in aesthetic experience could be related to the notion of truth. We only have to apply the character of potentiality, which is contained in the term 'faculties', to the concept of truth in order to see that the truth-content of the work of art is really its truth-*potential* – in the sense I have outlined above.

If aesthetic semblance can be understood as the arena of that pleasurable and free interplay of imaginative and intellectual-reflexive activities, in the Kantian sense to which we have just alluded, then the utopian 'lustre of semblance' would not in the end be totally isolated from truth and a real utopia. For the ecstatic moment of aesthetic experience, in which the continuum of historical time is exploded, can be understood as the 'point of entry' for forces which, in their non-aesthetic usage, might restore a continuity between art and living praxis. This is presumably also what Jauss means when he forges a connection between 'aesthetic enjoyment' and the 'conversion of aesthetic experience into symbolic or communicative action'.[6] But if this 'conversion' of aesthetic experience into communicative action indicates that works of art are closely involved in questions of truth, as we have just seen, then the emancipation of semblance cannot be total: semblance communicates secretly with truth and reconciliation, as Adorno believed, and yet in a sense that differs from what Adorno believed.

I have tried to show in what sense the relationship between Adorno's categories of truth, semblance and reconciliation can be developed into a complex constellation of categories such that the philosophical potential and the critical purpose of Adorno's aesthetics can be preserved. If we add a dimension of 'communicative rationality' to Adorno's concept of rationality, then it becomes possible to expand his aesthetics of truth in a pragmatic way. If the receiving, communicating and acting subjects are incorporated into the relationship between art, reality and utopia, this produces an effect of 'multi-dimensionality' by contrast with Adorno's own dialectically one-dimensional constructions. It would be worthwhile discussing issues of actionist, aleatoric, and popular art (towards which Adorno, almost a priori, adopted a critical atti-tude), as well as the issue of the 'dissolution of the concept of the work' about which we have heard so much recently, from this point of view. I believe that, on these issues too, we should have to give a new slant to Adorno's central arguments, which are frequently criticized today – and not without cause – as 'traditionalist'. But for present purposes I should like to limit myself to two partial aspects, namely the question of the mutability of the relationship between art and living praxis, which has been given prominence by P. Bürger in particular, on the one hand, and the question of the aesthetic valency of popular art forms on the other.

1   In my discussion of Habermas, I have interpreted the process of differenti-ation between the spheres of validity of science, law and morality, and art, in which problems are dealt with according to the special logic appropriate to the particular type of validity-claim in question, as the expression of an irreversible cultural learning process. If we keep to this interpretation, on the abstract level of dimensions of validity, then it is no longer possible for slogans like the 'sub-lation of art in the praxis of life', if we take them literally, to point the way towards a possibility of escaping from a condition in which art is ideologically *separated* from the reality of life. Those avant-garde movements that Bürger has analysed tried to convert the aesthetic *directly* into the practical,[7] and their failure was therefore rooted in a self-deception about the nature of their own activities, *amongst other things*. Bürger rightly points to the fact that 'what had become historically split off as the realm of aesthetics' cannot be made into 'the organizing centre of a liberating and liberated praxis of life'.[8] But nevertheless we can – and Bürger insists that we should – think of the *relationships* in which art and living praxis stand to each other as changeable. The process of differ-entiation between spheres of validity must be distinguished from particular forms of *institutional* differentiation. Bürger says of the bourgeois 'institution of art' that 'art as fully individuated subsystem is, at the same time, one whose individual products no longer tend to assume a social function'.[9] It is consis-tent with this view when Bürger demands a *transformation* of the institution of art, or at least of the norms that regulate it,[10] in order that art should regain its social relevance. Bürger's utopia of an avant-gardist transformation of the insti-tution of art so that 'all can freely develop their productive potential'[11] seems to me to represent an interpretation of the 'praxis of art', of its social function, that is weighted too heavily towards the aesthetics of production. It is only for this reason that he can play off the praxis of art against Adorno and against the idea of the (great) work of art.[12] If, on the other hand, we take the reception side into account, then it is not clear why a change in the function of art that is related to a democratic opening-up of society should exclude the idea of the great work of art. The opposite seems to me to be the case: without the paradigmatic

productions of 'great' art, in which the imagination, the accumulated knowledge and the skill of obsessively specialized artists is objectivized, a democratically generalized aesthetic production would presumably decline into an amateur arts-and-craftism. A similar case might be made here as for the elements of improvisation in recent music. Boulez and Dahlhaus have pointed out that music would suffer a regression if the moment of improvisation were to be treated as something absolute: improvisation is as a rule only an activation and variation of what is laid down in memory or, as Boulez says, it is 'manipulated recollection'.[13] John Cage hit upon the same problem when he said, 'I must find a way of liberating people without them going silly.'[14]

I argue on the assumption that a transformation of the 'institution of art' cannot mean the abolition of the 'culture of experts',[15] but that it would amount rather to the establishment of a tighter network of connections between the culture of experts and the lifeworld on the one hand, and the culture of experts and popular art on the other. Barriers to such a rapprochement between aesthetics and the practical sphere, between high and low culture, have been identified by Adorno and Horkheimer in their critique of the culture industry. But if we allow the course of history such a degree of ambiguity that we can still see it as possessing a potential for emancipation, then it is also possible to discover traces of a transformation of the relationship between art and the lifeworld in reality. On the basis of these traces we can defend the idea of an altered relationship between art and the lifeworld in which a democratic praxis would be able to draw productively on the innovative and communicative potential of art. My reflections on the truth of art were intended to show, amongst other things, that the perspective of *this sort* of 'sublation' of art in the praxis of life really is present in the concept of artistic beauty. In this connection, too, it would be possible to fetch an idea of Adorno's back from the realm of the inconceivable into the realm of the conceivable.

2   As we come to the end of this essay, it is only possible to take a cursory glance at a theme which is of great importance for Adorno, that of popular art. Adorno's critique of Benjamin is well known; his work on jazz can be understood as a reply to Benjamin's optimistic appraisal of modern mass culture in the essay on the 'Work of Art'. In connection with that essay, Adorno writes in a letter to Benjamin that Schönberg and the American film are the 'torn halves of an integral freedom'.[16] But in the same letter he makes it clear that he is *only* able to discern reification and ideology in mass culture, *not* freedom. What Adorno means with his phrase about the torn halves of freedom is basically, yet again, the polarity in art between the sensual, mimetic dimension and that of intellectual construction; the phrase should be read in conjunction with a passage from his *Dissonanzen* where Adorno emphasizes the liberating role of the sensual, expressive and superficial for the emergence of Viennese classicism, and thus for all the great music that comes after Bach:

Thus these deplored moments became part of great Western music: sensual stimulation as gateway to the harmonious dimension and finally to the coloristic one; the unrestrained individual as bearer of the expressive and humanizing dimensions of music; 'superficiality' as critique of the dumb objectivity of forms . . .[17]

Mozart's *Magic Flute* is, for Adorno, a moment of perfect coincidence between serious and light music; but it is also the last such moment. 'After the *Magic Flute*, serious and light music could no longer be forced into a common framework.'[18] For Adorno, the 'light' music of the present day is nothing but ideology and trash, a product of the culture industry just like film. Adorno utterly condemns jazz.

It seems to me that where Adorno passes judgements such as this, what is being expressed is not only a legitimate criticism of the culture industry, but also a traditionalist prejudice which similarly prevented him from recognizing the productive elements in Benjamin's interpretation of mass culture. There were, of course, powerful *theoretical* arguments behind Adorno's objections: the fundamental theses of the *Dialectic of Enlightenment*, for example, do reserve a certain degree of ambivalence in their treatment of 'great' art, but none for mass culture – which appears as fitting perfectly into the universal system of delusion. But in this case it seems to me that Benjamin's exploratory approach, which is theoretically less secure and unafraid of contradictions, is more productive. For whereas Adorno measures the products of the new mass culture by standards which can only make them appear primitive, inane or cynical, Benjamin sees something *aesthetically* new arising out of the interference of new technical procedures and new modes of reception; he sees new ways of processing reality aesthetically, which are aimed at producing an 'equilibrium between the human subject and the technical apparatus'.[19] Benjamin argues, for example, that the American grotesque film brings about a 'therapeutic exploding of the unconscious' which finds its expression in 'collective laughter'.[20] Under the impact of technology, art becomes a vaccine against those collective psychoses in which the enormous tensions that technological innovations generate in mass populations would otherwise vent themselves.[21]

In technologized mass culture, Benjamin sees elements of an antidote to the psychic destruction of humanity by industrial society, whereas Adorno regards it above all as a medium of conformism and psychic manipulation. It is only the antithesis as such that is interesting: it appears to me that Benjamin's analysis at least points towards a *positive potential* in modern mass culture – from film to rock music – which Adorno was unable to see because of his traditionalism and his theoretical preconceptions. Rock music as the 'folk music of the industrial age' would be a test case.[22] I think that there is just as much positive potential for democratization and the unleashing of aesthetic imagination as there is potential for cultural regression in rock music and in the attitudes, skills and modes of perception which have developed around it. It is *ambivalences* such as these, as in the case of jazz, that we ought to defend against Adorno.

An analysis of modern mass culture based on Benjamin's approach would have to investigate, amongst other things, the explosive mixtures of aesthetic and political imagination which have become characteristic of the new brand of subversive behaviour on the part of protest movements since the sixties. There is an argument of Benjamin's which might be extrapolated: he argued that it was in film that the Dadaist impulse had found its artistic medium, and in a similar way we might perhaps argue that it is only in the new political forms of action, and in the alternative and resistance movements, that artistic 'actions' and 'happenings' have found the context in which they can develop their aesthetic explosive force. And as Benjamin suggested, this politicization of aesthetics ought to be sharply distinguished from the aestheticization of politics that took place under fascism. The latter signifies a destruction of politics through the expropriation of the masses, who become degraded to mere extras in a cynically organized spectacle; but the former means, potentially at least, the appropriation of politics by a mass population grown conscious of its own power. In terms of ideal types, these two possibilities represent polar extremes. The fact that in the world of concrete phenomena the poles occasionally meet is a feature of a social condition which contains within itself the possibility of both political regression and a new potential for freedom.

In various ways we have come closer to a new interpretation of the relationship between the categories of truth, semblance and reconciliation in Adorno's writings. In the process, the truth of art has come to appear as a phenomenon of interference between the various dimensions of the everyday concept of truth. This concept is associated with a utopian perspective, however, namely that of non-violent communication. Just as the three dimensions of truth interact in the concept of the truth of art, so too are they interconnected in the idea of non-violent communication. But the *specific* utopian aspect contributed by art is also present in every single authentic artistic production, whether in the overcoming of speechlessness, or in the sensual crystallization of a meaning that is dispersed in empirical experience. What non-violent communication means, however, is not the *sublation* of art. The beauty of art does not stand for reason in its entirety; it is rather the case that reason needs art to illuminate it, for without aesthetic experience and the subversive potential it contains, our moral discourse would necessarily become blind and our interpretations of the world empty.

At the end of his *Aesthetic Theory*, Adorno at least hinted at a similar way of looking at things. In the final passage of the book he emphasizes once more the communicative potential of emancipated art as opposed to its 'progressive negativity', commenting, 'Perhaps a pacified society will reappropriate the art of the past which at present is the ideological complement of an unpacified one; however, if newly evolved art were then to return to a condition of peace and order, to affirmative representation, this would be the sacrifice of its freedom'.[23] What is remarkable is not that Adorno, even here, defends modern art against traditional art, but that he finds a place in emancipated society for emancipated art. In statements such as this, the solidarity of Adorno the Marxist, the theoretician of modernity, and the artist, with his times, breaks through the conceptual constraints of an overly narrow construction of history. The intention that has guided me in these reflections was to release the truth-content of Adorno's aesthetics and to develop it through critique and interpretation – in the fashion that Adorno postulated for works of art. In alluding to Adorno's conception of the interpretation of art here, I mean to offer more than simply an analogy: Adorno's writings on aesthetics themselves possess something of the qualities of a work of art, and thus may not be captured or surpassed by any process of interpretation. But interpretation and critique might nevertheless take on the function of a magnifying glass in relation to these texts; and if we read the texts with the aid of such a magnifying glass it might be that layers of meaning which appear fused to the naked eye would then separate out and distinguish themselves one from another. The image of a stereoscope would be better still: what would be achieved would be a three-dimensional image in which the latent depth of the texts became visible. By reading Adorno 'stereoscopically' in this way, we shall discover that Adorno's incomparable ability for the philosophical penetration of experience has permitted him, even within the limited medium of a philosophical dialectic of subject and object, to express, or at least to intimate, much that is actually resistant to presentation in that medium. My own reflections here were intended, apart from anything else, to promote just such a stereoscopic reading of Adorno.

Notes

1 *Translator's note*: The word 'semblance' has been used consistently to translate the German *'Schein'* in the sense it denotes in the context of Adorno's aesthetics. 'Semblance' is used frequently in the English translation of *Negative Dialectics*, though not in that of *Aesthetic Theory*.

2 Cf. F. Koppe, *Grundbegriffe der Ästhetik* (Frankfurt, 1983), p. 88.

3 See Martin Seel, *Die Kunst der Entzweiung. Zum Begriff der ästhetischen Rationalität*, (Frankfurt, 1985).

4 Cf. Theodor W. Adorno, *Aesthetic Theory*, trans. C. Lenhardt (London, 1984), p. 107 (*Ges. Schriften*, vol. 7, p. 281).

5 R. Bubner, 'Ueber einige Bedingungen gegenwärtiger Ästhetik', *Neue Hefte für Philosophie* (1973), Heft 5.

6 Cf. H. R. Jauss, *Aesthetic Experience and Literary Hermeneutics* (Minneapolis, 1982), pp. 19, 39ff.

7 Cf. Peter Bürger, *Theory of the Avantgarde* (Minneapolis, 1984).

8 Peter Bürger, *Zur Kritik der idealistischen Ästhetik*, p. 189.

9 Peter Bürger (1984), *Theory of the Avantgarde*.

10 Cf. Peter Bürger (1983), *Zur Kritikder Idealistischen Ästhetik*, p. 187.

11 Ibid., p. 135.

12 Cf. ibid., pp. 128ff.

13 Cf. Pierre Boulez, *Wille und Zufall. Gespräche mit Célestin Deliège und Hans Meyer* (Stuttgart and Zurich, 1976), p. 131.

14 Quoted in D. Schnebel, 'Wie ich das schaffe?'. In H.-K. Metzger and R. Riehn (eds), *Musik-Konzepte. Sonderband John Cage* (Munich, 1978), p. 51.

15 On this point, cf. Jürgen Habermas, 'Modernity vs. Postmodernity'. *New German Critique* 22 (Winter 1981), pp. 3–14.

16 Theodor W. Adorno, letter to Walter Benjamin, 18 March 1936, published in F. Jameson (ed.), *Aesthetics and Politics* (London, 1977), p. 123.

17 Theodor W. Adorno, 'On the Fetish Character of Music and the Regression of Listening'. In A. Arato and E. Gebhardt (eds), *The Essential Frankfurt School Reader* (New York, 1978), p. 272 (*Ges. Schriften*), vol. 14, p. 17.

18 Ibid.

19 Cf. Walter Benjamin, 'Das Kunstwerk im Zeitalter seiner technischen Reproduzierbarkeit'. *Ges. Schriften*, vol. 1.2 (Frankfurt, 1974), p. 460. [*Translator's note:* The passage in question is not included in the English edition; see Walter Benjamin, *Illuminations* (New York, 1969), pp. 217–52.]

20 Cf. ibid., p. 462.

21 Ibid.

22 On this point, cf. T. Kneif, *Einfuhrung in die Rockmusik* (Wilhelmshaven, 1979).

23 Theodor W. Adorno, *Asthetische Theorie (Gesammelte Schriften)*, vol. 7 (Frankfurt, 1970), p. 386; *Aesthetic Theory*, trans. C. Lenhardt (London, 1984), p. 369.

Part IV
Race, Multiculturalism, Difference

15

DissemiNation: Time, Narrative and the Margins of the Modern Nation

Homi K. Bhabha

How does one write the nation's modernity as the event of the everyday and the advent of the epochal?[1] The language of national belonging comes laden with atavistic apologues, which has led Benedict Anderson to ask: 'But why do nations celebrate their hoariness, not their astonishing youth?'[2] The nation's claim to modernity, as an autonomous or sovereign form of political rationality, is particularly questionable if, with Partha Chatterjee, we adopt the post-colonial perspective:

> Nationalism . . . seeks to represent itself in the image of the Enlightenment and fails to do so. For Enlightenment itself, to assert its sovereignty as the universal ideal, needs its Other; if it could ever actualise itself in the real world as the truly universal, it would in fact destroy itself.[3]

Such ideological ambivalence nicely supports Gellner's paradoxical point that the historical necessity of the idea of the nation conflicts with the contingent and arbitrary signs and symbols that signify the affective life of the national culture. The nation may exemplify modern social cohesion but

> Nationalism is not what it seems, and *above all not what it seems to itself* . . . The cultural shreds and patches used by nationalism are often arbitrary historical inventions. Any old shred would have served as well. But in no way does it follow that the principle of nationalism . . . is itself in the least contingent and accidental.[4]
> (My emphasis)

The problematic boundaries of modernity are enacted in these ambivalent temporalities of the nation-space. The language of culture and community is poised on the fissures of the present becoming the rhetorical figures of a national past. Historians transfixed on the event and origins of the nation never ask, and political theorists possessed of the 'modern' totalities of the nation – 'homogeneity, literacy and anonymity are the key traits'[5] – never pose, the essential question of the representation of the nation as a temporal process.

It is indeed only in the disjunctive time of the nation's modernity – as a knowledge caught between political rationality and its impasse, between the shreds and patches of cultural signification and the certainties of a nationalist pedagogy – that questions of nation as narration come to be posed. How do we plot the narrative of the nation that must mediate between the teleology of progress tipping over into the 'timeless' discourse of irrationality? How do we understand that 'homogeneity' of modernity – the people – which, if pushed too far, may assume something resembling the archaic body of the despotic or totalitarian mass? In the midst of progress and modernity, the language of ambivalence reveals a politics 'without duration', as Althusser once provocatively wrote: 'Space without places, time without duration.'[6] To write the story of the nation demands that we articulate that archaic ambivalence that informs the *time* of modernity. We may begin by questioning that progressive metaphor of modern social cohesion – *the many as one* – shared by organic theories of the holism of culture and community, and by theorists who treat gender, class or race as social totalities that are expressive of unitary collective experiences.

Out of many one: nowhere has this founding dictum of the political society of the modern nation – its spatial expression of a unitary people – found a more intriguing *image* of itself than in those diverse languages of literary criticism that seek to portray the great power of the idea of the nation in the disclosures of its everyday life; in the telling details that emerge as metaphors for national life. I am reminded of Bakhtin's wonderful description of a national *vision of emergence* in Goethe's *Italian Journey*, which represents the triumph of the Realistic component over the Romantic. Goethe's realist narrative produces a national-historical time that makes visible a specifically Italian day in the detail of its passing time: 'The bells ring, the rosary is said, the maid enters the room with a lighted lamp and says: *Felicissima notte!* . . . *If one were to force a German clockhand on them, they would be at a loss.*'[7] For Bakhtin, it is Goethe's vision of the microscopic, elementary, perhaps random, tolling of everyday life in Italy that reveals the profound history of its locality (*Lokalität*), the spatialization of historical time, 'a creative humanization of this locality, which transforms a part of terrestrial space into a place of historical life for people'.[8]

The recurrent metaphor of landscape as the inscape of national identity emphasizes the quality of light, the question of social visibility, the power of the eye to naturalize the rhetoric of national affiliation and its forms of collective expression. There is, however, always the distracting presence of another temporality that disturbs the contemporaneity of the national present, as we saw in the national discourses with which I began. Despite Bakhtin's emphasis on the realist vision in the emergence of the nation in Goethe's work, he acknowledges that the origin of the nation's visual *presence* is the effect of a narrative struggle. From the beginning, Bakhtin writes, the Realist and Romantic conceptions of time coexist in Goethe's work, but the ghostly (*Gespenstermässiges*), the terrifying (*Unerfreuliches*), and the unaccountable (*Unzuberechnendes*) are consistently surmounted by the structuring process of the visualization of time: 'the necessity of the past and the necessity of its place in a line of continuous development . . . finally the aspect of the past being linked to the necessary future'.[9] National time becomes concrete and visible in the chronotype of the local, particular, graphic, from beginning to end. The narrative structure of this *historical* surmounting of the 'ghostly' or the 'double' is seen in the intensification of narrative synchrony as a graphically visible position in space: 'to grasp the most elusive course of pure historical time and fix it through unmediated contemplation'.[10] But what kind of 'present' is this if it is a consistent process of surmounting the ghostly time of repetition? Can this national time–space be as fixed or as immediately visible as Bakhtin claims?

If in Bakhtin's 'surmounting' we hear the echo of another use of that word by Freud in his essay on 'The "uncanny"', then we begin to get a sense of the complex time of the national narrative. Freud associates *surmounting* with the repressions of a 'cultural' unconscious; a liminal, uncertain state of cultural belief when the archaic emerges in the midst of margins of modernity as a result of some psychic ambivalence or intellectual uncertainty. The 'double' is the figure most frequently associated with this uncanny process of 'the doubling, dividing and interchanging of the self'.[11] Such 'double-time' cannot be so simply represented as visible or flexible in 'unmediated contemplation'; nor can we accept Bakhtin's repeated attempt to read the national space as achieved only in the *fullness of time*. Such an apprehension of the 'double and split' time of national representation, as I am proposing, leads us to question the homogeneous and horizontal view associated with the nation's imagined community. We are led to ask whether the *emergence* of a national perspective – of an elite or subaltern nature – within a culture of social contestation, can ever articulate its 'representative' authority in that fullness of narrative time and visual synchrony of the sign that Bakhtin proposes.

Two accounts of the emergence of national narratives seem to support my suggestion. They represent the diametrically opposed world views of master and slave which, between them, account for the major historical and philosophical dialectic of modern times. I am thinking of John Barrell's[12] splendid analysis of the rhetorical and perspectival status of the 'English gentleman' within the social diversity of the eighteenth-century novel; and of Houston Baker's innovative reading of the 'new *national* modes of sounding, interpreting and speaking the Negro in the Harlem Renaissance'.[13]

In his concluding essay Barrell demonstrates how the demand for a holistic, representative vision of society could only be represented in a discourse that was *at the same time* obsessively fixed upon, and uncertain of, the boundaries of society, and the margins of the text. For instance, the hypostatized 'common language' which was the language of the gentleman whether he be Observer, Spectator, Rambler, 'Common to all by virtue of the fact that it manifested the peculiarities of none'[14] – was primarily defined through a process of negation – of regionalism, occupation, faculty – so that this centred vision of 'the gentleman' is so to speak 'a condition of empty potential, one who is imagined as being able to comprehend everything, and yet who may give no evidence of having comprehended anything.'[15]

A different note of liminality is struck in Baker's description of the 'radical maroonage' that structured the emergence of an insurgent Afro-American expressive culture in its expansive, 'national' phase. Baker's sense that the 'discursive project' of the Harlem Renaissance is modernist is based less on a strictly literary understanding of the term, and more on the agonistic enunciative conditions within which the Harlem Renaissance shaped its cultural practice. The transgressive, invasive structure of the black 'national' text, which thrives on rhetorical strategies of hybridity, deformation, masking, and inversion, is developed through an extended analogy with the guerilla warfare that became a way of life for the maroon communities of runaway slaves and fugitives who lived dangerously, and insubordinately, 'on the frontiers or margins of *all* American promise, profit and modes of production'.[16] From this liminal, minority position where, as Foucault would say, the relations of discourse are of the nature of warfare, the force of the people of an Afro-American nation emerge in the extended metaphor of maroonage. For 'warriors' read writers or even 'signs':

> these highly adaptable and mobile warriors took maximum advantage of local environments, striking and withdrawing with great rapidity, making extensive use of bushes to catch their adversaries in cross-fire, fighting only when and where they chose, depending on reliable intelligence networks among non-maroons (both slave and white settlers) and often communicating by horns.[17]

Both gentleman and slave, with different cultural means and to very different historical ends, demonstrate that forces of social authority and subversion or subalternity may emerge in displaced, even decentred strategies of signification. This does not prevent these positions from being effective in a political sense, although it does suggest that positions of authority may themselves be part of a process of ambivalent identification. Indeed the exercise of power may be both politically effective and psychically *affective* because the discursive liminality through which it is signified may provide greater scope for strategic manoeuvre and negotiation.

It is precisely in reading between these borderlines of the nation-space that we can see how the concept of the 'people' emerges within a range of discourses as a double narrative movement. The people are not simply historical events or parts of a patriotic body politic. They are also a complex rhetorical strategy of social reference: their claim to be representative provokes a crisis within the process of signification and discursive address. We then have a contested conceptual territory where the nation's people must be thought in double-time; the people are the historical 'objects' of a nationalist pedagogy, giving the discourse an authority that is based on the pre-given or constituted historical origin *in the past*; the people are also the 'subjects' of a process of signification that must erase any prior or originary presence of the nation-people to demonstrate the prodigious, living principles of the people as contemporaneity: as that sign of the *present* through which national life is redeemed and iterated as a reproductive process.

The scraps, patches and rags of daily life must be repeatedly turned into the signs of a coherent national culture, while the very act of the narrative performance interpellates a growing circle of national subjects. In the production of the nation as narration there is a split between the continuist, accumulative temporality of the pedagogical, and the repetitious, recursive strategy of the performative. It is through this process of splitting that the conceptual ambivalence of modern society becomes the site of *writing the nation*. [. . .]

Of Margins and Minorities

The difficulty of writing the history of the people as the insurmountable agonism of the living, the incommensurable experiences of struggle and survival in the construction of a national culture, is nowhere better seen than in Frantz Fanon's essay 'On national culture'.[18] I start with it because it is a warning against the intellectual appropriation of the 'culture of the people' (whatever that may be) within a representationalist discourse that may become fixed and reified in the annals of history. Fanon writes against that form of nationalist historicism that assumes that there is a moment when the differential temporalities of cultural histories coalesce in an immediately readable present. For my purposes, he focuses on the time of cultural representation, instead of immediately historicizing the event. He explores the space of the nation without immediately identifying it with the historical institution of the State. As my concern here is not with the history of nationalist movements, but only with certain traditions of writing that have attempted to construct narratives of the social imaginary of the nation-people, I am indebted to Fanon for liberating a certain, uncertain time of the people.

The knowledge of the people depends on the discovery, Fanon says, 'of a much more fundamental substance which itself is continually being renewed', a structure of repetition that is not visible in the translucidity of the people's customs or the obvious objectivities which seem to characterize the people. 'Culture abhors simplification,' Fanon writes, as he tries to locate the people in a performative time: 'the fluctuating movement that the people are *just* giving shape to'. The present of the people's history, then, is a practice that destroys the constant principles of the national culture that attempt to hark back to a 'true' national past, which is often represented in the reified forms of realism and stereotype. Such pedagogical knowledges and continuist national narratives miss the 'zone of occult instability where the people dwell' (Fanon's phrase). It is from this *instability* of cultural signification that the national culture comes to be articulated as a dialectic of various temporalities – modern, colonial, postcolonial, 'native' – that cannot be a knowledge that is stabilized in its enunciation: 'it is always contemporaneous with the act of recitation. It is the present act that on each of its occurrences marshalls in the ephemeral temporality inhabiting the space between the "I have heard" and "you will hear".'[19]

Fanon's critique of the fixed and stable forms of the nationalist narrative makes it imperative to question theories of the horizontal, homogeneous empty time of the nation's narrative. Does the language of culture's 'occult instability' have a relevance outside the situation of anticolonial struggle? Does the in-commensurable act of living – so often dismissed as ethical or empirical – have its own ambivalent narrative, its own history of theory? Can it change the way we identify the symbolic structure of the western nation?

A similar exploration of political time has a salutary feminist history in 'Women's time'.[20] It has rarely been acknowledged that Kristeva's celebrated essay of that title has its conjunctural, cultural history, not simply in psycho-analysis and semiotics, but in a powerful critique and redefinition of the nation as a space for the emergence of feminist political and psychic identifications. The nation as a symbolic denominator is, according to Kristeva, a powerful repository of cultural knowledge that erases the rationalist and progressivist logics of the 'canonical' nation. This symbolic history of the national culture is inscribed in the strange temporality of the future perfect, the effects of which are not dissimilar to Fanon's occult instability.

The borders of the nation Kristeva claims, are constantly faced with a double temporality: the process of identity constituted by historical sedimentation (the pedagogical); and the loss of identity in the signifying process of cultural identi-fication (the performative). The time and space of Kristeva's construction of the nation's finitude is analogous to my argument that the figure of the people emerges in the narrative ambivalence of disjunctive times and meanings. The concurrent circulation of linear, cursive and monumental time, in the same cultural space, constitutes a new historical temporality that Kristeva identifies with psychoanalytically informed, feminist strategies of political identification. What is remarkable is her insistence that the gendered sign can hold together such exorbitant historical times.

The political effects of Kristeva's multiple women's time leads to what she calls the 'demassification of difference'. The cultural moment of Fanon's 'occult instability' signifies the people in a fluctuating movement *which they are just giving shape to,* so that postcolonial time questions the teleological traditions of past and present, and the polarized historicist *sensibility* of the archaic and the modern. These are not simply attempts to invert the balance of power within an unchanged order of discourse. Fanon and Kristeva seek to redefine the symbolic process through which the social imaginary – nation, culture or community – becomes the subject of discourse, and the object of psychic identi-fication. These feminist and postcolonial temporalities force us to rethink the sign of history *within* those languages, political or literary, which designate the people 'as one'. They challenge us to think the question of community and communication *without* the moment of transcendence: how do we understand such forms of social contradiction?

Cultural identification is then poised on the brink of what Kristeva calls the 'loss of identity' or Fanon describes as a profound cultural 'undecidability'. The people as a form of address emerge from the abyss of enunciation where the subject splits, the signifier 'fades', the pedagogical and the performative are agonistically articulated. The language of national collectivity and cohesiveness is now at stake. Neither can cultural homogeneity nor the nation's horizontal space be authoritatively represented within the familiar territory of the *public sphere*: social causality cannot be adequately understood as a deterministic or overdetermined effect of a 'statist' centre; nor can the rationality of political choice be divided between the polar realms of the private and the public. The narrative of national cohesion can no longer be signified, in Anderson's words, as a 'sociological solidity'[21] fixed in a 'succession of *plurals*' – hospitals, prisons, remote villages – where the social space is clearly bounded by such repeated objects that represent a naturalistic, national horizon.

Such a pluralism of the national sign, where difference returns as the same, is contested by the signifier's 'loss of identity' that inscribes the narrative of the people in the ambivalent, 'double' writing of the performative and the pedagogical. The movement of meaning *between* the masterful image of the people and the movement of its sign interrupts the succession of plurals that produce the sociological solidity of the national narrative. The nation's totality is confronted with, and crossed by, a supplementary movement of writing. The heterogeneous structure of Derridean supplementarity in *writing* closely follows the agonistic, ambivalent movement between the pedagogical and performative that informs the nation's narrative address. A supplement, according to one meaning, 'cumulates and accumulates presence. It is thus that art, *techné* image, representation, convention, etc. come as supplements to nature and are rich with this entire cumulating function'[22] (pedagogical). The *double entendre* of the supplement suggests, however, that

> [It] intervenes or insinuates itself *in-the-place-of* . . . If it represents and makes an image it is by the *anterior* default of a presence . . . the supplement is an adjunct, a subaltern instance . . . As substitute, it is not simply added to the positivity of a presence, it produces no relief . . . Somewhere, something can be filled up of *itself* . . . only by allowing itself to be filled through sign and proxy.[23] (performative)

It is in this supplementary space of doubling – *not plurality* – where the image is presence and proxy, where the sign supplements and empties nature, that the disjunctive times of Fanon and Kristeva can be turned into the discourses of emergent cultural identities, within a non-pluralistic politics of difference.

This supplementary space of cultural signification that opens up – and holds together – the performative and the pedagogical, provides a narrative structure characteristic of modern political rationality: the marginal integration of individuals in a repetitious movement between the antinomies of law and order. From the liminal movement of the culture of the nation – at once opened up and held together – minority discourse emerges. Its strategy of intervention is similar to what British parliamentary procedure recognizes as a supplementary question. It is a question that is supplementary to what is stated on the 'order paper' for the minister's response. Coming 'after' the original, or in 'addition to' it, gives the supplementary question the advantage of introducing a sense of 'secondariness' or belatedness into the structure of the original demand. The supplementary strategy suggests that adding 'to' need not 'add up' but may disturb the calculation. As Gasché has succinctly suggested, 'supplements . . . are pluses that compensate for a minus in the origin.'[24] The supplementary strategy interrupts the successive seriality of the narrative of plurals and pluralism by radically changing their mode of articulation. In the metaphor of the national community as the 'many as one', the *one* is now both the tendency to totalize the social in a homogenous empty time, and the repetition of that minus in the origin, the less-than-one that intervenes with a metonymic, iterative temporality.

Notes

1   In memory of Paul Moritz Strimpel (1914–87): Pforzheim–Paris–Zurich–Ahmedabad–Bombay–Milan–Lugano.
2   B. Anderson, 'Narrating the nation'. *The Times Literary Supplement*.
3   P. Chatterjee, *Nationalist Thought and the Colonial World: A Derivative Discourse* (London: Zed, 1986), p. 17.
4   E. Gellner, *Nations and Nationalism* (Oxford: Basil Blackwell, 1983), p. 56.
5   Ibid., p. 38.
6   L. Althusser, *Montesquieu, Rousseau, Marx* (London: Verso, 1972), p. 78.
7   M. Bakhtin, *Speech Genres and Other Late Essays*, C. Emerson and M. Holquist (eds), trans. V. W. McGee (Austin, Texas: University of Texas Press, 1986), p. 31.
8   Ibid., p. 34.
9   Ibid., p. 36.
10 Ibid., pp. 47–9.
11 S. Freud, 'The "uncanny"'. In *The Standard Edition*, vol. XVII, J. Strachey (ed.) (London: The Hogarth Press, 1974), p. 234. See also pp. 236, 247.
12 J. Barrell, *English Literature in History, 1730–1780* (London: Hutchinson, 1983).
13 H. A. Baker, Jr., *Modernism and the Harlem Renaissance* (Chicago: Chicago University Press, 1987), esp. chs 8–9.
14 J. Barrell, *English Literature in History, 1730–1780*, p. 78.
15 Ibid., p. 203.
16 H.A. Baker, *Modernism and the Harlem Renaissance*, p. 77.
17 R. Price, *Maroon Societies*, quoted in Baker, ibid., p. 77.
18 F. Fanon, *The Wretched of the Earth* (Harmondsworth: Penguin, 1969). My quotations and references come from pp. 17–90.
19 J.-F. Lyotard, *The Postmodern Condition*, trans. G. Bennington and B. Massumi (Manchester: Manchester University Press, 1984), p. 22.

20   J. Kristeva, 'Women's time'. In T. Moi (ed.), *The Kristeva Reader* (Oxford: Blackwell, 1986), pp. 187–213. This passage was written in response to the insistent questioning of Nandini and Praminda in Prof. Tshome Gabriel's seminar on 'syncretic cultures' at the University of California, Los Angeles.
21   B. Anderson, 'Narrating the Nation', p. 35.
22   J. Derrida, *Of Grammatology*, trans. G. C. Spivak (trans.) (Baltimore, MD: Johns Hopkins University Press, 1976), pp. 144–5. Quoted in R. Gasché, *The Thin of the Mirror* (Cambridge, MA.: Harvard University Press, 1986), p. 208.
23   J. Derrida, ibid., p. 145.
24   R. Gasché, *The Thin of the Mirror* p. 211.

16

Sigmund Freud and the Epistemology of Race

Sander L. Gilman

For Sigmund Freud in the 1870s the idea of race was confining and limiting, as it implied a biological, immutable pattern of development. After the turn of the century, it came to acquire a more positive valence as a sign of the special status of the Jewish way of seeing the world. It moved from a purely biological category to a purely psychological one. In 1886, about the time Freud was studying with Jean-Martin Charcot in Paris, Gustave Le Bon, the anti-Semitic French sociologist, published his overt discussion of the inheritance of the psychological attributes of race, which he ascribed as much to biology as to social environment. (The American-Eastern Jewish psychiatrist A. A. Roback much later still accused Freud of putting Roback "to the test in piecing me together out of my environment ['Americanism'] and antecedents [Jewish 'Chuzpah'].")[1] Le Bon's views of the nature of the crowd were central to Freud's later work on the psychology of mass movements, which contains his unstated analyses of anti-Semitism. Freud's experience in Paris was as intensely anti-Semitic as that in his native Vienna had been. Freud wanted to reject Le Bon's biological view of race as "the innumerable common characteristics handed down from generation to generation, which constitute the genius of a race."[2] For Le Bon, race stood in the "first rank" of those factors that help shape the underlying attitudes of the crowd. Racial character "possesses, as the result of the laws of heredity, such power that its beliefs, institutions, and arts – in a word, all the elements of its civilization – are merely outward expressions of its genius."[3] And yet for the older Freud it was within the psyche, not the body, that the difference between Jew and Aryan existed.

Anthropologists such as Richard Andree evoked the unknowable essence of the Jew. Andree observed, concerning the conservative nature of the Jewish body and soul: "No other race but the Jews can be traced with such certainty backward for thousands of years, and no other race displays such a constancy of form, none resisted to such an extent the effects of time, as the Jews. Even when he adopts the language, dress, habits, and customs of the people among whom he lives, he still remains everywhere the same. All he adopts is but a cloak, under which the eternal Hebrew survives; he is the same in his facial features, in the structure of his body, his temperament, his character." Or, as a patient of the Viennese psychoanalyst Theodor Reik commented, "Once a Jew, always a Jew."[4] The body of the Jew is the sign of this immutability. Unlike Andree, Freud gave this essence a positive valence.

In 1926, Freud stated in an address to the B'nai B'rith on the occasion of his seventieth birthday that being Jewish meant sharing "many obscure emotional forces [*viele dunkle Gefühlsmächte*], which were the more powerful the less they could be expressed in words, as well as a clear consciousness of inner identity, the safe privacy of a common mental construction [*die Heimleichkeit der gleichen seelischen Identität*]."[5] His contemporaries, such as Theodor Reik (along with Freud and Eduard Hintschmann, the only psychoanalysts to be members of the B'nai B'rith), "were especially struck" by these words as the central definition of the Jew.[6]

Freud's version of the ethnopsychology of the Jew twisted Le Bon's claims concerning the biology of race. It evoked the Lamarckianism of William James's view of the transmission of "the same emotional propensities, the same habits, the same instincts, perpetuated without variation from one generation to another."[7] The uncanny nature of the known but repressed aspects of the mental life of an individual – about which Freud wrote in his essay on the uncanny – haunts Freud's image of the internal mental life defining the Jew. (Here it is the "uncanny" [*unheimlich*] that domesticates the "canny" [*heimlich*] nature of Jewish identity.) One of Freud's models is that of the ethnopsychology of the Jew – that there is a racial memory that exists in each generation. He observes (concerning "the uncanny associated with the omnipotence of thoughts") that "we – or our primitive forefathers – once believed that these possibilities were realities, and were convinced that they actually happened. . . . As soon as something actually happens in our lives which seems to confirm the old, discarded beliefs we get a feeling of the uncanny."[8] The affirmation through daily events – such as the exposure to anti-Semitism – revivifies the group memory, confirming the "common mental construction" of the Jew. This does not take place on the level of rationality, but within the unconscious. As he wrote to his Viennese Jewish "double," Arthur Schnitzler: "Judaism continues to mean much to me on an emotional level." The return of the repressed – not the ancient traditions of religious identity, but the suppressed discourse of anti-Semitism, expressed by Freud within the model of racial memory – haunted Freud. He articulated this discourse of the difference of the Jew within the phylogenetic model of the inheritance of racial memory.

The debate about the meaning of what Philip Rieff sees as the Victorian and Edwardian generalities about the "persistent character of the Jews" must be understood as part of the quest of scientific psychology in the late nineteenth century.[9] For Freud this sense of the psyche of the Jew had to do not only with the mental construction of the Jew but also with the Jew's emotional construction. Here he would have found substantial support in the work of William McDougall, whose study *The Group Mind* (1920) played a central role in shaping Freud's own argument about the psychology of the masses.[10] McDougall sees the fusing of the Hebrew tribes into a nation as having "played a vital part in its consolidation, implanted and fostered as it was by a succession of great teachers, the prophets. . . . The national self-consciousness thus formed has continued to be not only one factor, but almost the only factor or condition, of the continued existence of the Jewish people as a people, or at any rate the one fundamental condition on which all the others are founded – their exclusive religion, their objection to intermarriage with outsiders, their hope of a future restoration of the fortunes of the nation, and so forth."[11] Jewish self-consciousness leads to the establishment of institutions that preserve this "common mental construction." And these institutions reflect the emotional bonds of the Jews. For McDougall, but not necessarily for Freud, this sense of common purpose within the sphere of the political defines the Jew. Central, however, is that all aspects of the Jewish mind – including all the affective components – have their roots in this "common mental construction."

When Freud commented to his "brothers" in the B'nai B'rith about their "common mental construction," he was also specifically evoking the Jewish body. Freud's major association with Jews in the 1870s and 1880s was in joining (and helping form) a new lodge of the B'nai B'rith in Vienna.[12] "B'nai B'rith" means "sons of the Covenant." While the name was selected as a replacement for "Bundes-Brüder" – a German-Jewish lodge founded in New York in 1843 – it evoked, for *fin de siècle* Viennese Jews, the image of circumcision. As Theodor Reik noted in 1915: "The bond which the primordial fathers of the Jews concluded with their god is represented . . . as a glorified and emended account of an initiation ceremony. The connection of the *B'rith* with circumcision is just as little an accident as the covenant meal in which the worshippers of Jahve identified themselves with him; and the giving of the law – *B'rith* can also signify law – which stands in such an intimate relationship to the concluding of the covenant (Sinai) should be set side by side with the procedures of the puberty rites." The sense of "common mental construction" is associated closely with the special form of the Jew's body and the ritual bonding it signifies. Central to this is the act of circumcision and its resulting "feminization" of the male body.

There was a general assumption in Europe at the time that there was a "Jewish mind" that transcended conversion or adaptation.[13] This was usually understood as a fault. Ludwig Wittgenstein commented about Jews such as Freud that "even the greatest of Jewish thinkers is no more than talented. (Myself, for instance.) I think there is some truth to my idea that I really only think reproductively. . . . Can one take the case of Freud and Breuer as an example of Jewish reproductiveness?"[14] The Jewish mind has no true originality. The Jewish mind is prosaic, as Freud wrote to Emil Fluss in the

1870s: "How well I can imagine your feelings. To leave the native soil, dearly – beloved relatives, – the most beautiful surroundings – ruins close by – I must stop or I'll be as sad as you – and you yourself know best what you are leaving behind. . . . Oh Emil why are you a prosaic Jew? Journeymen imbued with Christian-Germanic fervor have composed beautiful lyrical poetry in similar circumstances."[15] This view echoes the negative interpretation of the "common mental construction" of the Jew as expressed in anthropological and cultural debates in the late nineteenth century. The "intellectual attributes of the Jews," whether in the desert or in the banks of Europe, "have remained constant for thousands of years."[16] The qualities of the Jewish mind, of the "common mental construction" that defined the Jew, usually were understood in *fin de siècle* culture as negative and destructive.[17] The Jews "possess no imagination. . . . All who have any claim at all to speak, testify unanimously that lack – or let us say poverty – of imagination is a fundamental trait of the Semite."[18] The "Jewish mind does not have the power to produce even the tiniest flower or blade of grass that has grown in the soil of another's mind and to put it into a comprehensive picture."[19] "Hence the Jewish people, despite all apparent intellectual qualities, is without any true culture, and especially without any culture of its own. For what sham culture the Jew today possesses is the property of other peoples, and for the most part it is ruined in his hands."[20]

Such views of the Jews are statements about their psychopathology. Freud concurred with the notion that the Jewish mind-set is pathological. In his lecture on anxiety (1917) he evoked the Lamarckian model of the inheritance of acquired characteristics in order to argue that the "core" of anxiety "is the repetition of some particular significant experience. This experience could only be a very early impression of a very general nature, placed in the prehistory not of the individual but of the species."[21] Or, one might add, in the prehistory of the race. Freud went on to note that this "affective state . . . [is] constructed in the same way as a hysterical attack and, like it, would be the precipitate of a reminiscence."[22] The anxiety of the Jew is analogous to but not identical with the suffering of the hysteric. [. . .]

The roots of this view lie deep in the theories of ethnopsychology as formulated by two Jews, the psychologist Moritz Lazarus and his brother-in-law, the philologist Heymann Steinthal, in the 1860s. In the opening issue of their journal for ethnopsychology and linguistics, *Zeitschrift für Völkerpsychologie und Sprachwissenschaft* (note the link between mind and language), they outlined assumptions about the knowability of the mind. Lazarus and Steinthal's object of study was the "psychology of human beings in groups [*Gemeinschaft*]." Unlike in other fields of psychology at the time, where laboratory and clinical work were demanded to define the arena of study, ethnopsychology depended on historical and cultural-ethnological data. Their work was highly medicalized: Lazarus had studied physiology with the materialist Johannes Müller and cofounded the Medical-Psychological Society with the Berlin neurologist Wilhelm Griesinger in 1867. While they wished to separate their psychology from materialistic physiology, they were bound by the scientific rhetoric of the materialistic arguments about inheritance. They subscribed to a Lamarckian theory of mnemonic inheritance in the construction of the mind. The great laboratory psychologist Wilhelm Wundt remained the major proponent of their views of "universal mental creations" well into the twentieth century.[23] And Freud made extensive use of Wundt's explication of these views in his *Psychopathology of Everyday Life* (1901) and *Totem and Taboo* (1913). The psychology of the individual, as one of Freud's other sources, the Princeton psychologist James Mark Baldwin, commented, recapitulates the history of the "race experience." One can expect "general analogies to hold between nervous development and mental development, one of which is the deduction of race history epoches from individual history epoches through the repetition of phylogenesis in ontogenesis, called in biology 'Recapitulation.'"[24] The history of the human race was to be found in the development of the individual. But "racial memory" has a very different connotation for a Jewish reader of Wundt and Baldwin.

Freud, like the ethnopsychologists, needed to separate the idea of the psyche from the body; he needed to eliminate the image of a fixed, immutable racial composition that determines all thoughts and actions. For these thinkers, the psyche was separate from, and yet still part of, the body. It seemed impossible, even given the need of such thinkers to avoid the pitfalls of race, truly to separate the mind from the body. [. . .]

Freud sees the construction of the mentality of a group as a reflex of biology tempered by the social context of the individual. But this mentality need not be empirically based. It may indeed be based on fantasies about others. The Jew forms for Freud the touchstone of difference. Thus, anti-Semitism is not wrong, an "error," but rather is an illusion of Aryans, the mental claim of their own superiority. In *The Future of an Illusion* (1927), Freud argued that the belief "of a former generation of doctors that *tabes dorsalis* [syphilis] is the result of sexual excess" was an outright error, as it was not based in fact. (This is an oblique reference to the common medical association of Jews, syphilis, and sexual excess.) But the belief that "the Indo-German race is the only one capable of civilization" is an illusion "derived from human wishes" rather than a misapprehension.[25] Freud here introduces the notion that there may be a "kernel of truth" in the origin of the Aryan view. The fantasy about the superiority of the Aryan, which provides the roots of anti-Semitism, is isolated in his construction of history from Freud's sense of the meaning of the active persecution of the Jews that resulted from the fantasies of the "Indo-German race."

In *Civilization and Its Discontents* (1930), Freud commented on the subjectivity of happiness: "No matter how much we may shrink with horror from certain situations – of a galley-slave in antiquity, of a peasant during the Thirty Years' War, of a victim of the Holy Inquisition, of a Jew awaiting a pogrom – it is nevertheless impossible for us to feel our way into such people – to divine the changes which original obtuseness of mind, a gradual stupefying process, the cessation of expectations, and cruder or more refined methods of narcotization have produced upon their receptivity to sensations of pleasure and unpleasure."[26] Freud separates himself and the reader (the "us") from the victim of the illusion of the persecutor.[27] This works in terms of the historical images he uses from antiquity, the seventeenth century, and the sixteenth century, but the image of the pogrom, while obliquely "historical" in that the term refers to the persecution of Russian Jewry at the end of the century, was also quite immediate to Freud, as "pogrom" was a term evoked in the Jew-baiting riots in Vienna and Berlin. In his narrative he displaces what was occurring in his own experience, even while he wrote *Civilization and Its Discontents*, into a "distant" past from which "he" and "we" stand apart as observers.

But officially and publicly (at least with non-Jews), as in his earlier review of Forel, Freud rejected traditional definitions of "race" as an operative category in science. During his analysis of Smiley Blanton, he commented: "My background as a Jew helped me to stand being criticized, being isolated, working alone. . . . All this was of help to me in discovering analysis. But that psychoanalysis itself is a Jewish product seems to me nonsense. As a scientific work, it is neither Jewish nor Catholic nor Gentile."[28] He wrote in a birthday greeting to Ernest Jones in 1929: "The first piece of work that it fell to psychoanalysis to perform was the discovery of the instincts that are common to all men living today – and not only to those living today but to those of ancient and of prehistoric times. It called for no great effort, therefore, for psychoanalysis to ignore the differences that arise among the inhabitants of the earth owing to the multiplicity of races, languages, and countries."[29] Yet this was written to an individual about whom he felt a "racial strangeness" (*Rassenfremdheit*) upon their first meeting in 1908.[30] Jones reported that Freud had said, during this meeting, that "from the shape of my [Jones's] head I could not be English and must be Welsh. It astonished me, first because it is uncommon for anyone on the Continent to know of the existence of my native country, and then because I had suspected my dolichocephalic skull might as well be Teutonic as Celtic."[31] Even Jones's response to Freud's remark is couched in the language of racial biology. Yet there was always the possibility that this view could erupt in anti-Semitic utterances. While Jones deplored the common discourse of anti-Semitism, when angered by the Viennese Jew Otto Rank in 1923 he lashed out at him as a "swindling Jew."

The Viennese-Jewish psychoanalyst Hanns Sachs, writing in the mid-1940s, was much more attuned to the implications of "seeing" race as written on the face: "I remember now, not without a note of sadness, that Freud, who had no trace of any 'racial' predilection one way or the other, in showing us [the pioneer hypnotist Ambroise Auguste] Liébeault's photograph pointed out how un-Latin (today the word would be 'Nordic') his face was and how well this was suited to his name which evidently was a variant of the Germanic *Luitpold*."[32] Likewise, when Freud sat for the sculptor Oscar Nemon in 1931 he described him in a letter to his Jewish colleague Max Eitingon as "from his appearance a Slavic Eastern Jew, Khazar or Kalmuck or something like that."[33] The use of these categories was at the time in no way questioned.

The apparent contradiction of his public claim of the neutrality of science in his letters to his Jewish colleagues is evidence of Freud's complicated resistance to and restructuring of the idea of a group mentality. His conviction of the compatibility of neutral science and ethnocentric perception is found in a letter written on June 8, 1913, to one of his most trusted Jewish followers, the Hungarian-Jewish psychoanalyst Sandor Ferenczi: "Certainly there are great differences between the Jewish and the Aryan spirit. We can observe that every day. Hence, there would assuredly be here and there differences in outlook on art and life. But there should not be such a thing as Aryan or Jewish science. Results in science must be identical, though the presentation of them may vary."[34] This difference in "spirit" is present and yet undefined. Many opponents of political anti-Semitism at the time acknowledged that there were "indeed, many scientific Jews, but I see nowhere a Jewish science," to quote Anatole Leroy-Beaulieu.[35] Yet it was clear that Freud understood that his own identification as a Jew provided the "ground" for the new science of psychoanalysis as well as limiting the access of this new field to the claims of a "neutral science." In 1910 he had confronted his Viennese colleagues at the second Psychoanalytic Congress and stated the case bluntly: "Most of you are Jews, and therefore you are incompetent to win friends for the new teaching. Jews must be content with the modest role of preparing the ground. It is absolutely essential that I should form ties in the world of general science. . . . The Swiss will save us."[36]

But the Swiss, at least Carl Gustav Jung, came to see psychoanalysis in Freud's formulation as a "Jewish" science. Jung noted the differences between a Jewish and an Aryan psychology as early as 1918. He stressed the rootlessness of the Jew, that "he is badly at a loss for that quality in man which roots him to the earth and draws new strength from below."[37] This view made the Jew's creativity, especially in the sphere of psychology, of value only for the Jew: "thus it is a quite unpardonable mistake to accept the conclusions of a Jewish psychology as generally valid."[38] This statement, made in 1927, was repeated virtually verbatim in 1934, at which point he noted that it was "no deprecation of Semitic psychology, any more than it is a deprecation of the Chinese to speak of the peculiar psychology of the Oriental."[39] He further qualified his view of the psychology of the Jew (and the very meaning of a Semitic psychology) by paraphrasing Ernest Renan; he wrote of the "Jew who is something of a nomad, has never yet created a cultural form of his own and as far as we can see never will, since all his instincts and talents require a more or less civilized nation to act as a host for their development."[40] Jung's private condemnation of the "essentially corrosive nature" of the "Jewish gospel" of Freud and Alfred Adler in a 1934 letter reflected his general view of the lack of value of the "Jewish points of view" that dominate Freudian psychoanalysis.[41] Jung based his thinking on a theory of racial memory that was part of early psychoanalysis, but he presented this view of racial memory within a clearly anti-Semitic discourse.

Jung also articulated one aspect of racial theory that came to have central importance for Freud and for many Jewish physicians dealing with the biology and psychology of human beings. For Jung, male Jews are feminized. They "have this peculiarity in common with women; being physically weaker they have to aim at the chinks in the armor of their adversary, and thanks to this technique which has been forced on them through the centuries, the Jews themselves are best protected where others are most vulnerable."[42] He does not mean that male Jews are women, only that they share certain characteristics with women. They are thus neither entirely masculine nor entirely feminine. It is this compensatory and feminized psyche of the Jews that generated psychoanalysis:

> In my opinion it has been a grave error in medical psychology up till now to apply Jewish categories – which are not even binding on all Jews – indiscriminately to Germanic and Slavic Christendom. Because of this the most precious secret of the Germanic peoples – their creative and intuitive depth of soul – has been explained as a morass of banal infantilism, while my own warning voice has for decades been suspected of anti-Semitism. This suspicion emanated from Freud. He did not understand the Germanic psyche any more than did his Germanic followers. Has the formidable phenomenon of National Socialism, on which the whole world gazes with astonished eyes, taught them better?[43]

Jewish males are "gender-benders"; they exist between the conventional categories of "normal" (and normative) sexuality, just as they exist between the categories of European national identity and ethnopsychology.

Jung's views were stated in the light of his understanding of the relationship between the Jewish body (weak like the body of his essential woman) and the Jewish mind. The entire field of Freudian psychoanalysis was merely a further representation of the weakness, of the sexualized disease of soul, that dismissed the Teutonic psyche as a "morass of banal infantilism." (Jung's reversal of the traditional anti-Semitic charges about the nature of the Jew's psyche is striking.) Jung's categories reflect the complex relationship between the structure of gender and that of race. No wonder the Jews desire to become but cannot become Christian Aryans: "Just as every Jew has a Christ complex, so every Negro has a white complex. . . . As a rule the colored man would give anything to change his skin, and the white man hates to admit that he has been touched by a black."[44] And the Jew cannot shed his Jewishness even though, to follow Jung's argument, he desperately desires to do so and the Aryan cringes at any contact with the Jew.

Freud's anger at Jung at the time of the rupture of their friendship (or, at least, of Jung's discipleship) was cast by him in racial terms. In 1913, when he learned of her pregnancy, he wrote to Sabina Spielrein, who had been Jung's mistress as well as his patient, that he "would like to take it that if the child turns out to be a boy, he will develop into a stalwart Zionist."[45] Freud commented that he was "cured of the last predilection for the Aryan cause. . . . He or it [the expected child] must be dark in any case, no more towheads. Let us banish all these will-o'-the-wisps!" In the next letter, following her announcement that the infant was a girl, Freud commented: "It is far better that the child should be a 'she.' Now we can think again about the blond Siegfried and perhaps smash that idol before his time comes." Freud's discourse about blond Aryans such as Jung and their eternal opposition to the "dark" Jews framed his conflict with Jung. It also simply reverses the rhetoric of race applied to him by Jung. But Freud did not articulate the difference in terms of gender – the imagined Jewish "boy" can become a Zionist, a Jewish nationalist, and the Jewish "girl" (Spielrein's daughter Renate) "will speak for herself." Jews, male and female, have a "common mental construction" as "dark" Jews.

Freud's romanticization of "darkness" is an acknowledgment of the "blackness" of the Jews and its glorification. But the image of the "dark" Jew is always linked to that of the "diseased" Jew. "Darkness" becomes a sign of the predisposition of the Jew to disease and the disqualification of the Jew as a physician, a neutral observer. Here one can return to the Hippocratic demand that the physician must appear healthy. Hippocrates opens *The Physician* with the observation that "the dignity of a physician requires that he should look healthy, and as plump as nature intended him to be; for the common crowd consider those who are not of excellent bodily condition to be unable to take care of others."[46] This tradition dominates even the modern view of the physician in which the doctor must have "a sound constitution and a healthy look, which indeed seem as necessary qualifications for a physician as a good life and virtuous behavior for a divine."[47] The dark Jew in turn-of-the-century Vienna would not fulfill this requirement and would be disqualified from becoming a true physician. Freud's romanticization of the "dark" Jew as the idealized Jew of the future also placed this "dark" Jew, male or female, in opposition to the claims of racial science about the intellectual and moral capacities of the Jew.

Freud was aware of the anti-Semitic association of the products of Jewish scientists with the nature of the Jewish mind. This tendency in the medical science of his day was evident when he commented to Smiley Blanton in 1930 that he had tried to place Jung at the head of the psychoanalytic movement because "there was a danger that people would consider psychoanalysis as primarily Jewish."[48] He said to Abraham Kardiner that he hated the idea that "psychoanalysis would founder because it would go down in history as a 'Jewish' science."[49] Psychoanalysis had to be freed from the perception that it was a "Jewish science," but it could not be freed from the Jewish mind, which, at least in Freud's view, constructed it.

Notes

1   A. A. Roback, *Freudiana* (Cambridge, MA: Sci-Art, 1957), p. 35.
2   Sigmund Freud, *The Standard Edition of the Complete Psychological Works of Sigmund Freud*. Translated from the German by James Strachey (London: Hogarth Press), vol. 18, p. 74.

3   Gustave Le Bon, *The Crowd: A Study of the Popular Mind* (New York: Viking Press, 1960), p. 83.

4   Theodor Reik (1951), "'Jessica, My Child.'" *American Imago* 8, pp. 3–27; here, p. 5.

5   Sigmund Freud, *The Standard Edition*, vol. 20, p. 274; alternatively, GW 17: 49–53.

6   Theodor Reik, *Jewish Wit* (New York: Gamut Press, 1962), p. 12.

7   William James, *The Principles of Psychology*, 2 vols (New York: Henry Holt, 1890), vol. 2, p. 678.

8   Sigmund Freud, *The Standard Edition*, vol. 17, p. 247–8.

9   Philip Rieff, *Freud: The Mind of the Moralist* (New York: Viking Press, 1959), p. 261.

10   Sigmund Freud, *The Standard Edition*, vol. 18, pp. 83–5, pp. 96–7.

11   William McDougall, *The Group Mind* (Cambridge: Cambridge University Press, 1920), pp. 159–60.

12   Hugo Knoepfmacher (1979), "Sigmund Freud and the B'nai B'rith." *Journal of the American Psychoanalytic Association*, vol. 27, pp. 441–9.

13   See the discussion of this concept, without any reference to the psychological or medical literature, in Stephen Beller, *Vienna and the Jews, 1867–1938: A Cultural History* (Cambridge: Cambridge University Press, 1989), pp. 73–83.

14   Ludwig Wittgenstein, *Culture and Value*, ed. by G. H. von Wright and Heikki Nyman (Oxford: Blackwell, 1980), pp. 18–19.

15   Sigmund Freud (1969), "Some Early Unpublished Letters." Trans. Ilse Scheier, *International Journal of Psychoanalysis* 50, pp. 419–27; here, p. 426.

16   Werner Sombart, *The Jews and Modern Capitalism*, trans. M. Epstein (Glencoe, IL: Free Press, 1951), p. 320.

17   Stephen Beller, *Vienna and the Jews*, pp. 78–83.

18   Houston Stewart Chamberlain, *Foundations of the Nineteenth Century*. Trans. John Lees, 2 vols (London: John Lane/The Bodley Head, 1913), 1, p. 418. On Freud's reading of Chamberlain, see: GW Nachtragsband, p. 787.

19   Ludwig Wittgenstein, *Culture and Value*, p. 19.

20   Adolf Hitler, *Mein Kampf*. Trans. Ralph Manheim (Boston: Houghton Mifflin, 1943), pp. 302–3.

21   Sigmund Freud, *The Standard Edition*, vol. 16, p. 396.

22   Ibid., p. 91.

23   Wilhelm Wundt, *Elements of Folk Psychology: Outlines of a Psychological History of the Development of Mankind*. Trans. Edward Leroy Schaub (London: Allen & Unwin, 1916), p. 2.

24   James Mark Baldwin, *Mental Development in the Child and the Race* (New York: Macmillan, 1898), pp. 14–15. See *The Standard Edition*, vol. 7, p. 173.

25   Sigmund Freud, *The Standard Edition*, vol. 21, pp. 30–1.

26   Ibid., vol. 21, p. 89.

27   In this context, see Dagmar Barnouw (1989), "Modernism in Vienna: Freud and a Normative Poetics of the Self." *Modern Austrian Literature*, vol. 22, pp. 327–44, on the question of Freud's construction of fictions of the self.

28   Smiley Blanton, *Diary of My Analysis with Sigmund Freud* (New York: Hawthorn Books, 1971), p. 43. No better indicator of Freud's sense of his double audience exists than the recently rediscovered text of an early draft of *Thoughts for the Times on War and Death* (1915), which he delivered to the Vienna lodge of the B'nai B'rith.

29   Sigmund Freud, *The Standard Edition*, vol. 21, p. 249.

30   *The Freud/Jung Letters: The Correspondence between Sigmund Freud and C. G. Jung*, ed.

William McGuire, trans. Ralph Manheim and R.F.C. Hull (Princeton: Princeton University Press, 1974), p. 145.

31 Ernest Jones, *The Life and Work of Sigmund Freud*, 3 vols, (New York: Basic Books, 1953–7), vol. 2, pp. 42–3.

32 Hanns Sachs, *Freud: Master and Friend* (Cambridge, MA: Harvard University Press, 1946), p. 48.

33 Cited by Michael Molnar (ed.) in *Freud, 1929–1939: A Record of the Final Decade* (New York: Scribner's, 1992), p. 100, from the letter of August 3, 1931, from Freud to Eitingon.

34 Ernest Jones, *The Life and Work of Sigmund Freud*, vol. 2, p. 168.

35 Anatole Leroy-Beaulieu, *Israel among the Nations: A Study of the Jews and Antisemitism*, trans. Frances Hellman (New York: Putnam's, 1895), p. 51.

36 Fritz Wittels, *Sigmund Freud: His Personality, His Teaching, and His School*, trans. Eden Paul and Ceder Paul (London: Allen & Unwin, 1924), p. 140. This translation corrected many errors (listed by Freud) in the original German.

37 Carl G. Jung, *Collected Works*, ed. Herbert Read et al., trans. R. F. C. Hull, 20 vols (London: Routledge, 1957–79), vol. 10, p. 13.

38 Ibid., vol. 7, p. 149, n. 8.

39 Ibid., vol. 10, p. 534.

40 Ibid., vol. 10, pp. 65–6.

41 Quoted by Mortimer Ostow (1977), "Letter to the Editor". *International Review of Psychoanalysis*, vol. 4, p. 377.

42 Carl G. Jung, *Collected Works*, vol. 10, p. 165.

43 Ibid., vol. 10, p. 166.

44 Ibid., vol. 10, p. 508.

45 Aldo Carotenuto, *A Secret Symmetry: Sabina Spielrein between Jung and Freud*. Trans. Arno Pomerans, John Shepley, and Krishna Winston (New York: Pantheon, 1982), pp. 120–1.

46 *Hippocrates*. Trans. W. H. S. Jones, 6 vols (Cambridge, MA: Harvard University Press, 1959), vol. 2, p. 311.

47 George A. Aitken (ed.), *The Tatler*, 4 vols (London: Duckworth, 1899), vol. 4, p. 162 (for September 19, 1710).

48 Smiley Blanton, *Diary of My Analysis with Sigmund Freud*, p. 43.

49 Abraham Kardiner, *My Analysis with Freud: Reminiscences* (New York: Norton, 1977), p. 70.

17

Masters, Mistresses, Slaves, and the Antinomies of Modernity

Paul Gilroy

If popular writers like Jürgen Habermas and Marshall Berman are to be believed, the unfulfilled promise of modernity's Enlightenment project remains a beleaguered but nonetheless vibrant resource which may even now be able to guide the practice of contemporary social and political struggles. In opposition to this view, I propose that the history of the African diaspora and a reassessment of the relationship between modernity and slavery may require a more complete revision of the terms in which the modernity debates have been constructed than any of its academic participants may be willing to concede.

Despite the many positive qualities of Berman's work, the persuasive generality of his argument leads him to speak rather hastily of the "intimate unity of the modern self and the modern environment." This is conveyed in an instinctive manner by "the first great wave of writers and thinkers about modernity – Goethe, Hegel, Marx, Stendhal and Baudelaire, Carlyle and Dickens, Herzen and Dostoevsky."[1] Their conspicuous Europeancentredness aside, remarks like this would seem not only to endorse the view of modernity as an absolute break with its past but also to deny the possibility that the distinctiveness of the modern self might reside in its being a necessarily fractured or compound entity. From Berman's perspective, the powerful impact of issues like "race" and gender on the formation and reproduction of modern selves can too easily be set aside. The possibility that the modern subject may be located in historically specific and unavoidably complex configurations of individualization and embodiment – black and white, male and female, lord and bondsman – is not entertained. Berman compounds these difficulties by arguing that "modern environments and experiences cut across *all* boundaries of geography and ethnicity, of class and nationality, of religion and ideology: in this sense modernity can be said to unite all mankind"[2] (emphasis added). This could be read as a suggestion that an all-encompassing modernity affects everyone in a uniform and essentially similar way. This approach therefore runs contrary to my own concern with the variations and discontinuities in modern experience and with the decentered and inescapably plural nature of modern subjectivity and identity.

Like Habermas, Berman makes some very bold claims for the Enlightenment's ideological and political bequest: "these images and ideas provide a rich legacy for modern political thought and form a sort of agenda for nearly all the radical movements of the past two centuries."[3] He notes perceptively, but rather ruefully, that Montesquieu and Rousseau "have given us an agenda, *but no utopia*"[4] (emphasis added). We shall see below that expressions of black Atlantic radicalism have consistently acquired and sometimes even refined their utopian tones. One of my aims is to defend this choice and illuminate the occasional strengths with which it has endowed diaspora politics and aesthetics.

Elsewhere, in an interesting exchange with Perry Anderson,[5] Berman goes so far as to suggest that his own entirely laudable desire to remain as close as possible to the insinuating rhythms of everyday life, and his admirable belief that left intellectuals should cultivate the capacity to read the signs in the street in defiance of contemporary pressures to retreat into a contemplative state, are both valuable products of this special modernist perspective. Though not immune to the lure of the esoteric, for a variety of reasons black intellectuals, most of whom have not held academic positions, have tended to find it easier to remain in contact with the level of culture which Berman so rightly finds invigorating.

The same set of issues emerges in even sharper focus when, in another article, Berman describes a return to the area of the South Bronx where he spent his boyhood.[6] The breakdancers and graffitists that he observes moving across the shadows of that desolate urban landscape are not so easily to be claimed for the overarching modernism he seeks to affirm. Their history, which for all its appeal does not enter directly into Berman's accounts of the dizzying allure and the democratic potential of modern society, originates in distinctively modern institutions of the western hemisphere like the sugar plantation.[7] It constitutes the lineage of a variety of social thought – a movement or sequence of movements in cultural politics and political culture – which is an extremely ambiguous component of his modernist vision and has little to do with the innocent, European modernity that appears in the wider debates in which he is participating.

Later on we shall see in detail how specific groups of black intellectuals – again not simply writers – have analyzed and sought to come to terms with their inherently ambivalent relationship to the West and its dubious political legacies. Here it is only necessary to note that the contemporary descendants and the protective cultural forms of black radicalism also raise queries about the assumption of symmetrical intersubjectivity which features in so much of this discourse on the nature of modernity and modernization. In view of this, it is unsurprising that Berman speaks of those who make it out of the ruins of the South Bronx simply as "working-class heroes,"[8] as if their membership of or affiliation to an identifiable and cohesive working class is a self-evident fact that somehow confirms his sense of the centripetal effects of modernity.

I should emphasize that Berman is not being singled out for attack here, and that I have a great deal of sympathy with his persuasive and stimulating account of modernity and its attendant political choices. Pointing to some of the lapses in his narrative of the modern should not lead one to overlook the fact that he, unlike many of his theoretical peers, does at least notice the black and Hispanic presence in the ruins of the modern city. He may not be concerned with the impact of racial categories and meanings in the work of "intuitive" modernists like Hegel, but he does recognize the contemporary cultural products of modern black history and seek to portray their positive value. Berman even appreciates that "not much of [their] art is produced in commodity form for sale."[9] However, none of these important insights interrupts his haste to annexe the cultural forms of the black Atlantic for an image of the working class. In a small way, Berman's inability to give due weight to the plurality that I believe is integral to the modern raises further profound problems about his presentation of the continuity of modern identity and the totalizing wholeness with which he invests his conception of modern experience.

Pointing out aspects of the particularity of modern black experiences should not be understood as an occasion for staging the confrontation between the regional values of a distinct sector or community and the supposed universalism of occidental rationality. I am not suggesting that the contemporary traces of black intellectual history comprise or even refer to a lifeworld that is incommensurable with that of the former slaveholders. That would be the easy way out, for in focusing on racial slavery and its aftermath we are required to consider a historical relationship in which dependency and antagonism are intimately associated and in which black critiques of modernity may also be, in some significant senses, its affirmation. The key to comprehending this lies not in the overhasty separation of the cultural forms particular to both groups into some ethnic typology but in a detailed and comprehensive grasp of their complex interpenetration.[10] The intellectual and cultural achievements of the black Atlantic populations exist partly inside and not always against the grand narrative of Enlightenment and its operational principles. Their stems have grown strong, supported by a lattice of western politics and letters. Though African linguistic tropes and political and philosophical themes are still visible for those who wish to see them, they have often been transformed and adapted by their New World locations to a new point where the dangerous issues of purified essences and simple origins lose all meaning. These modern black political formations stand simultaneously both inside and outside the western culture which has been their peculiar step-parent. This complex relationship points once again to the need to engage critically with the way in which modernity has been theorized and periodized by its most enthusiastic defenders and critics. Regrettably, both groups have been equally slow in perceiving the centrality of ideas of race and culture to their ongoing investigations.

Like Berman, whose work bears his influence, Jürgen Habermas's writings convey a deep faith in the democratic potential of modernity. Modernity is understood as a distinct configuration with its own spatial and temporal characteristics defined above all through the consciousness of novelty that surrounds the emergence of civil society, the modern state, and industrial capitalism. Neither writer would accept that the normative potential of this new era has been exhausted, but theirs is not a positivistic or naive enthusiasm. Modernity is apprehended through its counter-discourses and often defended solely through its counterfactual elements, yet their analyses remain substantially unaffected by the histories of barbarity which appear to be such a prominent feature of the widening gap between modern experience and modern expectation. There is a scant sense, for example, that the universality and rationality of enlightened Europe and America were used to sustain and relocate rather than eradicate an order of racial difference inherited from the pre-modern era. The figure of Columbus does not appear to complement the standard pairing of Luther and Copernicus that is implicitly used to mark the limits of this particular understanding of modernity. Locke's colonial interests and the effect of the conquest of the Americas on Descartes and Rousseau are simply non-issues. In this setting – it is hardly surprising that if it is perceived to be relevant at all – the history of slavery is somehow assigned to blacks. It becomes our special property rather than a part of the ethical and intellectual heritage of the West as a whole.[11] This is only just preferable to the conventional alternative response which views plantation slavery as a pre-modern residue that disappears once it is revealed to be fundamentally incompatible with enlightened rationality and capitalist industrial production.

Like a good many ex-slaves and abolitionists, Habermas is tenaciously committed to the course of making bourgeois civil society live up to its political and philosophical promises. Drawing his theory of modernity from the work of Kant and Hegel, he notes its contemporary crises but says that they can be resolved only from within modernity itself by the completion of the Enlightenment project. There is perhaps an irony in seeing the affiliates of historical materialism defending the very humanistic rationality which for many years was one of their major intellectual foes.

Habermas recognizes the intimate ties between the idea of modernity and the development of European art which is able to act as a reconciler of the fragmented moments of reason. Using Weber and Nietzsche, he also defines modernity through its supercession of religious world views and the process of cultural rationalization whereby science, morality, and art are separated into autonomous spheres, each governed by its own epistemological rules and procedures of validation. The differentiation of these spheres of value is characterized by an emphasis on decentration and reflexivity. Thus the modernization of the lifeworld sees the concepts of authenticity, aesthetics, and ethics sharply differentiated while the modern is identified in the rift between secular and sacred spheres of action opened up by the death of God and the consequent hole at the centre of the lifeworld. This divergence proceeds closely articulated with the reification of consciousness that can be apprehended in the severing of expert cultures from the lifeworld and the latter's "colonization" by debased forms of pseudo-reason which serve only to integrate and func-tionalize the social system. Under these conditions, everyday consciousness becomes a "fragmented consciousness" divorced from the opportunity to engage in reflexive, self-critical practice or the chance to analyze experience in terms of distinct, cognitive, practical, and aesthetic standards.

Habermas does not follow Hegel in arguing that slavery is itself a modern-izing force in that it leads both master and servant first to self-consciousness and then to disillusion, forcing both to confront the unhappy realization that the true, the good, and the beautiful do not have a single shared origin. This is probably because though Habermas's theory of modernity draws heavily on Hegel, its Kantian focus absolves it from exploring the dialectic of master and slave in which Hegel's allegory of consciousness and freedom is rooted. I will return to this point later on. It is interesting that when Habermas does finally touch on the master/slave relationship he is exclusively concerned with the psychological dimensions of the allegory. He cites Hegel's observation that it is only the "Wild Moguls" who have their Lords outside themselves whereas the authentic offspring of European modernity remain enslaved even as they carry their Lord inside themselves.[12] It is particularly disappointing that he has not found the modern demand that European masters take their enslaved other seriously worthy of more detailed comment. Habermas is acute in appreciating that Hegel's account of the master/slave relationship is secreted inside many of the writings of contemporary theorists of modernity. He gives this account of the special significance of Hegel's work in initiating the debates over modernity which prefigure contemporary discussions: "Hegel is not the first philosopher to belong to the modern age but he is the first for whom modernity became a problem. In his theory the constellation among modernity, time consciousness and rationality becomes visible for the first time. Hegel himself explodes this constellation, because rationality puffed up into absolute spirit neutralizes the conditions under which modernity attained a consciousness of itself."[13] These words endorse the idea that a journey back to Hegel may be worth making. Struggling to specify the value of the same difficult passages, the historian David Brion Davis describes them thus:

> It was Hegel's genius to endow lordship and bondage with such a rich resonance of meanings that the model could be applied to every form of physical and psychological domination . . . Above all, Hegel bequeathed a message that would have a profound impact on future thought . . . we can expect nothing from the mercy of God or from the mercy of those who exercise worldly lordship in His or other names; that man's true emancipation, whether physical or spiritual, must always depend on those who have endured and overcome some form of slavery.[14]

Brion Davis is not alone in seeking to defend a more directly social reading of Hegel's text than Habermas's own more strictly delimited and essentially psychological concerns would sanction. The writings of Alexander Kojève have been particularly important in popularizing an interpretation of the master/slave relationship which, without drifting towards a literal analysis, is both less psychological and more historically specific than is currently fashionable.[15] Kojève's identification of an existential impasse that develops out of the master's dependency on the slave is also interesting because it would seem to offer an interesting point of departure for the analysis of modern aesthetics. These passages in Hegel and Kojève's influential interpretation of them have been widely taken up in social and psychoanalytic theory, forming, for example, an important part of the background to Richard Wright's Parisian revisions of Marxism and appropriations of phenomenology and existentialism. They have also been of great interest to the feminist writers who have returned to Hegel's allegory (via the Lukács of *History and Class Consciousness*) as part of their clarifying the possibility of "standpoint epistemologies,"[16] particular sociological or experiential locations from which woman-centered knowledge about the world can proceed. This is a big debate and cannot be reconstructed in its entirety here. It has, however, been brought to bear on modern black history and political culture by a number of feminist authors, in particular Patricia Hill Collins, whose argument for the existence of a black women's standpoint epistemology is conducted in something of the same critical, reconstructive, and revisionist spirit that guides my thinking here.[17] Hill Collins argues that the western traditions of thinking and thinking about thinking to which the human sciences are bound have systematically tried to separate these privileged activities from mere being. This insight is linked in her argument to criticism of the pernicious effects of the dualistic, binary thinking in which one partner in the cognitive couple is always dominated by its repressed and subjugated other half – male/female, rational/irrational, nature/culture, light/dark.

Though I concur with most of Hill Collins's diagnosis of this state of affairs, I disagree with her responses to it. Her answer to the western separation of thinking (and thinking about thinking) from being is to collapse them back into each other so that they form a functional unity that can be uncritically celebrated. She utilizes a feminist version of this reasoning as an analogy for understanding what black women can do to produce a critical theory capable of addressing their experiences of marginalization from truth-seeking and interpretive activities. This begins in an argument for the social construction of "race" and gender. There is no essential woman or woman in general that can focus the emancipatory project of feminist politics; therefore a feminist epistemology must proceed to construct its own standpoint addressed to that lack. This is done in a spirit disabused of the belief that essentially feminine experience can act as the guarantor of feminist knowledge claims. In the (non-black) feminist discourse, the terms "woman" and "feminist" are distinguished and must remain separate for the critique to operate plausibly. There is no open counter-argument from Hill Collins for the superior value of an essentialist understanding of black female subjectivity. However, another version of racial essentialism is smuggled in through the back porch even as Hill Collins loudly banishes it from her front door. In her transposition, the term "black" does a double duty. It covers the positions of knowing and being. Its epistemological and ontological dimensions are entirely congruent. Their simple expressive unity joins an act of political affirmation to this philosophical stance: "being black encompasses both experiencing white domination and individual and group valuation of an independent, long-standing Afrocentric consciousness."[18] Her inconsistent deployment of the term Afrocentric, sometimes appearing as a synonym for black and sometimes as equivalent to the sense of the word "feminist" which was opposed to the word "woman," does little to solve the confusion that results from this: "Even though I will continue to use the term Afrocentric feminist thought interchangeably with the phrase Black feminist thought, I think they are conceptually distinct."[19]

Hill Collins repeatedly emphasizes that the standpoint she is exploring is "self-defined." This formulation appears at the point where a classically "Leninist" version of vanguardism is imported into her writing. The mass of black women have experiences that open the way forward to unique forms of consciousness. However, they are incapable of "articulating" the standpoint and need to be helped to do this by an elite cadre of black female intellectuals who vaccinate ordinary folk with the products of their critical theorizing, thereby generating resistance. This group also performs what appears to be a low-intensity disciplinary function in areas of black politics other than feminist struggles: "Black women intellectuals who articulate an autonomous, self-defined standpoint are in a position to examine the usefulness of coalitions with other groups, both scholarly and activist, in order to develop new models for social change."[20] Whatever one thinks of the political strategies implied in all this, it is striking how the image of an integral, humanist, and thoroughly Cartesian racial subject underpins and animates the construct of self that has been situated at the core of this "Black women's standpoint – those experiences and ideas shared by African-American women that provide a unique angle of vision on self, community, and society."[21] The elision of black and African-American in this passage is symptomatic of other problems that will be examined below. But what are we to make of the fact that self always comes first in this litany? What understanding of self is it to supply the subjectivity that can focus the subject of black politics?

Hill Collins's answers to these questions suggest that an embeddedness in Enlightenment assumptions continues despite the ostentatious gestures of disaffiliation. Experience-centered knowledge claims, mediated if at all by input from the intellectual vanguard, simply end up substituting the standpoint of black women for its forerunner rooted in the lives of white men. This may have some value as a short-term corrective, but it is less radical and less stimulating than the possibility that we might move beyond the desire to situate our claims about the world in the lives of these whole and stable, ideal subjects. For all its conspicuous masculinism and Eurocentrism, Hegel's allegory is relational. It can be used to point out the value of incorporating the problem of subject formation into both epistemology and political practice. This would also mean taking a cue from a politicized postmodernism and leaving the categories of enquiry open.[22]

My own interest in the famous section at the start of Hegel's *The Phenomenology of Mind*[23] is twofold: First, it can be used to initiate an analysis of modernity which is abjured by Habermas because it points directly to an approach which sees the intimate association of modernity and slavery as a fundamental conceptual issue. This is significant because it can be used to offer a firm rebuke to the mesmeric idea of history as progress and because it provides an opportunity to re-periodize and reaccentuate accounts of the dialectic of Enlightenment which have not always been concerned to look at modernity through the lenses of colonialism or scientific racism. Second, a return to Hegel's account of the conflict and the forms of dependency produced in the relationship between master and slave foregrounds the issues of brutality and terror which are also too frequently ignored. Taken together, these problems offer an opportunity to transcend the unproductive debate between a Eurocentric rationalism which banishes the slave experience from its accounts of modernity while arguing that the crises of modernity can be resolved from within, and an equally occidental anti-humanism which locates the origins of modernity's current crises in the shortcomings of the Enlightenment project.

Cornel West has pointed out that Hegel was the favourite philosopher of Dr. Martin Luther King, Jr.[24] The point of entry into the discourse of modernity which Hegel affords is doubly significant because, as we shall see, a significant number of intellectuals formed by the black Atlantic have engaged in critical dialogues with his writings. Their difficult and deeply ambivalent relationship to his work and the intellectual tradition in which it stands helps to locate their uncomfortable position relative to western politics and letters and to identify the distinctive perspectives on the modern world that they have expressed. Amiri Baraka's 1963 poem "Hegel" captures this ambivalence and shows that the appropriation of Hegelian themes is by no means always negative:

> I scream for help. And none comes, has ever
> come. No single redeeming hand
> has ever been offered . . .
> no single redeeming word, has come
> wringing out of flesh
> with the imperfect beautiful resolution
> that would release me from this heavy contract
> of emptiness.[25]

In *Being and Nothingness* Sartre makes the point that Hegel's analysis does not deal with lateral relations between masters or within the caste of slaves let alone with the impact of a free non-slave owning population on the institution of slavery.[26] However, despite these contextual failings, its insights and view of slavery as, in a sense, the premise of modernity also give us the chance to reopen discussion of the origins of black politics in the Euro-American age of revolution and the consequent relationship between the contrasting varieties of radicalism which energized the slaves' struggles for emancipation and racial justice, and which endure in the struggles of their dispersed descendants today. Plantation slavery was more than just a system of labor and a distinct mode of racial domination. Whether it encapsulated the inner essence of capitalism or was a vestigial, essentially precapitalist element in a dependant relationship to capitalism proper, it provided the foundations for a distinctive network of economic, social, and political relations. Above all, "its demise threw open the most fundamental questions of economy, society and polity,"[27] and it has retained a central place in the historical memories of the black Atlantic.

The way these populations continue to make creative, communicative use of the memory of slavery points constructively away from the twin positions that have overdetermined the debate on modernity so far – an uncritical and complacent rationalism and a self-conscious and rhetorical anti-humanism which simply trivializes the potency of the negative. Moving beyond these options requires consideration of what, following Walter Benjamin, can be called the primal history of modernity.[28] Although Benjamin was not attuned to the possibility that modern history could be seen as fractured along the axis that separates European masters and mistresses from their African slaves, there are elements of his thinking, particularly those which derive from his relationship to Jewish mysticism, which make it a valuable resource for my own critique.[29] The time has come for the primal history of modernity to be reconstructed from the slaves' points of view. These emerge in the especially acute consciousness of both life and freedom which is nurtured by the slave's "mortal terror of his sovereign master" and the continuing "trial by death" which slavery becomes for the male slave.[30] This primal history offers a unique perspective on many of the key intellectual and political issues in the modernity debates. I have already mentioned the idea of history as progress. Apart from that thorny perennial, the slaves' perspectives require a discrete view not just of the dynamics of power and domination in plantation societies dedicated to the pursuit of commercial profit but of such central categories of the Enlightenment project as the idea of universality, the fixity of meaning, the coherence of the subject, and, of course, the foundational ethnocentrism in which these have all tended to be anchored. Each of these issues has an impact on the formation of racial discourse and a relevance in understanding the development of racial politics. These problems aside, the slaves' perspectives necessitate a critical stance on the discourse of bourgeois humanism which several scholars have implicated in the rise and consolidation of scientific racism.[31] Using the memory of slavery as an interpretive device suggests that this humanism cannot simply be repaired by introducing the figures of black folks who had previously been confined to the intermediate category between animal and human that Du Bois identifies as a "tertium quid."[32]

In keeping with the spiritual components which also help to distinguish them from modern secular rationality, the slaves' perspectives deal only secondarily in the idea of a rationally pursued utopia. Their primary categories are steeped in the idea of a revolutionary or eschatological apocalypse – the Jubilee. They provocatively suggest that many of the advances of modernity are in fact insubstantial or pseudo-advances contingent on the power of the racially dominant grouping and that, as a result, the critique of modernity cannot be satisfactorily completed from within its own philosophical and political norms, that is, immanently. The representative figures [. . .] were all acutely aware of the promise and potential of the modern world. Nevertheless, their critical perspectives on it were only partly grounded in its own norms. However uneasily their work balanced its defences of modernity against its critiques, they drew deliberately and self-consciously on premodern images and symbols that gain an extra power in proportion to the brute facts of modern slavery. These have contributed to the formation of a vernacular variety of unhappy consciousness which demands that we rethink the meanings of rationality, autonomy, reflection, subjectivity, and power in the light of an extended meditation both on the condition of the slaves and on the suggestion that racial terror is not merely compatible with occidental rationality but cheerfully complicit with it. In terms of contemporary politics and social theory, the value of this project lies in its promise to uncover both an ethics of freedom to set alongside modernity's ethics of law and the new conceptions of selfhood and individuation that are waiting to be constructed from the slaves' standpoint – forever disassociated from the psychological and epistemic correlates of racial subordination. This unstable standpoint is to be understood in a different way from the clarion calls to epistemological narcissism and the absolute sovereignity of unmediated experience[33] which sometimes appear in association with the term. It can be summed up in Foucault's tentative extension of the idea of a *critical* self-inventory into the political field. This is made significantly in a commentary upon the Enlightenment: "The critical ontology of ourselves has to be considered not, certainly, as a theory, a doctrine, nor even as a permanent body of knowledge that is accumulating; it has to be conceived as an attitude, an ethos, a philosophical life in which the critique of what we are is at one and the same time the historical analysis of the limits that are imposed on us and an experiment with the possibility of going beyond them."[34]

Having recognized the cultural force of the term "modernity" we must also be prepared to delve into the special traditions of artistic expression that emerge from slave culture. The expressive cultures developed in slavery continue to preserve in artistic form needs and desires which go far beyond the mere satisfaction of material wants. In contradistinction to the Enlightenment assumption of a fundamental separation between art and life, these expressive forms reiterate the continuity of art and life. They celebrate the grounding of the aesthetic with other dimensions of social life. The particular aesthetic which the continuity of expressive culture preserves derives not from dispassionate and rational evaluation of the artistic object but from an inescapably subjective contemplation of the mimetic functions of artistic performance in the processes of struggles towards emancipation, citizenship, and eventually autonomy. Subjectivity is here connected with rationality in a contingent manner. It may be grounded in communication, but this form of interaction is not an equivalent and idealized exchange between equal citizens who reciprocate their regard for each other in grammatically unified speech. The extreme patterns of communication defined by the institution of plantation slavery dictate that we recognize the anti-discursive and extra-linguistic ramifications of power at work in shaping communicative acts. There may, after all, be no reciprocity on the plantation outside of the possibilities of rebellion and suicide, flight and silent mourning, and there is certainly no grammatical unity of speech to mediate communicative reason. In many respects, the plantation's inhabitants live non-synchronously. Their mode of communication is divided by the radically opposed political and economic interests that distinguish the master and mistress from their respective human chattels. Under these conditions, artistic practice retains its "cultic functions" while its superior claims to authenticity and historic witness may be actively preserved. It becomes diffuse throughout the subaltern racial collectivity where relations of cultural production and reception operate that are wholly different from those which define the public sphere of the slaveholders. In this severely restricted space, sacred or profane, art became the backbone of the slaves' political cultures and of their cultural history. It remains the means through which cultural activists even now engage in "rescuing critiques" of the present by both mobilizing memories of the past and inventing an imaginary pastness that can fuel their utopian hopes.

We can see now that the arts of darkness appear in the West at the point where modernity is revealed to be actively associated with the forms of terror legitimated by reference to the idea of "race." We must remember that however modern they may appear to be, the artistic practices of the slaves and their descendants are also grounded outside modernity. The invocation of anteriority as anti-modernity is more than a consistent rhetorical flourish linking contemporary Africalogy and its nineteenth-century precursors. These gestures articulate a memory of pre-slave history that can, in turn, operate as a mechanism to distil and focus the counter-power of those held in bondage and their descendants. This artistic practice is therefore inescapably both inside and outside the dubious protection modernity offers. It can be examined in relation to modern forms, themes, and ideas but carries its own distinct critique of modernity; a critique forged out of the particular experiences involved in being a racial slave in a legitimate and avowedly rational system of unfree labor. To put it another way, this artistic and political formation has come to relish its measure of autonomy from the modern – an independent vitality that comes from the syncopated pulse of non-European philosophical and aesthetic outlooks and the fallout from their impact on western norms. This autonomy developed further as slavery, colonialism, and the terror that attended them pitted the vital arts of the slaves against the characteristically modern conditions in which their oppression appeared – as a byproduct of the coerced production of commodities for sale on a world market. This system produced an ungenteel modernity, de-centered from the closed worlds of metropolitan Europe that have claimed the attention of theorists so far.

Notes

1   Marshall Berman, *All That Is Solid Melts into Air* (London: Verso, 1983), p. 132.
2   Ibid., p. 15.
3   Marshall Berman, *The Politics of Authenticity: Radical Individualism and the Emergence of Modern Society* (London: George Allen and Unwin, 1971), p. 317.
4   Ibid.
5   Marshall Berman (1984), "The Signs in the Street: A Response to Perry Anderson". *New Left Review*, 144.
6   Marshall Berman (1984), "Urbicide". *Village Voice*, 29, no. 36, Sept. 4.
7   Manuel Moreno Fraginals, *The Sugar Mill: The Socioeconomic Complex of Sugar in Cuba* (New York: Monthly Review Press, 1976).
8   Marshall Berman, "Urbicide". p. 25.
9   Ibid., p. 17.
10 Studies of cultural syncretism in terms of day-to-day experiences have begun to appear: Mechal Sobel's *The World They Made Together: Black and White Values in Eighteenth-Century Virginia* (Princeton, NJ: Princeton University Press, 1987) seems to me to be an exemplary text of this type.
11 The work of David Brion Davis is an important exception here, but he is an American and a historian.
12 Jürgen Habermas, *The Philosophical Discourse of Modernity* (Cambridge: Polity Press, 1987), p. 28.
13 Ibid., p. 43.
14 David Brion Davis, *The Problem of Slavery in the Age of Revolution, 1770–1823* (Ithaca and London: Cornell University Press, 1975).
15 A. Kojève, *Introduction to the Reading of Hegel* (New York: Basic Books, 1969); Hussein A. Bulhan, *Frantz Fanon and the Psychology of Oppression* (New York: Plenum Press, 1985). The division between those who, like Deleuze, argue that Hegel says the future belongs to the slave and those who interpret his words as pointing to a world beyond the master/slave relationship remains a deep one. See Giles Deleuze, *Nietzsche and Philosophy* (London: Athlone Press, 1983).
16 Sandra Harding, *The Science Question in Feminism* (Milton Keynes: Open University Press, 1986), p. 158; Nancy Hartsock, *Money, Sex and Power* (Boston: Northeastern University Press, 1983), p. 240.
17 Hill Collins's emphasis on the outsider within could, for example, be readily assimilated to the notions of "double consciousness," "double vision," and "dread-full objectivity" discussed elsewhere in this chapter. It is interesting that she does not attempt to link this theme in her own work with the history of these ideas in African-American political culture. See Patricia Hill Collins (1986), "Learning from the Outsider Within: The Sociological Significance of Black Feminist Thought". *Social Problems* 33, no. 6, pp. 14–32.
18 Patricia Hill Collins, *Black Feminist Thought: Knowledge, Consciousness and the Politics*

of Empowerment (New York and London: Routledge, 1991), p. 27. The deconstructive zeal with which Hill Collins urges her readers to take traditional epistemological assumptions apart is exhausted after tackling "woman" and "intellectual." It runs out long before she reaches the key words "black" and "Afrocentric," which appear to be immune to this critical operation (see p. 17).

19   Ibid., p. 40.

20   Ibid., pp. 32–3.

21   Ibid., p. 23.

22   Jane Flax, *Thinking Fragments* (Berkeley and Oxford: University of California Press, 1990).

23   G. W. F Hegel, *The Phenomenology of the Mind*, trans. J. B. Baillie (New York: Harper and Row, 1967), ch. 4.

24   Cornel West, "The Religious Foundations of the Thought of Martin Luther King, Jr.," in *We Shall Overcome: Martin Luther King and the Black Freedom Struggle*, ed. Peter J. Albert and Ronald Hoffman (New York: Pantheon, 1990).

25   Quoted by Kimberley Benston in *Baraka* (New Haven: Yale University Press, 1976), p. 90. For a discussion of the relationship between Baraka and Hegel see Esther M. Jackson, "LeRoi Jones (Imamu Amiri Baraka): Form and the Progression of Consciousness," in Kimberly W. Benston (ed.), *Imamu Amiri Baraka (LeRoi Jones): Twentieth Century Views* (Englewood Cliffs, NJ: Prentice Hall, 1978).

26   J.-P. Sartre, *Being and Nothingness* (London: Methuen, 1969), bk. 1, pp. 157–8.

27   Eric Foner, *Nothing but Freedom* (Baton Rouge and London: Louisiana State University Press, 1983), p. 1.

28   Walter Benjamin, "Paris: The Capital of the Nineteenth Century," in *Charles Baudelaire: A Lyric Poet in the Era of High Capitalism* (London: Verso, 1976), p. 159. See also Richard Wolin, *Walter Benjamin: An Aesthetic of Redemption* (New York: Columbia University Press, 1982).

29   Andrew Benjamin, "Tradition and Experience," in Andrew Benjamin, ed., *The Problems of Modernity* (London: Routledge, 1989).

30   See Orlando Patterson's discussion of Hegel in *Slavery and Social Death* (Cambridge, MA: Harvard University Press, 1982), pp. 97–101.

31   Dominique Lecourt, "On Marxism as a Critique of Sociological Theories," in M. O'Callaghan (ed.), *Sociological Theories: Race and Colonialism* (Paris: UNESCO, 1980), p. 267.

32   "... somewhere between men and cattle God had created a tertium quid, and called it Negro, – a clownish, simple creature, at times lovable within its limitations, but straitly foreordained to walk within the Veil." *The Souls of Black Folk* (1903; New York: Bantam, 1989), p. 63.

33   For a critique of these appeals see Joan Wallach Scott (1991), "The Evidence of Experience". *Critical Inquiry* 17, Summer, pp. 773–97.

34   Michel Foucault, "What Is Enlightenment?" in *The Foucault Reader*, ed. Paul Rabinow (Harmondsworth: Peregrine, 1986), p. 50.

18

Subaltern Studies: Deconstructing Historiography

Gayatri Chakravorty Spivak

Change and Crisis

The work of the Subaltern Studies group offers a theory of change. The insertion of India into colonialism is generally defined as a change from semi-feudalism into capitalist subjection. Such a definition theorizes the change within the great narrative of the modes of production and, by uneasy implication, within the narrative of the transition from feudalism to capitalism. Concurrently, this change is seen as the inauguration of politicization for the colonized. The colonial subject is seen as emerging from those parts of the indigenous elite which come to be loosely described as "bourgeois nationalist." The Subaltern Studies group seems to me to be revising this general definition and its theorization by proposing at least two things: first, that the moment(s) of change be pluralized and plotted as confrontations rather than transition (they would thus be seen in relation to histories of domination and exploitation rather than within the great modes-of-production narrative) and, secondly, that such changes are signalled or marked by a functional change in sign-systems. The most important functional change is from the religious to the militant. There are, however, many other functional changes in sign-systems indicated in these collections: from crime to insurgency, from bondsman to worker, and so on.

The most significant outcome of this revision or shift in perspective is that the agency of change is located in the insurgent or the "subaltern." [. . .]

A functional change in a sign-system is a violent event. Even when it is perceived as "gradual," or "failed," or yet "reversing itself," the change itself can only be operated by the force of a crisis. What Paul de Man writes of criticism can here be extended to a subalternity that is turning things "upside down": "In periods that are not periods of crisis, or in individuals bent upon avoiding crisis at all cost, there can be all kinds of approaches to [the social] . . . but there can be no [insurgency]."[1] Yet, if the space for a change (necessarily also an addition) had not been there in the prior function of the sign-system, the crisis could not have made the change happen. The change in signification-function supplements the previous function. "The movement of signification adds something . . . but this addition . . . comes to perform a vicarious function, to supplement a lack on the part of the signified."[2] The Subaltern Studies collective scrupulously annotates this double movement.

They generally perceive their task as making a theory of consciousness or culture rather than specifically a theory of change. It is because of this, I think, that the force of crisis, *although never far from their argument,* is not systematically emphasized in their work, and is sometimes disarmingly alluded to as "impingement," "combination," "getting caught up in a general wave," "circumstances for unification," "reasons for change," "ambiguity," "unease," "transit," "bringing into focus"; even as it is also described as "switch," "catching fire" and, pervasively, as "turning upside down" – all critical concept-metaphors that would indicate force.[3] Indeed, a general sobriety of tone will not allow them to emphasize sufficiently that they are themselves bringing hegemonic historiography to crisis. This leads them to describe the clandestine operation of supplementarity as the inexorable speculative logic of the dialectic. In this they seem to me to do themselves a disservice, for, as self-professed dialecticians, they open themselves to older debates between spontaneity and consciousness or structure and history. Their actual practice, which, I will argue, is closer to deconstruction, would put these oppositions into question. A theory of change as the site of the displacement of function between sign-systems – which is what they oblige me to read in them – is a theory of reading in the strongest possible general sense. The site of displacement of the function of signs is the name of reading as active transaction between past and future. This transactional reading as (the possibility of) action, even at its most dynamic, is perhaps what Antonio Gramsci meant by "elaboration," *e-laborare,* working out.[4] If seen in this way, the work of the Subaltern Studies group repeatedly makes it possible for us to grasp that the concept-metaphor of the "social text" is not the reduction of real life to the page of a book. My theoretical intervention is a modest attempt to remind us of this.

It can be advanced that their work presupposes that the entire socius, at least in so far as it is the object of their study, is what Nietzsche would call a *fortgesetzte Zeichenkette* – a "continuous sign-chain." The possibility of action lies in the dynamics of the disruption of this object, the breaking and relinking of the chain. This line of argument does not set consciousness over against the socius, but sees it as itself also constituted as and on a semiotic chain. It is thus an instrument of study which participates in the nature of the object of study. To see consciousness thus is to place the historian in a position of irreducible compromise. I believe it is because of this double bind that it is possible to unpack the aphoristic remark of Nietzsche's that follows the image of the sign-chain with reference to this double bind: "All concepts in which an entire process is comprehended [*sich zusammenfasst*] withdraws itself from [*sich entzieht*] definition; only that which has no history is definable."[5] At any rate these presuppositions are not, strictly speaking, consonant with a desire to find a consciousness (here of the subaltern) in a positive and pure state. My essay will also try to develop this discrepancy.

Cognitive Failure is Irreducible

All of the accounts of attempted discursive displacements provided by the group are accounts of failures. For the subaltern displacements, the reason for failure most often given is the much greater scope, organization, and strength of the colonial authorities. In the case of the nationalist movement for independence it is clearly pointed out that the bourgeoisie's "interested" refusal to recognize the importance of, and to ally themselves with, a politicized peasantry accounted for the failure of the discursive displacement that operated the peasants' politicization. Yet there is also an incipient evolutionism here which, trying perhaps to avoid a vulgar Marxist glorification of the peasant, lays the blame on "the existing level of peasant consciousness" for the fact "that peasant solidarity and peasant power were seldom sufficient or sustained enough."[6] This contradicts the general politics of the group – which sees the elite's hegemonic access to "consciousness" as an interpretable construct.

To examine this contradiction we must first note that discursive displacements wittingly or unwittingly operated from above are also failures. Chakrabarty, Das, and Chandra chart the failures of trade union socialism, functionalist entrepreneurialism and agrarian communism to displace a semifeudal into a "modern" discourse. Chatterjee shows how Gandhi's initial dynamic transaction with the discursive field of the Hindu religious Imaginary had to be travestied in order that his ethics of resistance could be displaced into the sign-system of bourgeois politics.[7] (No doubt if an "entity" like "bourgeois politics" were to be opened up to discursive analysis the same micro-dynamics of displacements would emerge.) My point is, simply, that failures or partial successes in discursive-field displacement do not necessarily relate, following a progressivist scale, to the "level of consciousness" of a class.

Let us now proceed to note that what has seemingly been thoroughly successful, namely elite historiography, on the right or the left, nationalist or colonialist, is itself, by the analysis of this group, shown to be constituted by cognitive failures. Indeed, if the theory of change as the site of the displacement of a discursive field is their most pervasive argument, this comes a close second. Here too no distinction is made, quite properly in my estimation, between witting and unwitting lapses. Hardiman points at the Nationalists' persistent (mis)cognition of discursive field-displacement on the part of the subaltern as the signature of Sanskritization.[8] He reads contemporary analysis such as Paul Brass's study of factionalism for the symptoms of what Edward Said has called "orientalism."[9] It is correctly suggested that the sophisticated vocabulary of much contemporary historiography *successfully* shields this cognitive *failure* and that this success-in-failure, this sanctioned ignorance, is inseparable from colonial domination. Das shows rational expectation theory, that hegemonic yet defunct (successful cognitive failure once again) mainstay of neo-colonialism, at work in India's "Green Revolution to Prevent A Red One."[10]

Within this tracking of successful cognitive failure, the most interesting maneuver is to examine the production of "evidence," the cornerstone of the edifice of historical truth,[11] and to anatomize the mechanics of the construction of the self-consolidating Other – the insurgent and insurgency. In this part of the project, Guha seems to radicalize the historiography of colonial India through a combination of Soviet and Barthesian semiotic analysis. The discursivity (cognitive failure) of disinterested (successful and therefore true) historiography is revealed. The Muse of History and counter-insurgency are shown to be complicit.[12]

I am suggesting, of course, that an implicitly evolutionist or progressivist set of presuppositions measuring failure or success in terms of level of consciousness is too simple for the practice of the collective. If we look at the varieties of activity treated by them, subaltern, insurgent, nationalist, colonialist, historiographic, it is a general field of failures that we see. In fact the work of the collective is making the distinction between success and failure indeterminate – for the most successful historical record is disclosed by them to be crosshatched by cognitive failure. Since in the case of the subaltern they are considering consciousness (however "negative") and culture (however determining); and in the case of the elite, culture and manipulation – the subaltern is also operating in the theatre of "cognition." At any rate, where does cognition begin and end? I will consider later the possible problems with such compartmentalized views of consciousness. Here suffice it to say that by the ordinary standards of coherence, and in terms of their own methodology, the possibility of failure cannot be derived from any criterion of success unless the latter is a theoretical fiction.[13]

A word on "alienation," as used by members of this group, to mean "a failure of self-cognition," is in order here.

> To overestimate . . . [the] lucidity or depth [of the subaltern consciousness] will be . . . ill-advised . . . This characteristic expression of a negative consciousness on the insurgent's part matched its other symptom, that is, his self-alienation. He was still committed to envisaging the coming war on the Raj as the project of a will independent of himself and his own role in it as no more than instrumental . . .

[In their own] parwana [proclamation] . . . the authors did not recognize even their own voice, but heard only that of God.[14]

To be sure, within his progressivist narrative taxonomy Hegel describes the march of history in terms of a diminution in the self-alienation of the so-called world historical agent. Kojève and his followers in France distinguished between this Hegel, the narrator of (a) history, and the speculative Hegel who outlined a system of logic.[15] Within the latter, alienation is irreducible in any act of consciousness. Unless the subject separates from itself to grasp the object there is no cognition, indeed no thinking, no judgment. Being and Absolute Idea, the first and last sections of *The Science of Logic,* two accounts of simple unalienability, are not accessible to individual or personal consciousness. From the strictly philosophical point of view, then, (a) elite historiography, (b) the bourgeois nationalist account, as well as (c) re-inscription by the Subaltern Studies group, are operated by alienation – *Verfremdung* as well as *Entäußerung.* Derrida's reading of Hegel as in *Glas* would question the argument for the inalienability even of Absolute Necessity and Absolute Knowledge, but here we need not move that far. We must ask the opposite question. How shall we deal with Marx's suggestion that man must strive toward self-determination and unalienated practice and Gramsci's that "the lower classes" must "achieve self-awareness via a series of negations?"[16]

Formulating an answer to this question might lead to far-reaching practical effects if the risks of the irreducibility of cognitive "failure" and of "alienation" are accepted. The group's own practice can then be graphed on this grid of "failures," with the concept of failure generalized and re-inscribed as I have suggested above. This subverts the inevitable vanguardism of a theory that otherwise criticizes the vanguardism of theory. This is why I hope to align them with deconstruction: "Operating necessarily from the inside, borrowing all the strategic and economic resources of subversion from the old structure, borrowing them structurally, that is to say without being able to isolate their elements and atoms, the enterprise of deconstruction always in a certain way falls prey to its own work."[17]

This is the greatest gift of deconstruction: to question the authority of the investigating subject without paralysing him, persistently transforming conditions of impossibility into possibility.[18] Let us pursue the implications of this in our particular case.

The group, as we have seen, tracks failures in attempts to displace discursive fields. A deconstructive approach would bring into focus the fact that they are themselves engaged in an attempt at displacing discursive fields, that they themselves "fail" (in the general sense) for reasons as "historical" as those they adduce for the heterogeneous agents they study; and would attempt to forge a practice that would take this into account. Otherwise, refusing to acknowledge the implications of their own line of work because that would be politically incorrect, they would, willy-nilly, "insidiously objectify" the subaltern,[19] control him through knowledge even as they restore versions of causality and self-determination to him,[20] become complicit, in their desire for totality (and therefore totalization),[21] with a "law [that] assign[s] a[n] undifferentiated [proper] name" to "the subaltern as such."[22]

Subaltern Studies and the European Critique of Humanism

A "religious idiom gave the hillmen [of the Eastern Ghats] a framework, within which to conceptualize their predicament and to seek solutions to it."[23] The idiom of recent European theories of interpretation seems to offer this collective a similar framework. As they work their displacement, they are, as I suggest above, expanding the semantic range of "reading" and "text," words that are, incidentally, not prominent in their vocabulary. This is a bold transaction and can be compared favorably to some similar attempts made by historians in the United States.[24] It is appropriately marked by attempts to find local parallels, as in the concept of *atidesa* in Guha's work, and to insert the local into the general, as in the pervasive invocation of English, French, German, and occasionally Italian insurgency in *Elementary Aspects of Peasant Insurgency in Colonial India*, and in the invocation of the anthropology of Africa in Partha Chatterjee's work on modes of power.

It is the force of a crisis that operates functional displacements in discursive fields. In my reading of the volumes of *Subaltern Studies*, this critical force or bringing-to-crisis can be located in the energy of the questioning of humanism in the post-Nietzschean sector of western European structuralism, for our group Michel Foucault, Roland Barthes, and a certain Lévi-Strauss. These structuralists question humanism by exposing its hero – the sovereign subject as author, the subject of authority, legitimacy, and power. There is an affinity between the imperialist subject and the subject of humanism. Yet the crisis of anti-humanism – *like all crises* – does not move our collective "fully." The rupture shows agent, totality, and upon a culturalism, that are discontinuous with the critique itself to be also a repetition. They fall back upon notions of consciousness – as of humanism. They seem unaware of the historico-political provenance of various western "collaborators." Vygotsky and Lotman, Victor Turner and Lévi-Strauss, Evans-Pritchard and Hindess and Hirst can, for them, fuel the same fire as Foucault and Barthes. Since one cannot accuse this group of the eclecticism of the supermarket consumer, one must see in their practice a repetition of as well as a rupture from the colonial predicament: the transactional quality of inter-conflicting metropolitan sources often eludes the (post)colonial intellectual.

I remind the reader that, in my view, such "cognitive failures" are irreducible. As I comment on the place of "consciousness" in the work of Subaltern Studies, it is therefore not my intent to suggest a formula for correct cognitive moves.

The Problem of Subaltern Consciousness

I have been trying to read the work of the group against the grain of their theoretical self-representation. Their figuration of peasant or subaltern consciousness makes such a reading particularly productive.

To investigate, discover, and establish a subaltern or peasant consciousness seems at first to be a positivistic project – a project which assumes that, if properly prosecuted, it will lead to firm ground, to some *thing* that can be disclosed. This is all the more significant in the case of recovering a consciousness because, within the post-Enlightenment tradition that the collective participates in as interventionist historians, consciousness is *the* ground that makes all disclosures possible.

And, indeed, the group is susceptible to this interpretation. There *is* a certain univocal reflection or signification-theory presupposed here by which "peasant action in famine as in rebellion" is taken to "reflect . . . a single underlying consciousness";[25] and "solidarity" is seen as a "signifier of consciousness," where signification is representation, figuration, propriation (stringent de-limitation within a unique and self-adequate outline), and imprinting.[26]

Yet even as "consciousness" is thus entertained as an indivisible self-proximate signified or ground, there is a force at work here which would contradict such a metaphysics. For consciousness here is not consciousness-in-general, but a historicized political species thereof, subaltern consciousness. In a passage where "transcendental" is used as "transcending, because informing a hegemonic narrative" rather than in a strictly philosophical sense, Guha puts this admirably: "Once a peasant rebellion has been assimilated to the career of the Raj, the Nation or the people [the hegemonic narratives], it becomes easy for the historian to abdicate the responsibility he has of exploring and describing the consciousness specific to that rebellion and be content to ascribe to it a transcendental consciousness . . . representing them merely as instruments of some other will."[27]

Because of this bestowal of a historical specificity to consciousness in the narrow sense, even as it implicitly operates as a metaphysical methodological presupposition in the general sense, there is always a counterpointing suggestion in the work of the group that subaltern consciousness is subject to the cathexis of the elite, that it is never fully recoverable, that it is always askew from its received signifiers, indeed that it is effaced even as it is disclosed, that it is irreducibly discursive. It is, for example, chiefly a matter of "negative consciousness" in the more theoretical of these essays. Although "negative consciousness" is conceived of here as an historical stage peculiar to the subaltern, there is no logical reason why, given that the argument is inevitably historicized, this "negative," rather than the grounding positive view of consciousness, should not be generalized as the group's methodological presupposition. One view of "negative consciousness," for instance, sees it as the consciousness not of the being of the subaltern, but of that of the oppressors.[28] Here, in vague Hegelian limnings, is the anti-humanist and anti-positivist position that it is always the desire for/of (the power of the Other) that produces an image of the self. If this is generalized, as in my reading of the "cognitive failure" argument, it is the subaltern who provides the model for a general theory of consciousness. And yet, since the "subaltern" cannot appear without the thought of the "elite," the generalization is by definition incomplete – in philosophical language "non-originary," or, in an earlier version of *"unursprünglich,"* non-primordial. This "instituted trace at the origin" is a representation of the deconstructive critique of simple origins. Of the practical consequences of recognizing the traces of this strategy in the work of the group I will speak below.

Another note in the counterpoint deconstructing the metaphysics of consciousness in these texts is provided by the reiterated fact that it is only the texts of counter-insurgency or elite documentation that give us the news of the consciousness of the subaltern. "The peasants' view of the struggle will probably never be recovered, and whatever we say about it at this stage must be very tentative";[29] "Given the problems of documenting the consciousness of the jute mill workers, their will to resist and question the authority of their employers can be read only in terms of the sense of crisis it produced among the people in authority";[30] "It should be possible to read the presence of a rebel consciousness as a necessary and pervasive element within that body of evidence."[31] To be sure, it is the vocabulary of "this stage," "will to resist," and "presence." Yet the language seems also to be straining to acknowledge that the subaltern's view, will, presence, can be no more than a theoretical fiction to entitle the project of reading. It cannot be recovered, "it will probably never be recovered." If I shifted to the slightly esoteric register of the language of French post-structuralism, I could put it thus: "Thought [here the thought of subaltern consciousness] is here for me a perfectly neutral name, the blank part of the text, the necessarily indeterminate index of a future epoch of difference."[32]

Once again, in the work of this group, what had seemed the historical predicament of the colonial subaltern can be made to become the allegory of the predicament of *all* thought, *all* deliberative consciousness, though the elite profess otherwise. [. . .]

Reading the work of Subaltern Studies from within but against the grain, I would suggest that elements in their text would warrant a reading of the project to retrieve the subaltern consciousness as the attempt to undo a massive historiographic metalepsis and "situate" the effect of the subject as subaltern. I would read it, then, as a *strategic* use of positivist essentialism in a scrupulously visible political interest. This would put them in line with the Marx who locates fetishization, the ideological determination of the "concrete," and spins the narrative of the development of the money-form, with the Nietzsche who offers us genealogy in place of historiography, the Foucault who plots the construction of a "counter-memory," the Barthes of semiotropy and the Derrida of "affirmative deconstruction." This would allow them to use the critical force of anti-humanism, in other words, even as they share its constitutive paradox: that the essentializing moment, the object of their criticism, is irreducible.

The strategy becomes most useful when "consciousness" is being used in the narrow sense, as self-consciousness. When "consciousness" is being used in that way, Marx's notion of un-alienated practice or Gramsci's notion of an "ideologically *coherent*," "spontaneous philosophy of the multitude" are plausible and powerful.[33] For class-consciousness does not engage the ground-level of consciousness – consciousness in general. "Class" is not, after all, an inalienable description of a human reality. Class-consciousness on the *descriptive* level is itself a strategic and artificial rallying awareness which, on the *transformative* level, seeks to destroy the mechanics which come to construct the outlines of the very class of which a collective consciousness has been situationally developed. "Any member of the insurgent community" – Guha spends an entire chapter showing how that collective consciousness of community develops – "who chooses to continue in such subalternity is regarded as hostile towards the inversive process initiated by the struggle and hence as being on the enemy's side."[34] The task of the "consciousness" of class or collectivity within a social field of exploitation and domination is thus necessarily self-alienating. The tradition of the English translations of Marx often obliterates this. Consider, for example, the following well-known passage from the *Communist Manifesto:* "If the proletariat in struggle [*im Kampfe*] against the bourgeoisie is compelled to unite itself in a class [*sich notwendig zum Klasse vereint*], and, by means of a revolution, it makes itself the ruling class, and, as such, sweeps away by force the old conditions of production, it thus sweeps away the conditions of class oppositions [*Klassengegensatz*] and of classes generally, and abolishes its own lordship [*Herrschaft*] as a class."[35] The phrases translated as "sweeps away," and "abolishes" are, in Marx's text *"aufhebt."* "'Aufheben' has a twofold meaning in the language: on the one hand it means to preserve, to maintain, and equally it also means to cause to cease, to put an end to. . . . The two definitions of 'Aufheben' which we have given can be quoted as two dictionary *meanings* of this word."[36] In this spirit of "maintain *and* cause to cease," we would rewrite "inversive" in the passage from *Elementary Aspects of Peasant Insurgency* as "displacing."

It is within the framework of a strategic interest in the self-alienating displacing move of and by a consciousness of collectivity, then, that self-determination and an unalienated self-consciousness can be broached. In the definitions of "consciousness" offered by the Subaltern Studies group there are plenty of indications that they are in fact concerned with consciousness not in the general, but in this crucial narrow sense.

Subaltern consciousness as self-consciousness of a sort is what inhabits "the whole area of independent thought and conjecture and speculation . . . on the part of the peasant,"[37] what offers the "clear proof of a distinctly independent interpretation of [Gandhi's] message,"[38] what animates the "parley[s] among . . . the principal [insurgents] seriously to weigh the pros and cons of any recourse to arms,"[39] indeed underwrites all invocations of the will of the subaltern.

Subaltern consciousness as emergent collective consciousness is one of the main themes of these books. Among the many examples that can be found, I will cite two: "what is indubitably represented in these extracts from Abdul Majid [a weaver]'s diary is a consciousness of the 'collective' – the community. Yet this consciousness of community was an ambiguous one, straddling as it did the religious fraternity, class *qasba*, and mohalla."[40] "[The tribe's] consciousness of itself as a body of insurgents was thus indistinguishable from its recognition of its ethnic self."[41] The group places this theory of the emergent collective subaltern consciousness squarely in the context of that tendency within western Marxism which would refuse class-consciousness to the precapitalist subaltern, especially in the theatres of Imperialism. Their gesture thus confronts E. J. Hobsbawm's notion of the "pre-political" as much as functionalist arguments from "reciprocity and moral economy" between "agrarian labourers" and "peasant proprietors," which are "an attempt to deny the relevance of class identities and class conflict to agrarian relations in Asia until a very recent date."[42] Chakrabarty's analysis of how historically unsound it is simply to reverse the gesture and try to impose a Marxian *working-class* consciousness upon the urban proletariat in a colonial context and, by implication, as Guha shows, upon the rural subaltern, takes its place within this confrontation.

For readers who notice the points of contact between the Subaltern Studies group and critics of humanism such as Barthes and Foucault, the confusion arises because of the use of the word "consciousness," unavoidably a post-phenomenological and post-psychoanalytic issue with such writers. I am not trying to clear the confusion by revealing through analysis that the Subaltern Studies group is not entertaining consciousness within that configuration at all, but is rather working exclusively with the second-level collective consciousness to be encountered in Marx and the classical Marxist tradition. I am suggesting, rather, that although the group does not wittingly engage with the post-structuralist understanding of "consciousness," our own transactional reading of them is enhanced if we see them as *strategically* adhering to the essentialist notion of consciousness, that would fall prey to an anti-humanist critique, within a historiographic practice that draws many of its strengths from that very critique.

Notes

1   Paul de Man, *Blindness and Insight: Essays in the Rhetoric of Contemporary Criticism* (Minneapolis: University of Minnesota Press, 1983), p. 8.
2   Jacques Derrida, *Writing and Difference*, trans. Alan Bass (Chicago: University of Chicago Press, 1982), p. 289. All translations modified when deemed necessary.
3   Ranajit Guha (ed.), *Subaltern Studies III: Writings on South Asian History and Society*

(Delhi: Oxford University Press, 1984), vol. 1, p. 83, p. 86 and p. 186.; vol. 2, p. 65 and p. 115; vol. 3, p. 21 and p. 71. Also Ranajit Guha, *Elementary Aspects of Peasant Insurgency in Colonial India* (Delhi: Oxford University Press, 1983), pp. 88, p. 226, p. 30 and p. 318.

4 See Edward W. Said, *The World, the Text, and the Critic* (Cambridge, MA: Harvard University Press, 1983), pp. 170–2 for a discussion of "elaboration" in Gramsci.

5 Friedrich Nietzsche, *On the Genealogy of Morals and Ecce Homo*, trans. Walter J. Kaufmann (New York: Vintage Books, 1969), p. 77 and p. 80.

6 Ranajit Guha (ed.) (1984), vol. 3, p. 52 and p. 115.

7 I am using the word "Imaginary" loosely in the sense given to it by Jacques Lacan. For a short definition, see Jean Laplanche and J. B. Pontalis, *The Language of Psycho-Analysis*, trans. David Nicholson-Smith (New York: Norton, 1973), p. 210.

8 Ranajit Guha (ed.) (1984), vol. 3, p. 214.

9 Ibid., vol. 1, p. 227.

10 Ibid., vol. 2, pp. 198–9.

11 Ibid., vol. 3, pp. 231–70.

12 Ibid., vol. 2, pp. 1–42; Ranajit Guha (1983).

13 As always my preferred example of a theoretical fiction remains the primary process in Freud, *The Complete Psychological Works*, trans. James Strachey et al. (London: Hogarth Press, 1961), vol. 5, p. 598f.

14 Ranajit Guha (1983), p. 28.

15 For an excellent discussion of this, see Judith Butler (1985), "Geist ist Zeit: French Interpretations of Hegel's Absolute". *Berkshire Review*, Summer.

16 Antonio Gramsci, cited in Ranajit Guha (1983), p. 28.

17 Jacques Derrida, *Of Grammatology*, trans. Spivak (Baltimore: Johns Hopkins University Press, 1976), p. 24.

18 Since the historian is gender-specific in the work of the collective (see pp. 33–43), I have consistently used "he."

19 Ranajit Guha (ed.) (1984), vol. 2, p. 262.

20 Ibid., vol. 2, p. 30.

21 Ibid., vol. 3, p. 317.

22 Ranajit Guha (1983), p. 159.

23 Ranajit Guha (ed.) (1984), vol. 1, pp. 140–1.

24 The most important example of this is Dominick LaCapra, *Rethinking Intellectual History* (Ithaca: Cornell University Press, 1983); and *History and Criticism* (Ithaca: Cornell University Press, 1984).

25 Ranajit Guha (ed.) (1984), vol. 3, p. 112.

26 Ranajit Guha (1983), p. 169.

27 Ranajit Guha (ed.) (1984), vol. 2, p. 38.

28 Ranajit Guha (1983), ch. 2; ibid., vol. 3, p. 183.

29 Ranajit Guha (ed.) (1984), ibid., vol. 1, p. 50.

30 Ibid., vol. 3, p. 121.

31 Ranajit Guha (1983), p. 15.

32 Jacques Derrida (1976), p. 93. Since my intention here is simply to offer a moment of transcoding, I have not undertaken to "explain" the Derridean passage.

33 Antonio Gramsci, *Prison Notebooks*, trans. Quentin Hoare and Geoffrey Nowell Smith (New York: International Publishers, 1971), p. 421.

34 Ranajit Guha (1983), p. 202.

35 Karl Marx and Friedrich Engels, "The Manifesto of the Communist Party," in *Selected Works* (Moscow: Foreign Languages Publishing House, 1951), p. 51.

36 Georg Friedrich Wilhelm Hegel, *The Science of Logic*, trans. A. V. Miller (New York: Humanities Press, 1976), p. 107.

37 Ranajit Guha (ed.) (1984), vol. 1, p. 188.

38 Ibid., vol. 3, p. 7.

39 Ibid., vol. 2, p. 1.

40 Ibid., vol. 3, p. 269.

41 Ranajit Guha (1983), p. 286.

42 Ranajit Guha (ed.) (1984), vol. 3, p. 78.

Part V

Feminism, Gender, and Sexual Difference

19

Gender Personality and the Reproduction of Mothering

Nancy Chodorow

In spite of the apparently close tie between women's capacities for childbearing and lactation on the one hand and their responsibilities for child care on the other, and in spite of the probable prehistoric convenience (and perhaps survival necessity) of a sexual division of labor in which women mothered, biology and instinct do not provide adequate explanations for how women come to mother. Women's mothering as a feature of social structure requires an explanation in terms of social structure. Conventional feminist and social psychological explanations for the genesis of gender roles – girls and boys are "taught" appropriate behaviors and "learn" appropriate feelings – are insufficient both empirically and methodologically to account for how women become mothers.

Methodologically, socialization theories rely inappropriately on individual intention. Ongoing social structures include the means for their own reproduction – in the regularized repetition of social processes, in the perpetuation of conditions which require members' participation, in the genesis of legitimating ideologies and institutions, and in the psychological as well as physical reproduction of people to perform necessary roles. Accounts of socialization help to explain the perpetuation of ideologies about gender roles. However, notions of appropriate behavior, like coercion, cannot in themselves produce parenting. Psychological capacities and a particular object-relational stance are central and definitional to parenting in a way that they are not to many other roles and activities.

Women's mothering includes the capacities for its own reproduction. This reproduction consists in the production of women with, and men without, the particular psychological capacities and stance which go into primary parenting. Psychoanalytic theory provides us with a theory of social reproduction that explains major features of personality development and the development of psychic structure, and the differential development of gender personality in particular. Psychoanalysts argue that personality both results from and consists in the ways a child appropriates, internalizes, and organizes early experiences in their family – from the fantasies they have, the defenses they use, the ways they channel and redirect drives in this object-relational context. A person subsequently imposes this intrapsychic structure, and the fantasies, defenses, and relational modes and preoccupations which go with it, onto external social situations. This reexternalization (or mutual reexternalization) is a major constituting feature of social and interpersonal situations themselves.

Psychoanalysis, however, has not had an adequate theory of the reproduction of mothering. Because of the teleological assumption that anatomy is destiny, and that women's destiny includes primary parenting, the ontogenesis of women's mothering has been largely ignored, even while the genesis of a wide variety of related disturbances and problems has been accorded widespread clinical attention. Most psychoanalysts agree that the basis for parenting is laid for both genders in the early relationship to a primary caretaker. Beyond that, in order to explain why *women* mother, they tend to rely on vague notions of a girl's subsequent identification with her mother, which makes her and not her brother a primary parent, or on an unspecified and uninvestigated innate femaleness in girls, or on logical leaps from lactation or early vaginal sensations to caretaking abilities and commitments.

The psychoanalytic account of male and female development, when reinterpreted, gives us a developmental theory of the reproduction of women's mothering. Women's mothering reproduces itself through differing object-relational experiences and differing psychic outcomes in women and men. As a result of having been parented by a woman, women are more likely than men to seek to be mothers, that is, to relocate themselves in a primary mother-child relationship, to get gratification from the mothering relationship, and to have psychological and relational capacities for mothering.

The early relation to a primary caretaker provides in children of both genders both the basic capacity to participate in a relationship with the features of the early parent-child one, and the desire to create this intimacy. However, because women mother, the early experience and preoedipal relationship differ for boys and girls. Girls retain more concern with early childhood issues in relation to their mother, and a sense of self involved with these issues. Their attachments therefore retain more preoedipal aspects. The greater length and different nature of their preoedipal experience, and their continuing preoccupation with the issues of this period, mean that women's sense of self is continuous with others and that they retain capacities for primary identification, both of which enable them to experience the empathy and lack of reality sense needed by a cared-for infant. In men, these qualities have been curtailed, both because they are early treated as an opposite by their mother and because their later attachment to her must be repressed. The relational basis for mothering is thus extended in women, and inhibited in men, who experience themselves as more separate and distinct from others.

The different structure of the feminine and masculine oedipal triangle and process of oedipal experience that results from women's mothering contributes further to gender personality differentiation and the reproduction of women's mothering. As a result of this experience, women's inner object world, and the affects and issues associated with it, are more actively sustained and more complex than men's. This means that women define and experience themselves relationally. Their heterosexual orientation is always in internal dialogue with both oedipal and preoedipal mother-child relational issues. Thus, women's heterosexuality is triangular and requires a third person – a child – for its structural and emotional completion. For men, by contrast, the heterosexual relationship alone recreates the early bond to their mother; a child interrupts it. Men, moreover, do not define themselves in relationship and have come to suppress relational capacities and repress relational needs. This prepares them to participate in the affect-denying world of alienated work, but not to fulfill women's needs for intimacy and primary relationships.

The oedipus complex, as it emerges from the asymmetrical organization of parenting, secures a psychological taboo on parent-child incest and pushes boys and girls in the direction of extrafamilial heterosexual relationships. This is one step toward the reproduction of parenting. The creation and maintenance of the incest taboo and of heterosexuality in girls and boys are different, however. For boys, superego formation and identification with their father, rewarded by the superiority of masculinity, maintain the taboo on incest with their mother, while heterosexual orientation continues from their earliest love relation with her. For girls, creating them as heterosexual in the first place maintains the taboo. However, women's heterosexuality is not so exclusive as men's. This makes it easier for them to accept or seek a male substitute for their fathers. At the same time, in a male-dominant society, women's exclusive emotional heterosexuality is not so necessary, nor is her repression of love for her father. Men are more likely to initiate relationships, and women's economic dependence on men pushes them anyway into heterosexual marriage.

Male dominance in heterosexual couples and marriage solves the problem of women's lack of heterosexual commitment and lack of satisfaction by making women more reactive in the sexual bonding process. At the same time, contradictions in heterosexuality help to perpetuate families and parenting by ensuring that women will seek relations to children and will not find heterosexual relationships alone satisfactory. Thus, men's lack of emotional availability and women's less exclusive heterosexual commitment help ensure women's mothering.

Women's mothering, then, produces psychological self-definition and capacities appropriate to mothering in women, and curtails and inhibits these capacities and this self-definition in men. The early experience of being cared for by a woman produces a fundamental structure of expectations in women and men concerning mothers' lack of separate interests from their infants and total concern for their infants' welfare. Daughters grow up identifying with these mothers, about whom they have such expectations. This set of expectations is generalized to the assumption that women naturally take care of children of all ages and the belief that women's "maternal" qualities can and should be extended to the nonmothering work that they do. All these results of women's mothering have ensured that women will mother infants and will take continuing responsibility for children.

The reproduction of women's mothering is the basis for the reproduction of women's location and responsibilities in the domestic sphere. This mothering, and its generalization to women's structural location in the domestic sphere, links the contemporary social organization of gender and social organization of production and contributes to the reproduction of each. That women mother is a fundamental organizational feature of the sex-gender system: It is basic to the sexual division of labor and generates a psychology and ideology of male dominance as well as an ideology about women's capacities and nature. Women, as wives and mothers, contribute as well to the daily and generational reproduction, both physical and psychological, of male workers and thus to the reproduction of capitalist production.

Women's mothering also reproduces the family as it is constituted in male-dominant society. The sexual and familial division of labor in which women mother creates a sexual division of psychic organization and orientation. It produces socially gendered women and men who enter into asymmetrical heterosexual relationships; it produces men who react to, fear, and act superior to women, and who put most of their energies into the nonfamilial work world and do not parent. Finally, it produces women who turn their energies toward nurturing and caring for children – in turn reproducing the sexual and familial division of labor in which women mother.

Social reproduction is thus asymmetrical. Women in their domestic role reproduce men and children physically, psychologically, and emotionally. Women in their domestic role as houseworkers reconstitute themselves physically on a daily basis and reproduce themselves as mothers, emotionally and psychologically, in the next generation. They thus contribute to the perpetuation of their own social roles and position in the hierarchy of gender.

Institutionalized features of family structure and the social relations of reproduction reproduce themselves. A psychoanalytic investigation shows that women's mothering capacities and commitments, and the general psychological capacities and wants which are the basis of women's emotion work, are built developmentally into feminine personality. Because women are themselves mothered by women, they grow up with the relational capacities and needs, and psychological definition of self-in-relationship, which commits them to mothering. Men, because they are mothered by women, do not. Women mother daughters who, when they become women, mother.

20

This Sex Which Is Not One

Luce Irigaray

Female sexuality has always been conceptualized on the basis of masculine parameters. Thus the opposition between "masculine" clitoral activity and "feminine" vaginal passivity, an opposition which Freud – and many others – saw as stages, or alternatives, in the development of a sexually "normal" woman, seems rather too clearly required by the practice of male sexuality. For the clitoris is conceived as a little penis pleasant to masturbate so long as castration anxiety does not exist (for the boy child), and the vagina is valued for the "lodging" it offers the male organ when the forbidden hand has to find a replacement for pleasure-giving.

In these terms, woman's erogenous zones never amount to anything but a clitoris-sex that is not comparable to the noble phallic organ, or a hole-envelope that serves to sheathe and massage the penis in intercourse: a non-sex, or a masculine organ turned back upon itself, self-embracing.

About woman and her pleasure, this view of the sexual relation has nothing to say. Her lot is that of "lack," "atrophy" (of the sexual organ), and "penis envy," the penis being the only sexual organ of recognized value. Thus she attempts by every means available to appropriate that organ for herself: through her somewhat servile love of the father–husband capable of giving her one, through her desire for a child–penis, preferably a boy, through access to the cultural values still reserved by right to males alone and therefore always masculine, and so on. Woman lives her own desire only as the expectation that she may at last come to possess an equivalent of the male organ.

Yet all this appears quite foreign to her own pleasure, unless it remains within the dominant phallic economy. Thus, for example, woman's auto-eroticism is very different from man's. In order to touch himself, man needs an instrument: his hand, a woman's body, language . . . And this self-caressing requires at least a minimum of activity. As for woman, she touches herself in and of herself without any need for mediation, and before there is any way to distinguish activity from passivity. Woman "touches herself" all the time, and moreover no one can forbid her to do so, for her genitals are formed of two lips in continuous contact. Thus, within herself, she is already two – but not divisible into one(s) – that caress each other.

This autoeroticism is disrupted by a violent break-in: the brutal separation of the two lips by a violating penis, an intrusion that distracts and deflects the woman from this "self-caressing" she needs if she is not to incur the disappearance of her own pleasure in sexual relations. If the vagina is to serve *also*, but *not only*, to take over for the little boy's hand in order to assure an articulation between autoeroticism and heteroeroticism in intercourse (the encounter with the totally other always signifying death), how, in the classic representation of sexuality, can the perpetuation of autoeroticism for woman be managed? Will woman not be left with the impossible alternative between a defensive virginity, fiercely turned in upon itself, and a body open to penetration that no longer knows, in this "hole" that constitutes its sex, the pleasure of its own touch? The more or less exclusive – and highly anxious – attention paid to erection in western sexuality proves to what extent the imaginary that governs it is foreign to the feminine. For the most part, this sexuality offers nothing but imperatives dictated by male rivalry: the "strongest" being the one who has the best "hard-on," the longest, the biggest, the stiffest penis, or even the one who "pees the farthest" (as in little boys' contests). Or else one finds imperatives dictated by the enactment of sadomasochistic fantasies, these in turn governed by man's relation to his mother: the desire to force entry, to penetrate, to appropriate for himself the mystery of this womb where he has been conceived, the secret of his begetting, of his "origin." Desire/need, also to make blood flow again in order to revive a very old relationship – intrauterine, to be sure, but also prehistoric – to the maternal.

Woman, in this sexual imaginary, is only a more or less obliging prop for the enactment of man's fantasies. That she may find pleasure there in that role, by proxy, is possible, even certain. But such pleasure is above all a masochistic prostitution of her body to a desire that is not her own, and it leaves her in a familiar state of dependency upon man. Not knowing what she wants, ready for anything, even asking for more, so long as he will "take" her as his "object" when he seeks his own pleasure. Thus she will not say what she herself wants; moreover, she does not know, or no longer knows, what she wants. As Freud admits, the beginnings of the sexual life of a girl child are so "obscure," so "faded with time," that one would have to dig down very deep indeed to discover beneath the traces of this civilization, of this history, the vestiges of a more archaic civilization that might give some clue to woman's sexuality. That extremely ancient civilization would undoubtedly have a different alphabet, a different language . . . Woman's desire would not be expected to speak the same language as man's; woman's desire has doubtless been submerged by the logic that has dominated the West since the time of the Greeks.

Within this logic, the predominance of the visual, and of the discrimination and individualization of form, is particularly foreign to female eroticism. Woman takes pleasure more from touching than from looking, and her entry into a dominant scopic economy signifies, again, her consignment to passivity: she is to be the beautiful object of contemplation. While her body finds itself thus eroticized, and called to a double movement of exhibition and of chaste retreat in order to stimulate the drives of the "subject," her sexual organ represents *the horror of nothing to see*. A defect in this systematics of representation and desire. A "hole" in its scoptophilic lens. It is already evident in Greek statuary that this nothing-to-see has to be excluded, rejected, from such a scene of representation. Woman's genitals are simply absent, masked, sewn back up inside their "crack."

This organ which has nothing to show for itself also lacks a form of its own. And if woman takes pleasure precisely from this incompleteness of form which allows her organ to touch itself over and over again, indefinitely, by itself, that pleasure is denied by a civilization that privileges phallomorphism. The value granted to the only definable form excludes the one that is in play in female autoeroticism. The *one* of form, of the individual, of the (male) sexual organ, of the proper name, of the proper meaning . . . supplants, while separating and dividing, that contact of *at least two* (lips) which keeps woman in touch with herself, but without any possibility of distinguishing what is touching from what is touched.

Whence the mystery that woman represents in a culture claiming to count everything, to number everything by units, to inventory everything as individualities. *She is neither one nor two.* Rigorously speaking, she cannot be identified either as one person, or as two. She resists all adequate definition. Further, she has no "proper" name. And her sexual organ, which is not *one* organ, is counted as *none*. The negative, the underside, the reverse of the only visible and morphologically designatable organ (even if the passage from erection to detumescence does pose some problems): the penis.

But the "thickness" of that "form," the layering of its volume, its expansions and contractions and even the spacing of the moments in which it produces itself as form – all this the feminine keeps secret. Without knowing it. And if woman is asked to sustain, to revive, man's desire, the request neglects to spell out what it implies as to the value of her own desire. A desire of which she is not aware, moreover, at least not explicitly. But one whose force and continuity are capable of nurturing repeatedly and at length all the masquerades of "feminity" that are expected of her.

It is true that she still has the child, in relation to whom her appetite for touch, for contact, has free rein, unless it is already lost, alienated by the taboo against touching of a highly obsessive civilization. Otherwise her pleasure will find, in the child, compensations for and diversions from the frustrations that she too often encounters in sexual relations per se. Thus maternity fills the gaps in a repressed female sexuality. Perhaps man and woman no longer caress each other except through that mediation between them that the child – preferably a boy – represents? Man, identified with his son, rediscovers the pleasure of maternal fondling; woman touches herself again by caressing that part of her body: her baby-penis-clitoris.

What this entails for the amorous trio is well known. But the Oedipal interdiction seems to be a somewhat categorical and factitious law – although it does provide the means for perpetuating the authoritarian discourse of fathers – when it is promulgated in a culture in which sexual relations are impracticable because man's desire and woman's are strangers to each other. And in which the two desires have to try to meet through indirect means, whether the archaic one of a sense-relation to the mother's body, or the present one of active or passive extension of the law of the father. These are regressive emotional behaviors, exchanges of words too detached from the sexual arena not to constitute an exile with respect to it: "mother" and "father" dominate the interactions of the couple, but as social roles. The division of labor prevents them from making love. They produce or reproduce. Without quite knowing how to use their leisure. Such little as they have, such little indeed as they wish to have. For what are they to do with leisure? What substitute for amorous resource are they to invent? Still . . .

Perhaps it is time to return to that repressed entity, the female imaginary. So woman does not have a sex organ? She has at least two of them, but they are not identifiable as ones. Indeed, she has many more. Her sexuality, always at least double, goes even further: it is *plural*. Is this the way culture is seeking to characterize itself now? Is this the way texts write themselves/are written now? Without quite knowing what censorship they are evading? Indeed, woman's pleasure does not have to choose between clitoral activity and vaginal passivity, for example. The pleasure of the vaginal caress does not have to be substituted for that of the clitoral caress. They each contribute, irreplaceably, to woman's pleasure. Among other caresses . . . Fondling the breasts, touching the vulva, spreading the lips, stroking the posterior wall of the vagina, brushing against the mouth of the uterus, and so on. To evoke only a few of the most specifically female pleasures. Pleasures which are somewhat misunderstood in sexual difference as it is imagined – or not imagined, the other sex being only the indispensable complement to the only sex.

But *woman has sex organs more or less everywhere*. She finds pleasure almost anywhere. Even if we refrain from invoking the hystericization of her entire body, the geography of her pleasure is far more diversified, more multiple in its differences, more complex, more subtle, than is commonly imagined – in an imaginary rather too narrowly focused on sameness.

"She" is indefinitely other in herself. This is doubtless why she is said to be whimsical, incomprehensible, agitated, capricious . . . not to mention her language, in which "she" sets off in all directions leaving "him" unable to discern the coherence of any meaning. Hers are contradictory words, somewhat mad from the standpoint of reason, inaudible for whoever listens to them with ready-made grids, with a fully elaborated code in hand. For in what she says, too, at least when she dares, woman is constantly touching herself. She steps ever so slightly aside from herself with a murmur, an exclamation, a whisper, a sentence left unfinished . . . When she returns, it is to set off again from elsewhere. From another point of pleasure, or of pain. One would have to listen with another ear, as if hearing *an "other meaning" always in the process of weaving itself, of embracing itself with words, but also of getting rid of words in order not to become fixed, congealed in them.* For if "she" says something, it is not, it is already no longer, identical with what she means. What she says is never identical with anything, moreover; rather, it is contiguous. *It touches (upon).* And when it strays too far from that proximity, she breaks off and starts over at "zero": her body-sex.

It is useless, then, to trap women in the exact definition of what they mean, to make them repeat (themselves) so that it will be clear; they are already elsewhere in that discursive machinery where you expected to surprise them. They have returned within themselves. Which must not be understood in the same way as within yourself. They do not have the interiority that you have, the one you perhaps suppose they have. Within themselves means *within the intimacy of that silent, multiple, diffuse touch.* And if you ask them insistently what they are thinking about, they can only reply: Nothing. Everything.

Thus what they desire is precisely nothing, and at the same time everything. Always something more and something else besides that *one* – sexual organ, for example – that you give them, attribute to them. Their desire is often interpreted, and feared, as a sort of insatiable hunger, a voracity that will swallow you whole. Whereas it really involves a different economy more than anything else, one that upsets the linearity of a project, undermines the goal-object of a desire, diffuses the polarization toward a single pleasure, disconcerts fidelity to a single discourse . . .

Must this multiplicity of female desire and female language be understood as shards, scattered remnants of a violated sexuality? A sexuality denied? The question has no simple answer. The rejection, the exclusion of a female imaginary certainly puts woman in the position of experiencing herself only fragmentarily, in the little-structured margins of a dominant ideology, as waste, or excess, what is left of a mirror invested by the (masculine) "subject" to reflect himself, to copy himself. Moreover, the role of "femininity" is prescribed by this masculine specula(riza)tion and corresponds scarcely at all to woman's desire, which may be recovered only in secret, in hiding, with anxiety and guilt.

But if the female imaginary were to deploy itself, if it could bring itself into play otherwise than as scraps, uncollected debris, would it represent itself, even so, in the form of *one* universe? Would it even be volume instead of surface? No. Not unless it were understood, yet again, as a privileging of the maternal over the feminine. Of a phallic maternal, at that. Closed in upon the jealous possession of its valued product. Rivaling man in his esteem for productive excess. In such a race for power, woman loses the uniqueness of her pleasure. By closing herself off as volume, she renounces the pleasure that she gets from the *nonsuture of her lips:* she is undoubtedly a mother, but a virgin mother; the role was assigned to her by mythologies long ago. Granting her a certain social power to the extent that she is reduced, with her own complicity, to sexual impotence.

(Re-)discovering herself, for a woman, thus could only signify the possibility of sacrificing no one of her pleasures to another, of identifying herself with none of them in particular, *of never being simply one.* A sort of expanding universe to which no limits could be fixed and which would not be incoherence nonetheless – nor that polymorphous perversion of the child in which the erogenous zones would lie waiting to be regrouped under the primacy of the phallus.

Woman always remains several, but she is kept from dispersion because the other is already within her and is autoerotically familiar to her. Which is not to say that she appropriates the other for herself, that she reduces it to her own property. Ownership and property are doubtless quite foreign to the feminine. At least sexually. But not *nearness.* Nearness so pronounced that it makes all discrimination of identity, and thus all forms of property, impossible. Woman derives pleasure from what is *so near that she cannot have it, nor have herself.* She herself enters into a ceaseless exchange of herself with the other without any possibility of identifying either. This puts into question all prevailing economies: their calculations are irremediably stymied by woman's pleasure, as it increases indefinitely from its passage in and through the other.

However, in order for woman to reach the place where she takes pleasure as woman, a long detour by way of the analysis of the various systems of oppression brought to bear upon her is assuredly necessary. And claiming to fall back on the single solution of pleasure risks making her miss the process of going back through a social practice that *her* enjoyment requires.

For woman is traditionally a use-value for man, an exchange value among men; in other words, a commodity. As such, she remains the guardian of material substance, whose price will be established, in terms of the standard of their work and of their need/desire, by "subjects": workers, merchants, consumers. Women are marked phallically by their fathers, husbands, procurers. And this branding determines their value in sexual commerce. Woman is never anything but the locus of a more or less competitive exchange between two men, including the competition for the possession of mother earth.

How can this object of transaction claim a right to pleasure without removing her/itself from established commerce? With respect to other merchandise in the marketplace, how could this commodity maintain a relationship other than one of aggressive jealousy? How could material substance enjoy her/itself without provoking the consumer's anxiety over the disappearance of his nurturing ground? How could that exchange – which can in no way be defined in terms "proper" to woman's desire – appear as anything but a pure mirage, mere foolishness, all too readily obscured by a more sensible discourse and by a system of apparently more tangible values?

A woman's development, however radical it may seek to be, would thus not suffice to liberate woman's desire. And to date no political theory or political practice has resolved, or sufficiently taken into consideration, this historical problem, even though Marxism has proclaimed its importance. But women do not constitute, strictly speaking, a class, and their dispersion among several classes makes their political struggle complex, their demands sometimes contradictory.

There remains, however, the condition of underdevelopment arising from women's submission by and to a culture that oppresses them, uses them, makes of them a medium of exchange, with very little profit to them. Except in the quasi monopolies of masochistic pleasure, the domestic labor force, and reproduction. The powers of slaves? Which are not negligible powers, moreover. For where pleasure is concerned, the master is not necessarily well served. Thus to reverse the relation, especially in the economy of sexuality, does not seem a desirable objective.

But if women are to preserve and expand their autoeroticism, their homosexuality, might not the renunciation of heterosexual pleasure correspond once again to that disconnection from power that is traditionally theirs? Would it not involve a new prison, a new cloister, built of their own accord? For women to undertake tactical strikes, to keep themselves apart from men long enough to learn to defend their desire, especially through speech, to discover the love of other women while sheltered from men's imperious choices that put them in the position of rival commodities, to forge for themselves a social status that compels recognition, to earn their living in order to escape from the condition of prostitute . . . these are certainly indispensable stages in the escape from their proletarization on the exchange market. But if their aim were simply to reverse the order of things, even supposing this to be possible, history would repeat itself in the long run, would revert to sameness: to phallocratism. It would leave room neither for women's sexuality, nor for women's imaginary, nor for women's language to take (their) place.

Note

This text was originally published as "Ce sexe qui n'en est pas un," in *Cahiers du Grif*, no. 5. English translation: "This Sex Which Is Not One," trans. Claudia Reeder, in *New French Feminisms*, ed. Elaine Marks and Isabelle de Courtivron (New York, 1981), pp. 99–106.

21

Subjects of Sex/Gender/Desire

Judith Butler

In Lacan, as in Irigaray's post-Lacanian reformulation of Freud, sexual difference is not a simple binary that retains the metaphysics of substance as its foundation. The masculine "subject" is a fictive construction produced by the law that prohibits incest and forces an infinite displacement of a heterosexualizing desire. The feminine is never a mark of the subject; the feminine could not be an "attribute" of a gender. Rather, the feminine is the signification of lack, signified by the Symbolic, a set of differentiating linguistic rules that effectively create sexual difference. The masculine linguistic position undergoes individuation and heterosexualization required by the founding prohibitions of the Symbolic law, the law of the Father. The incest taboo that bars the son from the mother and thereby instates the kinship relation between them is a law enacted "in the name of the Father." Similarly, the law that refuses the girl's desire for both her mother and father requires that she take up the emblem of maternity and perpetuate the rules of kinship. Both masculine and feminine positions are thus instituted through prohibitive laws that produce culturally intelligible genders, but only through the production of an unconscious sexuality that reemerges in the domain of the imaginary.

The feminist appropriation of sexual difference, whether written in opposition to the phallogocentrism of Lacan (Irigaray) or as a critical reelaboration of Lacan, attempts to theorize the feminine, not as an expression of the metaphysics of substance, but as the unrepresentable absence effected by (masculine) denial that grounds the signifying economy through exclusion. The feminine as the repudiated/excluded within that system constitutes the possibility of a critique and disruption of that hegemonic conceptual scheme. The works of Jacqueline Rose[1] and Jane Gallop[2] underscore in different ways the constructed status of sexual difference, the inherent instability of that construction, and the dual consequentiality of a prohibition that at once institutes a sexual identity and provides for the exposure of that construction's tenuous ground. Although Wittig and other materialist feminists within the

French context would argue that sexual difference is an unthinking replication of a reified set of sexed polarities, these criticisms neglect the critical dimension of the unconscious which, as a site of repressed sexuality, reemerges within the discourse of the subject as the very impossibility of its coherence. As Rose points out very clearly, the construction of a coherent sexual identity along the disjunctive axis of the feminine/masculine is bound to fail;[3] the disruptions of this coherence through the inadvertent reemergence of the repressed reveal not only that "identity" is constructed, but that the prohibition that constructs identity is inefficacious (the paternal law ought to be understood not as a deterministic divine will, but as a perpetual bumbler, preparing the ground for the insurrections against him).

The differences between the materialist and Lacanian (and post-Lacanian) positions emerge in a normative quarrel over whether there is a retrievable sexuality either "before" or "outside" the law in the mode of the unconscious or "after" the law as a postgenital sexuality. Paradoxically, the normative trope of polymorphous perversity is understood to characterize both views of alternative sexuality. There is no agreement, however, on the manner of delimiting that "law" or set of "laws." The psychoanalytic critique succeeds in giving an account of the construction of "the subject" – and perhaps also the illusion of substance – within the matrix of normative gender relations. In her existential–materialist mode, Wittig presumes the subject, the person, to have a presocial and pregendered integrity. On the other hand, "the paternal Law" in Lacan, as well as the monologic mastery of phallogocentrism in Irigaray, bear the mark of a monotheistic singularity that is perhaps less unitary and culturally universal than the guiding structuralist assumptions of the account presume.[4]

But the quarrel seems also to turn on the articulation of a temporal trope of a subversive sexuality that flourishes *prior* to the imposition of a law, *after* its overthrow, or during its reign as a constant challenge to its authority. Here it seems wise to reinvoke Foucault who, in claiming that sexuality and power are coextensive, implicitly refutes the postulation of a subversive or emancipatory sexuality which could be free of the law. We can press the argument further by pointing out that "the before" of the law and "the after" are discursively and performatively instituted modes of temporality that are invoked within the terms of a normative framework which asserts that subversion, destabilization, or displacement requires a sexuality that somehow escapes the hegemonic prohibitions on sex. For Foucault, those prohibitions are invariably and inadvertently productive in the sense that "the subject" who is supposed to be founded and produced in and through those prohibitions does not have access to a sexuality that is in some sense "outside," "before," or "after" power itself. Power, rather than the law, encompasses both the juridical (prohibitive and regulatory) and the productive (inadvertently generative) functions of differential relations. Hence, the sexuality that emerges within the matrix of power relations is not a simple replication or copy of the law itself, a uniform repetition of a masculinist economy of identity. The productions swerve from their original purposes and inadvertently mobilize possibilities of "subjects" that do not merely exceed the bounds of cultural intelligibility, but effectively expand the boundaries of what is, in fact, culturally intelligible.

The feminist norm of a postgenital sexuality became the object of significant criticism from feminist theorists of sexuality, some of whom have sought a specifically feminist and/or lesbian appropriation of Foucault. This utopian notion of a sexuality freed from heterosexual constructs, a sexuality beyond "sex," failed to acknowledge the ways in which power relations continue to construct sexuality for women even within the terms of a "liberated" hetero-sexuality or lesbianism.[5] The same criticism is waged against the notion of a specifically feminine sexual pleasure that is radically differentiated from phallic sexuality. Irigaray's occasional efforts to derive a specific feminine sexu-ality from a specific female anatomy have been the focus of anti-essentialist arguments for some time.[6] The return to biology as the ground of a specific feminine sexuality or meaning seems to defeat the feminist premise that biology is not destiny. But whether feminine sexuality is articulated here through a discourse of biology for purely strategic reasons,[7] or whether it is, in fact, a feminist return to biological essentialism, the characterization of female sexuality as radically distinct from a phallic organization of sexuality remains problematic. Women who fail either to recognize that sexuality as their own or understand their sexuality as partially constructed within the terms of the phallic economy are potentially written off within the terms of that theory as "male-identified" or "unenlightened." Indeed, it is often unclear within Irigaray's text whether sexuality is culturally constructed, or whether it is only culturally constructed within the terms of the phallus. In other words, is specifi-cally feminine pleasure "outside" of culture as its prehistory or as its utopian future? If so, of what use is such a notion for negotiating the contemporary struggles of sexuality within the terms of its construction?

The pro-sexuality movement within feminist theory and practice has effec-tively argued that sexuality is always constructed within the terms of discourse and power, where power is partially understood in terms of hetero-sexual and phallic cultural conventions. The emergence of a sexuality constructed (not determined) in these terms within lesbian, bisexual, and heterosexual contexts is, therefore, *not* a sign of a masculine identification in some reductive sense. It is not the failed project of criticizing phallogocentrism or heterosexual hegemony, as if a political critique could effectively undo the cultural construction of the feminist critic's sexuality. If sexuality is culturally constructed within existing power relations, then the postulation of a norma-tive sexuality that is "before," "outside," or "beyond" power is a cultural impossibility and a politically impracticable dream, one that postpones the concrete and contemporary task of rethinking subversive possibilities for sexu-ality and identity within the terms of power itself. This critical task presumes, of course, that to operate within the matrix of power is not the same as to repli-cate uncritically relations of domination. It offers the possibility of a repetition of the law which is not its consolidation, but its displacement. In the place of a "male-identified" sexuality in which "male" serves as the cause and irreducible meaning of that sexuality, we might develop a notion of sexuality constructed in terms of phallic relations of power that replay and redistribute the possibilities of that phallicism precisely through the subversive operation of "identifications" that are, within the power field of sexuality, inevitable. If "identifications," following Jacqueline Rose, can be exposed as phantasmatic, then it must be possible to enact an identification that displays its phantasmatic structure. If there is no radical repudiation of a culturally constructed sexuality, what is left is the question of how to acknowledge and "do" the construction one is invariably in. Are there forms of repetition that do not constitute a simple imitation, reproduction, and, hence, consolidation of the law (the anachronistic notion of "male identification" that ought to be discarded from a feminist vocabulary)? What possibilities of gender configurations exist among the various emergent and occasionally convergent matrices of cultural intelligibility that govern gendered life?

Within the terms of feminist sexual theory, it is clear that the presence of power dynamics within sexuality is in no sense the same as the simple consolidation or augmentation of a heterosexist or phallogocentric power regime. The "presence" of so-called heterosexual conventions within homosexual contexts as well as the proliferation of specifically gay discourses of sexual difference, as in the case of "butch" and "femme" as historical identities of sexual style, cannot be explained as chimerical representations of originally heterosexual identities. And neither can they be understood as the pernicious insistence of heterosexist constructs within gay sexuality and identity. The repetition of heterosexual constructs within sexual cultures both gay and straight may well be the inevitable site of the denaturalization and mobilization of gender categories. The replication of heterosexual constructs in non-heterosexual frames brings into relief the utterly constructed status of the so-called heterosexual original. Thus, gay is to straight *not* as copy is to original, but, rather, as copy is to copy. The parodic repetition of "the original" [. . .] reveals the original to be nothing other than a parody of the *idea* of the natural and the original.[8] Even if heterosexist constructs circulate as the available sites of power/discourse from which to do gender at all, the question remains: What possibilities of recirculation exist? Which possibilities of doing gender repeat and displace through hyperbole, dissonance, internal confusion, and proliferation the very constructs by which they are mobilized?

Consider not only that the ambiguities and incoherences within and among heterosexual, homosexual, and bisexual practices are suppressed and redescribed within the reified framework of the disjunctive and asymmetrical binary of masculine/feminine, but that these cultural configurations of gender confusion operate as sites for intervention, exposure, and displacement of these reifications. In other words, the "unity" of gender is the effect of a regulatory practice that seeks to render gender identity uniform through a compulsory heterosexuality. The force of this practice is, through an exclusionary apparatus of production, to restrict the relative meanings of "heterosexuality," "homosexuality," and "bisexuality" as well as the subversive sites of their convergence and resignification. That the power regimes of heterosexism and phallogocentrism seek to augment themselves through a constant repetition of their logic, their metaphysic, and their naturalized ontologies does not imply that repetition itself ought to be stopped – as if it could be. If repetition is bound to persist as the mechanism of the cultural reproduction of identities, then the crucial question emerges: What kind of subversive repetition might call into question the regulatory practice of identity itself?

If there is no recourse to a "person," a "sex," or a "sexuality" that escapes the matrix of power and discursive relations that effectively produce and regulate the intelligibility of those concepts for us, what constitutes the possibility of effective inversion, subversion, or displacement within the terms of a constructed identity? What possibilities exist *by virtue of* the constructed character of sex and gender? Whereas Foucault is ambiguous about the precise character of the "regulatory practices" that produce the category of sex, and Wittig appears to invest the full responsibility of the construction to sexual reproduction and its instrument, compulsory heterosexuality, yet other discourses converge to produce this categorial fiction for reasons not always clear or consistent with one another. The power relations that infuse the biological sciences are not easily reduced, and the medicolegal alliance emerging in nineteenth-century Europe has spawned categorial fictions that could not be anticipated in advance. The very complexity of the discursive map that constructs gender appears to hold out the promise of an inadvertent and generative convergence of these discursive and regulatory structures. If the regulatory fictions of sex and gender are themselves multiple contested sites of meaning, then the very multiplicity of their construction holds out the possibility of a disruption of their univocal posturing.

Clearly this project does not propose to lay out within traditional philosophical terms an *ontology* of gender whereby the meaning of *being* a woman or a man is elucidated within the terms of phenomenology. The presumption here is that the "being" of gender is *an effect*, an object of a genealogical investigation that maps out the political parameters of its construction in the mode of ontology. To claim that gender is constructed is not to assert its illusoriness or artificiality, where those terms are understood to reside within a binary that counterposes the "real" and the "authentic" as oppositional. As a genealogy of gender ontology, this inquiry seeks to understand the discursive production of the plausibility of that binary relation and to suggest that certain cultural configurations of gender take the place of "the real" and consolidate and augment their hegemony through that felicitous self-naturalization.

If there is something right in Beauvoir's claim that one is not born, but rather *becomes* a woman, it follows that *woman* itself is a term in process, a becoming, a constructing that cannot rightfully be said to originate or to end. As an ongoing discursive practice, it is open to intervention and resignification. Even when gender seems to congeal into the most reified forms, the "congealing" is itself an insistent and insidious practice, sustained and regulated by various social means. It is, for Beauvoir, never possible finally to become a woman, as if there were a *telos* that governs the process of acculturation and construction. Gender is the repeated stylization of the body, a set of repeated acts within a highly rigid regulatory frame that congeal over time to produce the appearance of substance, of a natural sort of being. A political genealogy of gender ontologies, if it is successful, will deconstruct the substantive appearance of gender into its constitutive acts and locate and account for those acts within the compulsory frames set by the various forces that police the social appearance of gender. To expose the contingent acts that create the appearance of a naturalistic necessity, a move which has been a part of cultural critique at least since Marx, is a task that now takes on the added burden of showing how the very notion of the subject, intelligible only through its appearance as gendered, admits of possibilities that have been forcibly foreclosed by the various reifications of gender that have constituted its contingent ontologies.

Notes

1 Jacqueline Rose, *Sexuality in the Field of Vision* (London: Verso, 1987).

2 Jane Gallop, *Reading Lacan* (Ithaca: Cornell University Press, 1985); *The Daughter's Seduction: Feminism and Psychoanalysis* (Ithaca: Cornell University Press, 1982).

3 "What distinguishes psychoanalysis from sociological accounts of gender (hence for me the fundamental impasse of Nancy Chodorow's work) is that whereas for the latter, the internalization of norms is assumed roughly to work, the basic premise and indeed starting point of psychoanalysis is that it does not. The unconscious constantly reveals the 'failure' of identity." Jacqueline Rose, *Sexuality in the Field of Vision*, p. 90.

4 It is, perhaps, no wonder that the singular structuralist notion of "the Law" clearly resonates with the prohibitive law of the Old Testament. The "paternal law" thus comes under a post-structuralist critique through the understandable route of a French reappropriation of Nietzsche. Nietzsche faults the Judeo-Christian "slave-morality" for conceiving the law in both singular and prohibitive terms. The will-to-power, on the other hand, designates both the productive and multiple possibilities of the law, effectively exposing the notion of "the Law" in its singularity as a fictive and repressive notion.

5 See Gayle Rubin, "Thinking Sex: Notes for a Radical Theory of the Politics of Sexuality." In *Pleasure and Danger*, ed. Carole S. Vance (Boston: Routledge and Kegan Paul, 1984), pp. 267–319. Also in *Pleasure and Danger*, see Carole S. Vance, "Pleasure and Danger: Towards a Politics of Sexuality," pp. 1–28; Alice Echols, "The Taming of the Id: Feminist Sexual Politics, 1968–83," pp. 50–72; Amber Hollibaugh, "Desire for the Future: Radical Hope in Pleasure and Passion," pp. 401–10. See Amber Hollibaugh and Cherríe Moraga, "What We're Rollin Around in Bed with: Sexual Silences in Feminism"; Alice Echols, "The New Feminism of Yin and Yang," in *Powers of Desire: The Politics of Sexuality*, ed. Ann Snitow, Christine Stansell, and Sharon Thompson (London: Virago, 1984); *Heresies*, vol. 12, 1981, the "sex issue"; Samois (ed.), *Coming to Power* (Berkeley: Samois, 1981); Deirdre English, Amber Hollibaugh, and Gayle Rubin, "Talking Sex: A

Conversation on Sexuality and Feminism." *Socialist Review*, no. 58, July–August, 1981; Barbara T. Kerr and Mirtha N. Quintanales, "The Complexity of Desire: Conversations on Sexuality and Difference." *Conditions* #8, vol. 3, no. 2, 1982, pp. 52–71.

6   Irigaray's perhaps most controversial claim has been that the structure of the vulva as "two lips touching" constitutes the nonunitary and autoerotic pleasure of women prior to the "separation" of this doubleness through the pleasure-depriving act of penetration by the penis. See Luce Irigaray, *Ce sexe qui n'en est pas un*. Along with Monique Plaza and Christine Delphy, Wittig has argued that Irigaray's valorization of that anatomical specificity is itself an uncritical replication of a reproductive discourse that marks and carves up the female body into artificial "parts" like "vagina," "clitoris," and "vulva." At a lecture at Vassar College, Wittig was asked whether she had a vagina, and she replied that she did not.

7   See a compelling argument for precisely this interpretation by Diana J. Fuss, *Essentially Speaking* (New York: Routledge, 1989).

8   If we were to apply Fredric Jameson's distinction between parody and pastiche, gay identities would be better understood as pastiche. Whereas parody, Jameson argues, sustains some sympathy with the original of which it is a copy, pastiche disputes the possibility of an "original" or, in the case of gender, reveals the "original" as a failed effort to "copy" a phantasmatic ideal that cannot be copied without failure. See Fredric Jameson, "Postmodernism and Consumer Society," in *The Anti-Aesthetic: Essays on Postmodern Culture*, ed. Hal Foster (Port Townsend, WA: Bay Press, 1983).

22

Living with Uncertainty

Jeffrey Weeks

'To speak of sexuality and the body, and not also speak of AIDS,' B. Ruby Rich has written, 'would be, well, obscene.'[1] I can only concur. Since the early 1980s AIDS, HIV disease, has haunted the sexual imaginary, embodying the danger and fear that trails in the wake of the body and its pleasures. Even as the epidemic becomes 'normalized' in large parts of the world, it becomes endemic in others, casting a shadow over the changes that are transforming the sexual world. [. . .]

The person with HIV or AIDS must live with the resulting uncertainty all the time: the uncertainty of diagnosis, of prognosis, of reactions of friends, families, loved ones, of anonymous and fearful or hate-filled others. Everyone else must live with the uncertainty too: the uncertainty bred of risk, of possible infection, of *not* knowing, of loss. [. . .]

Chance, accident, contingency: these are more than characteristics of a particular set of diseases. They appear as markers of the present. Things happen to us, without apparent rationale or justification. The hope of modernity – that we could control nature, become the masters of all we survey – may be brought to naught by random happenings in countries of which we know or care little – or by a microscopic organism unknown until the 1980s.

Yet though events may appear accidental and unexpected, the ways in which we respond are not. They have a history – in fact, many histories. AIDS may be a modern phenomenon, *the* disease of the *fin de millennium*, but it is a remarkably historicized phenomenon, framed with histories that burden people living with HIV and AIDS with a weight they should not have to bear.

There are histories of previous diseases, and response to diseases, which provided a rich source of comparisons between the impact of syphilis in the nineteenth century, and AIDS today.[2] There are histories of sexuality, especially the unorthodox sexualities, and histories of the ways in which sexuality has been regulated, telling a tale of power, the institutionalization of the heterosexual norm and the marginalization of the perverse.[3] There are histories of racial categorization, of development and undevelopment, which have constructed racialized minorities of the poor and disadvantaged, a Third World in the heart of the cities of the First World, as well as a developing world battling against poverty and disease.[4] There are histories of moral panics focusing on the vulnerable, of punitive interventions to contain the infected, of various forms of oppression of those who do not conform to the norms, and of resistance.[5] We are overwhelmed with histories, and with the lessons they could, but usually do not, teach us. But they have one thing in common. These histories are histories of difference and diversity.

Despite the common viral and immunological factors, HIV and AIDS are experienced differently by different groups of people. The suffering and loss felt by gay men in the urban communities of large western cities is neither less nor greater than the suffering or loss of the poor in the black and hispanic communities of New York, or in the cities and villages of Africa, Latin America or south-east Asia; but it is different, because the histories of the communities affected are different. As Simon Watney has written: 'Wherever we look in the world, it is invariably the case that people's experience of HIV infection and disease faithfully duplicates their socio-economic situation *before* the epidemic began'.[6] We can find here a key to the power of AIDS. It is a syndrome that can threaten catastrophe on an unprecedented scale. But it is experienced, directly or empathetically, as a particular, historically and culturally organized series of diseases. AIDS is both global and local in its impact, and this tells us something vital about the historic present in which we live.

The impact of, and response to, AIDS forcefully reminds us of the complexities and interdependence of the contemporary world. Migrations across countries and continents, from country to town, from 'traditional' ways of life to 'modern', in flight from persecution, poverty or sexual repression, made the spread of HIV possible. The modern information society, global programmes, international consultations and conferences, makes possible a world-wide response to threatening disaster.

Yet the very scale and speed of this globalization of experience produces, as if by a necessary reflex, a burgeoning of culturally and politically specific responses, as well as new identities, new communities and conflicting demands and obligations. In becoming aware of the global village, we seem to need to affirm and reaffirm our local needs, histories and loyalties. Identity and difference: these provide the site of many of the most acute political, social and cultural debates today.

We can see in the AIDS crisis, and in the response it has engendered, several tendencies which cast a sharp light on wider currents and concerns. First, there is a general sense of crisis, a 'sense of an ending', generated by rapid cultural and sexual change, which many have seen AIDS as reinforcing. AIDS did not *cause* this pervasive mood – on the contrary people with HIV have had to endure the consequences of it – but the epidemic rode in on the overwhelming waves of change, and we have to confront the results. AIDS, it has been argued, demonstrates how we as a culture '. . . struggle and negotiate about appropriate processes to deal with social change, especially in its radical form'.[7] And we find that process painfully difficult. Second, following from that, AIDS reminds us of the complexities of contemporary identities. It was the rise of new sexual identities and communities in the 1960s and 1970s, especially those of lesbians and gay men, which dramatized the fundamental reorientation of sexual ways of being that was taking place. The association of those identities with the threat of disease and death only served to underline the sense of sexual uncertainty that was already manifesting itself in a revival of moral absolutisms and cultural counter-attacks. Uncertainty about who and what we are feeds into wider anxieties and fears.

Third, related to this, AIDS speaks to an 'unfinished revolution' in sexual relationships: a collapse of the settled certainties of family life, an explosion of different lifestyles and life experiments, a potent but incomplete democratization of relationships, and an acute tension between individual desires and collective belongings. Not surprisingly, AIDS, as Seidman argues, has become a principal site to struggle over sexual ethics, and to clarify the meaning and morality of sex.[8]

But finally, these very changes, which seem to many to illustrate the final collapse of the enlightened hopes of modernity, have produced new solidarities as people grapple with the challenges of postmodernity in profoundly humane ways. HIV and AIDS mark you. They have also provided the challenge and opportunities for creating new sensibilities, forged in the furnace of suffering, loss and survival. Out of the pain, rage and anger has come care, mutuality and love, a testimony to the possibilities of realizing human bonds across the chasms of an unforgiving culture. Here we see, I believe, the real possibilities of a radical humanism, grounded in people's struggles, experiences, particular histories and elective traditions. [. . .]

Sexuality, Relationships and the Democratic Imagination

Modernity, Giddens has argued, is a post-traditional order in which the question 'how shall I live?' has to be answered in day-to-day decisions about who to be, how to behave, what to wear, what to eat, and, crucially for this discussion, how we should live together, whom we can love.[9] As the energies of postmodernity gather pace, undermining settled patterns and old certainties, so these questions come more and more to the fore, and nowhere more so than in what I shall call the sphere of the intimate, the domain of 'private life' and its infinitely malleable and promiscuous partner, the erotic.

Intimacy in its modern form, as Giddens suggests, implies a radical democratization of the interpersonal domain, because it assumes not only the individual being the ultimate maker of his or her own life, but also equality between partners and freedom to choose lifestyles and forms of partnership. This theme of democratization, and its dilemmas, is crucial to our understanding of changes in sexual mores. There are two key areas where it is especially significant: family and/or domestic arrangements; and sexuality and love.

We are currently in the midst of a sometimes fevered debate about the family and domestic arrangements. Among conservatives this takes the form of a lamentation at the decline of the family, a hallowed theme hardly new, as we have seen, to this *fin de siècle,* but given a new wind because of transparently dramatic changes to its form, and because it has become an easy symbol for wider changes. Among liberals and radicals, on the other hand, the 1960s theme of finding alternatives *to* the family has given way to a recognition that there are 'alternative families', differentiated in all sorts of ways: by class, ethnicity, life-cycle and so on, and by deliberate choice of lifestyle. We may anguish over some of these forms, and attempt to determine what is best for childrearing and social stability (two parents seem to be preferred over one, heterosexual parents are generally favoured over homosexual), but broadly, and with varying degrees of reluctance, there is a general recognition on the liberal left that domestic diversity is with us to stay.

The problem is that while we may recognize the fact of diversity, we have yet to forge a language or set of values by which we can measure the legitimacy of all these forms. 'Commuter-marriages', relationships carried out at a distance as partners stretch the bonds of intimacy by constant travel (and surely the best neologism in this area), are apparently acceptable; homosexual partnerships, however domesticated, regularly are not, despite the growing recognition of 'partnership rights' in a number of countries. The furore in the late 1980s over 'pretended family relationships', that other neologism for lesbian and gay relationships,[10] showed that at least in the United Kingdom the boundaries of acceptability may indeed have expanded, but not that far.

And yet one of the most remarkable features of domestic change has been the emergence of common patterns in both homosexual and heterosexual ways of life.[11] Contemporary lesbian and gay relationships, in principle at least, are freely chosen by autonomous individuals, and have to be constructed afresh each time.[12] They survive only as long as they offer a satisfactory framework for fulfilling the domestic, emotional and/or sexual needs of the freely contracting partners. Of course, there are always all sorts of inequality, of income, age, ethnicity and so on that structure these relationships, but in principle they are partnerships between free agents, carrying little historical baggage, except (a big exception I admit) that of public opprobrium.

Heterosexual relationships, by contrast, remain – in the well chosen words of Clark and Haldane – largely 'wedlocked', despite the secular decline in marriage rates and the massive rise in cohabitation.[13] In Britain, for example, most people still marry at some stage, often when children arrive, and regularly remarry when they (frequently) divorce. Even cohabitation is marriage-like, and the majority of children born outside marriage are registered in the name of both partners. Whatever the changes that have transformed the institution, most of us live or have lived in families, and we remain wedded to familial language. Recent surveys in the USA and Britain reveal a surprising conservatism in domestic and sexual arrangements, at least in the majority white populations.[14] Yet alongside this continuity there are profound changes rattling the doors. The rise in divorce (a third of marriages expected to end in divorce), the prevalence of premarital sex (the vast majority of partners now have had sex before marriage), the gradual fading away of the stigma of illegitimacy (a spiralling number of births outside marriage), the rise of one-parent families (90 per cent headed by women), even the judicial recognition that there can be rape in marriage:[15] all these are familiar facts, but their implications are often misunderstood. It does not necessarily imply 'a breakdown of the family' as our more conservative commentators used to see it. As has frequently been pointed out, the divorced very often remarry, and remarry. There is a constant effort to 'make a go of it'. But the underlying ideology is changing.

People try to make a go of it, sometimes several times over, for a variety of reasons, but the central drive is the search for a satisfactory relationship as a key element in personal affirmation. Marriage becomes more and more a relationship entered into and sustained only for as long as it delivers emotional satisfaction from close contact with others, from intimacy.[16] Of course, as Janet Finch and others have pointed out, there are still many obligations which hold relationships together, especially children, and these are structured along lines of gender more often than not, and it is still true that most marriages do not end prematurely in divorce.[17] But increasingly choice of involvements is the key, and the reasons for choice are the hopes, often dashed but resilient, that the new relationship will deliver the goods. And these goods are emotional involvement and satisfaction.

In other words, marriage is entered into less as a status transition (though it remains that) and more as a sign of commitment. But in that it is only a more symbolically potent form of the commitment that lies at the heart of many other forms of relationship, including non-heterosexual.

Marriage today embraces elements of what has been called a 'pure relationship'.[18] Pure relationships are sought and entered into only for what the relationship can bring to the contracting partners. They are inevitably mediated through a host of socio-economic and gender factors. They often survive through inertia, habit and mutual dependency, as well as because of the web of obligations that are negotiated through the relationship. But the principle is that the relationship survives only as long as the commitment survives, or until a more promising relationship offers itself. The pure relationship depends on mutual trust between the partners, which in turn is closely related to the achievement of the desired level of intimacy. If trust breaks down, so in the end does intimacy, and the search for a better arrangement renews. This involves a high degree of instability. There is a new contingency in personal relationships. But the emphasis on personal commitment as the key to emotional satisfaction also has radical implications. For commitment implies the involvement of consenting, more or less equal individuals. The pure relationship implies a democratization of intimate relationships: the emphasis on individual autonomy and choice provides a radicalizing dynamic that is making possible the transformation of personal life.

Two things are important here. First, the relationship, whatever its form, marital or non-marital, becomes the defining element of the sphere of the intimate that provides the framework for everyday life. Second, it is the focus of personal identity, in which the personal narrative is constructed and reconstructed to provide the provisional sense of unity of the self that is necessary in the world of postmodernity. The pure relationship is both a product of the reflexive self, and a focus for its realization. It offers a nodal point for personal meaning in the contemporary world. It is here that sexuality and love are important, because they provide some of the prime sites for the attainment of meaning today.

Since the nineteenth century at least, Foucault and others have argued, there has been a constant attempt to tell what you are by telling the assumed truth about your sexuality.[19] The great polarities that we take for granted in speaking about social and personal life, male/female, heterosexual/homosexual, were assumed to be located in fundamental divisions within our sexual natures. We are now more aware that these divides, that we so easily assume are inbuilt and natural, personal to us, are in fact deeply historical and social. In part these definitions have been impositions, a complex effect of the play of power. In part they have been the result of a long process of internal struggle, negotiation and self-definition.[20]

Giddens, in partial challenge to Foucault, has argued that sexuality has the importance it does in the contemporary world not because of its significance for the control systems of modernity but because it is a point of connection between two other processes: the separation of experiences into discrete categories of existence, which has led to the privatization of death as well as of sexuality (in fact it made the emergence of sexuality as a discrete area of life possible); and the transformation of intimacy which has democratized sexual relations, and opened the way to the pure relationship. Although presented as antagonistic theories, however, these positions are not in practice incompatible. The very fact that sexuality has been bound up with structures of domination and subordination, for women, the sexually transgressive and the colonized, internally and externally, it has inevitably meant that the sexual has been a prime site for the struggle for a sense of self and identity. Those struggles in turn have contributed to the democratization of relationships. Inevitably, then, our sense of our self, the meanings we attach to our lives, are closely shaped by our sense of our sexuality. Sexuality may be a 'historic construct' but it remains also a key site for the construction of personal meaning and social location.[21]

But in the process the meaning of sexuality has itself changed. For long locked into the history of reproduction, it has now to a large degree floated free of it, a process that was well developed long before the Pill promised a once and for all technological fix.[22] It continues to evoke images of sin, for many, violence, for children and women particularly, and perhaps for all of us, power.

It is still linked with the threat of disease, re-evoked by the presence of the HIV epidemic. It is, as Carole Vance put it, a site of danger as well as pleasure.[23] But in a complex process, its meanings have expanded. It has become for most what it always was in theory, polymorphous or 'plastic'. In principle, at least, the erotic arts have been opened up to all of us, via a thousand sex manuals on the joys of sex, a flourishing trade in sexual representations, and an explosion of discourse around the body and its pleasures. Sexuality has become an arena for experimentation. This is closely related to the question of relationships, because if commitment, intimacy, trying again, are keys to modern private life, so is their attainment through sexual satisfaction, which increasingly means the exploration of the erotic, in ever more exotic and intricate patterns. There are, of course, many types of relationship without sex, and a lot of sex without relationships. But it is not an accident that intimacy as a term is closely related to sexual activity. Modern intimacy is closely linked with the exploration and satisfaction of sexual desire.

Where does that leave love? It is easy to talk about sexuality without love, and love without sexuality. But it is clear that love also is increasingly something that is shaped contingently, as a focus for intimate relationships. Love, like sexuality, has become more fluid, less a prescription for eternal devotion, more a matter of personal choice and self-making, a mode of communication rather than an eternal truth.[24] Its meanings are made for and in specific circumstances. That does not mean that it is less important; on the contrary, its very mobility, its potentiality for transcending the divide between autonomous individuals, makes it an ever more vital ingredient of social as well as private life. But we cannot assume its form; it must be negotiated afresh each time. Love, Bauman argues, is insecurity incarnate.[25]

These changes are affecting men and women alike, but their impact is highly gendered. Giddens has argued that women are in fact in the vanguard of change, and there are certainly many signs of a new ability among women to take control of their lives and commitments: most divorces, for example, are initiated by women.[26] Changes in sexual mores may have sexualized women's bodies to an extraordinary degree, though often exploitatively; they have also opened up unprecedented spaces for autonomy and self-actualization. Yet the pragmatics of independence are always hazardous. In their study of young women's attitudes to their bodies and sexualities in the context of the risk of HIV and AIDS, Holland et al. show how the assertion of female sexuality remains geared to the exigencies of male needs.[27] The potential for autonomy is there, but so are the constraints:

> Sex connects bodies and this connexion gives women an intimate space within which men's powers can be subverted and resisted. If women can recognize and capture this space, they can negotiate relationships with men which upset the gender hierarchy and so are potentially socially destabilizing. We suggest that few young women recognize and capture this space because they lack a critical consciousness that they are living a disembodied femininity. Where women do

have a critical consciousness of the embodiment of their sexuality, and are comfortable with desires of their own, men's power can be directly threatened . . . which might help explain the prevalence of male violence in sexual encounters.[28]

Research such as this indicates that sexuality remains a battleground, where the meanings of sexuality and love are still fought over, even in those parts of the world where sex-talk is most open and explicit. And yet it also suggests that even in the most resilient interstices of male privilege the potential for change, for renegotiation of relationships, is apparent.

Like all developments these shifts and changes in personal relationships are highly uneven in their impact. They are the cutting edge, and their effects are transforming intimate life, but they are working through the residue of deeply sedimented traditions. Not only are the changes highly gendered, there are different patterns in different communities. In their study of mixed race relations in Britain Alibhai-Brown and Montague illustrate the complexities of choice where racial and ethnic identification intersect with sexual attraction and love.[29] Inter-racial relations are scarcely new, but they have always of necessity had to negotiate the hazards of group norms and shifting, yet institutionalized patterns of prejudice and discrimination. Increasingly they also have to live with the reassertion of more exclusive collective identities among racial and ethnic minorities, leading to reinforced social taboos against exogamy. The rise of fundamentalist commitments among these minority communities, affirming translocal loyalties to Islam or Hinduism or other all-encompassing belief systems as an aspect of passionate group loyalties, is regularly associated with concerns with the gendered and sexualized body, as if the essence of identity can be asserted only through bodily purification.[30] Yet at the same time, as Alibhai-Brown and Montague argue:

> just as there are many Asian and Black Britons who would now argue against mixed relationships, there are also many others whose lives have been enriched and transformed by them and who see this as a new dawn. It can no longer be assumed, as it once was, that white values would dominate – that the Black or Asian partner would turn 'white', give or take an occasional ethnic headscarf, or sari at the office Christmas party, which was commonplace in the previous two decades . . . Nothing is taken for granted.[31]

'Nothing is taken for granted.' This is becoming the leitmotif of sexual manners as individuals struggle, pragmatically, to define their needs in the fluctuating circumstances in which they live their sexual lives. Bauman argues that there are two characteristic strategies for coping with the potential flux in relationships that now opens up what he describes as 'fixing' and 'floating'.[32] Fixing takes place when the potential openness of 'confluent love' and sexuality is set firmly in place by the demands of duty.[33] 'Floating' is what occurs when the arduousness of the constant negotiation of the terms of the relationship leads to our 'cutting our losses', starting again, ever hopeful that this time we will get it right. Neither is particularly appealing. The first, at its most extreme, would seem to prefer an empty shell to the creativity of a living relationship. The second can result in what Bauman describes as a 'de-ethicized intimacy', where responsibility to others, especially children, is lost in the pursuit of personal satisfaction.[34] These are not, however, the only possibilities. The democratization of sexuality and relationships that is now on the cultural agenda, only partially realized though it may yet be, creates the space for rethinking the ethics and values of personal relationships, for exploring what we mean by terms like responsibility, care, concern and love. This is the challenge of the transformations of sexuality now taking place. In this postmodern world it is unlikely that we will ever rid ourselves of the spectre of uncertainty, but its presence might help us to realize that living without certainty is the best spur there is to thinking again about what we value, what we really want.

Notes

1   D. Crimp (1987), 'AIDS cultural analysis/cultural activism'. *October* 43, Winter 1987, p. 14.
2   E. Fee and D. M. Fox (eds), *AIDS: The Burdens of History* (Berkeley, Los Angeles and London: University of California Press, 1988); E. Fee and D. M. Fox (eds), *AIDS: The Making of a Chronic Disease* (Berkeley, Los Angeles and Oxford: University of California Press, 1992).
3   Michel Foucault, *The History of Sexuality, Volume 1, An Introduction* (London: Allen Lane, 1976/1979).
4   C. West, *Race Matters* (Boston: Beacon Press, 1993).
5   Jeffrey Weeks, *Against Nature: Essays on History, Sexuality and Identity* (London: Rivers Oram Press, 1991).
6   S. Watney (1989), 'The subject of AIDS'. In P. Aggleton, P. Davies and G. Hart, (eds), *AIDS: Social Representations: Social Practices* (London, New York and Philadelphia: The Falmer Press, 1989), p. 19.
7   D. Nelkin, D. P. Willis and S. V. Parris, (eds), *A Disease of Society: Cultural and Institutional Responses to AIDS* (Cambridge: Cambridge University Press, 1991), p. 3.
8   S. Seidman, *Embattled Eros: Sexual Politics and Ethics in Contemporary America* (London and New York: Routledge, 1992), p. 146.
9   Anthony Giddens, *The Transformation of Intimacy* (Cambridge: Polity Press, 1992).
10 J. Weeks, *Against Nature*, ch. 8.
11 H. Bech (1992a), 'Report from a rotten state: "marriage" and "homosexuality" in "Denmark"'. In K. Plummer (ed.), *Modern Homosexualities: Fragments of Lesbian and Gay Experience* (London and New York: Routledge, 1992); H. Bech (1992b), 'Living together in the (post) modern world'. A paper given at the European Conference of Sociology, Vienna 1992.
12 K. Weston, *Families we Choose: Lesbians, Gays, Kinship* (New York: Columbia University Press, 1991).
13 D. Clark and D. Haldane, *Wedlocked? Intervention and Research in Marriage* (Cambridge: Polity Press, 1990).

14   E. O. Laumann, R. T. Michael, J. H. Gagnon and S. Michaels, *The Social Organization of Sexuality: Sexual Practices in the United States* (Chicago: University of Chicago Press, 1994); K. Wellings, J. Field, A. M. Johnson, and J. Wadsworth, *Sexual Behaviour in Britain: The National Survey of Sexual Attitudes and Lifestyles* (London: Penguin, 1994).

15   J. Weeks (1993), 'An unfinished revolution: sexuality in the twentieth century'. In V. Harwood, D. Oswell, K. Parkinson, and A. Ward (eds), *Pleasure Principles: Politics, Sexuality and Ethics* (London: Lawrence and Wishart, 1993).

16   A. Giddens, *The Transformation of Intimacy*.

17   J. Finch, *Family Obligations and Social Change* (Cambridge: Polity Press, 1989).

18   A. Giddens, *The Transformation of Intimacy*.

19   M. Foucault, *The History of Sexuality*.

20   See S. Kern, *The Culture of Love: Victorians to Moderns* (Cambridge, MA and London: Harvard University Press, 1992).

21   M. Foucault, *The History of Sexuality*.

22   K. Wellings et al. (1994), *Sexual Behaviour in Britain*.

23   C. S. Vance (ed.), *Pleasure and Danger: Exploring Female Sexuality* (London and Boston: Routledge and Kegan Paul, 1984).

24   Niklas Luhmann, *Love as Passion* (Cambridge, Polity Press, 1986).

25   Zygmunt Bauman, *Postmodern Ethics* (Oxford: Blackwell, 1993), p. 98.

26   A. Giddens, *The Transformation of Intimacy*.

27   J. Holland, C. Ramazanoglu, S. Sharpe and R. Thomson (1994), 'Power and desire: the embodiment of female sexuality'. *Feminist Review* 46, Spring 1994.

28   Ibid., pp. 34–5.

29   Y. Alibhai-Brown and A. Montague (1992), *The Colour of Love: Mixed Race Relationships* (London: Virago, 1992).

30   C. Bhatt (1994), 'New foundations: contingency, indeterminacy and black trans-locality'. In J. Weeks (ed.), *The Lesser Evil and the Greater Good: The Theory and Politics of Social Diversity* (London: Rivers Oram Press, 1994).

31   Y. Alibhai-Brown and A. Montague, p. 15.

32   Z. Bauman, *Postmodern Ethics*, p. 98.

33   A. Giddens, *The Transformation of Intimacy*.

34   Z. Bauman, *Postmodern Ethics*, p. 106.

23

Situated Knowledges: The Science Question in Feminism and the Privilege of Partial Perspective

Donna J. Haraway

Academic and activist feminist enquiry has repeatedly tried to come to terms with the question of what *we* might mean by the curious and inescapable term 'objectivity'. We have used a lot of toxic ink and trees processed into paper decrying what *they* have meant and how it hurts *us*. The imagined 'they' constitute a kind of invisible conspiracy of masculinist scientists and philosophers replete with grants and laboratories; and the imagined 'we' are the embodied others, who are not allowed *not* to have a body, a finite point of view, and so an inevitably disqualifying and polluting bias in any discussion of consequence outside our own little circles, where a 'mass'-subscription journal might reach a few thousand readers composed mostly of science-haters. At least, I confess to these paranoid fantasies and academic resentments lurking underneath some convoluted reflections in print under my name in the feminist literature in the history and philosophy of science. We, the feminists in the debates about science and technology, are the Reagan era's 'special interest groups' in the rarefied realm of epistemology, where traditionally what can count as knowledge is policed by philosophers codifying cognitive canon law. Of course, a special interest group is, by Reaganoid definition, any collective historical subject which dares to resist the stripped-down atomism of Star Wars, hypermarket, postmodern, media-simulated citizenship. Max Headroom doesn't have a body; therefore, he alone *sees* everything in the great communicator's empire of the Global Network. No wonder Max gets to have a naive sense of humour and a kind of happily regressive, pre-oedipal sexuality, a sexuality which we ambivalently – and dangerously incorrectly – had imagined was reserved for lifelong inmates of female and colonized bodies, and maybe also white male computer hackers in solitary electronic confinement.

It has seemed to me that feminists have both selectively and flexibly used and been trapped by two poles of a tempting dichotomy on the question of objectivity. Certainly I speak for myself here, and I offer the speculation that there is a collective discourse on these matters. On the one hand, recent social studies of science and technology have made available a very strong social constructionist argument for *all* forms of knowledge claims, most certainly and especially scientific ones.[1] In these tempting views, no insider's perspective is privileged, because all drawings of inside–outside boundaries in knowledge are theorized as power moves, not moves towards truth. So, from the strong social constructionist perspective, why should we be cowed by scientists' descriptions of their activity and accomplishments; they and their patrons have stakes in throwing sand in our eyes. They tell parables about objectivity and scientific method to students in the first years of their initiation, but no practitioner of the high scientific arts would be caught dead *acting on* the textbook versions. Social constructionists make clear that official ideologies about objectivity and scientific method are particularly bad guides to how scientific knowledge is actually *made*. Just as for the rest of us, what scientists believe or say they do and what they really do have a very loose fit. [. . .]

I, and others, started out wanting a strong tool for deconstructing the truth claims of hostile science by showing the radical historical specificity, and so contestability, of *every* layer of the onion of scientific and technological constructions, and we end up with a kind of epistemological electroshock therapy, which far from ushering us into the high stakes tables of the game of contesting public truths, lays us out on the table with self-induced multiple personality disorder. We wanted a way to go beyond showing bias in science (that proved too easy anyhow), and beyond separating the good scientific sheep from the bad goats of bias and misuse. It seemed promising to do this by the strongest possible constructionist argument that left no cracks for reducing the issues to bias versus objectivity, use versus misuse, science versus pseudo-science. We unmasked the doctrines of objectivity because they threat-ened our budding sense of collective historical subjectivity and agency and our 'embodied' accounts of the truth, and we ended up with one more excuse for not learning any post-Newtonian physics and one more reason to drop the old feminist self-help practices of repairing our own cars. They're just texts anyway, so let the boys have them back. Besides these textualized postmodern worlds are scary, and we prefer our science fiction to be a bit more utopic, maybe like *Woman on the Edge of Time* or even *Wanderground*.

Some of us tried to stay sane in these disassembled and dissembling times by holding out for a feminist version of objectivity. Here, motivated by many of the same political desires, is the other seductive end of the duplicitous objectivity problem. Humanistic Marxism was polluted at the source by its structuring ontological theory of the domination of nature in the self-construction of man and by its closely related impotence to historicize anything women did that didn't qualify for a wage. But Marxism was still a promising resource in the form of epistemological feminist mental hygiene that sought our own doctrines of objective vision. Marxist starting points offered tools to get to our versions of standpoint theories, insistent embodiment, a rich tradition of critiques of hegemony without disempowering positivisms and relativisms, and nuanced theories of mediation. Some versions of psychoanalysis aided this approach immensely, especially anglophone object relations theory, which maybe did more for US socialist-feminism for a time than anything from the pen of Marx or Engels, much less Althusser or any of the late pretenders to sonship treating the subject of ideology and science.[2]

Another approach, 'feminist empiricism', also converges with feminist uses of Marxian resources to get a theory of science which continues to insist on legitimate meanings of objectivity and which remains leery of a radical constructivism conjugated with semiology and narratology. Feminists have to insist on a better account of the world; it is not enough to show radical historical contingency and modes of construction for everything. Here, we, as feminists, find ourselves perversely conjoined with the discourse of many practising scientists, who, when all is said and done, mostly believe they are describing and discovering things by *means of* all their constructing and arguing. Evelyn Keller has been particularly insistent on this fundamental matter, and Harding calls the goal of these approaches a successor science. Feminists have stakes in a successor science project that offers a more adequate, richer, better account of a world, in order to live in it well and in critical, reflexive relation to our own as well as others' practices of domination and the unequal parts of privilege and oppression that make up all positions. In traditional philosophical categories, the issue is ethics and politics perhaps more than epistemology.

So, I think my problem and 'our' problem is how to have *simultaneously* an account of radical historical contingency for all knowledge claims and knowing subjects, a critical practice for recognizing our own 'semiotic technologies' for making meanings, *and* a no-nonsense commitment to faithful accounts of a 'real' world, one that can be partially shared and friendly to earth-wide projects of finite freedom, adequate material abundance, modest meaning in suffering, and limited happiness. Harding calls this necessary multiple desire a need for a successor science project and a postmodern insistence on irreducible difference and radical multiplicity of local knowledges. *All* components of the desire are paradoxical and dangerous, and their combination is both contradictory and necessary. Feminists don't need a doctrine of objectivity that promises transcendence, a story that loses track of its mediations just where someone might be held responsible for something, and unlimited instrumental power. We don't want a theory of innocent powers to represent the world, where language and bodies both fall into the bliss of organic symbiosis. We also don't want to theorize the world, much less act within it, in terms of Global Systems, but we do need an earth-wide network of connections, including the ability partially to translate knowledges among very different – and power-differentiated – communities. We need the power of modern critical theories of how meanings and bodies get made, not in order to deny meaning and bodies, but in order to live in meanings and bodies that have a chance for a future.

Natural, social and human sciences have always been implicated in hopes like these. Science has been about a search for translation, convertibility, mobility of meanings, and universality – which I call reductionism, when one language (guess whose) must be enforced as the standard for all the translations and conversions. What money does in the exchange orders of capitalism, reductionism does in the powerful mental orders of global sciences: there is finally only one equation. That is the deadly fantasy that feminists and others have identified in some versions of objectivity doctrines in the service of hierarchical and positivist orderings of what can count as knowledge. That is one of the reasons the debates about objectivity matter, metaphorically and otherwise. Immortality and omnipotence are not our goals. But we could use some enforceable, reliable accounts of things not reducible to power moves and agnostic, high status games of rhetoric or to scientistic, positivist arrogance. This point applies whether we are talking about genes, social classes, elementary particles, genders, races or texts; the point applies to the exact, natural, social and human sciences, despite the slippery ambiguities of the words *objectivity* and *science* as we slide around the discursive terrain. In our efforts to climb the greased pole leading to a usable doctrine of objectivity, I and most other feminists in the objectivity debates have alternatively, or even simultaneously, held on to both ends of the dichotomy, which Harding describes in terms of successor science projects versus postmodernist accounts of difference and I have sketched [. . .] as radical constructivism versus feminist critical empiricism. It is, of course, hard to climb when you are holding on to both ends of a pole, simultaneously or alternately. It is, therefore, time to switch metaphors.

The Persistence of Vision[3]

I would like to proceed by placing metaphorical reliance on a much maligned sensory system in feminist discourse: vision. Vision can be good for avoiding binary oppositions. I would like to insist on the embodied nature of all vision, and so reclaim the sensory system that has been used to signify a leap out of the marked body and into a conquering gaze from nowhere. This is the gaze that mythically inscribes all the marked bodies, that makes the unmarked category claim the power to see and not be seen, to represent while escaping representation. This gaze signifies the unmarked positions of Man and White, one of the many nasty tones of the world *objectivity* to feminist ears in scientific and technological, late industrial, militarized, racist and male dominant societies, that is, here, in the belly of the monster, in the United States in the late 1980s. I would like a doctrine of embodied objectivity that accommodates paradoxical and critical feminist science projects: feminist objectivity means quite simply *situated knowledges*.

The eyes have been used to signify a perverse capacity – honed to perfection in the history of science tied to militarism, capitalism, colonialism, and male supremacy – to distance the knowing subject from everybody and everything in the interests of unfettered power. The instruments of visualization in multi-nationalist, postmodernist culture have compounded these meanings of disembodiment. The visualizing technologies are without apparent limit; the eye of any ordinary primate like us can be endlessly enhanced by sonography systems, magnetic resonance imaging, artificial intelligence-linked graphic manipulation systems, scanning electron microscopes, computer-aided tomography scanners, colour enhancement techniques, satellite surveillance systems, home and office VDTs, cameras for every purpose from filming the mucous membrane lining the gut cavity of a marine worm living in the vent gases on a fault between continental plates to mapping a planetary hemisphere elsewhere in the solar system. Vision in this technological feast becomes un-regulated gluttony; all perspective gives way to infinitely mobile vision, which no longer seems just mythically about the god-trick of seeing everything from nowhere, but to have put the myth into ordinary practice. And like the god-trick, this eye fucks the world to make techno-monsters. Zoe Sofoulis calls this the cannibal-eye of masculinist extra-terrestrial projects for excremental second birthing.

A tribute to this ideology of direct, devouring, generative and unrestricted vision, whose technological mediations are simultaneously celebrated and presented as utterly transparent, the volume celebrating the 100th anniversary of the National Geographic Society closes its survey of the magazine's quest literature, effected through its amazing photography, with two juxtaposed chapters. The first is on 'Space', introduced by the epigraph, 'The choice is the universe – or nothing'. Indeed. This chapter recounts the exploits of the space race and displays the colour-enhanced 'snapshots' of the outer planets reassembled from digitalized signals transmitted across vast space to let the viewer 'experience' the moment of discovery in immediate vision of the 'object'.[4] These fabulous objects come to us simultaneously as indubitable recordings of what is simply there and as heroic feats of techno-scientific production. The next chapter is the twin of outer space: 'Inner Space', intro-duced by the epigraph, 'The stuff of stars has come alive'. Here, the reader is brought into the realm of the infinitesimal, objectified by means of radiation outside the wave lengths that 'normally' are perceived by hominid primates, i.e., the beams of lasers and scanning electron microscopes, whose signals are processed into the wonderful full-colour snapshots of defending T cells and invading viruses.

But of course that view of infinite vision is an illusion, a god-trick. I would like to suggest how our insisting metaphorically on the particularity and embodiment of all vision (though not necessarily organic embodiment and including technological mediation), and not giving in to the tempting myths of vision as a route to disembodiment and second-birthing, allows us to construct a usable, but not an innocent, doctrine of objectivity. I want a feminist writing of the body that metaphorically emphasizes vision again, because we need to reclaim that sense to find our way through all the visualizing tricks and powers of modern sciences and technologies that have transformed the objectivity debates. We need to learn in our bodies, endowed with primate colour and stereoscopic vision, how to attach the objective to our theoretical and political scanners in order to name where we are and are not, in dimensions of mental and physical space we hardly know how to name. So, not so perversely, objectivity turns out to be about particular and specific embodiment, and definitely not about the false vision promising transcendence of all limits and responsibility. The moral is simple: only partial perspective promises objective vision. This is an objective vision that initiates, rather than closes off, the problem of responsibility for the generativity of all visual practices. Partial perspective can be held accountable for both its promising and its destructive monsters. All western cultural narratives about objectivity are allegories of the ideologies of the relations of what we call mind and body, of distance and responsibility, embedded in the science question in feminism. Feminist objectivity is about limited location and situated knowledge, not about transcendence and splitting of subject and object. In this way we might become answerable for what we learn how to see. [. . .]

Many currents in feminism attempt to theorize grounds for trusting especially the vantage points of the subjugated; there is good reason to believe vision is better from below the brilliant space platforms of the powerful. Linked to this suspicion, this chapter is an argument for situated and embodied knowledges and against various forms of unlocatable, and so irresponsible, knowledge claims. Irresponsible means unable to be called into account. There is a premium on establishing the capacity to see from the peripheries and the depths. But here lies a serious danger of romanticizing and/or appropriating the vision of the less powerful while claiming to see from their positions. To see from below is neither easily learned nor unproblematic, even if 'we' 'naturally' inhabit the great underground terrain of subjugated knowledges. The positionings of the subjugated are not exempt from critical re-examination, decoding, deconstruction and interpretation; that is, from both semiological and hermeneutic modes of critical enquiry. The standpoints of the subjugated are not 'innocent' positions. On the contrary, they are preferred because in principle they are least likely to allow denial of the critical and interpretative core of all knowledge. They are savvy to modes of denial through repression, forgetting and disappearing acts – ways of being nowhere while claiming to see comprehensively. The subjugated have a decent chance to be on to the god-trick and all its dazzling – and, therefore, blinding – illuminations. 'Subjugated' standpoints are preferred because they seem to promise more adequate, sustained, objective, transforming accounts of the world. But *how* to see from below is a problem requiring at least as much skill with bodies and language, with the mediations of vision, as the 'highest' techno-scientific visualizations.

Such preferred positioning is as hostile to various forms of relativism as to the most explicitly totalizing versions of claims to scientific authority. But the alternative to relativism is not totalization and single vision, which is always finally the unmarked category whose power depends on systematic narrowing and obscuring. The alternative to relativism is partial, locatable, critical knowledges sustaining the possibility of webs of connections called solidarity in politics and shared conversations in epistemology. Relativism is a way of being nowhere while claiming to be everywhere equally. The 'equality' of positioning is a denial of responsibility and critical enquiry. Relativism is the perfect mirror twin of totalization in the ideologies of objectivity; both deny the stakes in location, embodiment and partial perspective; both make it impossible to see well. Relativism and totalization are both 'god-tricks' promising vision from everywhere and nowhere equally and fully, common myths in rhetorics surrounding Science. But it is precisely in the politics and epistemology of partial perspectives that the possibility of sustained, rational, objective enquiry rests.

So, with many other feminists, I want to argue for a doctrine and practice of objectivity that privileges contestation, deconstruction, passionate construction, webbed connections and hope for transformation of systems of knowledge and ways of seeing. But not just any partial perspective will do; we must be hostile to easy relativisms and holisms built out of summing and subsuming parts. 'Passionate detachment' (Kuhn) requires more than acknowledged and self-critical partiality. We are also bound to seek perspective from those points of view, which can never be known in advance, which promise something quite extraordinary, that is, knowledge potent for constructing worlds less organized by axes of domination. In such a viewpoint, the unmarked category would *really* disappear – quite a difference from simply repeating a disappearing act. The imaginary and the rational – the visionary and objective vision – hover close together. I think Harding's plea for a successor science and for postmodern sensibilities must be read to argue that this close touch of the fantastic element of hope for transformative knowledge and the severe check and stimulus of sustained critical enquiry are jointly the ground of any believable claim to objectivity or rationality not riddled with breath-taking denials and repressions. It is even possible to read the record of scientific revolutions in terms of this feminist doctrine of rationality and objectivity. Science has been utopian and visionary from the start; that is one reason 'we' need it.

A commitment to mobile positioning and to passionate detachment is dependent on the impossibility of innocent 'identity' politics and epistemologies as strategies for seeing from the standpoints of the subjugated in order to see well. One cannot 'be' either a cell or molecule – or a woman, colonized person, labourer, and so on – if one intends to see and see from these positions critically. 'Being' is much more problematic and contingent. Also, one cannot relocate in any possible vantage point without being accountable for that movement. Vision is *always* a question of the power to see – and perhaps of the violence implicit in our visualizing practices. With whose blood were my eyes crafted? These points also apply to testimony from the position of 'oneself'. We are not immediately present to ourselves. Self-knowledge requires a semiotic-material technology linking meanings and bodies. Self-identity is a bad visual system. Fusion is a bad strategy of positioning. The boys in the human sciences have called this doubt about self-presence the 'death of the subject', that single ordering point of will and consciousness. That judgment seems bizarre to me. I prefer to call this generative doubt the opening of non-isomorphic subjects, agents and territories of stories unimaginable from the vantage point of the cyclopian, self-satiated eye of the master subject. The western eye has funda-mentally been a wandering eye, a travelling lens. These peregrinations have often been violent and insistent on mirrors for a conquering self – but not always. Western feminists also *inherit* some skill in learning to participate in revisualizing worlds turned upside down in earth-transforming challenges to the views of the masters. All is not to be done from scratch.

The split and contradictory self is the one who can interrogate positionings and be accountable, the one who can construct and join rational conver-sations and fantastic imaginings that change history.[5] Splitting, not being, is the privileged image for feminist epistemologies of scientific knowledge. 'Splitting' in this context should be about heterogeneous multiplicities that are simultaneously necessary and incapable of being squashed into isomorphic slots or cumulative lists. This geometry pertains within and among subjects. The topography of subjectivity is multidimensional; so, therefore, is vision. The knowing self is partial in all its guises, never finished, whole, simply there and original; it is always constructed and stitched together imperfectly, and *there-fore* able to join with another, to see together without claiming to be another. Here is the promise of objectivity: a scientific knower seeks the subject position not of identity, but of objectivity; that is, partial connection. There is no way to 'be' simultaneously in all, or wholly in any, of the privileged (subjugated) positions structured by gender, race, nation and class. And that is a short list of critical positions. The search for such a 'full' and total position is the search for the fetishized perfect subject of oppositional history, sometimes appearing in feminist theory as the essentialized Third World Woman. Subjugation is not grounds for an ontology; it might be a visual clue. Vision requires instruments of vision; an optics is a politics of positioning. Instruments of vision mediate standpoints; there is no immediate vision from the standpoints of the sub-jugated. Identity, including self-identity, does not produce science; critical positioning does, that is, objectivity. Only those occupying the positions of the dominators are self-identical, unmarked, disembodied, unmediated, trans-cendent, born again. It is unfortunately possible for the subjugated to lust for and even scramble into that subject position – and then disappear from view. Knowledge from the point of view of the unmarked is truly fantastic, distorted, and so irrational. The only position from which objectivity could not possibly be practised and honoured is the standpoint of the master, the Man, the One God, whose Eye produces, appropriates and orders all difference. No one ever accused the God of monotheism of objectivity, only of indifference. The god-trick is self-identical, and we have mistaken that for creativity and knowledge, omniscience even.

Positioning is, therefore, the key practice grounding knowledge organized around the imagery of vision, as so much western scientific and philosophic discourse is organized. Positioning implies responsibility for our enabling practices. It follows that politics and ethics ground struggles for the contests over what may count as rational knowledge. That is, admitted or not, politics and ethics ground struggles over knowledge projects in the exact, natural, social and human sciences. Otherwise, rationality is simply impossible, an optical illusion projected from nowhere comprehensively. Histories of science may be powerfully told as histories of the technologies. These technologies are ways of life, social orders, practices of visualization. Technologies are skilled practices. How to see? Where to see from? What limits to vision? What to see for? Whom to see with? Who gets to have more than one point of view? Who gets blinkered? Who wears blinkers? Who interprets the visual field? What other sensory powers do we wish to cultivate besides vision? Moral and political discourse should be the paradigm of rational discourse in the imagery and technologies of vision. Sandra Harding's claim, or observation, that movements of social revolution have most contributed to improvements in science might be read as a claim about the knowledge consequences of new technologies of positioning. But I wish Harding had spent more time remembering that social and scientific revolutions have not always been liberatory, even if they have always been visionary. Perhaps this point could be captured in another phrase: the science question in the military. Struggles over what will count as rational accounts of the world are struggles over *how* to see. The terms of vision: the science question in colonialism; the science question in exterminism; the science question in feminism.

The issue in politically engaged attacks on various empiricisms, reductionisms, or other versions of scientific authority should not be relativism, but location. A dichotomous chart expressing this point might look like this:

universal rationality	ethnophilosophies
common language	heteroglossia
new organon	deconstruction
unified field theory	oppositional positioning
world system	local knowledges
master theory	webbed accounts

But a dichotomous chart misrepresents in a critical way the positions of embodied objectivity which I am trying to sketch. The primary distortion is the illusion of symmetry in the chart's dichotomy, making any position appear, first, simply alternative and, second, mutually exclusive. A map of tensions and resonances between the fixed ends of a charged dichotomy better represents the potent politics and epistemologies of embodied, therefore accountable, objectivity. For example, local knowledges have also to be in tension with the productive structurings that force unequal translations and exchanges – material and semiotic – within the webs of knowledge and power. Webs *can* have the property of systematicity, even of centrally structured global systems with deep filaments and tenacious tendrils into time, space and consciousness, the dimensions of world history. Feminist accountability requires a knowledge tuned to resonance, not to dichotomy. Gender is a field of structured and structuring difference, where the tones of extreme localization, of the intimately personal and individualized body, vibrate in the same field with global high tension emissions. Feminist embodiment, then, is not about fixed location in a reified body, female or otherwise, but about nodes in fields, inflections in orientations, and responsibility for difference in material-semiotic fields of meaning. Embodiment is significant prosthesis; objectivity cannot be about fixed vision when what counts as an object is precisely what world history turns out to be about.

How should one be positioned in order to see resonances, transformations, resistances, and complicities in this situation of tensions? Here, primate vision is not immediately a very powerful metaphor or technology for feminist political-epistemological clarification, since it seems to present to consciousness already processed and objectified fields; things seem already fixed and distanced. But the visual metaphor allows one to go beyond fixed appearances, which are only the end products. The metaphor invites us to investigate the varied apparatuses of visual production, including the prosthetic technologies interfaced with our biological eyes and brains. And here we find highly particular machineries for processing regions of the electro-magnetic spectrum into our pictures of the world. It is in the intricacies of these visualization technologies in which we are embedded that we will find metaphors and means for understanding and intervening in the patterns of objectification in the world, that is, the patterns of reality for which we must be accountable. In these metaphors, we find means for appreciating simultaneously *both* the concrete, 'real' aspect and the aspect of semiosis and production in what we call scientific knowledge.

I am arguing for politics and epistemologies of location, positioning and situating, where partiality and not universality is the condition of being heard to make rational knowledge claims. These are claims on people's lives; the view from a body, always a complex, contradictory, structuring and structured body, versus the view from above, from nowhere, from simplicity. Only the god-trick is forbidden. Here is a criterion for deciding the science question in militarism, that dream science/technology of perfect language, perfect communication, final order.

Feminism loves another science: the sciences and politics of interpretation, translation, stuttering, and the partly understood. Feminism is about the sciences of the multiple subject with (at least) double vision. Feminism is about a critical vision consequent upon a critical positioning in inhomogeneous gendered social space.[6] Translation is always interpretative, critical and partial.

Here is a ground for conversation, rationality, and objectivity – which is power-sensitive, not pluralist, 'conversation'. It is not even the mythic cartoons of physics and mathematics – incorrectly caricatured in anti-science ideology as exact, hyper-simple knowledges – that have come to represent the hostile other to feminist paradigmatic models of scientific knowledge, but the dreams of the perfectly known in high-technology, permanently militarized scientific productions and positionings, the god-trick of a Star Wars paradigm of rational knowledge. So location is about vulnerability; location resists the politics of closure, finality, or, to borrow from Althusser, feminist objectivity resists 'simplification in the last instance'. That is because feminist embodiment resists fixation and is insatiably curious about the webs of differential positioning. There is no single feminist standpoint because our maps require too many dimensions for that metaphor to ground our visions. But the feminist standpoint theorists' goal of an epistemology and politics of engaged, accountable positioning remains eminently potent. The goal is better accounts of the world, that is, 'science'.

Above all, rational knowledge does not pretend to disengagement: to be from everywhere and so nowhere, to be free from interpretation, from being represented, to be fully self-contained or fully formalizable. Rational knowledge is a process of ongoing critical interpretation among 'fields' of interpreters and decoders. Rational knowledge is power-sensitive conversation:

> knowledge: community : : knowledge: power
> hermeneutics: semiology : : critical interpretation: codes.

Decoding and transcoding plus translation and criticism; all are necessary. So science becomes the paradigmatic model not of closure, but of that which is contestable and contested. Science becomes the myth not of what escapes human agency and responsibility in a realm above the fray, but rather of accountability and responsibility for translations and solidarities linking the cacophonous visions and visionary voices that characterize the knowledges of the subjugated. A splitting of senses, a confusion of voice and sight, rather than clear and distinct ideas, becomes the metaphor for the ground of the rational. We seek not the knowledges ruled by phallogocentrism (nostalgia for the presence of the one true Word) and disembodied vision, but those ruled by partial sight and limited voice. We do not seek partiality for its own sake, but for the sake of the connections and unexpected openings situated knowledges make possible. The only way to find a larger vision is to be somewhere in particular. The science question in feminism is about objectivity as positioned rationality. Its images are not the products of escape and transcendence of limits, i.e., the view from above, but the joining of partial views and halting voices into a collective subject position that promises a vision of the means of ongoing finite embodiment, of living within limits and contradictions, i.e., of views from somewhere.

Notes

1   For example, see Karin Knorr-Cetina and Michael Mulkay (eds), *Science Observed: Perspectives on the Social Study of Science* (Beverly Hills: Sage, 1983); Wiebe E. Bijker et al., *The Social Construction of Technological Systems* (Cambridge, MA: MIT Press, 1987); and especially, Bruno Latour, *Les microbes, guerre et paix, suivi des irréductions* (Paris: Métailie, 1984), and *The Pasteurization of France, followed by Irreductions: A Politico-Scientific Essay* (Cambridge, MA: Harvard University Press, 1988).

2   Crucial to this discussion are Sandra Harding, *The Science Question in Feminism* (Ithaca: Cornell University Press, 1986); Evelyn Fox Keller, *Reflections on Gender and Science* (New Haven: Yale University Press, 1985); Nancy Harstock, *Money, Sex, and Power* (New York: Longman, 1983); Jane Flax, 'Postmodernism and gender relations in feminist theory', *Signs* 12 (4), 1987 pp. 621–43; Hilary Rose, 'Women's work: women's knowledge', in Juliet Mitchell and Ann Oakley (eds), *What Is Feminism? A Reexamination* (New York: Pantheon, 1986); Donna Haraway, 'Manifesto for Cyborgs' in *Simians, Cyborgs and Women* (New York: Routledge, 1991), pp. 149–81; and Rosalind Petchesky, 'Fetal images', *Feminist Studies* 13 (2), pp. 263–92.

3   John Varley's science fiction short story called 'The Persistence of Vision' is part of the inspiration for this section. In the story, Varley constructs a utopian community designed and built by the deaf-blind. He then explores these people's technologies and other mediations of communication and their relations to sighted children and visitors. See Varley, *The Persistence of Vision* (New York: Dell, 1978), pp. 263–316.

4   I owe my understanding of the experience of these photographs to Jim Clifford, University of California at Santa Cruz, who identified their 'land ho!' effect on the reader.

5   Joan Scott reminded me that Teresa de Lauretis, in her *Feminist Studies/Critical Studies* (Bloomington: Indiana University Press, 1986), (1986a, pp. 14–15) put it like this:

> Differences among women may be better understood as differences within women. But once understood in their constitutive power – once it is understood, that is, that these differences not only constitute each woman's consciousness and subjective limits but all together define *the female subject of feminism* in its very specificity, its inherent and at least for now irreconcilable contradiction – these differences, then, cannot be again collapsed into a fixed identity, a sameness of all women as Woman, or a representation of Feminism as a coherent and available image.

6   Harding (1986, p. 18) suggested that gender has three dimensions, each historically specific: gender symbolism, the social-sexual division of labour, and processes of constructing individual gendered identity. [. . .]

The chart below begins an analysis by parallel dissections. In the chart (and in reality?), both gender and science are analytically asymmetrical; i.e., each term contains and obscures a structuring hierarchicalized binarism, sex/gender and nature/science. Each binarism orders the silent term by a logic of appropriation, as resource to product, nature to culture, potential to actual. Both poles of the binarism are constructed and structure each other dialectically. Within each voiced or explicit term, further asymmetrical splittings can be excavated, as from gender, masculine to feminine, and from science, hard sciences to soft sciences. This is a point about remembering how a particular analytical tool works, willy nilly, intended or not. The chart reflects common ideological aspects of discourse on science and gender and may help as an analytical tool to crack open mystified units like Science or Woman.

Gender	Science
symbolic system	symbolic system
social division of labour (by sex, by race, etc.)	social division of labour (by craft, industrial, or post-industrial logics)
individual identity/subject position (desiring/desired; autonomous/relational)	individual identity/subject position (knower/known; scientist/other)
material culture (gender paraphernalia and daily gender technologies: the narrow tracks on which sexual difference runs)	material culture (laboratories: the narrow tracks on which facts run)
dialectic of construction and discovery	dialectic of construction and discovery

Part VI
The Modernity/Postmodernity Debate

24

Postmodernism

David Harvey

Over the last two decades 'postmodernism' has become a concept to be wrestled with, and such a battleground of conflicting opinions and political forces that it can no longer be ignored. 'The culture of the advanced capitalist societist,' announce the editors of *PRECIS 6*,[1] 'has undergone a profound shift in the *structure of feeling*.' Most, I think, would now agree with Huyssens's more cautious statement:

> What appears on one level as the latest fad, advertising pitch and hollow spectacle is part of a slowly emerging cultural transformation in Western societies, a change in sensibility for which the term 'post-modern' is actually, at least for now, wholly adequate. The nature and depth of that transformation are debatable, but transformation it is. I don't want to be misunderstood as claiming that there is a wholesale paradigm shift of the cultural, social, and economic orders; any such claim clearly would be overblown. But in an important sector of our culture there is a noticeable shift in sensibility, practices and discourse formations which distinguishes a post-modern set of assumptions, experiences and propositions from that of a preceding period.[2]

With respect to architecture, for example, Charles Jencks dates the symbolic end of modernism and the passage to the postmodern as 3.32 p.m. on 15 July 1972, when the Pruitt-Igoe housing development in St Louis (a prize-winning version of Le Corbusier's 'machine for modern living') was dynamited as an uninhabitable environment for the low-income people it housed. Thereafter, the ideas of the CIAM, Le Corbusier, and the other apostles of 'high modernism' increasingly gave way before an onslaught of diverse possibilities, of which those set forth in the influential *Learning from Las Vegas* by Venturi, Scott Brown and Izenour (also published in 1972) proved to be but one powerful cutting edge. The point of that work, as its title implies, was to insist that architects had more to learn from the study of popular and vernacular landscapes (such as those of suburbs and commercial strips) than from the pursuit of some abstract, theoretical, and doctrinaire ideals. It was time, they said, to build for people rather than for Man. The glass towers, concrete blocks and steel slabs that seemed set fair to steamroller over every urban landscape from Paris to Tokyo and from Rio to Montreal, denouncing all ornament as crime, all individualism as sentimentality, all romanticism as kitsch, have progressively given way to ornamented tower blocks, imitation mediaeval squares and fishing villages, custom-designed or vernacular housing, reno-vated factories and warehouses, and rehabilitated landscapes of all kinds, all in the name of procuring some more 'satisfying' urban environment. So popular has this quest become that no less a figure than Prince Charles has weighed in with vigorous denunciations of the errors of postwar urban re-development and the developer destruction that has done more to wreck London, he claims, than the Luftwaffe's attacks in World War II.

In planning circles we can track a similar evolution. Douglas Lee's influential article 'Requiem for large-scale planning models' appeared in a 1973 issue of the *Journal of the American Institute of Planners* and correctly predicted the demise of what he saw as the futile efforts of the 1960s to develop large-scale, comprehensive, and integrated planning models (many of them specified with all the rigour that computerized mathematical modelling could then command) for metropolitan regions.[3] Shortly thereafter, the *New York Times* (13 June 1976) described as 'mainstream' the radical planners (inspired by Jane Jacobs) who had mounted such a violent attack upon the soulless sins of modernist urban planning in the 1960s. It is nowadays the norm to seek out 'pluralistic' and 'organic' strategies for approaching urban development as a 'collage' of highly differentiated spaces and mixtures, rather than pursuing grandiose plans based on functional zoning of different activities. 'Collage city' is now the theme and 'urban revitalization' has replaced the vilified 'urban renewal' as the key buzz-word in the planners' lexicon. 'Make no little plans', Daniel Burnham wrote in the first wave of modernist planning euphoria at the end of the nineteenth century, to which a postmodernist like Aldo Rossi can now more modestly reply: 'To what, then, could I have aspired in my craft? Certainly to small things, having seen that the possibility of great ones was historically precluded.'

Shifts of this sort can be documented across a whole range of diverse fields. The postmodern novel, McHale argues, is characterized by a shift from an 'epistemological' to an 'ontological' dominant.[4] By this he means a shift from the kind of perspectivism that allowed the modernist to get a better bearing on the meaning of a complex but nevertheless singular reality, to the fore-grounding of questions as to how radically different realities may coexist, collide, and interpenetrate. The boundary between fiction and science fiction has, as a consequence, effectively dissolved, while postmodernist characters often seem confused as to which world they are in, and how they should act with respect to it. Even to reduce the problem of perspective to autobiography, says one of Borges' characters, is to enter the labyrinth: 'Who was I? Today's self, bewildered, yesterday's, forgotten; tomorrow's, unpredictable?' The question marks tell it all.

In philosophy, the intermingling of a revived American pragmatism with the post-Marxist and post-structuralist wave that struck Paris after 1968 produced what Bernstein calls 'a rage against humanism and the Enlightenment legacy'.[5] This spilled over into a vigorous denunciation of abstract reason and a deep aversion to any project that sought universal human emancipation through mobilization of the powers of technology, science, and reason. Here, also, no less a person that Pope John Paul II has entered the fray on the side of the post-modern. The Pope 'does not attack Marxism or liberal secularism because they are the wave of the future', says Rocco Buttiglione, a theologian close to the Pope, but because the 'philosophies of the twentieth century have lost their appeal, their time has already passed'. The moral crisis of our time is a crisis of Enlightenment thought. For while the latter may indeed have allowed man to emancipate himself 'from community and tradition of the Middle Ages in which his individual freedom was submerged', the Enlightenment affirmation of 'self without God' in the end negated itself because reason, a means, was left, in the absence of God's truth, without any spiritual or moral goal. If lust and power are 'the only values that don't need the light of reason to be discovered', then reason had to become a mere instrument to subjugate others (*Baltimore Sun*, 9 September 1987). The postmodern theological project is to reaffirm God's truth without abandoning the powers of reason.

With such illustrious (and centrist) figures as the Prince of Wales and Pope John Paul II resorting to postmodernist rhetoric and argumentation, there can be little doubt as to the breadth of change that has occurred in 'the structure of feeling' in the 1980s. Yet there is still abundant confusion as to what the new 'structure of feeling' might entail. Modernist sentiments may have been under-mined, deconstructed, surpassed, or bypassed, but there is little certitude as to the coherence or meaning of the systems of thought that may have replaced them. Such uncertainty makes it peculiarly difficult to evaluate, interpret and explain the shift that everyone agrees has occurred.

Does postmodernism, for example, represent a radical break with mod-ernism, or is it simply a revolt within modernism against a certain form of 'high modernism' as represented, say, in the architecture of Mies van der Rohe and the blank surfaces of minimalist abstract expressionist painting? Is post-modernism a style (in which case we can reasonably trace its precursors back to Dada, Nietzsche, or even, as Kroker and Cook prefer,[6] to St Augustine's *Confessions* in the fourth century) or should we view it strictly as a periodizing concept (in which case we debate whether it originated in the 1950s, 1960s, or 1970s)? Does it have a revolutionary potential by virtue of its opposition to all forms of meta-narratives (including Marxism, Freudianism, and all forms of Enlightenment reason) and its close attention to 'other worlds' and to 'other voices' that have for too long been silenced (women, gays, blacks, colonized peoples with their own histories)? Or is it simply the commercial-ization and domestication of modernism, and a reduction of the latter's already tarnished aspirations to a *laissez-faire*, 'anything goes' market eclecticism? Does it, therefore, undermine or integrate with neo-conservative politics? And do we attach its rise to some radical restructuring of capitalism, the emergence of some 'postindustrial' society, view it, even, as the 'art of an inflationary era' or as the 'cultural logic of late capitalism' (as Newman and Jameson have proposed)?

We can, I think, begin to get a grip on these difficult questions by casting an eye over the schematic differences between modernism and postmodernism as laid out by Hassan (see table 24.1).[7] Hassan sets up a series of stylistic oppositions in order to capture the ways in which postmodernism might be portrayed as a reaction to the modern. I say 'might' because I think it dangerous (as does Hassan) to depict complex relations as simple polarizations, when almost certainly the true state of sensibility, the real 'structure of feeling' in both the modern and postmodern periods, lies in the manner in which these stylistic oppositions are synthesized. Nevertheless, I think Hassan's tabular schema provides a useful starting point.

Table 24.1 Schematic differences between modernism and postmodernism[8]

modernism	postmodernism
romanticism/Symbolism	paraphysics/Dadaism
form (conjunctive, closed)	antiform (disjunctive, open)
purpose	play
design	chance
hierarchy	anarchy
mastery/logos	exhaustion/silence
art object/finished work	process/performance/happening
distance	participation
creation/totalization/synthesis	decreation/deconstruction/antithesis
presence	absence
centring	dispersal
genre/boundary	text/intertext
semantics	rhetoric
paradigm	syntagm
hypotaxis	parataxis
metaphor	metonymy
selection	combination
root/depth	rhizome/surface
interpretation/reading	against interpretation /misreading
signified	signifier
lisible (readerly)	scriptible (writerly)
narrative/*grand histoire*	anti-narrative/*petite histoire*
master code	idiolect
symptom	desire
type	mutant
genital/phallic	polymorphous/androgynous
paranoia	schizophrenia

origin/cause	difference-difference/trace
God the Father	The Holy Ghost
metaphysics	irony
determinacy	indeterminacy
transcendence	immanence

There is much to contemplate in this schema, drawing as it does on fields as diverse as linguistics, anthropology, philosophy, rhetoric, political science and theology. Hassan is quick to point out how the dichotomies are themselves insecure, equivocal. Yet there is much here that captures a sense of what the differences might be. 'Modernist' town planners, for example, do tend to look for 'mastery' of the metropolis as a 'totality' by deliberately designing a 'closed form', whereas postmodernists tend to view the urban process as uncontrollable and 'chaotic', one in which 'anarchy' and 'change' can 'play' in entirely 'open' situations. 'Modernist' literary critics do tend to look at works as examples of a 'genre' and to judge them by the 'master code' that prevails within the 'boundary' of the genre, whereas the 'postmodern' style is simply to view a work as a 'text' with its own particular 'rhetoric' and 'idiolect', but which can in principle be compared with any other text of no matter what sort. Hassan's oppositions may be caricatures, but there is scarcely an arena of present intellectual practice where we cannot spot some of them at work. In what follows I shall try and take up a few of them in the richer detail they deserve.

I begin with what appears to be the most startling fact about postmodernism: its total acceptance of the ephemerality, fragmentation, discontinuity and the chaotic that formed the one half of Baudelaire's conception of modernity. But postmodernism responds to the fact of that in a very particular way. It does not try to transcend it, counteract it, or even to define the 'eternal and immutable' elements that might lie within it. Postmodernism swims, even wallows, in the fragmentary and the chaotic currents of change as if that is all there is. Foucault instructs us, for example, to 'develop action, thought, and desires by proliferation, juxtaposition, and disjunction', and 'to prefer what is positive and multiple, difference over uniformity, flows over unities, mobile arrangements over systems. Believe that what is productive is not sedentary but nomadic'.[9] To the degree that it does try to legitimate itself by reference to the past, therefore, postmodernism typically harks back to that wing of thought, Nietzschean in particular, that emphasizes the deep chaos of modern life and its intractability before rational thought. This does not imply, however, that postmodernism is simply a version of modernism; real revolutions in sensibility can occur when latent and dominated ideas in one period become explicit and dominant in another. Nevertheless, the continuity of the condition of fragmentation, ephemerality, discontinuity, and chaotic change in both modernist and postmodernist thought is important. I shall make much of it in what follows.

Embracing the fragmentation and ephemerality in an affirmative fashion

implies a whole host of consequences that bear directly on Hassan's oppositions. To begin with, we find writers like Foucault and Lyotard explicitly
attacking any notion that there might be a meta-language, meta-narrative, or
meta-theory through which all things can be connected or represented.
Universal and eternal truths, if they exist at all, cannot be specified.
Condemning meta-narratives (broad interpretative schemas like those
deployed by Marx or Freud) as 'totalizing', they insist upon the plurality of
'power-discourse' formations (Foucault), or of 'language games' (Lyotard).
Lyotard in fact defines the postmodern simply as 'incredulity towards meta-
narratives'.

Foucault's ideas – particularly as developed in his early works – deserve
attention since they have been a fecund source for postmodernist argument.
The relation between power and knowledge is a central theme there. But
Foucault breaks with the notion that power is ultimately located within the
state,[10] and abjures us to 'conduct an *ascending* analysis of power, starting, that
is, from its infinitesimal mechanisms, which each have their own history, their
own trajectory, their own techniques and tactics, and then see how these mechanisms of power have been – and continue to be – invested, colonized, utilized,
involuted, transformed, displaced, extended, etc. by ever more general mechanisms and by forms of global domination'. Close scrutiny of the micro-politics
of power relations in different localities, contexts, and social situations leads
him to conclude that there is an intimate relation between the systems of knowledge ('discourses') which codify techniques and practices for the exercise of
social control and domination within particular localized contexts. The prison,
the asylum, the hospital, the university, the school, the psychiatrist's office, are
all examples of sites where a dispersed and piecemeal organization of power
is built up independently of any systematic strategy of class domination. What
happens at each site cannot be understood by appeal to some overarching
general theory. Indeed the only irreducible in Foucault's scheme of things is
the human body, for that is the 'site' at which all forms of repression are ultimately registered. So while there are, in Foucault's celebrated dictum, 'no
relations of power without resistances', he equally insists that no utopian
scheme can ever hope to escape the power-knowledge relation in non-
repressive ways. He here echoes Max Weber's pessimism as to our ability to
avoid the 'iron cage' of repressive bureaucratic-technical rationality. More
particularly, he interprets Soviet repression as the inevitable outcome of a
utopian revolutionary theory (Marxism) which appealed to the same techniques and knowledge systems as those embedded in the capitalist system it
sought to replace. The only way open to 'eliminate the fascism in our heads' is
to explore and build upon the open qualities of human discourse, and thereby
intervene in the way knowledge is produced and constituted at the particular
sites where a localized power-discourse prevails. Foucault's work with homo-
sexuals and prisoners was not aimed at producing reforms in state practices,
but dedicated to the cultivation and enhancement of localized resistance to the
institutions, techniques and discourses of organized repression.

Foucault evidently believed that it was only through such a multifaceted and pluralistic attack upon localized practices of repression that any global challenge to capitalism might be mounted without replicating all the multiple repressions of capitalism in a new form. His ideas appeal to the various social movements that sprang into existence during the 1960s (feminists, gays, ethnic and religious groupings, regional autonomists, etc.) as well as to those disillusioned with the practices of communism and the politics of communist parties. Yet it leaves open, particularly so in the deliberate rejection of any holistic theory of capitalism, the question of the path whereby such localized struggles might add up to a progressive, rather than regressive, attack upon the central forms of capitalist exploitation and repression. Localized struggles of the sort that Foucault appears to encourage have not generally had the effect of challenging capitalism, though Foucault might reasonably respond that only struggles fought in such a way as to challenge all forms of power-discourse might have such a result.

Lyotard, for his part, puts a similar argument, though on a rather different basis. He takes the modernist preoccupation with language and pushes it to extremes of dispersal. While 'the social bond is linguistic', he argues, it 'is not woven with a single thread' but by an 'indeterminate number' of 'language games'. Each of us lives 'at the intersection of many of these' and we do not necessarily establish 'stable language combinations and the properties of the ones we do establish are not necessarily communicable'. As a consequence, 'the social subject itself seems to dissolve in this dissemination of language games'. Interestingly, Lyotard here employs a lengthy metaphor of Wittgenstein's (the pioneer of the theory of language games), to illuminate the condition of postmodern knowledge: 'Our language can be seen as an ancient city: a maze of little streets and squares, of old and new houses, and of houses with additions from different periods; and this surrounded by a multitude of new boroughs with straight regular streets and uniform houses'.

The 'atomization of the social into flexible networks of language games' suggests that each of us may resort to a quite different set of codes depending upon the situation in which we find ourselves (at home, at work, at church, in the street or pub, at a memorial service, etc.). To the degree that Lyotard (like Foucault) accepts that 'knowledge is the principal force of production' these days, so the problem is to define the locus of that power when it is evidently 'dispersed in clouds of narrative elements' within a heterogeneity of language games. Lyotard (again like Foucault) accepts the potential open qualities of ordinary conversations in which rules can bend and shift so as 'to encourage the greatest flexibility of utterance'. He makes much of the seeming contradiction between this openness and the rigidities with which institutions (Foucault's 'non-discursive domains') circumscribe what is or is not admissible within their boundaries. The realms of law, of the academy, of science and bureaucratic government, of military and political control, of electoral politics, and corporate power, all circumscribe what can be said and how it can be said in important ways. But the 'limits the institution imposes on potential language "moves" are never established once and for all', they are 'themselves the stakes and provisional results of language strategies, within the institution and without'. We ought not, therefore, to reify institutions prematurely, but to recognize how the differentiated performance of language games creates institutional languages and powers in the first place. If 'there are many different language games – a heterogeneity of elements' we have then also to recognize that they can 'only give rise to institutions in patches – local determinism'.

Such 'local determinisms' have been understood by others as 'interpretative communities',[11] made up of both producers and consumers of particular kinds of knowledge, of texts, often operating within a particular institutional context (such as the university, the legal system, religious groupings), within particular divisions of cultural labour (such as architecture, painting, theatre, dance), or within particular places (neighbourhoods, nations, etc.) Individuals and groups are held to control mutually within these domains what they consider to be valid knowledge.

To the degree that multiple sources of oppression in society and multiple foci of resistance to domination can be identified, so this kind of thinking has been taken up in radical politics, even imported into the heart of Marxism itself. We thus find Aronowitz arguing in *The Crisis of Historical Materialism* that 'the multiple, local, autonomous struggles for liberation occurring throughout the postmodern world make all incarnations of master discourses absolutely illegitimate'.[12] Aronowitz is here seduced, I suspect, by the most liberative and therefore most appealing aspect of postmodern thought – its concern with 'otherness'. Huyssens particularly castigates the imperialism of an enlightened modernity that presumed to speak for others (colonized peoples, blacks and minorities, religious groups, women, the working class) with a unified voice.[13] The very title of Carol Gilligan's *In a Different Voice* – a feminist work which challenges the male bias in setting out fixed stages in the moral development of personality – illustrates a process of counterattack upon such universalizing presumptions.[14] The idea that all groups have a right to speak for themselves, in their own voice, and have that voice accepted as authentic and legitimate is essential to the pluralistic stance of postmodernism. Foucault's work with marginal and interstitial groups has influenced a whole host of researchers, in fields as diverse as criminology and anthropology, into new ways to re-construct and represent the voices and experiences of their subjects. Huyssens, for his part, emphasizes the opening given in postmodernism to understanding difference and otherness, as well as the liberatory potential it offers for a whole host of new social movements (women, gays, blacks, ecologists, regional auton-omists, etc.). Curiously, most movements of this sort, though they have definitely helped change 'the structure of feeling', pay scant attention to post-modernist arguments.[15] [. . .]

Interestingly, we can detect this same preoccupation with 'otherness' and 'other worlds' in postmodernist fiction. McHale, in emphasizing the pluralism of worlds that coexist within postmodernist fiction, finds Foucault's concept of a *heterotopia* a perfectly appropriate image to capture what that fiction is striving to depict. By heterotopia, Foucault means the coexistence in 'an impossible space' of a 'large number of fragmentary possible worlds' or, more simply, incommensurable spaces that are juxtaposed or superimposed upon each other. Characters no longer contemplate how they can unravel or unmask a central mystery, but are forced to ask, 'Which world is this? What is to be done in it? Which of myselves is to do it?' instead. The same shift can be detected in the cinema. In a modernist classic like *Citizen Kane* a reporter seeks to unravel the mystery of Kane's life and character by collecting multiple reminiscences and perspectives from those who had known him. In the more postmodernist format of the contemporary cinema we find, in a film like *Blue Velvet*, the central character revolving between two quite incongruous worlds – that of a conventional 1950s small-town America with its high school, drugstore culture, and a bizarre, violent, sex-crazed underworld of drugs, dementia and sexual perversion. It seems impossible that these two worlds should exist in the same space, and the central character moves between them, unsure which is the true reality, until the two worlds collide in a terrible denouement. A postmodernist painter like David Salle likewise tends to 'collage together incompatible source materials as an alternative to choosing between them'.[16] Pfeil even goes so far as to depict the total field of postmodernism as 'a distilled representation of the whole antagonistic, voracious world of otherness'.[17]

But to accept the fragmentation, the pluralism, and the authenticity of other voices and other worlds poses the acute problem of communication and the means of exercising power through command thereof. Most postmodernist thinkers are fascinated by the new possibilities for information and knowledge production, analysis and transfer. Lyotard, for example, firmly locates his arguments in the context of new technologies of communication and, drawing upon Bell's and Touraine's theses of the passage to a 'post-industrial' information-based society, situates the rise of postmodern thought in the heart of what he sees as a dramatic social and political transition in the languages of communication in advanced capitalist societies.[18] He looks closely at the new technologies for the production, dissemination and use of that knowledge as a 'principal force of production'. The problem, however, is that knowledge can now be coded in all kinds of ways, some of which are more accessible than others. There is more than a hint in Lyotard's work, therefore, that modernism has changed because the technical and social conditions of communication have changed.

Postmodernists tend to accept, also, a rather different theory as to what language and communication are all about. Whereas modernists had presupposed that there was a tight and identifiable relation between what was being said (the signified or 'message') and how it was being said (the signifier or 'medium'), post-structuralist thinking sees these as 'continually breaking apart and re-attaching in new combinations'. 'Deconstructionism' (a movement initiated by Derrida's reading of Martin Heidegger in the late 1960s) here enters the picture as a powerful stimulus to postmodernist ways of thought. Deconstructionism is less a philosophical position than a way of thinking about and 'reading' texts. Writers who create texts or use words do so on the basis of all the other texts and words they have encountered, while readers deal with them in the same way. Cultural life is then viewed as a series of texts intersecting with other texts, producing more texts (including that of the literary critic, who aims to produce another piece of literature in which texts under consideration are intersecting freely with other texts that happen to have affected his or her thinking). This intertextual weaving has a life of its own. Whatever we write conveys meanings we do not or could not possibly intend, and our words cannot say what we mean. It is vain to try and master a text because the perpetual interweaving of texts and meanings is beyond our control. Language works through us. Recognizing that, the deconstructionist impulse is to look inside one text for another, dissolve one text into another, or build one text into another.

Derrida considers, therefore, collage/montage as the primary form of postmodern discourse. The inherent heterogeneity of that (be it in painting, writing, architecture) stimulates us, the receivers of the text or image, 'to produce a signification which could be neither univocal nor stable'. Both producers and consumers of 'texts' (cultural artefacts) participate in the production of significations and meanings (hence Hassan's emphasis upon 'process', 'performance', 'happening', and 'participation' in the postmodernist style). Minimizing the authority of the cultural producer creates the opportunity for popular participation and democratic determinations of cultural values, but at the price of a certain incoherence or, more problematic, vulnerability to massmarket manipulation. However this may be, the cultural producer merely creates raw materials (fragments and elements), leaving it open to consumers to recombine those elements in any way they wish. The effect is to break (deconstruct) the power of the author to impose meanings or offer a continuous narrative. Each cited element says Derrida, 'breaks the continuity or the linearity of the discourse and leads necessarily to a double reading: that of the fragment perceived in relation to its text of origin; that of the fragment as incorporated into a new whole, a different totality'. Continuity is given only in 'the trace' of the fragment as it moves from production to consumption. The effect is to call into question all the illusions of fixed systems of representation.[19]

There is more than a hint of this sort of thinking within the modernist tradition (directly from surrealism, for example) and there is a danger here of thinking of the meta-narratives in the Enlightenment tradition as more fixed and stable than they truly were. Marx, as Ollman observes, deployed his concepts relationally, so that terms like value, labour, capital, are 'continually breaking apart and re-attaching in new combinations' in an open-ended struggle to come to terms with the totalizing processes of capitalism.[20] Benjamin, a complex thinker in the Marxist tradition, worked the idea of collage/montage to perfection, in order to try and capture the many-layered and fragmented relations between economy, politics and culture without ever abandoning the standpoint of a totality of practices that constitute capitalism. Taylor likewise concludes, after reviewing the historical evidence of its use (particularly by Picasso), that collage is a far from adequate indicator of difference between modernist and postmodernist painting.[21]

But if, as the postmodernists insist, we cannot aspire to any unified representation of the world, or picture it as a totality full of connections and differentiations rather than as perpetually shifting fragments, then how can we possibly aspire to act coherently with respect to the world? The simple postmodernist answer is that since coherent representation and action are either repressive or illusionary (and therefore doomed to be self-dissolving and self-defeating), we should not even try to engage in some global project. Pragmatism (of the Dewey sort) then becomes the only possible philosophy of action. We thus find Rorty, one of the major US philosophers in the postmodern movement, dismissing 'the canonical sequence of philosophers from Descartes to Nietzsche as a distraction from the history of concrete social engineering which made the contemporary North American culture what it is now, with all its glories and all its dangers.'[22] Action can be conceived of and decided only within the confines of some local determinism, some interpretative community, and its purported meanings and anticipated effects are bound to break down when taken out of these isolated domains, even when coherent within them. We similarly find Lyotard arguing that 'consensus has become an outmoded and suspect value' but then adding, rather surprisingly, that since 'justice as a value is neither outmoded nor suspect' (how it could remain such a universal, untouched by the diversity of language games, he does not tell us), we 'must arrive at an idea and practice of justice that is not linked to that of consensus'.[23]

It is precisely this kind of relativism and defeatism that Habermas seeks to combat in his defence of the Enlightenment project. While Habermas is more than willing to admit what he calls 'the deformed realization of reason in history' and the dangers that attach to the simplified imposition of some meta-narrative on complex relations and events, he also insists that 'theory can locate a gentle, but obstinate, a never silent although seldom redeemed claim to reason, a claim that must be recognized de facto whenever and wherever there is to be consensual action'. He, too, turns to the question of language, and in *The Theory of Communicative Action* insists upon the dialogical qualities of human communication in which speaker and hearer are necessarily oriented to the task of reciprocal understanding. Out of this, Habermas argues, consensual and normative statements do arise, thus grounding the role of universalizing reason in daily life. It is this that allows 'communicative reason to operate in history as an avenging force'. Habermas's critics are, however, more numerous than his defenders.

The portrait of postmodernism I have so far sketched in seems to depend for its validity upon a particular way of experiencing, interpreting, and being in the world. This brings us to what is, perhaps, the most problematic facet of postmodernism, its psychological pre-suppositions with respect to personality, motivation and behaviour. Preoccupation with the fragmentation and instability of language and discourses carries over directly, for example, into a certain conception of personality. Encapsulated, this conception focuses on schizophrenia (not, it should be emphasized, in its narrow clinical sense), rather than on alienation and paranoia (see Hassan's schema). Jameson explores this theme to very telling effect.[24] He uses Lacan's description of schizophrenia as a linguistic disorder, as a breakdown in the signifying chain of meaning that creates a simple sentence. When the signifying chain snaps, then 'we have schizophrenia in the form of a rubble of distinct and unrelated signifiers'. If personal identity is forged through 'a certain temporal unification of the past and future with the present before me', and if sentences move through the same trajectory, then an inability to unify past, present and future in the sentence betokens a similar inability to 'unify the past, present and future of our own biographical experience or psychic life'. This fits, of course, with postmodernism's preoccupation with the signifier rather than the signified, with participation, performance and happening rather than with an authoritative and finished art object, with surface appearances rather than roots (again, see Hassan's schema). The effect of such a breakdown in the signifying chain is to reduce experience to 'a series of pure and unrelated presents in time'. Offering no counterweight, Derrida's conception of language colludes in the production of a certain schizophrenic effect, thus, perhaps, explaining Eagleton's and Hassan's characterization of the typical postmodernist artefact as schizoid. Deleuze and Guattari, in their supposedly playful exposition *Anti-Oedipus*, hypothesize a relationship between schizophrenia and capitalism that prevails 'at the deepest level of one and the same economy, one and the same production process,' concluding that 'our society produces schizos the same way it produces Prell shampoo or Ford cars, the only difference being that the schizos are not saleable'.[25]

A number of consequences follow from the domination of this motif in postmodernist thought. We can no longer conceive of the individual as alienated in the classical Marxist sense, because to be alienated presupposes a coherent rather than a fragmented sense of self from which to be alienated. It is only in terms of such a centred sense of personal identity that individuals can pursue projects over time, or think cogently about the production of a future significantly better than time present and time past. Modernism was very much about the pursuit of better futures, even if perpetual frustration of that aim was conducive to paranoia. But postmodernism typically strips away that possibility by concentrating upon the schizophrenic circumstances induced by fragmentation and all those instabilities (including those of language) that prevent us even picturing coherently, let alone devising strategies to produce, some radically different future. Modernism, of course, was not without its schizoid moments – particularly when it sought to combine myth with heroic modernity – and there has been a sufficient history of the 'deformation of reason' and of 'reactionary modernisms' to suggest that the schizophrenic circumstance, though for the most part dominated, was always latent within the modernist movement. Nevertheless, there is good reason to believe that 'alienation of the subject is displaced by fragmentation of the subject' in postmodern aesthetics.[26] If, as Marx insisted, it takes the alienated individual to pursue the Enlightenment project with a tenacity and coherence sufficient to bring us to some better future, then loss of the alienated subject would seem to preclude the conscious construction of alternative social futures.

The reduction of experience to 'a series of pure and unrelated presents' further implies that the 'experience of the present becomes powerfully, overwhelmingly vivid and "material": the world comes before the schizophrenic with heightened intensity, bearing the mysterious and oppressive charge of affect, glowing with hallucinatory energy'.[27] The image, the appearance, the spectacle can all be experienced with an intensity (joy or terror) made possible only by their appreciation as pure and unrelated presents in time. So what does it matter 'if the world thereby momentarily loses its depth and threatens to become a glossy skin, a stereoscopic illusion, a rush of filmic images without density?'[28] The immediacy of events, the sensationalism of the spectacle (political, scientific, military, as well as those of entertainment), become the stuff of which consciousness is forged.

Notes

1   *PRECIS* 6 *The culture of fragments* (New York: Columbia University Graduate School of Architecture, 1987).
2   A. Huyssens (1984), 'Mapping the post-modern', *New German Critique*, 33, pp. 5–52.
3   Douglas Lee (1973), 'Requiem for large-scale planning models', *Journal of the American Institute of Planners* 39, pp. 117–42.
4   B. McHale, *Postmodernist Fiction* (London, 1987).
5   R. Bernstein (ed.), *Habermas and Modernity* (Oxford, 1985), p. 25.
6   A. Kroker and D. Cook, *The Postmodern Scene: excremental culture and hyper-aesthetics* (New York, 1986).
7   I. Hassan, *Paracriticisms: seven speculations of the times* (Urbana, IL, 1975); I. Hassan (1985), 'The culture of postmodernism', *Theory, Culture and Society* 2, (3), pp. 119–32.
8   Ibid., pp. 123–4.
9   Michel Foucault, *The Foucault Reader*, ed. P. Rabinow (Harmondsworth, 1984), p. xiii.
10 Michel Foucault, *Power/knowledge* (New York, 1972), p. 159.
11 Stanley Fish, *Is there a Text in this Class? The authority of interpretive communities* (Cambridge, MA, 1980).
12 P. Bove (1986), 'The ineluctability of difference: scientific pluralism and the critical intelligence.' In J. Arac (ed.), *Postmodernism and Politics* (Manchester, 1986), p. 18.
13 A. Huyssens, 'Mapping the post-modern'.
14 Carol Gilligan, *In a Different Voice: psychological theory and women's development* (Cambridge, MA, 1982).
15 N. Hartsock (1987), 'Rethinking modernism: minority versus majority theories', *Cultural Critique* 7, pp. 187–206.
16 B. Taylor, *Modernism, Post-modernism, Realism: a critical perspective for art* (Winchester, 1987), p. 8.

17   F. Pfeil, 'Postmodernism as a "structure of feeling".' In C. Nelson and L. Grossberg (eds), *Marxism and the Interpretation of Culture* (Urbana, IL, 1988).
18   Jean-François Lyotard, *The Postmodern Condition* (Manchester, 1984).
19   H. Foster (ed.), *The Anti-aesthetic: essays on postmodern culture* (Port Townsend, Washington, 1983), p. 142.
20   B. Ollman, *Alienation* (Cambridge, 1971).
21   B. Taylor (1987), *Modernism, Post-modernism, Realism,* pp. 53–65.
22   Richard Rorty, 'Habermas and Lyotard on postmodernity.' In R. Bernstein (ed.), *Habermas and modernity* (Oxford, 1985), p. 173.
23   Jean-François Lyotard (1984), *The Postmodern Condition*, p. 66.
24   Fredric Jameson (1984b), 'Postmodernism, or the cultural logic of late capitalism', *New Left Review* 146, pp. 53–92.
25   G. Deleuze and F. Guattari, *Anti-Oedipus: capitalism and schizophrenia* (London, 1984), p. 245.
26   Fredric Jameson (1984a), 'The politics of theory: ideological positions in the post-modernism debate', *New German Critique* 33, p. 63.
27   Fredric Jameson (1984b), 'Postmodernism, or the cultural logic of late capitalism, p. 120.
28   Ibid.

The Postmodern Condition

Jean-François Lyotard

The Field: Knowledge in Computerized Societies

Our working hypothesis is that the status of knowledge is altered as societies enter what is known as the post-industrial age and cultures enter what is known as the postmodern age.[1] This transition has been under way since at least the end of the 1950s, which for Europe marks the completion of reconstruction. The pace is faster or slower depending on the country, and within countries it varies according to the sector of activity: the general situation is one of temporal disjunction which makes sketching an overview difficult.[2] A portion of the description would necessarily be conjectural. At any rate, we know that it is unwise to put too much faith in futurology.[3]

Rather than painting a picture that would inevitably remain incomplete, I will take as my point of departure a single feature, one that immediately defines our object of study. Scientific knowledge is a kind of discourse. And it is fair to say that for the last forty years the "leading" sciences and technologies have had to do with language: phonology and theories of linguistics,[4] problems of communication and cybernetics,[5] modern theories of algebra and informatics,[6] computers and their languages,[7] problems of translation and the search for areas of compatibility among computer languages,[8] problems of information storage and data banks,[9] telematics and the perfection of intelligent terminals,[10] paradoxology.[11] The facts speak for themselves (and this list is not exhaustive).

These technological transformations can be expected to have a considerable impact on knowledge. Its two principal functions – research and the transmission of acquired learning – are already feeling the effect, or will in the future. With respect to the first function, genetics provides an example that is accessible to the layman: it owes its theoretical paradigm to cybernetics. Many other examples could be cited. As for the second function, it is common knowledge that the miniaturization and commercialization of machines is already changing the way in which learning is acquired, classified, made available, and exploited. It is reasonable to suppose that the proliferation of information-processing machines is having, and will continue to have, as much of an effect on the circulation of learning as did advancements in human circulation (transportation systems) and later, in the circulation of sounds and visual images (the media).[12]

The nature of knowledge cannot survive unchanged within this context of general transformation. It can fit into the new channels, and become operational, only if learning is translated into quantities of information.[13] We can predict that anything in the constituted body of knowledge that is not translatable in this way will be abandoned and that the direction of new research will be dictated by the possibility of its eventual results being translatable into computer language. The "producers" and users of knowledge must now, and will have to, possess the means of translating into these languages whatever they want to invent or learn. Research on translating machines is already well advanced.[14] Along with the hegemony of computers comes a certain logic, and therefore a certain set of prescriptions determining which statements are accepted as "knowledge" statements.

We may thus expect a thorough exteriorization of knowledge with respect to the "knower," at whatever point he or she may occupy in the knowledge process. The old principle that the acquisition of knowledge is indissociable from the training (*Bildung*) of minds, or even of individuals, is becoming obsolete and will become ever more so. The relationship of the suppliers and users of knowledge to the knowledge they supply and use is now tending, and will increasingly tend, to assume the form already taken by the relationship of commodity producers and consumers to the commodities they produce and consume – that is, the form of value. Knowledge is and will be produced in order to be sold, it is and will be consumed in order to be valorized in a new production: in both cases, the goal is exchange. Knowledge ceases to be an end in itself, it loses its use-value.[15]

It is widely accepted that knowledge has become the principle force of production over the last few decades;[16] this has already had a noticeable effect on the composition of the work force of the most highly developed countries[17] and constitutes the major bottleneck for the developing countries. In the post-industrial and postmodern age, science will maintain and no doubt strengthen its preeminence in the arsenal of productive capacities of the nation-states. Indeed, this situation is one of the reasons leading to the conclusion that the gap between developed and developing countries will grow ever wider in the future.[18]

But this aspect of the problem should not be allowed to overshadow the other, which is complementary to it. Knowledge in the form of an informational commodity indispensable to productive power is already, and will continue to be, a major – perhaps *the* major – stake in the worldwide competition for power. It is conceivable that the nation-states will one day fight for control of information, just as they battled in the past for control over territory, and afterwards for control of access to and exploitation of raw materials and cheap labor. A new field is opened for industrial and commercial strategies on the one hand, and political and military strategies on the other.[19]

However, the perspective I have outlined above is not as simple as I have made it appear. For the mercantilization of knowledge is bound to affect the privilege the nation-states have enjoyed, and still enjoy, with respect to the production and distribution of learning. The notion that learning falls within the purview of the State, as the brain or mind of society, will become more and more outdated with the increasing strength of the opposing principle, according to which society exists and progresses only if the messages circulating within it are rich in information and easy to decode. The ideology of communicational "transparency," which goes hand in hand with the commercialization of knowledge, will begin to perceive the State as a factor of opacity and "noise." It is from this point of view that the problem of the relationship between economic and State powers threatens to arise with a new urgency.

Already in the last few decades, economic powers have reached the point of imperiling the stability of the State through new forms of the circulation of capital that go by the generic name of *multinational corporations*. These new forms of circulation imply that investment decisions have, at least in part, passed beyond the control of the nation-states.[20] The question threatens to become even more thorny with the development of computer technology and telematics. Suppose, for example, that a firm such as IBM is authorized to occupy a belt in the earth's orbital field and launch communications satellites or satellites housing data banks. Who will have access to them? Who will determine which channels or data are forbidden? The State? Or will the State simply be one user among others? New legal issues will be raised, and with them the question: "who will know?"

Transformation in the nature of knowledge, then, could well have repercussions on the existing public powers, forcing them to reconsider their relations (both de jure and de facto) with the large corporations and, more generally, with civil society. The reopening of the world market, a return to vigorous economic competition, the breakdown of the hegemony of American capitalism, the decline of the socialist alternative, a probable opening of the Chinese market – these and many other factors are already, at the end of the 1970s, preparing States for a serious reappraisal of the role they have been accustomed to playing since the 1930s: that of guiding, or even directing investments.[21] In this light, the new technologies can only increase the urgency of such a re-examination, since they make the information used in decision making (and therefore the means of control) even more mobile and subject to piracy.

It is not hard to visualize learning circulating along the same lines as money, instead of for its "educational" value or political (administrative, diplomatic, military) importance; the pertinent distinction would no longer be between knowledge and ignorance, but rather, as is the case with money, between "payment knowledge" and "investment knowledge" – in other words, between units of knowledge exchanged in a daily maintenance frame-work (the reconstitution of the work force, "survival") versus funds of knowledge dedicated to optimizing the performance of a project.

If this were the case, communicational transparency would be similar to liberalism. Liberalism does not preclude an organization of the flow of money in which some channels are used in decision making while others are only good for the payment of debts. One could similarly imagine flows of knowledge traveling along identical channels of identical nature, some of which would be reserved for the "decision makers," while the others would be used to repay each person's perpetual debt with respect to the social bond. [. . .]

Delegitimation

In contemporary society and culture – post-industrial society, postmodern culture[22] – the question of the legitimation of knowledge is formulated in different terms. The grand narrative has lost its credibility, regardless of what mode of unification it uses, regardless of whether it is a speculative narrative or a narrative of emancipation.

The decline of narrative can be seen as an effect of the blossoming of tech-niques and technologies since World War II, which has shifted emphasis from the ends of action to its means; it can also be seen as an effect of the redeploy-ment of advanced liberal capitalism after its retreat under the protection of Keynesianism during the period 1930–60, a renewal that has eliminated the communist alternative and valorized the individual enjoyment of goods and services.

Anytime we go searching for causes in this way we are bound to be dis-appointed. Even if we adopted one or the other of these hypotheses, we would still have to detail the correlation between the tendencies mentioned and the decline of the unifying and legitimating power of the grand narratives of specu-lation and emancipation.

It is, of course, understandable that both capitalist renewal and prosperity and the disorienting upsurge of technology would have an impact on the status of knowledge. But in order to understand how contemporary science could have been susceptible to those effects long before they took place, we must first locate the seeds of "delegitimation"[23] and nihilism that were inherent in the grand narratives of the nineteenth century.

First of all, the speculative apparatus maintains an ambigious relation to knowledge. It shows that knowledge is only worthy of that name to the extent that it reduplicates itself ("lifts itself up," *hebt sich auf*, is sublated) by citing its own statements in a second-level discourse (autonymy) that functions to legiti-mate them. This is as much as to say that, in its immediacy, denotative discourse bearing on a certain referent (a living organism, a chemical property, a physical phenomenon, etc.) does not really know what it thinks it knows. Positive science is not a form of knowledge. And speculation feeds on its suppression. The Hegelian speculative narrative thus harbors a certain skepticism toward positive learning, as Hegel himself admits.[24]

A science that has not legitimated itself is not a true science; if the discourse that was meant to legitimate it seems to belong to a prescientific form of knowledge, like a "vulgar" narrative, it is demoted to the lowest rank, that of an ideology or instrument of power. And this always happens if the rules of the science game that discourse denounces as empirical are applied to science itself.

Take for example the speculative statement: "A scientific statement is knowledge if and only if it can take its place in a universal process of engendering." The question is: Is this statement knowledge as it itself defines it? Only if it can take its place in a universal process of engendering. Which it can. All it has to do is to presuppose that such a process exists (the Life of spirit) and that it is itself an expression of that process. This presupposition, in fact, is indispensable to the speculative language game. Without it, the language of legitimation would not be legitimate; it would accompany science in a nosedive into nonsense, at least if we take idealism's word for it.

But this presupposition can also be understood in a totally different sense, one which takes us in the direction of postmodern culture: we could say, in keeping with the perspective we adopted earlier, that this presupposition defines the set of rules one must accept in order to play the speculative game.[25] Such an appraisal assumes first that we accept that the "positive" sciences represent the general mode of knowledge and second, that we understand this language to imply certain formal and axiomatic presuppositions that it must always make explicit. This is exactly what Nietzsche is doing, though with a different terminology, when he shows that "European nihilism" resulted from the truth requirement of science being turned back against itself.[26]

There thus arises an idea of perspective that is not far removed, at least in this respect, from the idea of language games. What we have here is a process of delegitimation fueled by the demand for legitimation itself. The "crisis" of scientific knowledge, signs of which have been accumulating since the end of the nineteenth century, is not born of a chance proliferation of sciences, itself an effect of progress in technology and the expansion of capitalism. It represents, rather, an internal erosion of the legitimacy principle of knowledge. There is erosion at work inside the speculative game, and by loosening the weave of the encyclopedic net in which each science was to find its place, it eventually sets them free.

The classical dividing lines between the various fields of science are thus called into question – disciplines disappear, overlappings occur at the borders between sciences, and from these new territories are born. The speculative hierarchy of learning gives way to an immanent and, as it were, "flat" network of areas of inquiry, the respective frontiers of which are in constant flux. The old "faculties" splinter into institutes and foundations of all kinds, and the universities lose their function of speculative legitimation. Stripped of the responsibility for research (which was stifled by the speculative narrative), they limit themselves to the transmission of what is judged to be established knowledge, and through didactics they guarantee the replication of teachers rather than the production of researchers. This is the state in which Nietzsche finds and condemns them.[27]

The potential for erosion intrinsic to the other legitimation procedure, the emancipation apparatus flowing from the *Aufklärung*, is no less extensive than the one at work within speculative discourse. But it touches a different aspect. Its distinguishing characteristic is that it grounds the legitimation of science and truth in the autonomy of interlocutors involved in ethical, social, and political praxis. As we have seen, there are immediate problems with this form of legitimation: the difference between a denotative statement with cognitive value and a prescriptive statement with practical value is one of relevance, therefore of competence. There is nothing to prove that if a statement describing a real situation is true, it follows that a prescriptive statement based upon it (the effect of which will necessarily be a modification of that reality) will be just.

Take, for example, a closed door. Between "The door is closed" and "Open the door" there is no relation of consequence as defined in propositional logic. The two statements belong to two autonomous sets of rules defining different kinds of relevance, and therefore of competence. Here, the effect of dividing reason into cognitive or theoretical reason on the one hand, and practical reason on the other, is to attack the legitimacy of the discourse of science. Not directly, but indirectly, by revealing that it is a language game with its own rules (of which the a priori conditions of knowledge in Kant provide a first glimpse) and that it has no special calling to supervise the game of praxis (nor the game of aesthetics, for that matter). The game of science is thus put on a par with the others.

If this "delegitimation" is pursued in the slightest and if its scope is widened (as Wittgenstein does in his own way, and thinkers such as Martin Buber and Emmanuel Lévinas in theirs)[28] the road is then open for an important current of postmodernity: science plays its own game; it is incapable of legitimating the other language games. The game of prescription, for example, escapes it. But above all, it is incapable of legitimating itself, as speculation assumed it could.

The social subject itself seems to dissolve in this dissemination of language games. The social bond is linguistic, but is not woven with a single thread. It is a fabric formed by the intersection of at least two (and in reality an indeterminate number) of language games, obeying different rules. Wittgenstein writes: "Our language can be seen as an ancient city: a maze of little streets and squares, of old and new houses, and of houses with additions from various periods; and this surrounded by a multitude of new boroughs with straight regular streets and uniform houses."[29] And to drive home that the principle of unitotality – or synthesis under the authority of a metadiscourse of knowledge – is inapplicable, he subjects the "town" of language to the old sorites paradox by asking: "how many houses or streets does it take before a town begins to be a town?"[30]

New languages are added to the old ones, forming suburbs of the old town: "the symbolism of chemistry and the notation of the infinitesimal calculus."[31] Thirty-five years later we can add to the list: machine languages, the matrices of game theory, new systems of musical notation, systems of notation for nondenotative forms of logic (temporal logics, deontic logics, modal logics), the language of the genetic code, graphs of phonological structures, and so on.

We may form a pessimistic impression of this splintering: nobody speaks all of those languages, they have no universal metalanguage, the project of the system–subject is a failure, the goal of emancipation has nothing to do with science, we are all stuck in the positivism of this or that discipline of learning, the learned scholars have turned into scientists, the diminished tasks of research have become compartmentalized and no one can master them all.[32] Speculative or humanistic philosophy is forced to relinquish its legitimation duties,[33] which explains why philosophy is facing a crisis wherever it persists in arrogating such functions and is reduced to the study of systems of logic or the history of ideas where it has been realistic enough to surrender them.[34]

Turn-of-the-century Vienna was weaned on this pessimism: not just artists such as Musil, Kraus, Hofmannsthal, Loos, Schönberg, and Broch, but also the philosophers Mach and Wittgenstein.[35] They carried awareness of and theoretical and artistic responsibility for delegitimation as far as it could be taken. We can say today that the mourning process has been completed. There is no need to start all over again. Wittgenstein's strength is that he did not opt for the positivism that was being developed by the Vienna Circle,[36] but outlined in his investigation of language games a kind of legitimation not based on performativity. That is what the postmodern world is all about. Most people have lost the nostalgia for the lost narrative. It in no way follows that they are reduced to barbarity. What saves them from it is their knowledge that legitimation can only spring from their own linguistic practice and communicational interaction. Science "smiling into its beard" at every other belief has taught them the harsh austerity of realism.[37]

Notes

1   Alain Touraine, *La Société postindustrielle* (Paris: Denoël, 1969) [Eng. trans. by Leonard Mayhew, *The Post-Industrial Society* (London: Wildwood House, 1974)]; Daniel Bell, *The Coming of Post-Industrial Society* (New York: Basic Books, 1973); Ihab Hassan, *The Dismemberment of Orpheus: Toward a PostModern Literature* (New York: Oxford University Press, 1971); Michel Benamou and Charles Caramello (eds), *Performance in Postmodern Culture* (Wisconsin: Center for Twentieth Century Studies & Coda Press, 1977); M. Köhler (1977), "Postmodernismus: ein begriffgeschichtlicher Ueberblick." *Amerikastudien* 22, p. 1.

2   An already classic literary expression of this is provided in Michel Butor, *Mobile: Etude pour une représentation des Etats-Unis* (Paris: Gallimard, 1962).

3   Jib Fowles (ed.), *Handbook of Futures Research* (Westport, Conn.: Greenwood Press, 1978).

4   Nikolai S. Trubetskoi, *Grundzüge der Phonologie* (Prague: Travaux du cercle linguistique de Prague, vol. 7, 1939) [Eng. trans. by Christiane Baltaxe *Principles of Phonology* (Berkeley: University of California Press, 1969)].

5   Norbert Wiener, *Cybernetics and Society: The Human Use of Human Beings* (Boston: Houghton Mifflin, 1949); William Ross Ashby, *An Introduction to Cybernetics* (London: Chapman & Hall, 1956).

6   See the work of Johannes von Neumann (1903–57).

7   S. Bellert, "La Formalisation des systémes cybernétiques." In *Le Concept d'information dans la science contemporaine* (Paris: Minuit, 1965).

8   Georges Mounin, *Les Problémes théoriques de la traduction* (Paris: Gallimard, 1963). The computer revolution dates from 1965, with the new generation of IBM 360s; R. Moch, "Le Tournant informatique." *Documents contributifs*, Annex 4, *L'Informatisation de la société* (Paris: La Documentation française, 1978); R. M. Ashby (1970), "La Seconde Génération de la micro-électronique." *La Recherche* 2, June, pp. 127ff.

9   C. L. Gaudfernan and A. Taïb, "Glossaire." In P. Nora and A. Minc, *L'Informatisation de la sociétié* (Paris: La Documentation française, 1978); R. Béca, "Les Banques de données." *Nouvelle informatique et nouvelle croissance*, Annex 1, *L'Informatisation de la sociétié*.

10 L. Joycux, "Les Applications avancées de l'informatique." *Documents contributifs*. [. . .]

11 Paul Watzlawick, Janet Helmick-Beavin, and Don D. Jackson, *Pragmatics of Human Communication: A Study of Interactional Patterns, Pathologies, and Paradoxes* (New York: Norton, 1967).

12 L. Brunel, *Des Machines et des hommes* (Montréal: Québec Science, 1978): Jean-Louis Missika and Dominique Wolton, *Les réseaux pensants* (Librairie technique et documentaire, 1978). [. . .]

13 The unit of information is the bit. For these definitions see Gaudfernan and Taïb, "Glossaire." This is discussed in René Thom (1973), "Un protée de la sémantique: l'information." In *Modéles mathématiques de la morphogenése* (Paris: Union Générale d'Edition, 1974). In particular, the transcription of messages into code allows ambiguities to be eliminated: see Watzlawick et al., *Pragmatics of Human Communication*, p. 98.

14 The firms Craig and Lexicon have announced the commercial production of pocket translators: four modules for four different languages with simultaneous reception, each containing 1,500 words, with memory. Weidner Communication Systems Inc. produces a *Multilingual Word Processor* that allows the capacity of an average translator to be increased from 600 to 2,400 words per hour. It includes a triple memory: bilingual dictionary, dictionary of synonyms, grammatical index (*La Semaine media* 6, December 6, 1978, p. 5).

15 Jürgen Habermas, *Erkenntnis und Interesse* (Frankfurt: Suhrkamp, 1968) [Eng. trans. by Jeremy Shapiro, *Knowledge and Human Interests* (Boston: Beacon, 1971), p. 1].

16 "Man's understanding of nature and his mastery over it by virtue of his presence as a social body . . . appears as the great foundation-stone [Grundpfeiler] of production and of wealth," so that "general social knowledge becomes a *direct force of production,*" writes Marx in the *Grundrisse* (1857–8) [(Berlin: Dietz Verlag, 1953), p. 593; Eng. trans. by Martin Nicolaus (New York: Vintage, 1973), p. 705]. However, Marx concedes that it is not "only in the form of knowledge, but also as immediate organs of social practice" that learning becomes force, in other words, as machines:

machines are *"organs of the human brain created by human hand; the power of knowledge, objectified"* [p. 7061.] See Paul Mattick, *Marx and Keynes: The Limits of the Mixed Economy* (Boston: Extending Horizons Books, 1969). This point is discussed in Lyotard, "La place de l'aliénation dans le retournement marxiste" (1969), in *Dérive à partir de Marx et Freud* (Paris: Union Générale d'Edition 1973), pp. 78–166.

17 The composition of the labor force in the United States changed as follows over a twenty-year period (1950–71):

	1950	1971
Factory, service sector, or agricultural workers	62.5%	51.4%
Professionals and technicians	7.5	14.2
White-collar	30.0	34.0

(*Statistical Abstracts*, 1971)

18 Because of the time required for the "fabrication" of a high level technician or the average scientist in comparison to the time needed to extract raw materials and transfer money-capital. At the end of the 1960s, Mattick estimated the net rate of investment in underdeveloped countries at 3–5 percent of the GNP and at 10–15 percent in the developed countries (*Marx and Keynes,* p. 248.]

19 Nora and Minc, *L'Informatisation de la sociétié*, especially Pt. 1, "Les défis;" Y. Stourdzé, "Les Etats-Unis et la guerre des communications." *Le Monde*, December 13–15, 1978. In 1979, the value of the world market of telecommunications devices was $30 billion; it is estimated that in ten years it will reach $68 billion (*La Semaine media* 19, March 8, 1979).

20 F. De Combret, "Le redéploiement industriel." *Le Monde*, April 1978; M. Lepage, *Demain le capitalisme* (Paris: Le Livre de Poche, 1978); Alain Cotta, *La France et l'impératif mondial* (Paris: Presses Universitaires de France, 1978).

21 It is a matter of "weakening the administration," of reaching the "minimal state." This is the decline of the Welfare State, which is accompanying the "crisis" that began in 1974.

22 See note 1. Certain scientific aspects of postmodernism are inventoried by: Ihab Hassan (1978), "Culture, Indeterminacy, and Immanence: Margins of the (Postmodern) Age." *Humanities in Society* 1, pp. 51–85.

23 Claus Mueller uses the expression "a process of delegitimation" in *The Politics of Communication* (New York: Oxford University Press, 1973), p. 164.

24 "Road of doubt . . . road of despair . . . skepticism," writes Hegel in the preface to the *Phenomenology of Spirit* to describe the effect of the speculative drive on natural knowledge.

25 For fear of encumbering this account, I have postponed until a later study the exposition of this group of rules. [See (1981) "Analyzing Speculative Discourse as Language-Game," *The Oxford Literary Review* 4, no. 3, pp. 59–67.]

26 Friedrich Nietzsche, "Der europäische Nihilismus" (MS. N VII 3); "der Nihilism, ein normaler Zustand" (MS. W II 1); "Kritik der Nihilism" (MS. W VII 3); "Zum Plane" (MS. W II 1), in *Nietzches Werke kritische Gesamtausgabe* vol. 7, pts. 1 and 2 (1887–9) (Berlin: De Gruyter, 1970). These texts have been the object of a commentary by K. Ryjik, *Nietzsche, le manuscrit de Lenzer Heide* (typescript, Département de philosophie, Université de Paris VIII [Vincennes]).

27 Friedrich Nietzsche, "On the future of our educational institutions." In A. Mugge (ed.), *Complete Works* (London: T. N. Fowlis, 1911; reprint, New York: Gordon Press, 1974), note 35, vol. 3.

28 Martin Buber, *Ich und Du* (Berlin: Schocken Verlag, 1922) [Eng. trans. by Ronald G. Smith, *I and Thou* (New York: Charles Scribner's Sons, 1937)], and *Dialogisches Leben* (Zurich: Müller, 1947); Emmanuel Lévinas, *Totalité et Infinité* (La Haye: Nijhoff, 1961) [Eng. trans. by Alphonso Lingis, *Totality and Infinity: An Essay on Exteriority* (Pittsburgh: Duquesne University Press, 1969)], and "Martin Buber und die Erkenntnis theorie" (1958), in *Philosophen des 20. Jahrhunderts* (Stuttgart: Kohlhammer, 1963) [French trans. "Martin Buber et la théorie de la connaissance." In *Noms Propres* (Montpellier: Fata Morgana, 1976)].

29 Ludwig Wittgenstein, *Philosophical Investigations*, trans. by G. E. M Anscombe (New York: Macmillan, 1953), sec. 18, p. 8.

30 Ibid.

31 Ibid.

32 See for example, "La taylorisation de la recherche," in *(Auto)critique de la science* (note 26), pp. 291–3. And especially D. J. de Solla Price, *Little Science, Big Science* (New York: Columbia University Press, 1963), who emphasizes the split between a small number of highly productive researchers (evaluated in terms of publication) and a large mass of researchers with low productivity. The number of the latter grows as the square of the former, so that the number of high productivity researchers only really increases every twenty years. Price concludes that science considered as a social entity is "undemocratic" (p. 59) and that "the eminent scientist" is a hundred years ahead of "the minimal one" (p. 56).

33 See J. T. Desanti, "Sur le rapport traditionnel des sciences et de la philosophie." In *La Philosophie silencieuse, ou critique des philosophies de la science* (Paris: Seuil, 1975).

34 The reclassification of academic philosophy as one of the human sciences in this respect has a significance far beyond simply professional concerns. I do not think that philosophy as legitimation is condemned to disappear, but it is possible that it will not be able to carry out this work, or at least advance it, without revising its ties to the university institution. See on this matter the preamble to the *Projet d'un institut polytechnique de philosophie* (typescript, Département de philosophie, Université de Paris VIII [Vincennes], 1979).

35 See Allan Janik and Stephan Toulmin, *Wittgenstein's Vienna* (New York: Sirnon & Schuster, 1973); and J. Piel (1975), (ed.), "Vienne début d'un siécle," *Critique*, pp. 339–40.

36 See Jürgen Habermas, "Dogmatismus, Vernunft unt Entscheidung – Zu Theorie und Praxis in der verwissenschaftlichen Zivilisation" (1963) in *Theorie und Praxis* [*Theory and Practice*, abr. edn. of 4th German edn., trans. by John Viertel (Boston: Beacon Press, 1971)].

37 "Science Smiling into its Beard" is the title of chap. 72, vol. 1 of Musil's *The Man Without Qualities*. Cited and discussed by J. Bouveresse in "La Problématique du sujet."

26

The Precession of Simulacra

Jean Baudrillard

Abstraction today is no longer that of the map, the double, the mirror or the concept. Simulation is no longer that of a territory, a referential being or a substance. It is the generation by models of a real without origin or reality: a hyperreal. The territory no longer precedes the map, nor survives it. Henceforth, it is the map that precedes the territory – PRECESSION OF SIMULACRA – it is the map that engenders the territory and if we were to revive the fable today, it would be the territory whose shreds are slowly rotting across the map. It is the real, and not the map, whose vestiges subsist here and there, in the deserts which are no longer those of the Empire, but our own. *The desert of the real itself.*

In fact, even inverted, the fable is useless. Perhaps only the allegory of the Empire remains. For it is with the same Imperialism that present-day simulators try to make the real, all the real, coincide with their simulation models. But it is no longer a question of either maps or territory. Something has disappeared: the sovereign difference between them that was the abstraction's charm. For it is the difference which forms the poetry of the map and the charm of the territory, the magic of the concept and the charm of the real. This representational imaginary, which both culminates in and is engulfed by the cartographer's mad project of an ideal coextensivity between the map and the territory, disappears with simulation – whose operation is nuclear and genetic, and no longer specular and discursive. With it goes all of metaphysics. No more mirror of being and appearances, of the real and its concept. No more imaginary coextensivity: rather, genetic miniaturization is the dimension of simulation. The real is produced from miniaturized units, from matrices, memory banks and command models – and with these it can be reproduced an indefinite number of times. It no longer has to be rational, since it is no longer measured against some ideal or negative instance. It is nothing more than operational. In fact, since it is no longer enveloped by an imaginary, it is no longer real at all. It is a hyperreal, the product of an irradiating synthesis of combinatory model in a hyperspace without atmosphere.

In this passage to a space whose curvature is no longer that of the real, nor of truth, the age of simulation thus begins with a liquidation of all referentials – worse: by their artificial resurrection in systems of signs, a more ductile material than meaning, in that it lends itself to all systems of equivalence, all binary oppositions and all combinatory algebra. It is no longer a question of imitation, nor of reduplication, nor even of parody. It is rather a question of substituting signs of the real for the real itself, that is, an operation to deter every real process by its operational double, a metastable, programmatic, perfect descriptive machine which provides all the signs of the real and short-circuits all its vicissitudes. Never again will the real have to be produced – this is the vital function of the model in a system of death, or rather of anticipated resurrection which no longer leaves any chance even in the event of death. A hyperreal henceforth sheltered from the imaginary, and from any distinction between the real and the imaginary, leaving room only for the orbital recurrence of models and the simulated generation of difference. [. . .]

Hyperreal and Imaginary

Disneyland is a perfect model of all the entangled orders of simulation. To begin with it is a play of illusions and phantasms: Pirates, the Frontier, Future World, etc. This imaginary world is supposed to be what makes the operation successful. But what draws the crowds is undoubtedly much more the social microcosm, the miniaturized and *religious* revelling in real America, in its delights and drawbacks. You park outside, queue up inside, and are totally abandoned at the exit. In this imaginary world the only phantasmagoria is in the inherent warmth and affection of the crowd, and in that sufficiently ex-cessive number of gadgets used there to specifically maintain the multitudinous effect. The contrast with the absolute solitude of the parking lot – a veritable concentration camp – is total. Or rather: inside, a whole range of gadgets magnetize the crowd into direct flows – outside, solitude is directed onto a single gadget: the automobile. By an extraordinary coincidence (one that undoubtedly belongs to the peculiar enchantment of this universe), this deep-frozen infantile world happens to have been conceived and realized by a man who is himself now cryogenized: Walt Disney, who awaits his resurrection at minus 180 degrees centigrade.

The objective profile of America, then, may be traced throughout Disneyland, even down to the morphology of individuals and the crowd. All its values are exalted here, in miniature and comic strip form. Embalmed and pacified. Whence the possibility of an ideological analysis of Disneyland (L. Marin does it well in *Utopies, jeux d'espaces*): digest of the American way of life, panegyric to American values, idealized transposition of a contradictory reality. To be sure. But this conceals something else, and that "ideological" blanket exactly serves to cover over a *third-order simulation:* Disneyland is there to conceal the fact that it is the "real" country, all of "real" America, which *is* Disneyland (just as prisons are there to conceal the fact that it is the social in its entirety, in its banal omnipresence, which is carceral). Disneyland is presented as imaginary in order to make us believe that the rest is real, when in fact all of Los Angeles and the America surrounding it are no longer real, but of the order of the hyperreal and of simulation. It is no longer a question of a false representation of reality (ideology), but of concealing the fact that the real is no longer real, and thus of saving the reality principle.

The Disneyland imaginary is neither true nor false; it is a deterrence machine set up in order to rejuvenate in reverse the fiction of the real. Whence the debility, the infantile degeneration of this imaginary. It is meant to be an infantile world, in order to make us believe that the adults are elsewhere, in the "real" world, and to conceal the fact that real childishness is everywhere, particularly amongst those adults who go there to act the child in order to foster illusions as to their real childishness.

Moreover, Disneyland is not the only one. Enchanted Village, Magic Mountain, Marine World: Los Angeles is encircled by these imaginary stations which feed reality, reality-energy, to a town whose mystery is precisely that it is nothing more than a network of endless, unreal circulation – a town of fabulous proportions, but without space or dimensions. As much as electrical and nuclear power stations, as much as film studios, this town, which is nothing more than an immense script and a perpetual motion picture, needs this old imaginary made up of childhood signals and faked phantasms for its sympathetic nervous system.

Political Incantation

Watergate. Same scenario as Disneyland (an imaginary effect concealing that reality no more exists outside than inside the bounds of the artificial perimeter): though here it is a scandal effect concealing that there is no difference between the facts and their denunciation (identical methods are employed by the CIA and the *Washington Post* journalists). Same operation, though this time tending towards scandal as a means to regenerate a moral and political principle, towards the imaginary as a means to regenerate a reality principle in distress.

The denunciation of scandal always pays homage to the law. And Watergate above all succeeded in imposing the idea that Watergate *was* a scandal – in this sense it was an extraordinary operation of intoxication. The reinjection of a large dose of political morality on a global scale. It could be said along with Bourdieu that: "The specific character of every relation of force is to dissimulate itself as such, and to acquire all its force only because it is so dissimulated," understood as follows: capital, which is immoral and unscrupulous, can only function behind a moral superstructure, and whoever regenerates this public morality (by indignation, denunciation, etc.) spontaneously furthers the order of capital, as did the *Washington Post* journalists.

But this is still only the formula of ideology, and when Bourdieu enunciates it, he takes "relation of force" to mean the *truth* of capitalist domination, and he *denounces* this relation of force as itself a *scandal* – he therefore occupies the same deterministic and moralistic position as the *Washington Post* journalists. He does the same job of purging and reviving moral order, an order of truth wherein the genuine symbolic violence of the social order is engendered, well beyond all relations of force, which are only its indifferent and shifting configuration in the moral and political consciousness of men.

All that capital asks of us is to receive it as rational or to combat it in the name of rationality, to receive it as moral or to combat it in the name of morality. For they are *identical*, meaning *they can be read another way*: before, the task was to dissimulate scandal; today, the task is to conceal the fact that there is none.

Watergate is not a scandal: this is what must be said at all cost, for this is what everyone is concerned to conceal, this dissimulation masking a strengthening of morality, a moral panic as we approach the primal (mise en) scène of capital: its instantaneous cruelty, its incomprehensible ferocity, its fundamental immorality – this is what is scandalous, unaccountable for in that system of moral and economic equivalence which remains the axiom of leftist thought, from Enlightenment theory to communism. Capital doesn't give a damn about the idea of the contract which is imputed to it – it is a monstrous unprincipled undertaking, nothing more. Rather, it is "enlightened" thought which seeks to control capital by imposing rules on it. And all that recrimination which replaced revolutionary thought today comes down to reproaching capital for not following the rules of the game. "Power is unjust, its justice is a class justice, capital exploits us, etc." – as if capital were linked by a contract to the society it rules. It is the Left which holds out the mirror of equivalence, hoping that capital will fall for this phantasmagoria of the social contract and fulfull its obligation towards the whole of society (at the same time, no need for revolution: it is enough that capital accepts the rational formula of exchange).

Capital in fact has never been linked by a contract to the society it dominates. It is a sorcery of the social relation, it is a *challenge to society* and should be responded to as such. It is not a scandal to be denounced according to moral and economic rationality, but a challenge to take up according to symbolic law.

Moebius – Spiralling Negativity

Hence Watergate was only a trap set by the system to catch its adversaries – a simulation of scandal to regenerative ends. This is embodied by the character called "Deep Throat", who was said to be a Republican grey eminence manipulating the leftist journalists in order to get rid of Nixon – and why not? All hypotheses are possible, although this one is superfluous: the work of the Right is done very well, and spontaneously, by the Left on its own. Besides, it would be naive to see an embittered good conscience at work here. For the Right itself also spontaneously does the work of the Left. All the hypotheses of manipulation are reversible in an endless whirligig. For manipulation is a floating causality where positivity and negativity engender and overlap with one another, where there is no longer any active or passive. It is by putting an *arbitrary* stop to this revolving causality that a principle of political reality can be saved. It is by the *simulation* of a conventional, restricted perspective field, where the premises and consequences of any act or event are calculable, that a political credibility can be maintained (including, of course, "objective" analysis, struggle, etc.). But if the entire cycle of any act or event is envisaged in a system where linear continuity and dialectical polarity no longer exist, in a field *unhinged by simulation*, then all determination evaporates, every act terminates at the end of the cycle having benefited everyone and been scattered in all directions.

Is any given bombing in Italy the work of leftist extremists, or of extreme right-wing provocation, or staged by centrists to bring every terrorist extreme into disrepute and to shore up its own failing power, or again, is it a police-inspired scenario in order to appeal to public security? All this is equally true, and the search for proof, indeed the objectivity of the fact does not check this vertigo of interpretation. We are in a logic of simulation which has nothing to do with a logic of facts and an order of reasons. Simulation is characterized by a *precession of the model*, of all models around the merest fact – the models come first, and their orbital (like the bomb) circulation constitutes the genuine magnetic field of events. Facts no longer have any trajectory of their own, they arise at the intersection of the models; a single fact may even be engendered by all the models at once. This anticipation, this precession, this short-circuit, this confusion of the fact with its model (no more divergence of meaning, no more dialectical polarity, no more negative electricity or implosion of poles) is what each time allows for all the possible interpretations, even the most contradictory – all are true, in the sense that their truth is exchangeable, in the image of the models from which they proceed, in a generalized cycle.

The communists attack the socialist party as though they wanted to shatter the Union of the Left. They sanction the idea that their reticence stems from a more radical political exigency. In fact, it is because they don't want power. But do they not want it at this conjuncture because it is unfavorable for the Left in general, or because it is unfavorable for them within the Union of the Left – or do they not want it by definition? When Berlinguer declares: "We mustn't be frightened of seeing the communists seize power in Italy," this means simultaneously:

- that there is nothing to fear, since the communists, if they come to power, will change nothing in its fundamental capitalist mechanism;
- that there isn't any risk of their ever coming to power (for the reason that they don't want to) – and even if they did take it up, they will only ever wield it by proxy;

- that in fact power, genuine power, no longer exists, and hence there is no risk of anybody seizing it or taking it over;
- but more: I, Berlinguer, am not frightened of seeing the communists seize power in Italy – which might appear evident, but not that much, since this can also mean the contrary (no need of psychoanalysis here): *I am frightened* of seeing the communists seize power (and with good reason, even for a communist).

All the above is simultaneously true. This is the secret of a discourse that is no longer only ambiguous, as political discourses can be, but that conveys the impossibility of a determinate position of power, the impossibility of a determinate position of discourse. And this logic belongs to neither party. It traverses all discourses without their wanting it.

Who will unravel this imbroglio? The Gordian knot can at least be cut. As for the Moebius strip, if it is split in two, it results in an additional spiral without there being any possibility of resolving its surfaces (here the reversible continuity of hypotheses). Hades of simulation, which is no longer one of torture, but of the subtle, maleficent, elusive twisting of meaning – where even those condemned at Burgos are still a gift from Franco to western democracy, which finds in them the occasion to regenerate its own flagging humanism, and whose indignant protestation consolidates in return Franco's regime by uniting the Spanish masses against foreign intervention? Where is the truth in all that, when such collusions admirably knit together without their authors even knowing it?

The conjunction of the system and its extreme alternative like two ends of a curved mirror, the "vicious" curvature of a political space henceforth magnetized, circularized, reversibilized from right to left, a torsion that is like the evil demon of commutation, the whole system, the infinity of capital folded back over its own surface: transfinite? And isn't it the same with desire and libidinal space? The conjunction of desire and value, of desire and capital. The conjunction of desire and the law – the ultimate joy and metamorphosis of the law (which is why it is so well received at the moment): only capital takes pleasure, Lyotard said, before coming to think that *we* take pleasure in capital. Overwhelming versatility of desire in Deleuze, an enigmatic reversal which brings this desire that is "revolutionary by itself, and as if involuntarily, in wanting what it wants," to want its own repression and to invest in paranoid and fascist systems? A malign torsion which reduces this revolution of desire to the same fundamental ambiguity as the other, historical revolution.

All the referentials intermingle their discourses in a circular, Moebian compulsion. Not so long ago sex and work were savagely opposed terms: today both are dissolved into the same type of demand. Formerly the discourse on history took its force from opposing itself to the one on nature, the discourse on desire to the one on power – today they exchange their signifiers and their scenarios.

It would take too long to run through the whole range of operational negativity, of all those scenarios of deterrence which, like Watergate, try to regenerate a moribund principle by simulated scandal, phantasm, murder – a sort of hormonal treatment by negativity and crisis. It is always a question of proving the real by the imaginary, proving truth by scandal, proving the law by transgression, proving work by the strike, proving the system by crisis and capital by revolution, as for that matter proving ethnology by the dispossession of its object (the Tasaday) – without counting:

- proving theatre by anti-theatre
- proving art by anti-art
- proving pedagogy by anti-pedagogy
- proving psychiatry by anti-psychiatry, etc., etc.

Everything is metamorphosed into its inverse in order to be perpetuated in its purged form. Every form of power, every situation speaks of itself by denial, in order to attempt to escape, by simulation of death, its real agony. Power can stage its own murder to rediscover a glimmer of existence and legitimacy. Thus with the American presidents: the Kennedys are murdered because they still have a political dimension. Others – Johnson, Nixon, Ford – only had a right to puppet attempts, to simulated murders. But they nevertheless needed that aura of an artificial menace to conceal that they were nothing other than mannequins of power. In olden days the king (also the god) had to die – that was his strength. Today he does his miserable utmost to pretend to die, so as to preserve the *blessing* of power. But even this is gone.

To seek new blood in its own death, to renew the cycle by the mirror of crisis, negativity and anti-power: this is the only alibi of every power, of every institution attempting to break the vicious circle of its irresponsibility and its fundamental nonexistence, of its dèja-vu and its dèja-mort.

Strategy of the Real

Of the same order as the impossibility of rediscovering an absolute level of the real, is the impossibility of staging an illusion. Illusion is no longer possible, because the real is no longer possible. It is the whole *political* problem of the parody, of hypersimulation or offensive simulation, which is posed here.

For example: it would be interesting to see whether the repressive apparatus would not react more violently to a simulated hold-up than to a real one? For the latter only upsets the order of things, the right of property, whereas the other interferes with the very principle of reality. Transgression and violence are less serious, for they only contest the *distribution* of the real. Simulation is infinitely more dangerous, however, since it always suggests, over and above its object, that *law and order themselves might really be nothing more than a simulation.*

But the difficulty is in proportion to the peril. How to feign a violation and put it to the test? Go and simulate a theft in a large department store: how do you convince the security guards that it is a simulated theft? There is no "objective" difference: the same gestures and the same signs exist as for a real theft; in fact the signs incline neither to one side nor the other. As far as the established order is concerned, they are always of the order of the real.

Go and organize a fake hold-up. Be sure to check that your weapons are harmless, and take the most trustworthy hostage, so that no life is in danger (otherwise you risk committing an offence). Demand ransom, and arrange it so that the operation creates the greatest commotion possible – in brief, stay close to the "truth", so as to test the reaction of the apparatus to a perfect simulation. But you won't succeed: the web of artificial signs will be inextricably mixed up with real elements (a police officer will really shoot on sight; a bank customer will faint and die of a heart attack; they will really turn the phoney ransom over to you) – in brief, you will unwittingly find yourself immediately in the real, one of whose functions is precisely to devour every attempt at simulation, to reduce everything to some reality – that's exactly how the established order is, well before institutions and justice come into play.

In this impossibility of isolating the process of simulation must be seen the whole thrust of an order that can only see and understand in terms of some reality, because it can function nowhere else. The simulation of an offence, if it is patent, will either be punished more lightly (because it has no "consequences") or be punished as an offence to public office (for example, if one triggered off a police operation "for nothing") – but *never as simulation*, since it is precisely as such that no equivalence with the real is possible, and hence no repression either. The challenge of simulation is irreceivable by power. How can you punish the simulation of virtue? Yet as such it is as serious as the simulation of crime. Parody makes obedience and transgression equivalent, and that is the most serious crime, since it *cancels out the difference upon which the law is based*. The established order can do nothing against it, for the law is a second-order simulacrum whereas simulation is third-order, beyond true and false, beyond equivalences, beyond the rational distinctions upon which function all power and the entire social. Hence, *failing the real*, it is here that we must aim at order.

This is why order always opts for the real. In a state of uncertainty, it always prefers this assumption (thus in the army they would rather take the simulator as a true madman). But this becomes more and more difficult, for it is practically impossible to isolate the process of simulation, through the force of inertia of the real which surrounds us, the inverse is also true (and this very reversibility forms part of the apparatus of simulation and of power's impotency): namely, *it is now impossible to isolate the process of the real*, or to prove the real.

Thus all hold-ups, hijacks and the like are now as it were simulation hold-ups, in the sense that they are inscribed in advance in the decoding and orchestration rituals of the media, anticipated in their mode of presentation and possible consequences. In brief, where they function as a set of signs dedicated exclusively to their recurrence as signs, and no longer to their "real" goal at all. But this does not make them inoffensive. On the contrary, it is as hyper-real events, no longer having any particular contents or aims, but indefinitely refracted by each other (for that matter like so-called historical events: strikes, demonstrations, crises, etc., that they are precisely unverifiable by an order which can only exert itself on the real and the rational, on ends and means: a referential order which can only dominate referentials, a determinate power which can only dominate a determined world, but which can do nothing about that indefinite recurrence of simulation, about that weightless nebula no longer obeying the law of gravitation of the real – power itself eventually breaking apart in this space and becoming a simulation of power (disconnected from its aims and objectives, and dedicated to *power effects* and mass simulation).

The only weapon of power, its only strategy against this defection, is to reinject realness and referentiality everywhere, in order to convince us of the reality of the social, of the gravity of the economy and the finalities of produc-tion. For that purpose it prefers the discourse of crisis, but also – why not? – the discourse of desire. "Take your desires for reality!" can be understood as the ultimate slogan of power, for in a nonreferential world even the confusion of the reality principle with the desire principle is less dangerous than con-tagious hyperreality. One remains among principles, and there power is always right.

Hyperreality and simulation are deterrents of every principle and of every objective; they turn against power this deterrence which is so well utilized for a long time itself. For, finally, it was capital which was the first to feed throughout its history on the destruction of every referential, of every human goal, which shattered every ideal distinction between true and false, good and evil, in order to establish a radical law of equivalence and exchange, the iron law of its power. It was the first to practice deterrence, abstraction, disconnec-tion, deterritorialization, etc.; and if it was capital which fostered reality, the reality principle, it was also the first to liquidate it in the extermination of every use value, of every real equivalence, of production and wealth, in the very sensation we have of the unreality of the stakes and the omnipotence of manipulation. Now, it is this very logic which is today hardened even more *against* it. And when it wants to fight this catastrophic spiral by secreting one last glimmer of reality, on which to found one last glimmer of power, it only multiplies the *signs* and accelerates the play of simulation.

As long as it was historically threatened by the real, power risked deterrence and simulation, disintegrating every contradiction by means of the production of equivalent signs. When it is threatened today by simulation (the threat of vanishing in the play of signs), power risks the real, risks crisis, it gambles on remanufacturing artificial, social, economic, political stakes. This is a question of life or death for it. But it is too late.

Whence the characteristic hysteria of our time: the hysteria of production and reproduction of the real. The other production, that of goods and commodities, that of *la belle epoque* of political economy, no longer makes any sense of its own, and has not for some time. What society seeks through production, and overproduction, is the restoration of the real which escapes it. That is why *contemporary "material" production is itself hyperreal*. It retains all the features, the whole discourse of traditional production, but it is nothing more than its scaled-down refraction (thus the hyperrealists fasten in a striking resemblance a real from which has fled all meaning and charm, all the profundity and energy of representation). Thus the hyperrealism of simulation is expressed everywhere by the real's striking resemblance to itself.

Power, too, for some time now produces nothing but signs of its resemblance. And at the same time, another figure of power comes into play: that of a collective demand for *signs* of power – a holy union which forms around the disappearance of power. Everybody belongs to it more or less in fear of the collapse of the political. And in the end the game of power comes down to nothing more than the *critical* obsession with power – an obsession with its death, an obsession with its survival, the greater the more it disappears. When it has totally disappeared, logically we will be under the total spell of power – a haunting memory already foreshadowed everywhere, manifesting at one and the same time the compulsion to get rid of it (nobody wants it any more, everybody unloads it on others) and the apprehensive pining over its loss. Melancholy for societies without power: this has already given rise to facism, that overdose of a powerful referential in a society which cannot terminate its mourning.

But we are still in the same boat: none of our societies knows how to manage its mourning for the real, for power, for the *social itself*, which is implicated in this same breakdown. And it is by an artificial revitalization of all this that we try to escape it. *Undoubtedly this will even end up in socialism.* By an unforeseen twist of events and an irony which no longer belongs to history, it is through the death of the social that socialism will emerge – as it is through the death of God that religions emerge. A twisted coming, a perverse event, an unintelligible reversion to the logic of reason. As is the fact that power is no longer present except to conceal that there is none. A simulation which can go on indefinitely, since – unlike "true" power which is, or was, a structure, a strategy, a relation of force, a stake – this is nothing but the object of a social *demand*, and hence subject to the law of supply and demand, rather than to violence and death. Completely expunged from the *political* dimension, it is dependent, like any other commodity, on production and mass consumption. Its spark has disappeared – only the fiction of a political universe is saved.

Likewise with work. The spark of production, the violence of its stake no longer exists. Everybody still produces, and more and more, but work has subtly become something else: a need (as Marx ideally envisaged it, but not at all in the same sense), the object of a social "demand," like leisure, to which it is equivalent in the general run of life's options. A demand exactly proportional to the loss of stake in the work process. The same change in fortune as for power: the *scenario* of work is there to conceal the fact that the work-real, the production-real, has disappeared. And for that matter so has the strike-real too, which is no longer a stoppage of work, but its alternative pole in the ritual scansion of the social calendar. It is as if everyone has "occupied" their work place or work post, after declaring the strike, and resumed production, as is the custom in a "self-managed" job, in exactly the same terms as before, by declaring themselves (and virtually being) in a state of permanent strike.

This isn't a science-fiction dream: everywhere it is a question of a doubling of the work process. And of a double or locum for the strike process-strikes which are incorporated like obsolescence in objects, like crisis in production. Then there are no longer any strikes or work, but both simultaneously, that is to say something else entirely: a *wizardry of work*, a *trompe l'oeil*, a scenodrama (not to say melodrama) of production, collective dramaturgy upon the empty stage of the social.

It is no longer a question of the *ideology* of work – of the traditional ethic that obscures the "real" labour process and the "objective" process of exploitation – but of the scenario of work. Likewise, it is no longer a question of the ideology of power, but of the *scenario* of power. Ideology only corresponds to a betrayal of reality by signs; simulation corresponds to a short-circuit of reality and to its reduplication by signs. It is always the aim of ideological analysis to restore the objective process; it is always a false problem to want to restore the truth beneath the simulacrum.

This is ultimately why power is so in accord with ideological discourses and discourses on ideology, for these are all discourses of *truth* – always good, even and especially if they are revolutionary, to counter the mortal blows of simulation.

27

The Cultural Logic of
Late Capitalism

Fredric Jameson

The crisis in historicity now dictates a return, in a new way, to the question of temporal organization in general in the postmodern force field, and indeed, to the problem of the form that time, temporality, and the syntagmatic will be able to take in a culture increasingly dominated by space and spatial logic. If, indeed, the subject has lost its capacity actively to extend its pro-tensions and re-tensions across the temporal manifold and to organize its past and future into coherent experience, it becomes difficult enough to see how the cultural productions of such a subject could result in anything but "heaps of fragments" and in a practice of the randomly heterogeneous and fragmentary and the aleatory. These are, however, very precisely some of the privileged terms in which postmodernist cultural production has been analyzed (and even defended, by its own apologists). They are, however, still privative features; the more substantive formulations bear such names as textuality, *écriture*, or schizophrenic writing, and it is to these that we must now briefly turn.

I have found Lacan's account of schizophrenia useful here not because I have any way of knowing whether it has clinical accuracy but chiefly because – as description rather than diagnosis – it seems to me to offer a suggestive aesthetic model.[1] I am obviously very far from thinking that any of the most significant postmodernist artists – Cage, Ashbery, Sollers, Robert Wilson, Ishmael Reed, Michael Snow, Warhol, or even Beckett himself – are schizophrenics in any clinical sense. Nor is the point some culture-and-personality diagnosis of our society and its art, as in psychologizing and moralizing culture critiques of the type of Christopher Lasch's influential *The Culture of Narcissism*, from which I am concerned to distance the spirit and the methodology of the present remarks: there are, one would think, far more damaging things to be said about our social system than are available through the use of psychological categories.

Very briefly, Lacan describes schizophrenia as a breakdown in the signifying chain, that is, the interlocking syntagmatic series of signifiers which constitutes an utterance or a meaning. I must omit the familial or more orthodox psychoanalytic background to this situation, which Lacan transcodes into language by describing the Oedipal rivalry in terms not so much of the biological individual who is your rival for the mother's attention but rather of what he calls the Name-of-the-Father, paternal authority now considered as a linguistic function.[2] His conception of the signifying chain essentially presupposes one of the basic principles (and one of the great discoveries) of Saussurean structuralism, namely, the proposition that meaning is not a one-to-one relationship between signifier and signified, between the materiality of language, between a word or a name, and its referent or concept. Meaning on the new view is generated by the movement from signifier to signifier. What we generally call the signified – the meaning or conceptual content of an utterance – is now rather to be seen as a meaning-effect, as that objective mirage of signification generated and projected by the relationship of signifiers among themselves. When that relationship breaks down, when the links of the signifying chain snap, then we have schizophrenia in the form of a rubble of distinct and unrelated signifiers. The connection between this kind of linguistic malfunction and the psyche of the schizophrenic may then be grasped by way of a twofold proposition: first, that personal identity is itself the effect of a certain temporal unification of past and future with one's present; and, second, that such active temporal unification is itself a function of language, or better still of the sentence, as it moves along its hermeneutic circle through time. If we are unable to unify the past, present, and future of the sentence, then we are similarly unable to unify the past, present, and future of our own biographical experience or psychic life. With the breakdown of the signifying chain, therefore, the schizophrenic is reduced to an experience of pure material signifiers, or, in other words, a series of pure and unrelated presents in time. We will want to ask questions about the aesthetic or cultural results of such a situation in a moment; let us first see what it feels like:

I remember very well the day it happened. We were staying in the country and I had gone for a walk alone as I did now and then. Suddenly, as I was passing the school, I heard a German song; the children were having a singing lesson. I stopped to listen, and at that instant a strange feeling came over me, a feeling hard to analyze but akin to something I was to know too well later – a disturbing sense of unreality. It seemed to me that I no longer recognized the school, it had become as large as a barracks; the singing children were prisoners, compelled to sing. It was as though the school and the children's song were set apart from the rest of the world. At the same time my eye encountered a field of wheat whose limits I could not see. The yellow vastness, dazzling in the sun, bound up with the song of the children imprisoned in the smooth stone school-barracks, filled me with such anxiety that I broke into sobs. I ran home to our garden and began to play "to make things seem as they usually were," that is, to return to reality. It was the first appearance of those elements which were always present in later sensations of unreality: illimitable vastness, brilliant light, and the gloss and smoothness of material things.[3]

In our present context, this experience suggests the following: first, the breakdown of temporality suddenly releases this present of time from all the activities and intentionalities that might focus it and make it a space of praxis; thereby isolated, that present suddenly engulfs the subject with indescribable vividness, a materiality of perception properly overwhelming, which effectively dramatizes the power of the material – or better still, the literal – signifier in isolation. This present of the world or material signifier comes before the subject with heightened intensity, bearing a mysterious charge of affect, here described in the negative terms of anxiety and loss of reality, but which one could just as well imagine in the positive terms of euphoria, a high, an intoxicatory or hallucinogenic intensity.

What happens in textuality or schizophrenic art is strikingly illuminated by such clinical accounts, although in the cultural text, the isolated signifier is no longer an enigmatic state of the world or an incomprehensible yet mesmerizing fragment of language but rather something closer to a sentence in free-standing isolation. Think, for example, of the experience of John Cage's music, in which a cluster of material sounds (on the prepared piano, for example) is followed by a silence so intolerable that you cannot imagine another sonorous chord coming into existence and cannot imagine remembering the previous one well enough to make any connection with it if it does. Some of Beckett's narratives are also of this order, most notably *Watt*, where a primacy of the present sentence in time ruthlessly disintegrates the narrative fabric that attempts to reform around it. My example, however, will be a less somber one, a text by a younger San Francisco poet whose group or school – so-called Language Poetry or the New Sentence – seem to have adopted schizophrenic fragmentation as their fundamental aesthetic.

China

We live on the third world from the sun. Number three. Nobody tells us what to do.
The people who taught us to count were being very kind.
It's always time to leave.
If it rains, you either have your umbrella or you don't.
The wind blows your hat off.
The sun rises also.
I'd rather the stars didn't describe us to each other; I'd rather we do it for ourselves.
Run in front of your shadow.
A sister who points to the sky at least once a decade is a good sister.
The landscape is motorized.
The train takes you where it goes.
Bridges among water.
Folks straggling along vast stretches of concrete, heading into the plane.

Don't forget what your hat and shoes will look like when you are nowhere to
be found.
Even the words floating in air make blue shadows.
If it tastes good we eat it.
The leaves are falling. Point things out.
Pick up the right things.
Hey guess what? What? *I've learned how to talk.* Great.
The person whose head was incomplete burst into tears.
As it fell, what could the doll do? Nothing.
Go to sleep.
You look great in shorts. And the flag looks great too.
Everyone enjoyed the explosions.
Time to wake up.
But better get used to dreams.

Bob Perelman[4]

Many things could be said about this interesting exercise in discontinuities; not
the least paradoxical is the re-emergence here across these disjoined sentences
of some more unified global meaning. Indeed, insofar as this is in some curious
and secret way a political poem, it does seem to capture something of the
excitement of the immense, unfinished social experiment of the New China –
unparalleled in world history – the unexpected emergence, between the two
superpowers, of "number three," the freshness of a whole new object world
produced by human beings in some new control over their collective destiny;
the signal event, above all, of a collectivity which has become a new "subject of
history" and which, after the long subjection of feudalism and imperialism,
again speaks in its own voice, for itself, as though for the first time.

But I mainly wanted to show the way in which what I have been calling
schizophrenic disjunction or *écriture*, when it becomes generalized as a cultural
style, ceases to entertain a necessary relationship to the morbid content we
associate with terms like schizophrenia and becomes available for more joyous
intensities, for precisely that euphoria which we saw displacing the older
affects of anxiety and alienation.

Consider, for example, Jean-Paul Sartre's account of a similar tendency in
Flaubert:

His sentence closes in on the object, seizes it, immobilizes it, and breaks its back,
wraps itself around it, changes into stone and petrifies its object along with itself.
It is blind and deaf, bloodless, not a breath of life; a deep silence separates it from
the sentence which follows; it falls into the void, eternally, and drags its prey
down into that infinite fall. Any reality, once described, is struck off the
inventory.[5]

I am tempted to see this reading as a kind of optical illusion (or photographic
enlargement) of an unwittingly genealogical type, in which certain latent or

subordinate, properly postmodernist, features of Flaubert's style are anachronistically foregrounded. However, it affords an interesting lesson in periodization and in the dialectical restructuring of cultural dominants and subordinates. For these features, in Flaubert, were symptoms and strategies in that whole posthumous life and resentment of praxis which is denounced (with increasing sympathy) throughout the three thousand pages of Sartre's *Family Idiot*. When such features become themselves the cultural norm, they shed all such forms of negative affect and become available for other, more decorative uses.

But we have not yet fully exhausted the structural secrets of Perelman's poem, which turns out to have little enough to do with that referent called China. The author has, in fact, related how, strolling through Chinatown, he came across a book of photographs whose idiogrammatic captions remained a dead letter to him (or perhaps, one should say, a material signifier). The sentences of the poem in question are then Perelman's own captions to those pictures, their referents another image, another absent text; and the unity of the poem is no longer to be found within its language but outside itself, in the bound unity of another, absent book. There is here a striking parallel to the dynamics of so-called photorealism, which looked like a return to representation and figuration after the long hegemony of the aesthetics of abstraction until it became clear that their objects were not to be found in the "real world" either but were themselves photographs of that real world, this last now transformed into images, of which the "realism" of the photorealist painting is now the simulacrum.

This account of schizophrenia and temporal organization might, however, have been formulated in a different way, which brings us back to Heidegger's notion of a gap or rift between Earth and World, albeit in a fashion that is sharply incompatible with the tone and high seriousness of his own philosophy. I would like to characterize the postmodernist experience of form with what will seem, I hope, a paradoxical slogan: namely, the proposition that "difference relates." Our own recent criticism, from Macherey on, has been concerned to stress the heterogeneity and profound discontinuities of the work of art, no longer unified or organic, but now a virtual grab bag or lumber room of disjoined subsystems and random raw materials and impulses of all kinds. The former work of art, in other words, has now turned out to be a text, whose reading proceeds by differentiation rather than by unification. Theories of difference, however, have tended to stress disjunction to the point at which the materials of the text, including its words and sentences, tend to fall apart into random and inert passivity, into a set of elements which entertain separations from one another.

In the most interesting postmodernist works, however, one can detect a more positive conception of relationship, which restores its proper tension to the notion of difference itself. This new mode of relationship through difference may sometimes be an achieved new and original way of thinking and perceiving; more often it takes the form of an impossible imperative to achieve that new mutation in what can perhaps no longer be called consciousness. I believe that the most striking emblem of this new mode of thinking relationships can be found in the work of Nam June Paik, whose stacked or scattered television screens, positioned at intervals within lush vegetation, or winking down at us from a ceiling of strange new video stars, recapitulate over and over again prearranged sequences or loops of images which return at dyssynchronous moments on the various screens. The older aesthetic is then practiced by viewers, who, bewildered by this discontinuous variety, decided to concentrate on a single screen, as though the relatively worthless image sequence to be followed there had some organic value in its own right. The postmodernist viewer, however, is called upon to do the impossible, namely, to see all the screens at once, in their radical and random difference; such a viewer is asked to follow the evolutionary mutation of David Bowie in *The Man Who Fell to Earth* (who watches fifty-seven television screens simultaneously) and to rise somehow to a level at which the vivid perception of radical difference is in and of itself a new mode of grasping what used to be called relationship: something for which the word *collage* is still only a very feeble name. [. . .]

The conception of postmodernism outlined here is a historical rather than a merely stylistic one. I cannot stress too greatly the radical distinction between a view for which the postmodern is one (optional) style among many others available and one which seeks to grasp it as the cultural dominant of the logic of late capitalism: the two approaches in fact generate two very different ways of conceptualizing the phenomenon as a whole: on the one hand, moral judgments (about which it is indifferent whether they are positive or negative), and, on the other, a genuinely dialectical attempt to think our present of time in History.

Of some positive moral evaluation of postmodernism little needs to be said: the complacent (yet delirious) camp-following celebration of this aesthetic new world (including its social and economic dimension, greeted with equal enthusiasm under the slogan of "post-industrial society") is surely unacceptable, although it may be somewhat less obvious that current fantasies about the salvational nature of high technology, from chips to robots – fantasies entertained not only by both left and right governments in distress but also by many intellectuals – are also essentially of a piece with more vulgar apologias for postmodernism.

But in that case it is only consequent to reject moralizing condemnations of the postmodern and of its essential triviality when juxtaposed against the Utopian "high seriousness" of the great modernisms: judgments one finds both on the Left and on the radical Right. And no doubt the logic of the simulacrum, with its transformation of older realities into television images, does more than merely replicate the logic of late capitalism; it reinforces and intensifies it. Meanwhile, for political groups which seek actively to intervene in history and to modify its otherwise passive momentum (whether with a view toward channeling it into a socialist transformation of society or diverting it into the regressive re-establishment of some simpler fantasy past), there cannot but be much that is deplorable and reprehensible in a cultural form of image addiction which, by transforming the past into visual mirages, stereotypes, or texts, effectively abolishes any practical sense of the future and of the collective project, thereby abandoning the thinking of future change to fantasies of sheer catastrophe and inexplicable cataclysm, from visions of "terrorism" on the social level to those of cancer on the personal. Yet if postmodernism is a historical phenomenon, then the attempt to conceptualize it in terms of moral or moralizing judgments must finally be identified as a category mistake. All of which becomes more obvious when we interrogate the position of the cultural critic and moralist; the latter, along with all the rest of us, is now so deeply immersed in postmodernist space, so deeply suffused and infected by its new cultural categories, that the luxury of the old-fashioned ideological critique, the indignant moral denunciation of the other, becomes unavailable.

The distinction I am proposing here knows one canonical form in Hegel's differentiation of the thinking of individual morality or moralizing (*Moralität*) from that whole very different realm of collective social values and practices (*Sittlichkeit*).[6] But it finds its definitive form in Marx's demonstration of the materialist dialectic, most notably in those classic pages of the *Manifesto* which teach the hard lesson of some more genuinely dialectical way to think historical development and change. The topic of the lesson is, of course, the historical development of capitalism itself and the deployment of a specific bourgeois culture. In a well-known passage Marx powerfully urges us to do the impossible, namely, to think this development positively and negatively all at once; to achieve, in other words, a type of thinking that would be capable of grasping the demonstrably baleful features of capitalism along with its extraordinary and liberating dynamism simultaneously within a single thought, and without attenuating any of the force of either judgment. We are somehow to lift our minds to a point at which it is possible to understand that capitalism is at one and the same time the best thing that has ever happened to the human race, and the worst. The lapse from this austere dialectical imperative into the more comfortable stance of the taking of moral positions is inveterate and all too human: still, the urgency of the subject demands that we make at least some effort to think the cultural evolution of late capitalism dialectically, as catastrophe and progress all together.

Such an effort suggests two immediate questions, with which we will conclude these reflections. Can we in fact identify some "moment of truth" within the more evident "moments of falsehood" of postmodern culture? And, even if we can do so, is there not something ultimately paralyzing in the dialectical view of historical development proposed above; does it not tend to demobilize us and to surrender us to passivity and helplessness by systematically obliterating possibilities of action under the impenetrable fog of historical inevitability? It is appropriate to discuss these two (related) issues in terms of current possibilities for some effective contemporary cultural politics and for the construction of a genuine political culture.

To focus the problem in this way is, of course, immediately to raise the more genuine issue of the fate of culture generally, and of the function of culture specifically, as one social level or instance, in the postmodern era. Everything in the previous discussion suggests that what we have been calling postmodernism is inseparable from, and unthinkable without the hypothesis of, some fundamental mutation of the sphere of culture in the world of late capitalism, which includes a momentous modification of its social function. Older discussions of the space, function, or sphere of culture (mostly notably Herbert Marcuse's classic essay "The Affirmative Character of Culture") have insisted on what a different language would call the "semiautonomy" of the cultural realm: its ghostly, yet Utopian, existence, for good or ill, above the practical world of the existent, whose mirror image it throws back in forms which vary from the legitimations of flattering resemblance to the contestatory indictments of critical satire or Utopian pain.

What we must now ask ourselves is whether it is not precisely this semi-autonomy of the cultural sphere which has been destroyed by the logic of late capitalism. Yet to argue that culture is today no longer endowed with the relative autonomy it once enjoyed as one level among others in earlier moments of capitalism (let alone in precapitalist societies) is not necessarily to imply its disappearance or extinction. Quite the contrary; we must go on to affirm that the dissolution of an autonomous sphere of culture is rather to be imagined in terms of an explosion: a prodigious expansion of culture throughout the social realm, to the point at which everything in our social life – from economic value and state power to practices and to the very structure of the psyche itself – can be said to have become "cultural" in some original and yet untheorized sense. This proposition is, however, substantively quite consistent with the previous diagnosis of a society of the image or the simulacrum and a transformation of the "real" into so many pseudoevents.

It also suggests that some of our most cherished and time-honored radical conceptions about the nature of cultural politics may thereby find themselves outmoded. However distinct those conceptions – which range from slogans of negativity, opposition, and subversion to critique and reflexivity – may have been, they all shared a single, fundamentally spatial, presupposition, which may be resumed in the equally time-honored formula of "critical distance." No theory of cultural politics current on the Left today has been able to do without one notion or another of a certain minimal aesthetic distance, of the possibility of the positioning of the cultural act outside the massive Being of capital, from which to assault this last. What the burden of our preceding demonstration suggests, however, is that distance in general (including "critical distance" in particular) has very precisely been abolished in the new space of post-modernism. We are submerged in its henceforth filled and suffused volumes to the point where our now postmodern bodies are bereft of spatial coordinates and practically (let alone theoretically) incapable of distantiation; meanwhile, it has already been observed how the prodigious new expansion of multi-national capital ends up penetrating and colonizing those very precapitalist enclaves (Nature and the Unconscious) which offered extraterritorial and Archimedean footholds for critical effectivity. The shorthand language of co-optation is for this reason omnipresent on the left, but would now seem to offer a most inadequate theoretical basis for understanding a situation in which we all, in one way or another, dimly feel that not only punctual and local counter-cultural forms of cultural resistance and guerrilla warfare but also even overtly political interventions like those of *The Clash* are all somehow secretly disarmed and reabsorbed by a system of which they themselves might well be considered a part, since they can achieve no distance from it.

What we must now affirm is that it is precisely this whole extraordinarily demoralizing and depressing original new global space which is the "moment of truth" of postmodernism. What has been called the postmodernist "sublime" is only the moment in which this content has become most explicit, has moved the closest to the surface of consciousness as a coherent new type of space in its own right – even though a certain figural concealment or disguise is still at work here, most notably in the high-tech thematics in which the new spatial content is still dramatized and articulated. Yet the earlier features of the postmodern which were enumerated above can all now be seen as themselves partial (yet constitutive) aspects of the same general spatial object.

The argument for a certain authenticity in these otherwise patently ideolog-ical productions depends on the prior proposition that what we have been calling postmodern (or multinational) space is not merely a cultural ideology or fantasy but has genuine historical (and socioeconomic) reality as a third great original expansion of capitalism around the globe (after the earlier ex-pansions of the national market and the older imperialist system, which each had their own cultural specificity and generated new types of space ap-propriate to their dynamics). The distorted and unreflexive attempts of newer cultural production to explore and to express this new space must then also, in their own fashion, be considered as so many approaches to the representation of (a new) reality (to use a more antiquated language). As paradoxical as the terms may seem, they may thus, following a classic interpretive option, be read as peculiar new forms of realism (or at least of the mimesis of reality), while at the same time they can equally well be analyzed as so many attempts to distract and divert us from that reality or to disguise its contradictions and resolve them in the guise of various formal mystifications.

As for that reality itself, however – the as yet untheorized original space of some new "world system" of multinational or late capitalism, a space whose negative or baleful aspects are only too obvious – the dialectic requires us to hold equally to a positive or "progressive" evaluation of its emergence, as Marx did for the world market as the horizon of national economies, or as Lenin did for the older imperialist global network. For neither Marx nor Lenin was socialism a matter of returning to smaller (and thereby less repressive and comprehensive) systems of social organization; rather, the dimensions attained by capital in their own times were grasped as the promise, the framework, and the precondition for the achievement of some new and more comprehensive socialism. Is this not the case with the yet more global and totalizing space of the new world system, which demands the intervention and elaboration of an internationalism of a radically new type? The disastrous realignment of socialist revolution with the older nationalisms (not only in south-east Asia), whose results have necessarily aroused much serious recent left reflection, can be adduced in support of this position.

But if all this is so, then at least one possible form of a new radical cultural politics becomes evident, with a final aesthetic proviso that must quickly be noted. Left cultural producers and theorists – particularly those formed by bourgeois cultural traditions issuing from romanticism and valorizing spontaneous, instinctive, or unconscious forms of "genius," but also for very obvious historical reasons such as Zhdanovism and the sorry consequences of political and party interventions in the arts – have often by reaction allowed themselves to be unduly intimidated by the repudiation, in bourgeois aesthetics and most notably in high modernism, of one of the age-old functions of art – the pedagogical and the didactic. The teaching function of art was, however, always stressed in classical times (even though it there mainly took the form of moral lessons), while the prodigious and still imperfectly understood work of Brecht reaffirms, in a new and formally innovative and original way, for the moment of modernism proper, a complex new conception of the relationship between culture and pedagogy. The cultural model I will propose similarly foregrounds the cognitive and pedagogical dimensions of political art and culture, dimensions stressed in very different ways by both Lukács and Brecht (for the distinct moments of realism and modernism, respectively).

We cannot, however, return to aesthetic practices elaborated on the basis of historical situations and dilemmas which are no longer ours. Meanwhile, the conception of space that has been developed here suggests that a model of political culture appropriate to our own situation will necessarily have to raise spatial issues as its fundamental organizing concern. I will therefore provisionally define the aesthetic of this new (and hypothetical) cultural form as an aesthetic of *cognitive mapping*.

In a classic work, *The Image of the City*, Kevin Lynch taught us that the alienated city is above all a space in which people are unable to map (in their minds) either their own positions or the urban totality in which they find themselves: grids such as those of Jersey City, in which none of the traditional markers (monuments, nodes, natural boundaries, built perspectives) obtain, are the most obvious examples. Disalienation in the traditional city, then, involves the practical reconquest of a sense of place and the construction or reconstruction of an articulated ensemble which can be retained in memory and which the individual subject can map and remap along the moments of mobile, alternative trajectories. Lynch's own work is limited by the deliberate restriction of his topic to the problems of city form as such; yet it becomes extraordinarily suggestive when projected outward onto some of the larger national and global spaces we have touched on here. Nor should it be too hastily assumed that his model – while it clearly raises very central issues of representation as such – is in any way easily vitiated by the conventional post-structural critiques of the "ideology of representation" or mimesis. The cognitive map is not exactly mimetic in that older sense; indeed, the theoretical issues it poses allow us to renew the analysis of representation on a higher and much more complex level.

There is, for one thing, a most interesting convergence between the empirical problems studied by Lynch in terms of city space and the great Althusserian (and Lacanian) redefinition of ideology as "the representation of the subject's *Imaginary* relationship to his or her *Real* conditions of existence."[7] Surely this is exactly what the cognitive map is called upon to do in the narrower framework of daily life in the physical city: to enable a situational representation on the part of the individual subject to that vaster and properly unrepresentable totality which is the ensemble of society's structures as a whole.

Yet Lynch's work also suggests a further line of development insofar as cartography itself constitutes its key mediatory instance. A return to the history of this science (which is also an art) shows us that Lynch's model does not yet, in fact, really correspond to what will become mapmaking. Lynch's subjects are rather clearly involved in precartographic operations whose results traditionally are described as itineraries rather than as maps: diagrams organized around the still subject-centered or existential journey of the traveler, along which various significant key features are marked – oases, mountain ranges, rivers, monuments, and the like. The most highly developed form of such diagrams is the nautical itinerary, the sea chart, or *portulans*, where coastal features are noted for the use of Mediterranean navigators who rarely venture out into the open sea.

Yet the compass at once introduces a new dimension into sea charts, a dimension that will utterly transform the problematic of the itinerary and allow us to pose the problem of a genuine cognitive mapping in a far more complex way. For the new instruments – compass, sextant, and theodolite – correspond not merely to new geographic and navigational problems (the difficult matter of determining longitude, particularly on the curving surface of the planet, as opposed to the simpler matter of latitude, which European navigators can still empirically determine by ocular inspection of the African coast); they also introduce a whole new coordinate: the relationship to the totality, particularly as it is mediated by the stars and by new operations like that of triangulation. At this point, cognitive mapping in the broader sense comes to require the co-ordination of existential data (the empirical position of the subject) with unlived, abstract conceptions of the geographic totality.

Finally, with the first globe (1490) and the invention of the Mercator projection at about the same time, yet a third dimension of cartography emerges, which at once involves what we would today call the nature of representational codes, the intrinsic structures of the various media, the intervention, into more naive mimetic conceptions of mapping, of the whole new fundamental question of the languages of representation itself, in particular the unresolvable (well-nigh Heisenbergian) dilemma of the transfer of curved space to flat charts. At this point it becomes clear that there can be no true maps (at the same time it also becomes clear that there can be scientific progress, or better still, a dialectical advance, in the various historical moments of mapmaking).

Transcoding all this now into the very different problematic of the Althusserian definition of ideology, one would want to make two points. The first is that the Althusserian concept now allows us to rethink these specialized geographical and cartographic issues in terms of social space – in terms, for example, of social class and national or international context, in terms of the ways in which we all necessarily also cognitively map our individual social relationship to local, national, and international class realities. Yet to reformulate the problem in this way is also to come starkly up against those very difficulties in mapping which are posed in heightened and original ways by that very global space of the postmodernist or multinational moment which has been under discussion here. These are not merely theoretical issues; they have urgent practical political consequences, as is evident from the conventional feelings of First World subjects that existentially (or "empirically") they really do inhabit a "post-industrial society" from which traditional production has disappeared and in which social classes of the classical type no longer exist – a conviction which has immediate effects on political praxis.

The second point is that a return to the Lacanian underpinnings of Althusser's theory can afford some useful and suggestive methodological enrichments. Althusser's formulation remobilizes an older and henceforth classical Marxian distinction between science and ideology that is not without value for us even today. The existential – the positioning of the individual subject, the experience of daily life, the monadic "point of view on the world" to which we are necessarily, as biological subjects, restricted – is in Althusser's formula implicitly opposed to the realm of abstract knowledge, a realm which, as Lacan reminds us, is never positioned in or actualized by any concrete subject but rather by that structural void called *le sujet supposé savoir* (the subject supposed to know), a subject-place of knowledge. What is affirmed is not that we cannot know the world and its totality in some abstract or "scientific" way. Marxian "science" provides just such a way of knowing and conceptualizing the world abstractly, in the sense in which, for example, Mandel's great book offers a rich and elaborated *knowledge* of that global world system, of which it has never been said here that it was unknowable but merely that it was unrepresentable, which is a very different matter. The Althusserian formula, in other words, designates a gap, a rift, between existential experience and scientific knowledge. Ideology has then the function of somehow inventing a way of articulating those two distinct dimensions with each other. What a historicist view of this definition would want to add is that such coordination, the production of functioning and living ideologies, is distinct in different historical situations, and, above all, that there may be historical situations in which it is not possible at all – and this would seem to be our situation in the current crisis.

But the Lacanian system is threefold, and not dualistic. To the Marxian—Althusserian opposition of ideology and science correspond only two of Lacan's tripartite functions: the Imaginary and the Real, respectively. Our digression on cartography, however, with its final revelation of a properly representational dialectic of the codes and capacities of individual languages or media, reminds us that what has until now been omitted was the dimension of the Lacanian Symbolic itself.

An aesthetic of cognitive mapping – a pedagogical political culture which seeks to endow the individual subject with some new heightened sense of its place in the global system – will necessarily have to respect this now enormously complex representational dialectic and invent radically new forms in order to do it justice. This is not then, clearly, a call for a return to some older kind of machinery, some older and more transparent national space, or some more traditional and reassuring perspectival or mimetic enclave: the new political art (if it is possible at all) will have to hold to the truth of postmodernism, that is to say, to its fundamental object – the world space of multinational capital – at the same time at which it achieves a breakthrough to some as yet unimaginable new mode of representing this last, in which we may again begin to grasp our positioning as individual and collective subjects and regain a capacity to act and struggle which is at present neutralized by our spatial as well as our social confusion. The political form of postmodernism, if there ever is any, will have as its vocation the invention and projection of a global cognitive mapping, on a social as well as a spatial scale.

Notes

1   The basic reference, in which Lacan discusses Schreber, is "D'une question préliminaire á tout traitement possible de la psychose," in *Ecrits*, trans. Alan Sheridan (New York, 1977), pp. 179–225. Most of us have received this classical view of psychosis by way of Deleuze and Guattari's *Anti-Oedipus*.

2   See my "Imaginary and Symbolic in Lacan." In *The Ideologies of Theory*, vol. I (Minnesota, 1988), pp. 75–115.

3   Marguerite Séchehaye, *Autobiography of a Schizophrenic Girl*, trans. G. Rubin-Rabson (New York, 1968), p. 19.

4   *Primer* (Berkeley, CA, 1978).

5   Jean-Paul Sartre, *What Is Literature?* (Cambridge, MA, 1988).

6   See my "Morality and Ethical Substance", *The Ideologies of Theory* (1988).

7   Louis Althusser, "Ideological State Apparatuses." In *Lenin and Philosophy* (New York, 1972).

28

Feminism and the Question of Postmodernism

Seyla Benhabib

In her book *Thinking Fragments: Psychoanalysis, Feminism and Postmodernism in the Contemporary West*, Jane Flax characterizes the postmodern position as subscription to the theses of the death of Man, of History and of Metaphysics.[1]

The Death of Man. "Postmodernists wish to destroy," she writes, "all essentialist conceptions of human being or nature . . . In fact Man is a social, historical or linguistic artifact, not a noumenal or transcendental Being . . . Man is forever caught in the web of fictive meaning, in chains of signification, in which the subject is merely another position in language."[2]

The Death of History. "The idea that History exists for or is his Being is more than just another precondition and justification for the fiction of Man. This idea also supports and underlies the concept of Progress, which is itself such an important part of Man's story . . . Such an idea of Man and History privileges and presupposes the value of unity, homegeneity, totality, closure and identity."[3]

The Death of Metaphysics. According to postmodernists, "Western metaphysics has been under the spell of the 'metaphysics of presence' at least since Plato . . . For postmodernists this quest for the Real conceals most Western philosophers' desire, which is to master the world once and for all by enclosing it within an illusory but absolute system they believe represents or corresponds to a unitary Being beyond history, particularity and change . . . Just as the Real is the ground of Truth, so too philosophy as the privileged representative of the Real and interrogator of truth claims must play a 'foundational' role in all 'positive knowledge'."[4]

Flax's clear and cogent characterization of the postmodernist position will enable us to see why feminists find in this critique of the ideals of western rationalism and the Enlightenment more than a congenial ally. But let me also note certain important discrepancies between my formulation of the conceptual options made possible by the end of the classical episteme of representation and Flax's version of postmodernism. First, whereas in the course of the transition from "nineteenth-century idealism to twentieth-century contextualism,"[5] I see a move toward the radical situatedness and contextualization of the subject, Flax follows the French tradition in stipulating the "death of the subject." Second, whereas I see a transformation in the object as well the medium of epistemological representation from consciousness to language, from claims about truth and reality to a more limited investigation of the conditions under which a community of inquirers can make warranted assertions about truth and the real, Flax maintains that "philosophy as the privileged representative of the Real" has not been transformed but has died off. So far, I have not dealt with the thesis of the Death of History, but as I shall argue below, of all the claims associated with postmodernist positions this one is the least problematical. Critical theorists as well as postmodernists, liberals as well as cornmunitarians, could agree upon some version of the thesis of the "death of history," in the sense of a teleologically determined progression of historical transformations; but the controversial questions concern the relation of historical narrative to the interests of present actors in their historical past. These discrepancies between Flax's formulations and my own as to how to characterize the epistemic options of the present will play a larger role as the argument progresses.

Consider for the time being how, like postmodernism, feminist theory as well has created its own versions of the three theses concerning the death of Man, History and Metaphysics.

The feminist counterpoint to the postmodernist theme of the *Death of Man* can be named the "Demystification of the Male Subject of Reason." Whereas postmodernists substitute for Man, or the sovereign subject of the theoretical and practical reason of the tradition, the study of contingent, historically changing and culturally variable social, linguistic and discursive practices, feminists claim that "gender" and the various practices contributing to its constitution are one of the most crucial contexts in which to situate the purportedly neutral and universal subject of reason.[6] The western philosophical tradition articulates the deep structures of the experiences and consciousness of a self which it claims to be representative for humans as such. The deepest categories of western philosophy obliterate differences of gender as these shape and structure the experience and subjectivity of the self. Western reason posits itself as the discourse of the one self-identical subject, thereby blinding us to and in fact delegitimizing the presence of otherness and difference which do not fit into its categories. From Plato over Descartes to Kant and Hegel western philosophy thematizes the story of the male subject of reason.

The feminist counterpoint to the *Death of History* would be the "Engendering of Historical Narrative." If the subject of the western intellectual tradition has usually been the white, propertied, Christian, male head of household, then History as hitherto recorded and narrated has been "his story." Furthermore, the various philosophies of history which have dominated since the

Enlightenment have forced historical narrative into unity, homegeneity and linearity with the consequence that fragmentation, heterogeneity, and above all the varying pace of different temporalities as experienced by different groups, have been obliterated.[7] We need only remember Hegel's belief that Africa has no history.[8] Until very recently neither did women have their own history, their own narrative with different categories of periodization and with different structural regularities.

The feminist counterpoint to the *Death of Metaphysics* would be "Feminist Skepticism Toward the Claims of Transcendent Reason." If the subject of reason is not a suprahistorical and context-transcendent being, but the theoretical and practical creations and activities of this subject bear in every instance the marks of the context out of which they emerge, then the subject of philosophy is inevitably embroiled with knowledge-governing interests which mark and direct its activities. For feminist theory, the most important "knowledge-guiding interest" in Habermas's terms, or disciplinary matrix of truth and power in Foucault's terms, are gender relations and the social, economic, political and symbolic constitution of gender differences among human beings.[9]

Despite this "elective affinity" between feminism and postmodernism, each of the three theses enumerated above can be interpreted to permit if not contradictory then at least radically divergent theoretical strategies. And for feminists which set of theretical claims they adopt as their own cannot be a matter of indifference. As Linda Alcoff has recently observed, feminist theory is undergoing a profound identity crisis at the moment.[10] The postmodernist position(s) thought through to their conclusions may eliminate not only the specificity of feminist theory but place in question the very emancipatory ideals of the women's movements altogether.

Feminist Skepticism toward Postmodernism

The following discussion will formulate two versions of the three theses enumerated above with the goal of clarifying once more the various conceptual options made available with the demise of the episteme of representations. Put in a nutshell, my argument is that strong and weak versions of the theses of the death of Man, of History and of Metaphysics are possible. Whereas the weak versions of these theses entail premises around which critical theorists as well as postmodernists and possibly even liberals and communitarians can unite, their strong versions undermine the possibility of normative criticism at large. Feminist theory can ally itself with this strong version of postmodernism only at the risk of incoherence and self-contradictoriness.

(a) Let us begin by considering the thesis of the Death of Man for a closer understanding of the conceptual option(s) allowed by the end of the episteme of representation. The weak version of this thesis would *situate* the subject in the context of various social, linguistic, and discursive practices. This view would by no means question the desirability and theoretical necessity of articulating a more adequate, less deluded, and less mystified vision of subjectivity than those provided by the concepts of the Cartesian cogito, the "transcendental unity of apperception," "Geist and consciousness," or "das Man" (the they). The traditional attributes of the philosophical subject of the West, like self-reflexivity, the capacity for acting on principles, rational accountability for one's actions, and the ability to project a life-plan into the future, in short, some form of autonomy and rationality, could then be reformulated by taking account of the radical situatedness of the subject.

The strong version of the thesis of the Death of the Man is perhaps best captured in Flax's own phrase that "Man is forever caught in the web of fictive meaning, in chains of signification, *in which the subject is merely another position in language.*" The subject thus dissolves into the chain of significations of which it was supposed to be the initiator. Along with this dissolution of the subject into yet "another position in language" disappear of course concepts of intentionality, accountability, self-reflexivity, and autonomy. The subject that is but another position in language can no longer master and create that distance between itself and the chain of significations in which it is immersed such that it can reflect upon them and creatively alter them.

The strong version of the Death of the Subject thesis is not compatible with the goals of feminism.[11] Surely, a subjectivity that would not be structured by language, by narrative, and by the symbolic codes of narrative available in a culture is unthinkable. We tell of who we are, of the "I" that we are, by means of a narrative. "I was born on such and such a date, as the daughter of such and such . . ." etc. These narratives are deeply colored and structured by the codes of expectable and understandable biographies and identities in our cultures.[12] We can concede all that, but nevertheless we must still argue that we are not merely extensions of our histories, that *vis-à-vis* our own stories we are in the position of author and character at once. The situated and gendered subject is heteronomously determined but still strives toward autonomy. I want to ask how in fact the very project of female emancipation would be thinkable without such a regulative ideal of enhancing the agency, autonomy, and selfhood of women.

Feminist appropriations of Nietzsche on this question can only be incoherent. In her recent book, *Gender Trouble: Feminism and the Subversion of Identity,* Judith Butler wants to extend the limits of reflexivity in thinking about the self beyond the dichotomy of "sex" and "gender." Her convincing and original arguments rejecting this dichotomous reasoning within which feminist theory has operated until recently get clouded, however, by the claim that to reject this dichotomy would mean subscribing to the view that the "gendered self" does not exist; all that the self is, is a series of performances. "Gender," writes Butler, "is not to culture as sex is to nature; gender is also the discursive/cultural means by which 'sexed nature' or a 'natural sex' is produced and established as 'prediscursive,' prior to culture, a politically neutral surface *on which* culture acts."[13] For Butler the myth of the already sexed body is the epistemological equivalent of the myth of the given: just as the given can only be identified within a discursive framework, so too it is the culturally available codes of gender that "sexualize" a body and that construct the directionality of that body's sexual desire.[14]

But Butler also maintains that to think beyond the univocality and dualisms of gender categories, we must bid farewell to the "doer behind the deed," to the self as the subject of a life-narrative. "In an application that Nietzsche himself would not have anticipated or condoned, we might state as a corollary: There is no gender identity behind the expressions of gender; that identity is performatively constituted by the very 'expressions' that are said to be its results."[15] Yet if this view of the self is adopted, is there any possibility of transforming those "expressions" which constitute us? If we are no more than the sum total of the gendered expressions we perform, is there ever any chance to stop the performance for a while, to pull the curtain down, and only let it rise if one can have a say in the production of the play itself? Isn't this what the struggle over gender is all about? Surely we can criticize the "metaphysical presuppositions of identity politics" and challenge the supremacy of heterosexist positions in the women's movement. Yet is such a challenge only thinkable via a complete debunking of any concepts of selfhood, agency, and autonomy? What follows from this Nietzschean position is a vision of the self as a masquerading performer, except of course we are now asked to believe that there is no self behind the mask. Given how fragile and tenuous women's sense of selfhood is in many cases, how much of a hit-and-miss affair their struggles for autonomy are, this reduction of female agency to a "doing without the doer" at best appears to me to be making a virtue out of necessity.

The view that gendered identity is constituted by "deeds without the doer," or by performances without a subject, not only undermines the normative vision of feminist politics and theory. It is also impossible to get rid of the subject altogether and claim to be a fully accountable participant in the community of discourse and inquiry: the strong thesis of the death of the subject undermines the discourse of the theorist herself. If the subject who produces discourse is but a product of the discourse it has created, or better still is but "another position in language," then the responsibility for this discourse cannot be attributed to the author but must be attributable to some fictive "authorial position," constituted by the intersection of "discursive planes." (I am tempted to add that in geometry the intersection of planes produces a line!) Butler entertains this possibility in the introduction to her work: "Philosophy is the predominant disciplinary mechanism that currently mobilizes this author-subject."[16] The "subject" here means also the "object of the discourse;" not the one who utilizes the discourse but the one who is utilized by the discourse itself. Presumably that is why Butler uses the language of "a discourse mobilizing an author/subject." The center of motility is not the thinking, acting and feeling self but "discourses," "systems of signification," "chains of signs," etc. But how then should we read *Gender Trouble*?

The kind of reading I am engaging here presupposes that there is a thinking author who has produced this text, who has intentions, purposes and goals in communicating with me; that the task of theoretical reflection begins with the attempt to understand what the author meant. Certainly, language always says much more than what the author means; there will always be a discrepancy between what we mean and what we say; but we engage in communication, theoretical no less than everyday communication, to gain some basis of mutual understanding and reasoning. The view that the subject is not reducible to "yet another position in language," but that no matter how constituted by language the subject retains a certain autonomy and ability to rearrange the significations of language, is a regulative principle of all communication and social action. Not only feminist politics, but also coherent theorizing becomes impossible if the speaking and thinking self is replaced by "authorial positions," and if the self becomes a ventriloquist for discourses operating through her or "mobilizing" her.[17]

Perhaps I have overstated the case against Butler.[18] Perhaps Butler does not want, any more than Flax herself, to dispense with women's sense of selfhood, agency and autonomy. In the concluding reflections to *Gender Trouble* Butler returns to questions of agency, identity, and politics. She writes:

> The question of locating "agency" is usually associated with the viability of the "subject," where the subject is understood to have some stable existence prior to the cultural field that it negotiated. Or, if the subject is culturally constructed, it is nevertheless vested with an agency, usually figured as the capacity for reflexive mediation, that remains intact regardless of its cultural embeddedness. On such a model, "culture" and "discourse" *mire* the subject, but do not constitute that subject. This move to qualify and to enmire the preexisting subject has appeared necessary to establish a point of agency that is not fully *determined* by that culture and discourse. And yet, this kind of reasoning falsely presumes (a) agency can only be established through recourse to a prediscursive "I," even if that "I" is found in the midst of a discursive convergence, and (b) that to be *constituted* by discourse is to be *determined* by discourse, where determination forecloses the possibility of agency."[19]

Butler rejects that identity can only be established through recourse to an "'I' that preexists signification."[20] She points out that "the enabling conditions for an assertion of 'I' are provided by the structure of signification, the rules that regulate the legitimate and illegitimate invocation of that pronoun, the practices that establish the terms of intelligibility by which that pronoun can circulate." The narrative codes of a culture then define the content with which this pronoun will be invested, the appropriate instances when it can be invoked, by whom and how. Yet one can agree with all that and still maintain that no individual is merely a blank slate upon whom are inscribed the codes of a culture, a kind of Lockean tabula rasa in latter-day Foucaultian garb! [. . .]

(b) Consider now the thesis of the Death of History. Of all positions normally associated with postmodernism this particular one appears to me to be the least problematical. Disillusionment with the ideals of progress, awareness of the atrocities committed in this century in the name of technological and economic progress, the political and moral bankruptcy of the natural sciences which put themselves in the service of the forces of human and planetary destruction – these are the shared sentiments of our century. Intellectuals and philosophers in the twentieth century are to be distinguished from one another less as being friends and opponents of the belief in progress but more in terms of the following: whether the farewell from the "meta-narratives of the Enlightenment" can be exercised in terms of a continuing belief in the power of rational reflection or whether this farewell is but a prelude to a departure from such reflection.

Interpreted as a *weak* thesis, the Death of History could mean two things: theoretically, this could be understood as a call to end the practice of "grand narratives" which are essentialist and monocausal. It is futile, let us say, to search for an essence of "motherhood," as a cross-cultural universal; just as it is futile to seek to produce a single grand theory of female oppression and male dominance across cultures and societies – be such a theory psychoanalytic, anthropological or biological. Politically, the end of such grand narratives would mean rejecting the hegemonial claims of any group or organization to "represent" the forces of history, to be moving with such forces, or to be acting in their name. The critique of the various totalitarian and totalizing movements of our century from National Socialism and Fascism to Stalinism and other forms of authoritarianism is certainly one of the most formative political experiences of postmodernist intellectuals like Lyotard, Foucault, and Derrida.[21] This is also what makes the Death of History thesis interpreted as the end of "grand narratives" so attractive to feminist theorists. Nancy Fraser and Linda J. Nicholson write for example:

> the practice of feminist politics in the 1980s has generated a new set of pressures which have worked against metanarratives. In recent years, poor and working-classs [sic] women, women of color, and lesbians have finally won a wider hearing for their objections to feminist theories which fail to illuminate their lives and address their problems. They have exposed the earlier quasi-metanarratives, with their assumptions of universal female dependence and confinement to the domestic sphere, as false extrapolations from the experience of the white, middle-class, heterosexual women who dominated the beginnings of the second wave . . . Thus, as the class, sexual, racial and ethnic awareness of the movement has altered, so has the preferred conception of theory. It has become clear that quasi-metanarratives hamper rather than promote sisterhood, since they elide differences among women and among the forms of sexism to which different women are differentially subject.[22]

The *strong* version of the thesis of the Death of History would imply, however, a prima facie rejection of any historical narrative that concerns itself with the long duree and that focusses on macro- rather than on micro-social practices. Nicholson and Fraser also warn against this "nominalist" tendency in Lyotard's work.[23] I agree with them that it would be a mistake to interpret the death of "grand narratives" as sanctioning in the future local stories as opposed to global history. The decision as to how local or global a historical narrative or piece of social-scientific research need be cannot be determined by epistemological arguments extraneous to the task at hand. It is the empirical researcher who should answer this question; the philosopher has no business legislating the scope of research to the empirical scientist. To the extent that Lyotard's version of postmodernism seems to sanctify the "small" or "local narrative" over the grand one, he engages in unnecessary a priorism with regard to openended questions of scientific inquiry.

The more difficult question suggested by the strong thesis of the "death of history" appears to me to be different: even while we dispense with grand narratives, how can we rethink the relationship between politics, historiography and historical memory? Is it possible for struggling groups not to interpret history in light of a moral-political imperative, namely, the imperative of the future interest in emancipation? Think for a moment not only of the way in which feminist historians in the last two decades have discovered women and their hitherto invisible lives and work, but of the manner in which they have also revalorized and taught us to see with different eyes such traditionally female and previously denigrated activities like gossip, quiltmaking, and even forms of typically female sickness like headaches, hysteria and taking to bed during menstruation.[24] In this process of the "feminist transvaluation of values" our *present* interest in women's strategies of survival and historical resistance has led us to imbue these *past* activities, which were wholly uninteresting from the standpoint of the traditional historian, with new meaning and significance.

While it is no longer possible or desirable to produce "grand narratives" of history, the "death of history" thesis occludes the epistemological interest in history and in historical narrative which accompany the aspirations of all struggling historical actors. Once this "interest" in recovering the lives and struggles of those "losers" and "victims" of history are lost, can we produce engaged feminist theory?

Defenders of "postmodern historiography" like Fraser and Nicholson who issue calls for a "postmodern feminist theory" look away from these difficulties in part because what they mean by this kind of theorizing is less "postmodernist" but more "neopragmatist." By "postmodern feminist theory" they mean a theory that would be pragmatic and fallibilistic, that "would tailor its method and categories to the specific task at hand, using multiple categories when appropriate and forswearing the metaphysical comfort of a single feminist method or feminist epistemology."[25] Yet this evenhanded and commonsensical approach to tailoring theory to the tasks at hand is not postmodernist. Fraser and Nicholson can reconcile their political commitments with their theoretical sympathies for postmodernism, only because they have substituted theoretical pragmatism for, in effect, the "hyper-theoretical" claims of postmodern historiography. [. . .]

(c) Finally, let me articulate strong and weak versions of the Death of

Metaphysics thesis. In considering this point it would be important to note right at the outset that much of the postmodernist critique of western metaphysics itself proceeds under the spell of a meta-narrative, namely, the narrative first articulated by Heidegger and then developed by Derrida that "Western metaphysics has been under the spell of the 'metaphysics of presence' at least since Plato . . ." This characterization of the philosophical tradition allows postmodernists the rhetorical advantage of presenting what they are arguing against in its least defensible versions: listen again to Flax's words: "For postmodernists this quest for the Real conceals the philosophers' desire, which is to master the world" or "Just as the Real is the ground of Truth, so too philosophy as the privileged representative of the Real . . ." etc. But is the philosophical tradition so monolithic and so essentialist as postmodernists would like to claim? Would not even Thomas Hobbes shudder at the suggestion that the "Real is the ground of Truth"? What would Kant say when confronted with the claim that "philosophy is the privileged representative of the Real"? Would not Hegel consider the view that concepts and language are one sphere and the "real" yet another merely a version of a naive correspondence theory of truth which the chapter on "Sense Certainty" in the *Phenomenology of Spirit* so eloquently dispensed with? In its strong version, the Death of Metaphysics thesis suffers not only from a subscription to a grandiose meta-narrative, but more significantly, this grandiose meta-narrative flattens out the history of modern philosophy and the competing conceptual schemes it contains to the point of unrecognizability. Once this history is rendered unrecognizable then the conceptual and philosophical problems involved in this bravado proclamation of the Death of Metaphysics can be neglected.

The weak version of the Death of Metaphysics thesis which is today more influential than the strong Heidegger–Derrida thesis about the "metaphysics of presence" is Richard Rorty's account. In *Philosophy and the Mirror of Nature* Rorty has shown in subtle and convincing manner that empiricist as well as rationalist projects in the modern period presupposed that philosophy, in contradistinction from the developing natural sciences in this period, could articulate the basis of validity of right knowledge and correct action. Rorty names this the project of "epistemology;"[26] this is the view that philosophy is a metadiscourse of legitimation, articulating the criteria of validity presupposed by all other discourses. Once it ceases to be a discourse of justification, philosophy loses its raison d'être. This is indeed the crux of the matter. Once we have detranscendentalized, contextualized, historicized, genderized the subject of knowledge, the context of inquiry, and even the methods of justification, what remains of philosophy?[27] Does not philosophy become a form of genealogical critique of regimes of discourse and power as they succeed each other in their endless historical monotony? Or maybe philosophy becomes a form of thick cultural narration of the sort that hitherto only poets had provided us with? Or maybe all that remains of philosophy is a form of sociology of knowledge, which instead of investigating the conditions of the validity of knowledge and action, investigates the empirical conditions under which communities of interpretation generate such validity claims?

Why is this question concerning the identity and future and maybe the possibility of philosophy of interest to feminists? Can feminist theory not flourish without getting embroiled in the arcane debates about the end or transformation of philosophy? The inclination of the majority of feminist theorists at the present is to argue that we can side-step this question; even if we do not want to ignore it, we must not be committed to answer it one way or another. Fraser and Nicholson ask: "How can we conceive a version of criticism without philosophy which is robust enough to handle the tough job of analyzing sexism in all its endless variety and monotonous similarity?"[28] My answer is that we cannot, and it is this which makes me doubt that as feminists we can adopt postmodernism as a theoretical ally. Social criticism without some form of philosophy is not possible, and without social criticism the project of a feminist theory which is at once committed to knowledge and to the emancipatory interests of women is inconceivable.

Notes

1   Jane Flax, *Psychoanalysis, Feminism and Postmodernism in the Contemporary West,* (Berkeley: University of California Press, 1990), pp. 32ff.
2   Ibid., p. 32.
3   Ibid., p. 33.
4   Ibid., p. 34.
5   R. Rorty, "Nineteenth-Century Idealism and Twentieth-Century Contextualism." In *Consequences of Pragmatism* (Minneapolis: University of Minnesota Press, 1982), pp. 139–60.
6   Luce Irigaray, *Speculum of the Other Woman*, trans. Gillian C. Gill (Ithaca: Cornell University Press, 1985), pp. 133ff; Genevieve Lloyd, *The Man of Reason: Male and Female in Western Philosophy* (Minneapolis: University of Minnesota Press, 1984); Sandra Harding and M. Hintikka (eds), *Discovering Reality: Feminist Perspectives on Epistemology, Metaphysics, Methodology and Philosophy of Science* (Dordrecht: Reidel, 1983).
7   Joan Kelly Gadol, "The Social Relations of the Sexes: Methodological Implications of Women's History," and "Did Women Have a Renaissance?" In *Women, History and Theory* (Chicago: University of Chicago Press, 1984), pp. 1–19, 19–51.
8   G. W. F. Hegel: "At this point we leave Africa not to mention it again. For it is no historical part of the world: it has no movement or development to exhibit. Historical movements in it – that is in the northern part – belong to the Asiatic or European World . . . What we properly understand by Africa, is the Unhistorical, Undeveloped Spirit, still involved in the conditions of mere nature. . . ." In *The Philosophy of History*, trans. J. Sibree, introd. C. J. Friedrich (New York: Dover, 1956), p. 99.
9   For a provocative utilization of a Foucaultian framework for gender analysis, cf. Judith Butler, *Gender Trouble: Feminism and the Subversion of Identity* (New York and London: Routledge, 1990).

10   Linda Alcoff (1988), "Poststructuralism and Cultural Feminism," *Signs* 13.3, pp. 4–36. See also Christine di Stefano, "Dilemmas of Difference: Feminism, Modernity, and Postmodernism." In Linda J. Nicholson (ed.), *Feminism/Postmodernism* (New York: Routledge, 1990), pp. 63–83; Susan Bordo, "Feminism, Postmodernism, and Gender Skepticism." In Linda J. Nicholson (1990), ibid., pp. 133–57; and more recently, Nancy Hartsock (1989), "Postmodernism and Political Change: Issues for Feminist Theory." In *Cultural Critique*, no. 14 (Winter 1989–90), pp. 15–35, for misgivings about the political and theoretical implications of postmodernism for feminism.

11   Similar concerns are raised by Daryl McGowan Tress in her comment on Jane Flax's "Postmodernism and Gender Relations in Feminist Theory" (a briefer version of arguments subsequently presented in Flax's book, in *Signs* 12.4 (1987), pp. 621–43); cf. Tress and Flax's reply in *Signs* 14.1 (Autumn 1988), pp. 196–203. See also Rosi Braidotti (1990), "Patterns of Dissonance: Women and/in Philosophy," in *Feministische Philosophie* (ed.) Herta NaglDocekal (Oldenburg: Vienna and Munich, 1990), pp. 108–23; Herta NaglDocekal, "Antigones Trauer und der Tod des Subjekts," lecture held at the Philosophinnen-Ringvorlesung at the Institute of Philosophy, Freie Universität Berlin, on May 25, 1990.

12   Patricia J. Williams's "On Being the Object of Property," is a fascinating example of discursive transgressions which in turn forces us to rethink the various narrative codes sanctifying some forms of speech, authority, and identity in our cultures. In *Signs* 14.1 (Autumn 1988), pp. 5–25.

13   Judith Butler, *Gender Trouble*, p. 7. While I applaud Butler's trenchant analysis of the dichotomous reasoning which has operated with a simple juxtaposition of sex and gender, my disagreement with her is whether the directionality of the desire of the body is one that is merely "constructed" through the "order of compulsory heterosexuality." A great deal hinges upon how we want to understand "construct" here. See next footnote for a further elaboration.

14   1 would want to distinguish here as well between the "social and cultural construction of sexuality" on the one hand, and the "shaping of the directionality of the body's desire" on the other. Given all the information we have today about the sheer multiplicity and variety of human erotic and sexual rituals, games, fantasies, myths, and ideals – from the homoeroticism of ancient Greek culture to the quasi-magical and bountiful eroticism of the ancient Indian art of love-making (kamasutran), from the elaborate courting and seduction rituals of ancient Islamic cultures to the flaunting of an obvious and flat sexuality in western mass democracies as a commodity to be obtained like any other at a certain price – given all this, to dispute the social and cultural construction of sexuality would be foolhardy. Yet the shaping of the directionality of desire for the human individual is an extremely complex process, in which the "memory of the body," of the "soma," of the "flesh" plays a crucial role. Culture does not "construct" everything – the human body is not a tabula rasa on which all is inscribed by mechanisms of agency and socialization. The body is an active medium with its own dispositions and "habits," which process, channel, and deflect the influences which come to it from the outside, in accordance with its own accumulated modality of being toward the world. On this issue as well, the disagreement between myself and Butler concerns the role of "agency," intentionality and ultimately the sources of human individual resistance to culture and society.

15   Judith Butler, *Gender Trouble*, p. 25.

16 Ibid., p. xiii.
17 The difficulties in this position derive from the views of the subject and subjectivity of Foucault, upon whom Butler relies. Although Butler critiques Foucault's own understanding of sexuality and particularly his concept of "pleasure" (*Gender Trouble*, pp. 96ff.), she relies upon his methodological framework in viewing the "subject" as a self constituted or constructed by the impact of various regimes of "power/knowledge." The social-scientific deficit of Foucault's work – his inadequate conceptions of social action and social movements, his inability to explain social change except as the discontinuous displacement of one "power/knowledge" regime by another – and his thin concepts of self and identity-formation are ultimately related.
18 I would like to thank Nancy Fraser for helping me see this point.
19 Judith Butler, *Gender Trouble*, p. 143. Emphasis in the text.
20 Ibid.
21 Cf. Vincent Descombes, *Modern French Philosophy* (New York: Cambridge University Press, 1980). See the excellent analysis by Peter Dews of the political experiences of the 1968 generation in France, as it has formed contemporary French philosophy, in *Logics of Disintegration – Post-Structuralist Thought and the Claims of Critical Theory* (New York: New Left Books, 1987).
22 Nancy Fraser and Linda J. Nicholson (1990), "Social Criticism Without Philosophy: An Encounter Between Feminism and Postmodernism." In *Feminism/ Postmodernism*, ed. Linda J. Nicholson, p. 33. Iris Young makes the same point in her "The Ideal of Community and the Politics of Difference," in the same volume, pp. 300–1.
23 Ibid., p. 34.
24 See the pioneering anthology by R. Bridenthal, C. Koonz, and S. Stuard (eds), *Becoming Visible: Women in European History* (Boston: Houghton Mifflin, 1987).
25 Nancy Fraser and Linda J. Nicholson, "Social Criticism Without Philosophy," p. 35.
26 Richard Rorty, *Philosophy and the Mirror of Nature* (Princeton: University Press, Princeton, 1979), pp. 131ff.
27 For trenchant accounts of the various problems and issues involved in this "sublation" and "transformation" of philosophy, see Kenneth Baynes, James Bohman, and Thomas McCarthy (eds), *After Philosophy: End or Transformation?* (Cambridge, MA: MIT Press, 1987).
28 Nancy Fraser and Linda J. Nicholson, "Social Criticism Without Philosophy," p. 34.

29

Postmodernity, or Living with Ambivalence

Zygmunt Bauman

The collapse of 'grand narratives' (as Lyotard put it) – the dissipation of trust in supra-individual and supra-communal courts of appeal – has been eyed by many observers with fear, as an invitation to the 'everything goes' situation, to universal permissiveness and hence, in the end, to the demise of all moral, and thus social, order. Mindful of Dostoyevsky's dictum 'if there is no God, every-thing is permitted', and of Durkheim's identification of asocial behaviour with the weakening of collective consensus, we have grown to believe that unless an awesome and incontestable authority – sacred or secular, political or philosophical – hangs over each and every human individual, then anarchy and universal carnage are likely to follow. This belief supported well the modern determination to install an artificial order: a project that made all spon-taneity suspect until proven innocent, that proscribed everything not explicitly prescribed and identified ambivalence with chaos, with 'the end of civilization' as we know it and as it could be imagined. Perhaps the fear emanated from the suppressed knowledge that the project was doomed from the start; perhaps it was cultivated deliberately, since it served a useful role as an emotional bulwark against dissention; perhaps it was just a side-effect, an intellectual afterthought born of the socio-political practice of cultural crusade and enforced assimilation. One way or the other, modernity bent on the bulldozing of all unauthorized difference and all wayward life-patterns could not but gestate the horror of deviation and render deviation synonymous with diversity. As Adorno and Horkheimer commented, the lasting intellectual and emotional scar left by the philosophical project and political practice of mod-ernity was the fear of the void; and the void was the absence of a universally binding, unambiguous and enforceable standard.

Of the popular fear of the void, of the anxiety born of the absence of clear instruction that leaves nothing to the harrowing necessity of choice, we know from the worried accounts narrated by intellectuals, the appointed or self-appointed interpreters of social experience. The narrators are never absent from their narration, though, and it is a hopeless task to try to sift out their presence from their stories. It may well be that at all times there was life outside philosophy, and that such life did not share the worries of the narrators; that it did quite well without being regimented by rationally proved and philosophically approved universal standards of truth, goodness and beauty. It may well even be that much of that life was liveable, orderly and moral *because* it was *not* tinkered with, manipulated and corrupted by the self-acclaimed agents of the 'universal ought'.[1] There is hardly any doubt, however, that one form of life can fare but badly without the prop of universally binding and apodictically valid standards: the form of life of the narrators themselves (more precisely, such form of life as contains the stories those narrators were telling through most of modern history).

It was that form of life first and foremost that lost its foundation once social powers abandoned their ecumenical ambitions, and felt therefore more than anyone else threatened by the fading out of universalistic expectations. As long as modern powers clung resolutely to their intention of constructing a better, reason-guided, and thus ultimately universal order, intellectuals had little difficulty in articulating their own claim to the crucial role in the process: universality was their domain and their field of expertise. As long as the modern powers insisted on the elimination of ambivalence as the measure of social improvement, intellectuals could consider their own work – the promotion of universally valid rationality – as a major vehicle and driving force of progress. As long as the modern powers continued to decry and banish and evict the Other, the different, the ambivalent, intellectuals could rely on mighty support for their authority of passing judgement and sorting out truth from falsity, knowledge from mere opinion. Like the adolescent hero of Cocteau's *Orphée*, convinced that the sun would not rise without his guitar and serenade, the intellectuals grew convinced that the fate of morality, civilized life and social order hangs on their solution of the problem of universality: on their clinching and final proof that the human 'ought' is unambiguous, and that its non-ambiguity has unshakeable and totally reliable foundations.

This conviction translated into two complementary beliefs: that there will be no good in the world *unless* its necessity has been proven; and that proving such a necessity, if and when accomplished, will have a similar effect on the world as that imputed to the legislative acts of a ruler: it will replace chaos with order and make the opaque transparent. Husserl was perhaps the last great philosopher of the modern era spurred into action by those twin beliefs. Appalled by the idea that whatever we see as truth may be founded but in beliefs, that our knowledge has merely a psychological grounding, that we might have adopted logic as a secure guide to correct thinking simply because this is how people happen on the whole to think, Husserl (like Descartes, Kant and other recognized giants of modern thought before him) made a gigantic effort to cut reason free from its worldly habitat (or was it prison?): to return it to where it belonged – a *transcendental*, out-worldly region, towering above the daily human bustle at a height at which it cannot be reached – neither glimpsed nor tarnished – from the lowly world of common daily experience. The latter could not be the domicile of reason, as it was precisely the world of the common and the ordinary and the spontaneous that was to be remade and reformed and transformed by the verdicts of reason. Only the few, capable of the formidable effort of transcendental reduction (an experience not unlike the shaman's trances, or forty days of desert meditation) can travel to those esoteric places where truth comes into view. For the time of their journey, they must forget – suspend and bracket out – the 'mere existing', so that they may become one with the transcendental subject – that thinking subject that thinks the truth because it does not think anything else, because it is free from its worldly interests and the common errors of the worldly way.

The world which Husserl left behind while embarking on his solitary expedition to the sources of certainty and truth took little note. This was a world of evil on the loose, of concentration camps and of growing stockpiles of bombs and poison gas. The most spectacular and lasting effect of absolute truth's last stand was not so much its *inconclusiveness*, stemming as some would say from the errors of design, but its utter *irrelevance* to the worldly fate of truth and goodness. The latter fate was decided far away from philosophers' desks, down in the world of daily life where struggles for political freedom raged and the limits of the state ambition to legislate social order, to define, to segregate, to organize, to constrain and to suppress were pushed forward and rolled backwards.

It seems that the more advanced is the cause of freedom at home the less demand there is for the services of explorers of distant lands where absolute truth is reputed to reside. When one's own truth seems secure and the truth of the other does not seem to be a challenge or a threat, truth can live well without sycophants assuring it of being 'the truest of them all' and the warlords determined to make sure that no one disagrees. Once the difference ceases to be a crime, it may be enjoyed at peace, and enjoyed for what it is, rather than for what it represents or what it is destined to become. Once the politicians abandon their search for empires, there is little demand for the philosophers' search for universality.[2] Empires of unconfined and unchallenged sovereignty, and the truth of unlimited and uncontested universality were the two arms with which modernity wished to remould the world according to the design of perfect order. Once the intention is no more, both arms find themselves without use.

In all probability the diversity of truths, standards of goodness and beauty does not grow once the intention is gone; neither does it become more resilient and stubborn than before; it only looks less alarming. It was, after all, the modern intention that made difference into an offence: *the* offence, the most mortal and least forgivable sin, to be precise. The pre-modern eye viewed difference with equanimity; as if it was in the pre-ordained order of things that they are and should remain different. Being unemotional, difference was also safely out of the cognitive focus. After a few centuries during which human diversity lived in hiding (a concealment enforced by the threat of exile) and it learned to be embarrassed about its stigma of iniquity, the postmodern eye (that is, the modern eye liberated from modern fears and inhibitions) views difference with zest and glee: difference is beautiful and no less good for that.

The appearance of sequence is, to be sure, itself an effect of the modern knack for neat divisions, clean breaks and pure substances. The postmodern celebration of difference and contingency has not displaced the modern lust for uniformity and certainty. Moreover, it is unlikely ever to do it; it has no capacity of doing so. Being what it is, postmodern mentality and practice cannot displace or eliminate or even margalize anything. As it is always the case with the notoriously ambivalent (multi-final: opening more than one option, pointing to more than one line of future change) human condition, the gains of postmodernity are simultaneously its losses; what gives it its strength and attraction is also the source of its weakness and vulnerability.

There is no clean break or unambiguous sequence. Postmodernity is weak on exclusion. Having declared limits off limits, it cannot but include and incorporate modernity into the very diversity that is its distinctive mark. It cannot refuse admission lest it should lose its identity. (Paradoxically, refusal would be equivalent to the ceding of the whole real estate to the rejected applicant.) It cannot but admit the rights of a legitimate resident even to such a lodger as denies its right to admit residents and the right of other residents to share its accommodation. Modern mentality is a born litigant and an old hand in lawsuits. Postmodernity cannot defend its case in court, as there is no court whose authority it would recognize. It might be forced instead to follow the Christian injunction of offering another cheek to the assailant's blows. It certainly is doomed to a long and hard life of cohabitation with its sworn enemy as a room-mate.

To the modern determination to seek or enforce consensus, postmodern mentality may only respond with its habitual tolerance of dissent. This makes the antagonists' chances unequal, with the odds heavily on the side of the resolute and strong-willed. Tolerance is too wan a defence against willfulness and lack of scruples. By itself, tolerance remains a sitting target – an easy prey for the unscrupulous. It can repulse assaults only when reforged into solidarity: into the universal recognition that difference is one universality that is not open to negotiation and that attack against the universal right to be different is the only departure from universality that none of the solidary agents, however different, may tolerate otherwise than at its own, and all the other agents', peril.

And so the transformation of the *fate* into a *destiny*, of tolerance into solidarity, is not just a matter of moral perfection, but a condition of survival. Tolerance as 'mere tolerance' is moribund; it can survive only in the form of solidarity. It just would not do to rest satisfied that the other's difference does not confine or harm my own – as some differences, of some others, are most evidently bent on constraining and damaging. Survival in the world of contingency and diversity is possible only if each difference recognizes another difference as the necessary condition of the preservation of its own. Solidarity, unlike tolerance, its weaker version, means readiness to fight; and joining the battle for the sake of the other's difference, not one's own. Tolerance is ego-centred and contemplative; solidarity is socially oriented and militant.

Like all other human conditions, postmodern tolerance and diversity has its dangers and its fears. Its survival is not guaranteed – not by God's design, universal reason, laws of history, or any other supra-human force. In this respect, of course, the postmodern condition does not differ at all from all other conditions; it differs only by knowing about it, by its knowledge of living without guarantee, of being on its own. This makes it exceedingly anxiety-prone. And this also gives it a chance. [. . .]

The Postmodern Political Agenda

Nothing merely ends in history, no project is ever finished and done with. Clean borders between epochs are but projections of our relentless urge to separate the inseparable and order the flux. Modernity is still with us. It lives as the pressure of unfulfilled hopes and interests ossified in self-reproducing institutions; as the zeal of perforce belated imitators, wishing to join the feast that those who are now leaving it with distaste once proudly enjoyed; as the shape of the world modern labours have left behind – for us to inhabit; as the 'problems' those labours spawned and defined for us, as well as our histori-cally trained, yet by now instinctive way of thinking about problems and reacting to them. This is, perhaps, what people like Habermas refer to when they speak of the 'unfinished project of modernity'.

And yet – whether or not the project keeps its remembered shape – some-thing has surely occurred to us, to the people who undertake and finish projects. The very fact that we now speak of modernity as a *project* (a design with intentions, ends and means) testifies most convincingly to the change that happened in us. Our ancestors did not talk of the 'project' when they were busily engaged in what now looks to us like unfinished business.

Michael Phillipson gave his recently published book the title *In Modernity's Wake*. A felicitous phrase, evoking a powerful image: the ship has passed by; its passage roughened the waters, left a turbulence so that all sailors around have to rework the course of their boats – while those who fell into the water must swim hard to reach them. Once the waters quieten down again, though, we, the sailors and former passengers alike, can have a closer look at the ship that caused this all. That ship is still quite near, huge and clearly visible in all its weighty bulk, but we are now *behind* it and we do not stand any more on its deck. Thus we can see it in all its impressive shape, fore to aft, scan it, appreciate it, plot the direction it takes. We may now decide whether to follow its course. We may also better judge the wisdom of its navigation, and even protest against the captain's commands.

Living 'in the wake' means turbulence, but also wider vistas and the new wisdom they offer. In modernity's wake, its passengers become aware of serious faults in the design of the ship that brought them where they are now. They also are reconciled to the fact that it could not bring them to a more pleasant destination, and are ready to look again, with a fresh and critical eye, at the old navigatory principles.

What is truly new in our situation today is, in other words, our vantage point. While still in the close neighbourhood of the modern era, and feeling the effects of the turbulence it caused on its way, we *can* now (better still, we are *prepared* and *willing to*) take a cool and critical view of modernity in its totality, evaluate its performance, pass judgement on the solidity and congruence of its construction. This is ultimately what the idea of *postmodernity* stands for: an existence fully determined and defined by the fact of being '*post*' (coming *after*) and over-whelmed by the awareness of being in such a condition. Postmodernity does not necessarily mean the end, the discreditation or the rejection of modernity. Postmodernity is no more (but no less either) than the modern mind taking a long, attentive and sober look at itself, at its condition and its past works, not fully liking what it sees and sensing the urge to change. Postmodernity is modernity coming of age: modernity looking at itself at a distance rather than from inside, making a full inventory of its gains and losses, psychoanalysing itself, discovering the intentions it never before spelled out, finding them mutu-ally cancelling and incongruous. Postmodernity is modernity coming to terms with its own impossibility; a self-monitoring modernity, one that consciously discards what it was once unconsciously doing.

In the process, the triple alliance of the values of liberty, equality and brother-hood that dominated the modern political battlefield did not escape scrutiny and the ensuing censure. No wonder; however hard political designers tried, they found themselves constantly in a trade-off situation, vainly struggling to reach all three at the same time. They found liberty militating against equality, equality giving short shrift to the dream of liberty, and brotherhood of doubtful virtue as long as the other two values failed to find a *modus coexistendi*. They came also to think that – given the huge and yet untapped energy of human liberty – the objectives of equality and brotherhood sold human potential too cheaply. Equality could not be easily distanced from the prospect of uniformity. Brotherhood smacked all too often of enforced unity and a demand that the ostensible siblings should sacrifice individuality in the name of a putative common cause. Not that the means fared better than the values. The conquest of nature brought more waste than human happiness. One thing in which industrial expansion succeeded most spectacularly was the multipli-cation of risks: more risks, bigger risks, unheard-of risks. For some time now, most 'economic growth' has been propelled by the need to defuse the risks it manufactured: risks of overpopulation, undernourishment, losing the climati-cally indispensable rainforests and creating socially devastating urban jungles, overheating the atmosphere, contaminating water supplies, poisoning food and air, spreading 'new and improved' diseases. More and more, the conquest of nature looked like the very illness it was alleged to cure.

And so the values began to shift. First at the bizarre, idiosyncratic margins, easy to pooh-pooh and dismiss as 'untypical' or downright loony. But then the slow movement turned into a stampede. It can be ignored no more that the new triple-value alliance gains in popularity at the expense of the old one. The new horizons that seem to inflame today human imagination and inspire human action are those of *liberty, diversity* and *tolerance*. These are new values that inform the postmodern *mentality*. As for postmodern *practice*, however, it does not look a whit less flawed than its predecessor.

Liberty is as truncated as before – though the parts of its body that have now been amputated are different from those that were removed in the past. In post-modern practice, liberty boils down to consumer choice. To enjoy it, one must be a consumer first. This preliminary condition leaves out millions. As throughout the modern era, in the postmodern world poverty disqualifies. Freedom in its new, market interpretation is as much a privilege as it was in its old versions. But there are new problems as well: with communal needs trans-lated into individual acts of acquisition, the maiming of liberty cannot but affect *everybody*, rich and poor alike, exemplary or flawed consumers: there are needs that cannot be met by no matter how many personal purchases, and so anybody's freedom of choice looks severely limited. One cannot buy privately one's way out from polluted air, a broken ozone layer or a rising radiation level; one cannot buy one's way into the forest immune to acid rain or seacoast protected against toxic algae thriving on the lush nourishment of chemically processed sewage. In the few instances when buying oneself out seems plausible – like escaping dilapidated public transport in a private car, or running away from the squalor of public health into a private clinic – the choice only adds to the problem that made it necessary in the first place, adding to the misery that prompted the escape. The choice therefore becomes ineffective the moment it is taken, at best a few moments later. There are plenty of flawed, weak consumers or disqualified consumers who must yet gain that freedom that the consumer society officially recognizes; but there are also weak, uncared for, deprived aspects of *everybody's* life (including the life of the ostensibly free consumers) yet to be protected by communal effort.

Diversity thrives; and the market-place thrives with it. More precisely, only such diversity is allowed to thrive as benefits the market. As the humourless, power-greedy and jealous national state did before, the market abhors self-management and autonomy – the wilderness it cannot control. As before, autonomy has to be fought for, if diversity is to mean anything but variety of marketable life-styles – a thin varnish of changeable fashions meant to hide the uniformly market-dependent condition. What is to be fought for is above all the right to secure communal, as distinct from individual, diversity; a diversity stemming from a communally chosen and communally serviced form of life. Such diversity can struggle for recognition and its share of services, but cannot (unless proved profitable) hope to be supported, let alone guaranteed, by the cornucopia of merchandized identities. If the standards of marketability are not met, the best one can count on is the market's indifference. At worst, the hostility of the market is to be reckoned with. Communally managed collective identities may jar with the idea of individually chosen life-styles – an idea that the market must hold tight to, with the most sincere and unqualified sympathy.

If the slogan of brotherhood is translated as the practice of pastoral power, as obtrusive interference with alternative ways of life, as insistence on uniformity, as defining all difference as a sign of retardation, deviation and a 'problem' requiring 'solutions' – *tolerance* translates as 'Let's live and let others live'. Where tolerance rules, difference is no more bizarre or challenging. Difference has been, so to speak, privatized. The urge to proselytize has wilted, the crusader spirit has dissipated. The age of cultural hegemony seems to have passed: cultures are meant to be enjoyed, not fought for. In our type of society, economic and political domination may well do without hegemony; it found the way of reproducing itself under conditions of cultural variety. The new tolerance means irrelevance of cultural choice for the stability of domination. And irrelevance rebounds in *indifference*. Alternative forms of life arouse but spectator interest of the type offered by a sparkling and spicy variety show; they may even trigger less resentment (particularly if viewed at a safe distance or through the secure shield of the TV screen), but no fellow-feeling either; they belong to the outer world of theatre and entertainment, not to the inner world of the politics of life. They stand beside each other, yet do not belong together. Like the market-promoted life-styles they bear no other value than one inserted by free choice. Most certainly, their presence imposes no obligation, breeds no responsibility. As practised by market-led postmodernity, tolerance degenerates into estrangement; the growth of spectator curiosity means fading of human interest. When alien forms of life descend from the safe seclusion of the TV screens or congeal into live and self-assertive communities next door instead of confining their existence to the multi-cultural cookbooks, ethnic restaurants and fashionable trinkets, they transgress their province of meaning: the province of theatre, of entertainment, of variety show – the only one that contains the precept of tolerance, of suspension of estrangement. A sudden jump from one province of meaning to another is at all times shocking – and so forms of life previously regarded as picturesque and amusing are now experienced as a threat. They arouse anger and hostility.

In other words, market-promoted tolerance does not lead to solidarity: it *fragments*, instead of uniting. It services well communal separation and the reduction of the social bond to a surface gloss. It survives as long as it remains to be lived in the airy world of the symbolic game of representation and does not spill over into the realm of daily coexistence thanks to the expedient of territorial and functional segregation. Most importantly, such tolerance is fully compatible with the practice of social domination. It may be preached and exercised without fear because it reaffirms rather than questions the superiority and privilege of the tolerant: the other, by being different, loses the entitlement to equal treatment – indeed, inferiority of the other is fully justified by the difference. Abandonment of the converting zeal comes together with the withdrawal of the very promise of equality. With mutual links reduced to tolerance, difference means perpetual distance, non-cooperation, and hierarchy. The 'fusion of horizons' hardly steps beyond the widening range of ethnic take-aways.

This much for the values postmodernity promotes. As to the means – the rape of nature has been replaced by the concern with the preservation of natural balance; reason-induced artificiality, the warring cry of modernity is fast losing an audience, and as an object of popular cult is equally fast replaced by the wisdom of nature. Fewer people believe today in the magical capacity of economic growth and technological expansion. One thing people trust technology to deliver without fail and on a growing pace is yet more discomfort and more danger – new, less calculable, less curable risks.

Under the power-politics management, and operated by market forces, new concerns and new sensitivities are used, however, to reinforce the very processes they abhor and condemn. The clash between the social nature of risks and privatized means of their containment is the postmodern version of the old contradiction of capitalism (one between the social means of pro-duction and their private ownership) singled out by Marx as the main cause of the system's imminent downfall. In the result of this clash, risks are not reduced, let alone extinguished. They are only removed from public sight and thus made, at least for a time, safe from criticism. (Risks tend to travel over the globe in a direction opposite to that of riches; the rich countries have an awe-some capacity to sell out their own poison as the poor people's meat; the only meat the poor can hope for.) Such technology-generated risks as cannot be moved are subdued with more technology – to (at least temporary) public applause. 'Nature conscious', 'ozone friendly' and 'green', petrol, aerosols, detergents or bleaches turn into big business and bring 'new and improved' profits. Ecology-conscious designers reduce the amount of carbon dioxide released by existing car engines so that more cars can be released onto more roads. (By 2015, Europe expects four times more cars than today; it is difficult to imagine a prosperous Europe without them, as one in every seven persons derives his or her livelihood from car production. It is equally difficult to imagine Europe with cars multiplying at the present speed, as the Acropolis has decayed more in the last twenty years than it did in the previous twenty-four centuries, and as Alpine forests which experts protect are fast sharing the fate of the rainforests of the upper Amazon which experts destroy.) As before, problems are formulated as demands for new (marketable, of course) technical gadgets and stuffs; as before, those desirous to be free from discomfort and risks are reminded that such freedom 'must pay for itself' and the big bills of social catastrophe are alleged to be cleared with the small change of private shopping concerns. In the process, the global origin of problems is effectively hidden from view, and the crusade against known risks may go on producing more and more sinister – yet unknown – risks, thus undermining its own future chance of success.

This is, though, but a minor part of the deception. Another, still greater and more seminal part, is the confinement of new sensitivity in the frame of technological discourse: both the salvation and the grudgingly admitted sins are hermetically sealed in the depoliticized ('politically neutral') discourse of technology and expertise, thereby reinforcing the social framework which makes sins inevitable and salvation unattainable. What is left outside the confines of rational discourse is the very issue that stands a chance of making the discourse rational and perhaps even practically effective: the *political* issue of democratic control over technology and expertise, their purposes and their desirable limits – the issue of politics as self-management and collectively made choices.

Whatever value or means championed by postmodernity we consider, they all point (if only tacitly or by elimination) to politics, democracy, full-blown citizenship as the sole vehicles of their implementation. With politics those values and means look like a chance of a better society; without politics, abandoned fully to the care of the market, they look more like deceitful slogans at best, sources of new and yet unfathomed dangers at worst. Postmodernity is not the end of politics, as it is not an end of history. On the contrary, whatever may be attractive in the postmodern promise calls for more politics, more political engagement, more political effectivity of individual and communal action (however much the call is stifled by the hubbub of consumer bustle, and however inaudible it becomes in a world made up of shopping malls and Disneylands, where all that matters is an enjoyable piece of theatre, and thus nothing matters really much).

Thus far, the postmodern condition has brought a massive withdrawal of would-be citizenry from the traditional (or at least traditionally lauded, if not always practised) form of politics. The seduced – those who benefit or believe to benefit – call for more small change in their pockets and would not listen to the reminders of unpaid social bills. The repressed accept the majority verdict that casts them as flawed consumers and believe much as everyone else that social bills are best cleared with small change in private pockets. Their sufferings do not add up, do not cumulate; the remedy, like the ailment, appears thoroughly privatized. The illness is the dearth of shopping; the cure is shopping unlimited. The combined result is massive political indifference. Its pressure flattens the political process into the screen-deep contest of show-business personalities, with election results replicating popularity ratings. Does all this augur the end of politics?

There are signs that the postmodern era may generate political forms of its own. The way in which many an old-style, absolutist regime collapsed in recent years in parts of the world as distant from each other and apparently unconnected as Chile and Czechoslovakia, hints at such a possibility. Without any anterior theoretical articulation, rebellions that led to the collapse seemed to manifest in practice a new vision of politics and political power: a vision in which the traditional modern imagery of solid and tough 'materiality' of political domination was bafflingly yet blatantly absent.

Let us name just a few common features of such rebellions. First, they were not 'designed revolutions', planned and prepared by an organized core of conspirators with a clandestine network of alternative leadership and a blue-print for future policies. Leadership, if any, surfaced in the course of the events, followed rather than anticipated the popular movement. Second, events unravelled without plan, following solely the logic of episodic succession and taking by surprise both the protesters and the targets of popular ire. Much as the battle gestated its own troops, the gradually opening possibilities generated their own strategies. Third, few if any buildings were targeted, stormed or taken, before their occupants left them or their occupancy lost political meaning; it was as if the actors did not see power as 'thing-like', residing in a specific location where it can be stored and from which it can be taken; as if instead they intuited government, rule, domination as an on-going process of communicative exchange, a series of acts rather than a set of possessions; something that can be interrupted, dismantled and later returned to and reassembled, rather than expropriated and redistributed. Fourth, the decisive blow and the ultimate cause of the collapse was not an overwhelming force of the rebels and military defeat of the rulers, but the uncompromising irony of the protesters reluctant to be manoeuvred out of their carnival-like mood of insouciant, obstreperous disrespect for the high and mighty. Single shots, when fired, met with universal outcry not just because of the suffering they caused the individual victims, but for their outlandishness, for their complete lack of resonance with the character of the event; echoes of another era, they sounded jarringly out of tune with the mood of a popular festival, celebrating the rediscovered freedom of the streets.

What the described events might have demonstrated is that even if state power does not need popular consent for its daily operation, it cannot survive an explicit refusal of such consent: means of coercion are not substitutes for consent; it is the availability of consent that makes such means effective in the first place. This could be a revelation to enlighten the era of new *postmodern* politics: armed with such new knowledge politics may turn into an entirely new kind of game, with consequences as yet exceedingly difficult to predict. This is, however, but one of the possible interpretations. The obliging speed with which the seemingly cast-iron edifices of oppressive power crumbled at the first whiff of popular refusal of meekness might have been a *local* phenomenon: a testimony to the obsoleteness of the modern state, for too long kept artificially alive by equally ageing and jaded communist regimes, and now brought into sudden relief by the practices of postmodern societies.

It is possible that what we have witnessed was the collapse of a *patronage state* – a social/political/economic formation singularly unfit for an era dominated by the postmodern values of novelty, of rapid (preferably inconsequential and episodic) change, of individual enjoyment and consumer choice. In exchange for the promise of personal provision and security, the patronage state demands surrender of the right to choose and to self-determine. The patronage state strives to be a monopolistic source of needs-satisfaction, social status and self-esteem; it transforms its subjects into clients and asks them to be grateful for what they have received today and will receive tomorrow. But for the same reason for which he feels entitled to demand gratitude, the patron cannot shake off his responsibility for the misfortune of his clients. Frustration is immediately reforged into a grievance which 'naturally' hits the patron, and his policy, as the obvious cause of suffering. Under postmodern conditions, when the exhilarating experience of ever-new needs rather than the satisfaction of the extant ones becomes the main measure of a happy life (and thus the production of new enticements turns to be the major vehicle of social integration and peaceful coexistence), the patronage state, adjusted to the task of defining and circumscribing the needs of its subjects, cannot stand competition with systems operated by the consumer market. And as it remains the only target within sight of the discontent that results, the odds are that the accumulated dissent will soon outweigh its capacity for purchasing consent and resolving conflicts. No wonder that the managers of the patronage state have apparently lost their determination to perpetuate a system geared to dictatorship over needs and the state's responsibility for their satisfaction – alongside their ability to govern.

Writing from the depth of a dissenting artist's experience, the Hungarian author Miklós Haraszti observed that in a society where the major (the only?) constraint shackling artistic freedom came from the market, 'The artist could express hatred, even towards this constraint, as long as his work was marketable . . . [but] planning, unlike the market, is not a placid sacred cow. It cannot tolerate contempt.'[3] The all-consuming ambition of the planning, designing, gardening state of modernity (one of which the communist state was a faithful disciple, even if a disciple who through his very diligence inadvertently exposed the inanity of the teaching) proved to be in the end its main drawback and fatal calamity. It kept embroiling it in potentially incapacitating crises.

The successor of the modern state places its bet on the expedient of privatizing and diffusing dissent, rather than collectivizing it and prompting it to accumulate. Having abandoned the designing ambitions, it can do with less coercion and little, if any, ideological mobilization. It seems to count on popular disaffection to remain scattered and to pass it by; to pass it by because it has been scattered. It may even be counting on such disaffection, as long as it stays scattered, to take care of the system's reproduction. Once declared to be a mortal danger to all social and political order, ambivalence is not an 'enemy at the gate' any more. On the contrary: like everything else, it has been made into one of the stage props in the play called postmodernity.

Notes

1   It is a prominent feature of the postmodern mentality that these and similar doubts are more and more widely shared by intellectual observers. Suddenly a growing number of social scientists discover that normative regulation of daily

life is often sustained through 'grass roots' initiative frequently of a heterodox ('deviationary' in official parlance) nature, and has to be protected against encroachments from above. Compare, for example, Michel de Certeau's analysis of *la peruque* (*The Practice of Everyday Life* [Berkeley: University of California Press, 1984], pp. 25ff) as the tool of defence of the self-regulated sphere of autonomy; or Hebdidge's brilliant characterization of subculture (normally the object of officially inspired 'moral panics' and detracted as a hiccup of barbarism, as a product of disintegration of order) as a phenomenon which 'forms up in the space between surveillance and the evasion of surveillance' and 'translates the fact of being under scrutiny into the pleasure of being watched. It is a hiding in the light'. Subculture, in Hebdidge's interpretation, is a 'declaration of independence, of otherness, of alien intent, a refusal of anonymity, of subordinate status. It is an *in*subordination. And at the same time it is also a confirmation of the fact of powerlessness, a celebration of impotence. Subcultures are both a play for attention and a refusal, once attention has been granted, to be read according to the book'. (*Hiding in the Light* [London: Routledge, 1988], p. 35.) Subculture is deliberate or semi-deliberate politics; it has its conscious or subconscious motive, programme and strategy. It often reaches its purpose: it gains attention, and then it is closely scrutinized so that its inner nature as a defence of autonomy can be gleaned. There are, however, much more massive though less vociferous and hence less visible territories of daily life that do not attract the obtrusive attention of the law-enforcing authorities and thus also the curiosity of intellectual commentators.

2   Emperor Shih Huang Ti, the hero of Borges' story, was credited with ordering the construction of the Chinese Wall and the burning of all the books that had been written before his time. He also boasted in his inscriptions that all things under his reign had the names that befitted them. And he decreed that his heirs should be called Second Emperor, Third Emperor, Fourth Emperor, and so on to infinity (Jorge Luis Borges, "The Walls and the Books", in *Other Inquisitions, 1937–1952*, trans. Ruth L. C. Simms [New York: Washington Square Press, 1966], pp. 1–2.) The four decrees of Shih Huang Ti represent modern ambition at its fullest and most logically coherent. The Wall guarded the perfect kingdom against interference by other coercive pressures; the destruction of books stopped infiltration of other ideas. With the kingdom secure on both fronts, no wonder all things finally received their right and proper names, and, starting with Shih Huang Ti's reign, future history was to be only more of the same.

3   Miklós Haraszti, *The Velvet Prison: Artists under State Socialism*, trans. Katalin and Stephen Landesmann with the help of Steve Wasserman (London: Penguin, 1989), pp. 80–1. Haraszti observes that the existence of censorship in state socialism is based on identity of interests between censor and censored (p. 8). Writing in the early 1980s, Haraszti added the adjective 'lasting' to the noun 'identity': a system that successfully 'absorbed the language of its victims' seemed then to Haraszti, like to virtually everybody else, destined to last forever. With the benefit of retrospective wisdom we may say that what seemed to be the strongest foundation of the system's security proved to be its undoing. Having assumed full charge of 'common interests' the communist power put its fate into the hands of its subjects; it could not survive the latter's withdrawal of consent. If in the unwritten yet binding contract between the communist rulers and the ruled one could not 'note any distinction drawn between the authorization for the domination of values and

the domination of the valuable ones' (p. 26), then any protest against the type of values enforced by the rulers must immediately have turned into a protest against the principle of value-enforcement as such. All dissent turned into *systemic* crisis (whereas in a society where needs, values and dissent itself are privatized similar dissent would reinforce the market-based mechanism of systemic reproduction).

Index